Love Hina

By

Ken Akamatsu

Volume 13

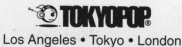

Los Angeles • Tokyo • London

Translator - Nan Rymer
English Adaptation - Adam Arnold
Associate Editors - Paul Morrissey & Tim Beedle
Retouch and Lettering - Marnie Echols
Cover Layout - Anna Kernbaum

Editor - Mark Paniccia
Managing Editor - Jill Freshney
Production Coordinator - Antonio DePietro
Production Manager - Jennifer Miller
Art Director - Matthew Alford
Editorial Director - Jeremy Ross
VP of Production - Ron Klamert
President & C.O.O. - John Parker
Publisher & C.E.O. - Stuart Levy

Email: editor@TOKYOPOP.com
Come visit us online at www.TOKYOPOP.com

A 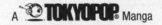 Manga

TOKYOPOP Inc.
5900 Wilshire Blvd. Suite 2000
Los Angeles, CA 90036

Love Hina volume 13

ISBN: 1-59182-119-3

First TOKYOPOP® printing: August 2003

10 9 8 7 6 5 4 3
Printed in the USA

Love Hina

The Story Thus Far...

Some promises are meant to be kept. For Keitaro Urashima, a promise he made with a little girl during his childhood has been the driving force for him to make it into Tokyo University. After studying and failing his exam three times, he finally managed to do the impossible and fulfill his promise...or did he? Having broken his leg prior to the university's opening ceremony, Keitaro made a shocking bedside confession of his love for Naru, and soon got it into his thick skull that he wanted to leave for half a year so he could study abroad! But perhaps we are getting ahead of ourselves.

This chapter in Keitaro Urashima's life began over two years ago when he inherited from his globe-trotting grandmother the Hinata House, an all-girls dormitory whose clientele was none too pleased that their live-in landlord is a man...or as close to a man as poor Keitaro can be. The lanky loser incessantly (and accidentally) crashes their sessions in the hot springs, walks in on them changing, and pokes his nose pretty much everywhere that it can get broken, if not by the hot-headed Naru—possibly the mystery girl from fifteen years ago—then by one of the other Hinata inmates—Kitsune, an alcoholic with a diesel libido and knack for gambling; Motoko, a swordsman who struggles with her feminine identity; Shinobu, a pre-teen princess with a colossal crush on Keitaro; Su, a foreign girl with a big appetite and some mean hacker skills; Sarah, an orphaned ward resentful of being left by her globe-trotting archeologist guardian, Seta; Mutsumi, an accident-prone lily also studying for her exams; Haruka, Keitaro's aunt and de facto matriarch of Hinata House; and now Kanako, Keitaro's little sister with a knack for impersonations and a bizarre love for her brother.

Just as the Hinata crew was beginning to get on with their lives without Keitaro around, Kanako Urashima arrived on the scene and instituted a number of changes. The biggest of these was the refurbishing of Hinata House into a full-service bed and breakfast. As tensions mount, the girls are forced to take sides against their tyrannical new landlord and her unlikely cohort, Naru. Just as things are about to get ugly, Keitaro makes his grand entrance and breaks up a coup d'etat staged by the dorm residents to overthrow Kanako.

As Keitaro slowly reacclimates himself to his former life, his desire to rekindle his relationship with Naru grows until late one night he asks her to join him at the mysterious annex behind Hinata House, a place where lovers can be forever bound together. Unfortunately for him, Kanako shows up and the plan goes haywire. Naru's ego takes a nosedive and she bolts on a journey of self-discovery that not only makes her a wanted terrorist, but also helps her to finally come to terms with her "true" feelings for Keitaro.

CONTENTS

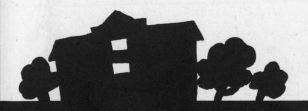

LOVE♡HINA

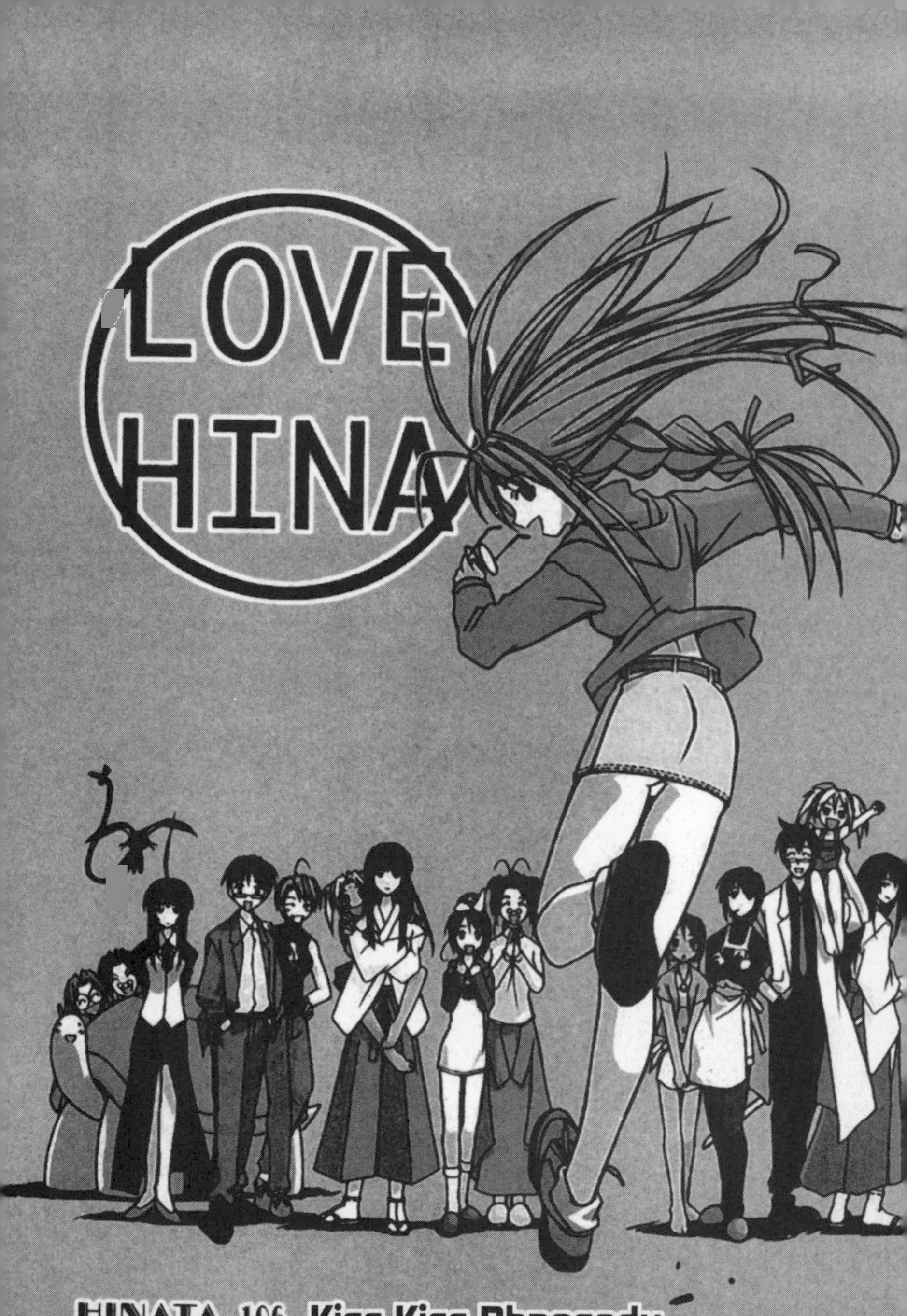
LOVE
HINA

HINATA.106 Kiss Kiss Rhapsody

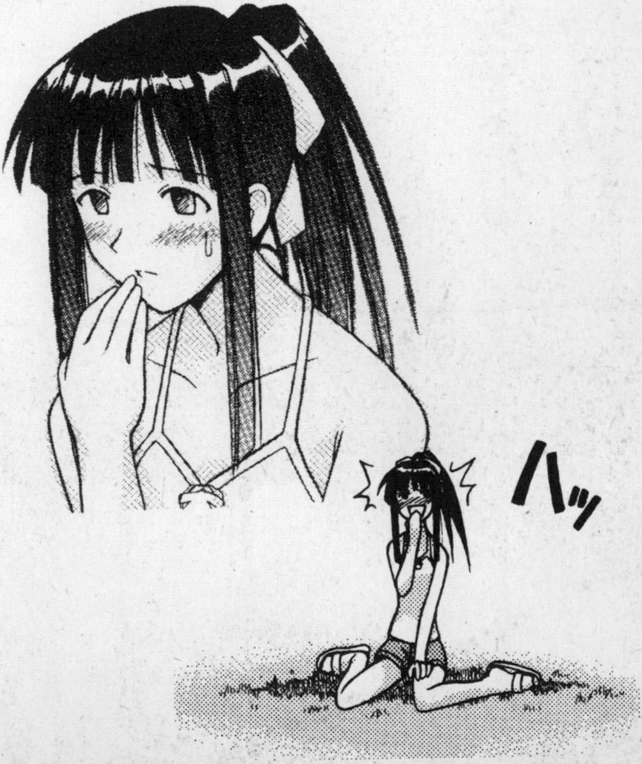
ハッ

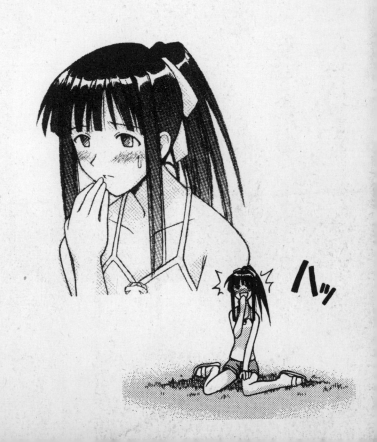

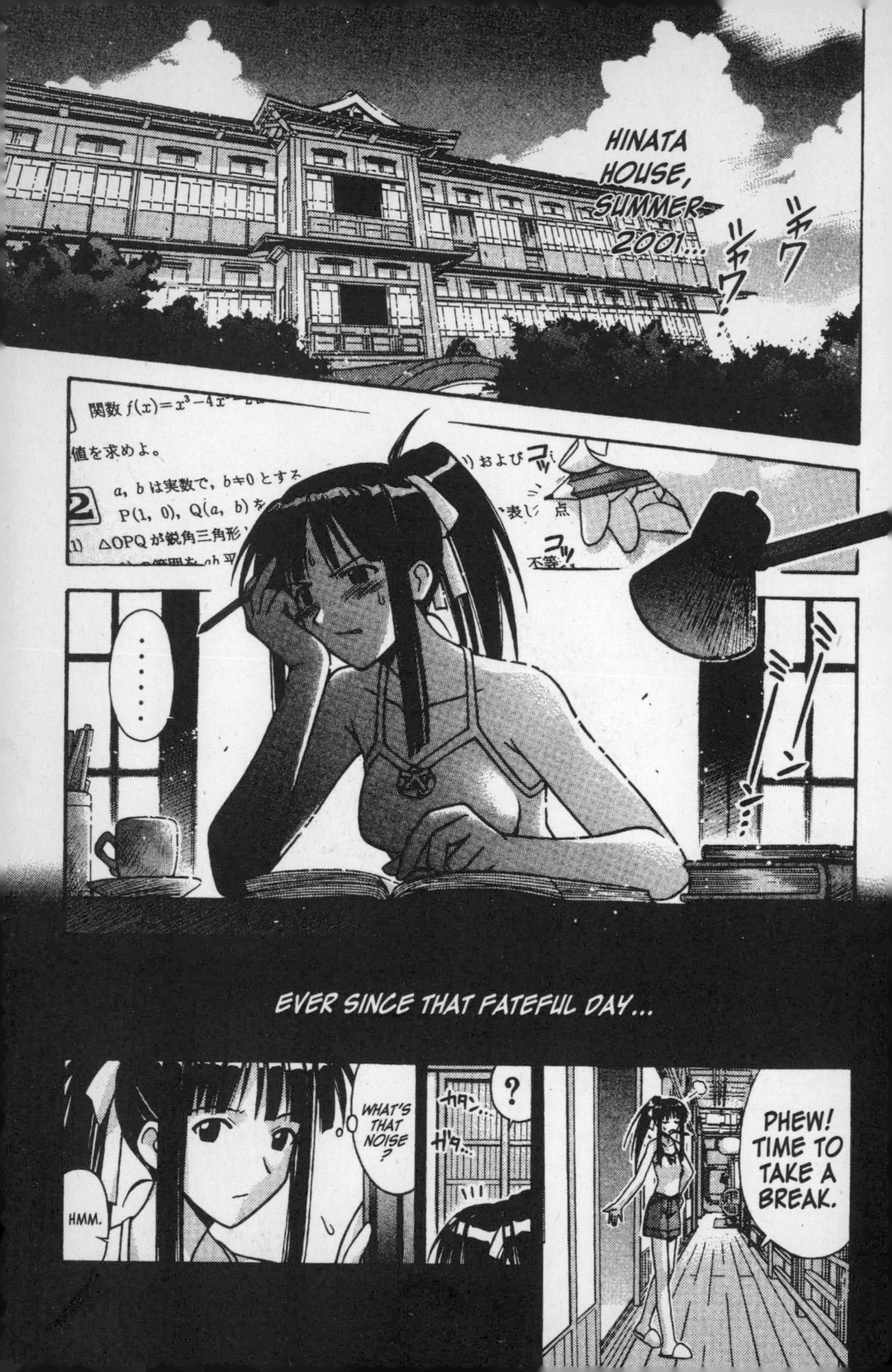
HINATA HOUSE, SUMMER 2001...
ジワ
ジワ…
関数 $f(x)=x^3-4x$
値を求めよ。
a, b は実数で, $b \neq 0$ とする
P(1, 0), Q(a, b) を
(1) △OPQ が鋭角三角形
りおよび
か表し
点
不等
コッ
コッ
……
ミーン
EVER SINCE THAT FATEFUL DAY...
PHEW! TIME TO TAKE A BREAK.
?
カタン…
ガタ…
WHAT'S THAT NOISE?
HMM.

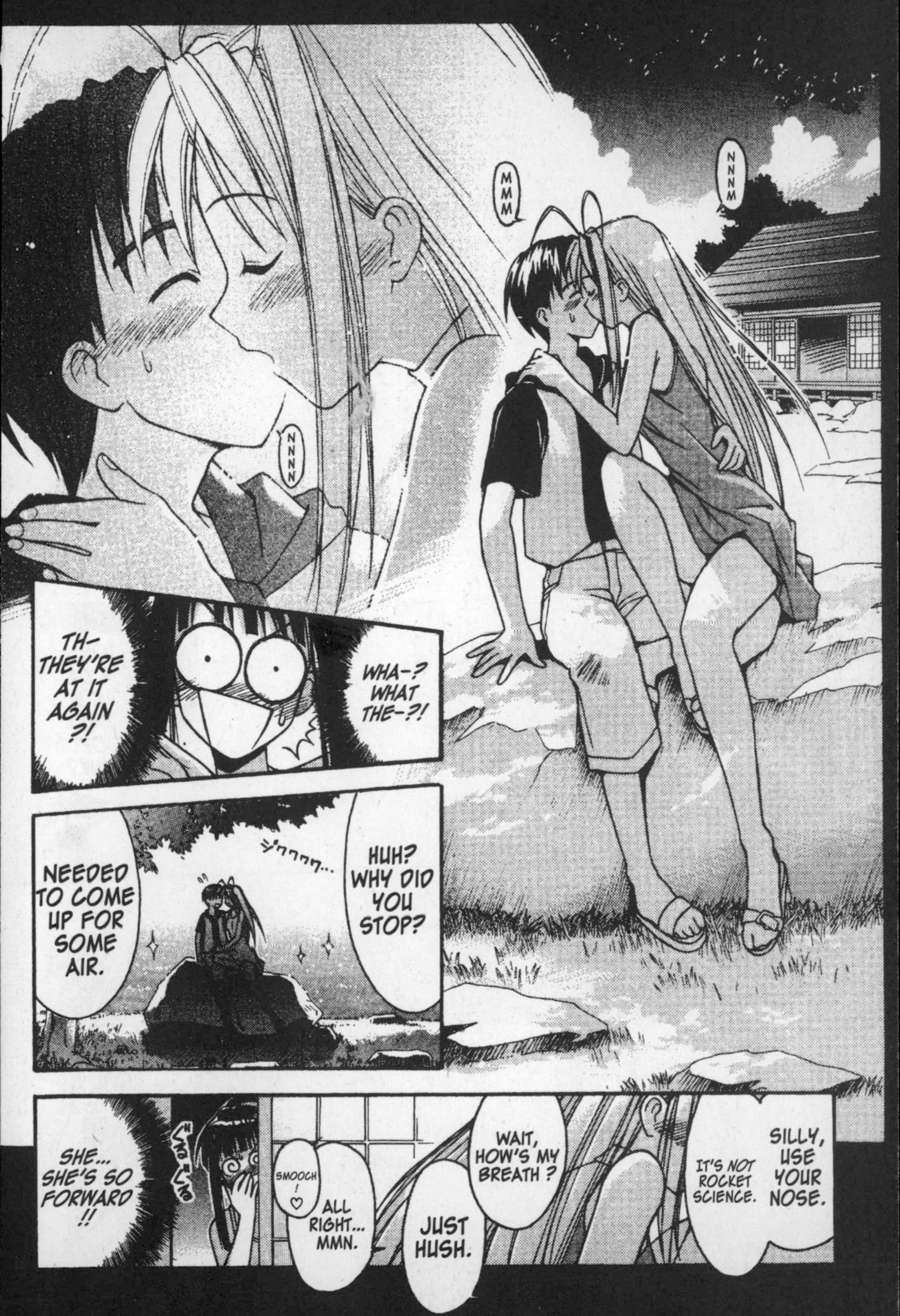
NNNM
MMM
NNNN
WHA-? WHAT THE-?!
TH- THEY'RE AT IT AGAIN ?!
HUH? WHY DID YOU STOP?
NEEDED TO COME UP FOR SOME AIR.
SILLY, USE YOUR NOSE.
IT'S NOT ROCKET SCIENCE.
WAIT, HOW'S MY BREATH ?
JUST HUSH.
ALL RIGHT... MMN.
SMOOCH! ♡
SHE... SHE'S SO FORWARD !!

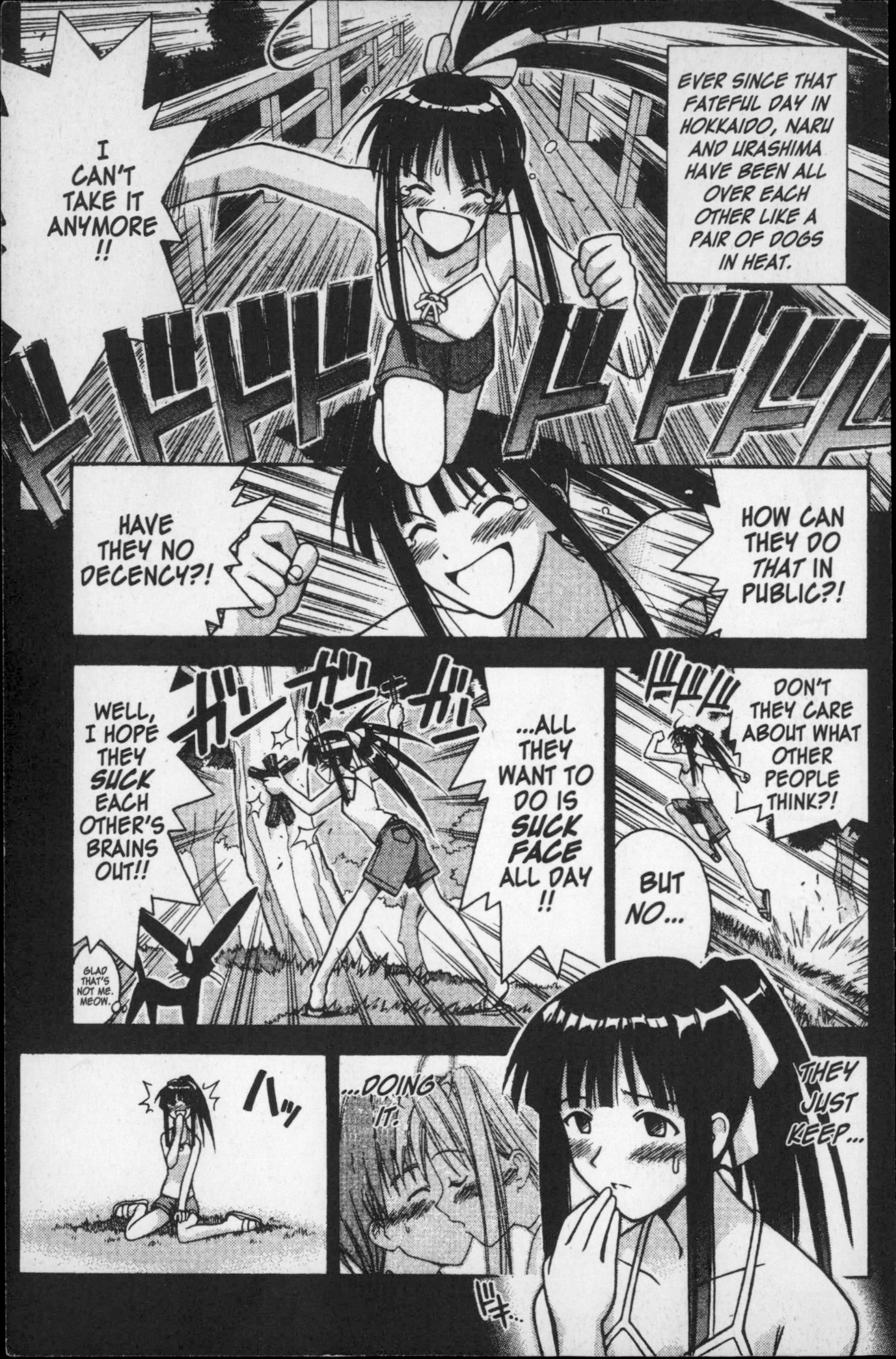

EVER SINCE THAT FATEFUL DAY IN HOKKAIDO, NARU AND URASHIMA HAVE BEEN ALL OVER EACH OTHER LIKE A PAIR OF DOGS IN HEAT.
I CAN'T TAKE IT ANYMORE !!
HOW CAN THEY DO THAT IN PUBLIC?!
HAVE THEY NO DECENCY?!
DON'T THEY CARE ABOUT WHAT OTHER PEOPLE THINK?!
BUT NO...
...ALL THEY WANT TO DO IS SUCK FACE ALL DAY !!
WELL, I HOPE THEY SUCK EACH OTHER'S BRAINS OUT!!
GLAD THAT'S NOT ME. MEOW.
THEY JUST KEEP...
...DOING IT.
ドキ...
ハッ

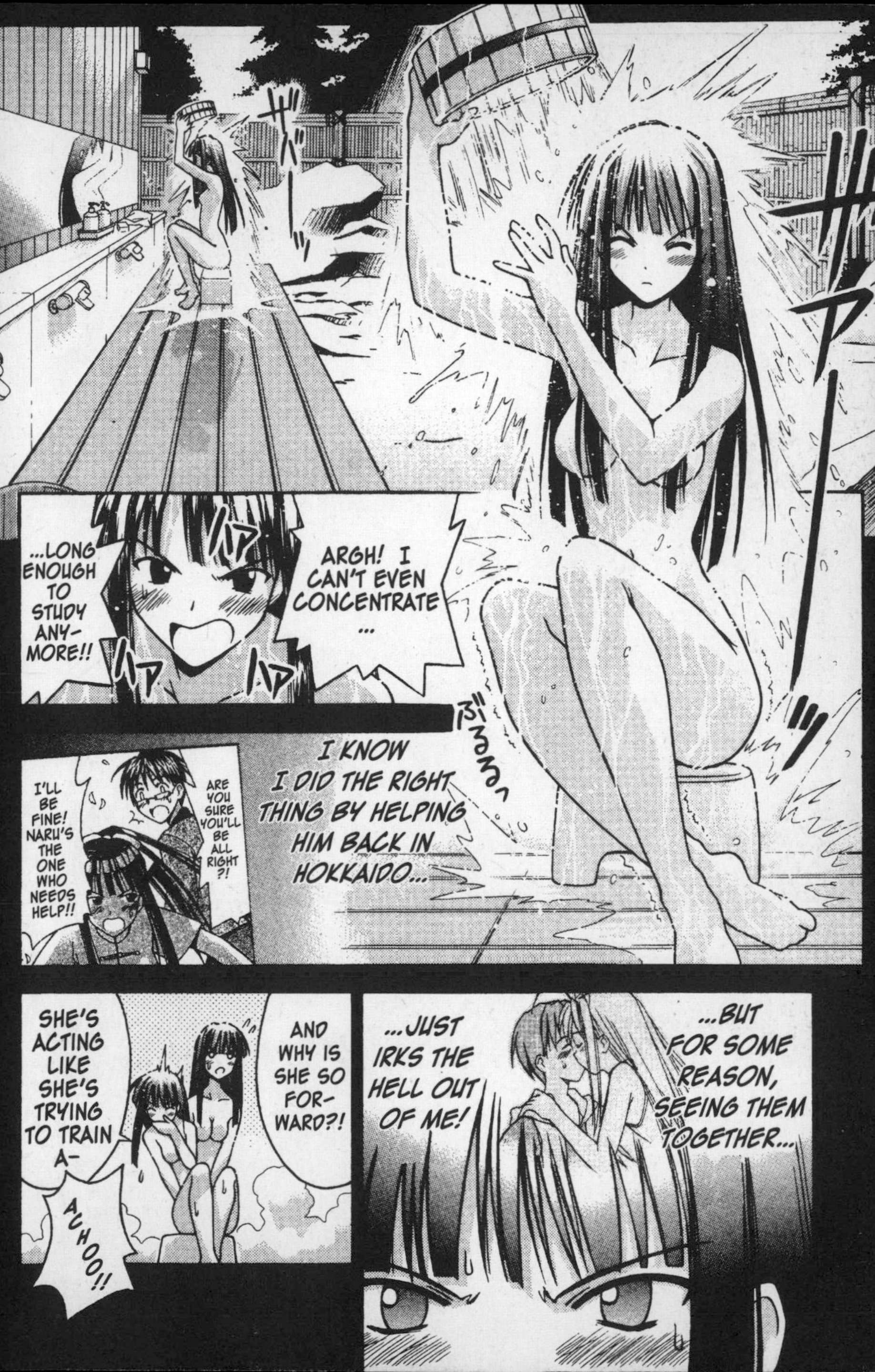
I KNOW I DID THE RIGHT THING BY HELPING HIM BACK IN HOKKAIDO...
ARGH! I CAN'T EVEN CONCENTRATE...
...LONG ENOUGH TO STUDY ANYMORE!!
ARE YOU SURE YOU'LL BE ALL RIGHT?!
I'LL BE FINE! NARU'S THE ONE WHO NEEDS HELP!!
...BUT FOR SOME REASON, SEEING THEM TOGETHER...
...JUST IRKS THE HELL OUT OF ME!
AND WHY IS SHE SO FOR-WARD?!
SHE'S ACTING LIKE SHE'S TRYING TO TRAIN A-
ACHOO!!

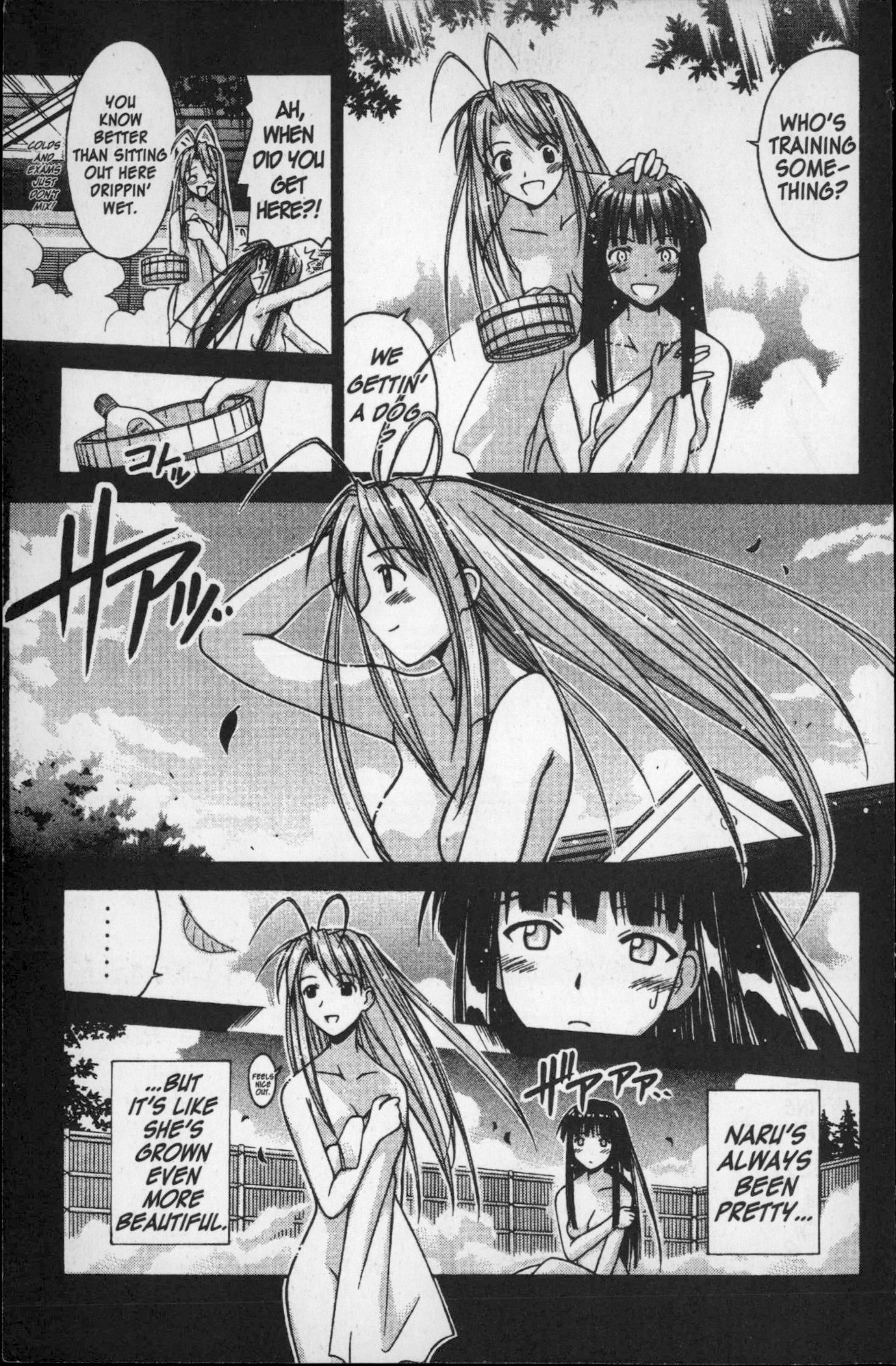
WHO'S TRAINING SOME-THING?
WE GETTIN' A DOG?
AH, WHEN DID YOU GET HERE?!
YOU KNOW BETTER THAN SITTING OUT HERE DRIPPIN' WET.
COLDS AND EXAMS JUST DON'T MIX!
コトッ
......
NARU'S ALWAYS BEEN PRETTY...
FEELS NICE OUT.
...BUT IT'S LIKE SHE'S GROWN EVEN MORE BEAUTIFUL.

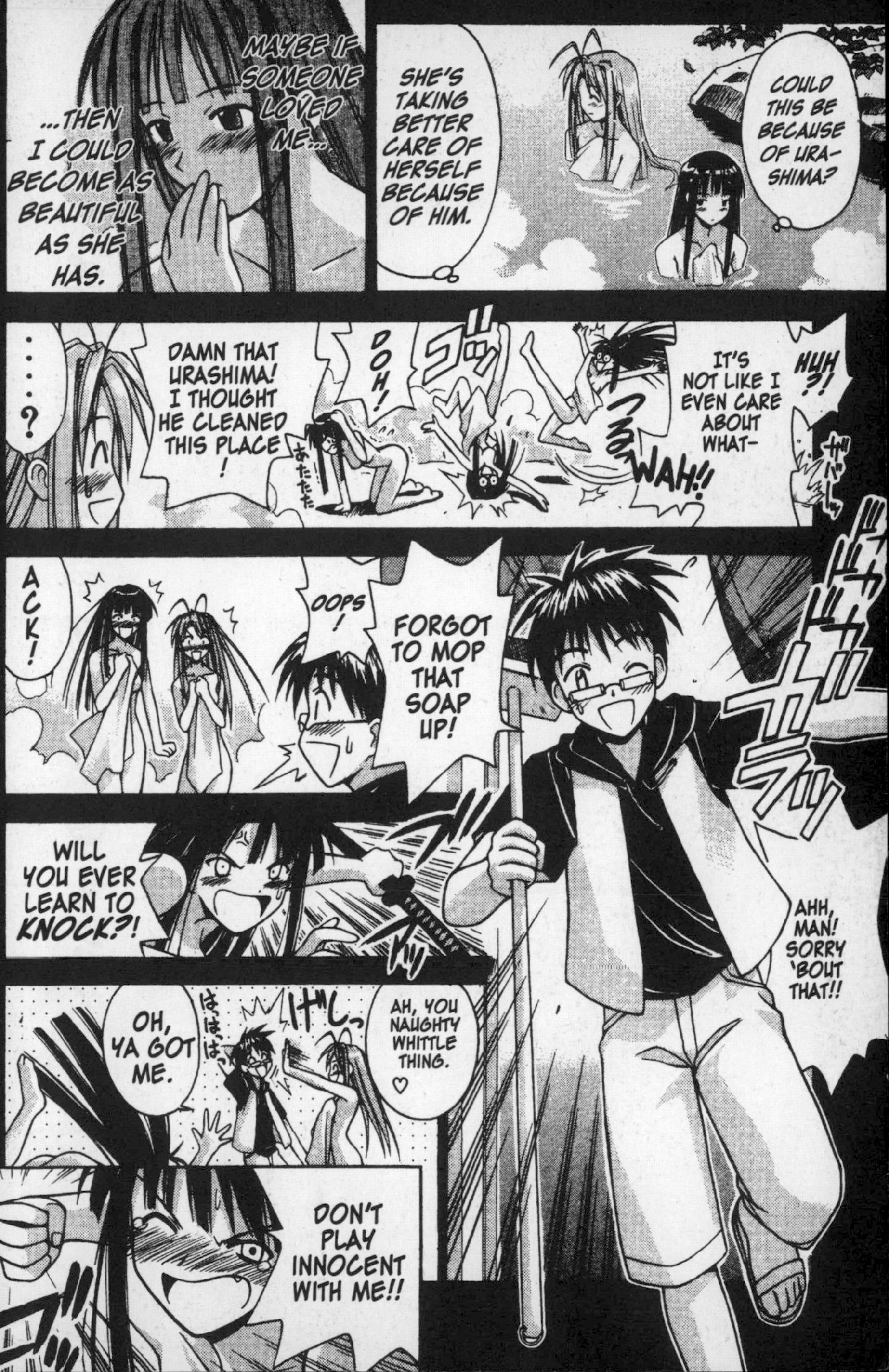
COULD THIS BE BECAUSE OF URA-SHIMA?
SHE'S TAKING BETTER CARE OF HERSELF BECAUSE OF HIM.
MAYBE IF SOMEONE LOVED ME...
...THEN I COULD BECOME AS BEAUTIFUL AS SHE HAS.
HUH?!
IT'S NOT LIKE I EVEN CARE ABOUT WHAT-
WAH!!
DOH!
あたたた
DAMN THAT URASHIMA! I THOUGHT HE CLEANED THIS PLACE!
...?
FORGOT TO MOP THAT SOAP UP!
OOPS!
ACK!
AHH, MAN! SORRY 'BOUT THAT!!
WILL YOU EVER LEARN TO KNOCK?!
AH, YOU NAUGHTY WHITTLE THING. ♡
げしっ
はは、は
OH, YA GOT ME.
DON'T PLAY INNOCENT WITH ME!!

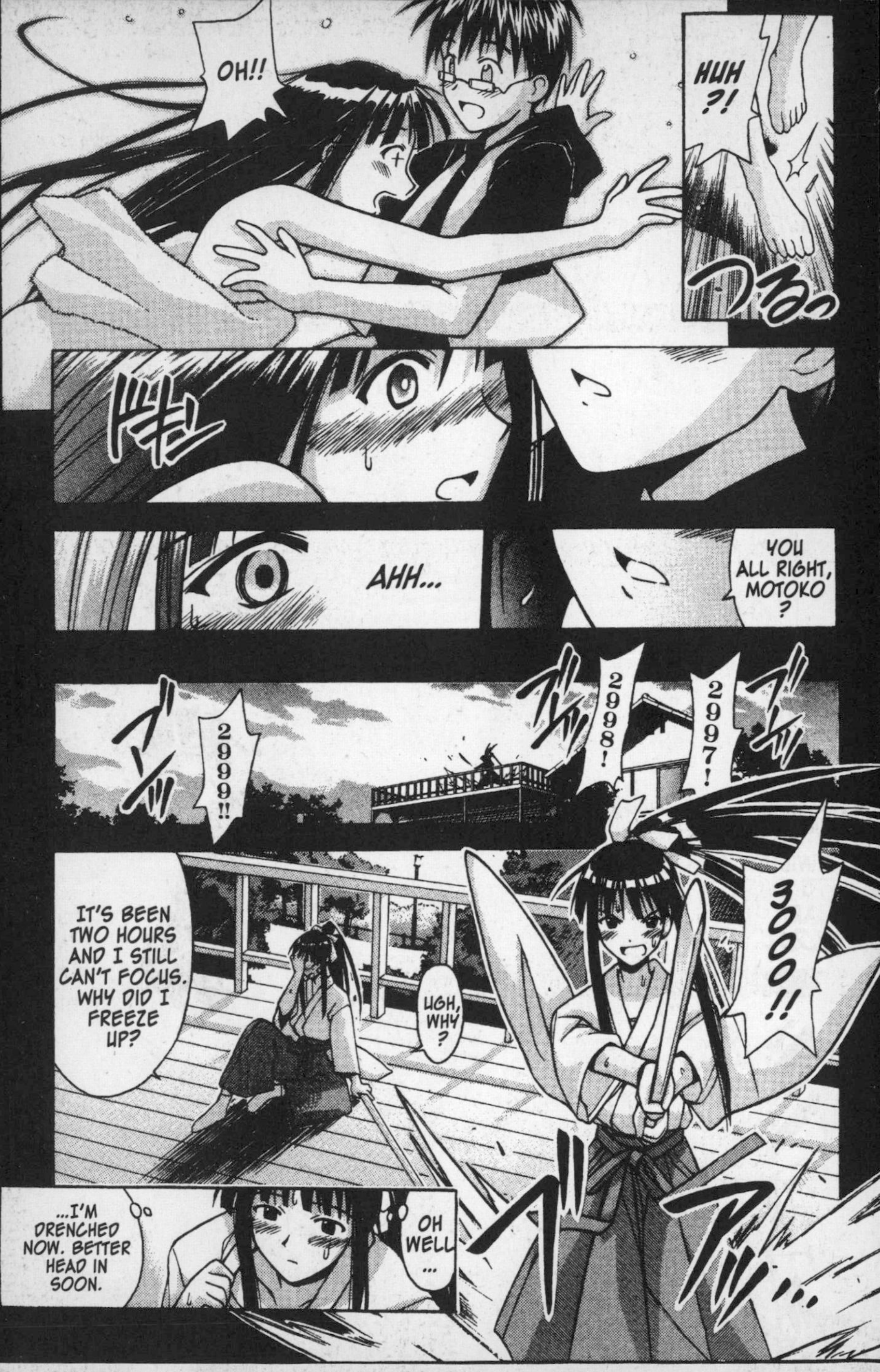
HUH ?!
つるっ
OH!!
ドキッ
YOU ALL RIGHT, MOTOKO ?
AHH...
2997!
2998!
2999!!
3000!!
UGH, WHY ?
IT'S BEEN TWO HOURS AND I STILL CAN'T FOCUS. WHY DID I FREEZE UP?
OH WELL ...
...I'M DRENCHED NOW. BETTER HEAD IN SOON.

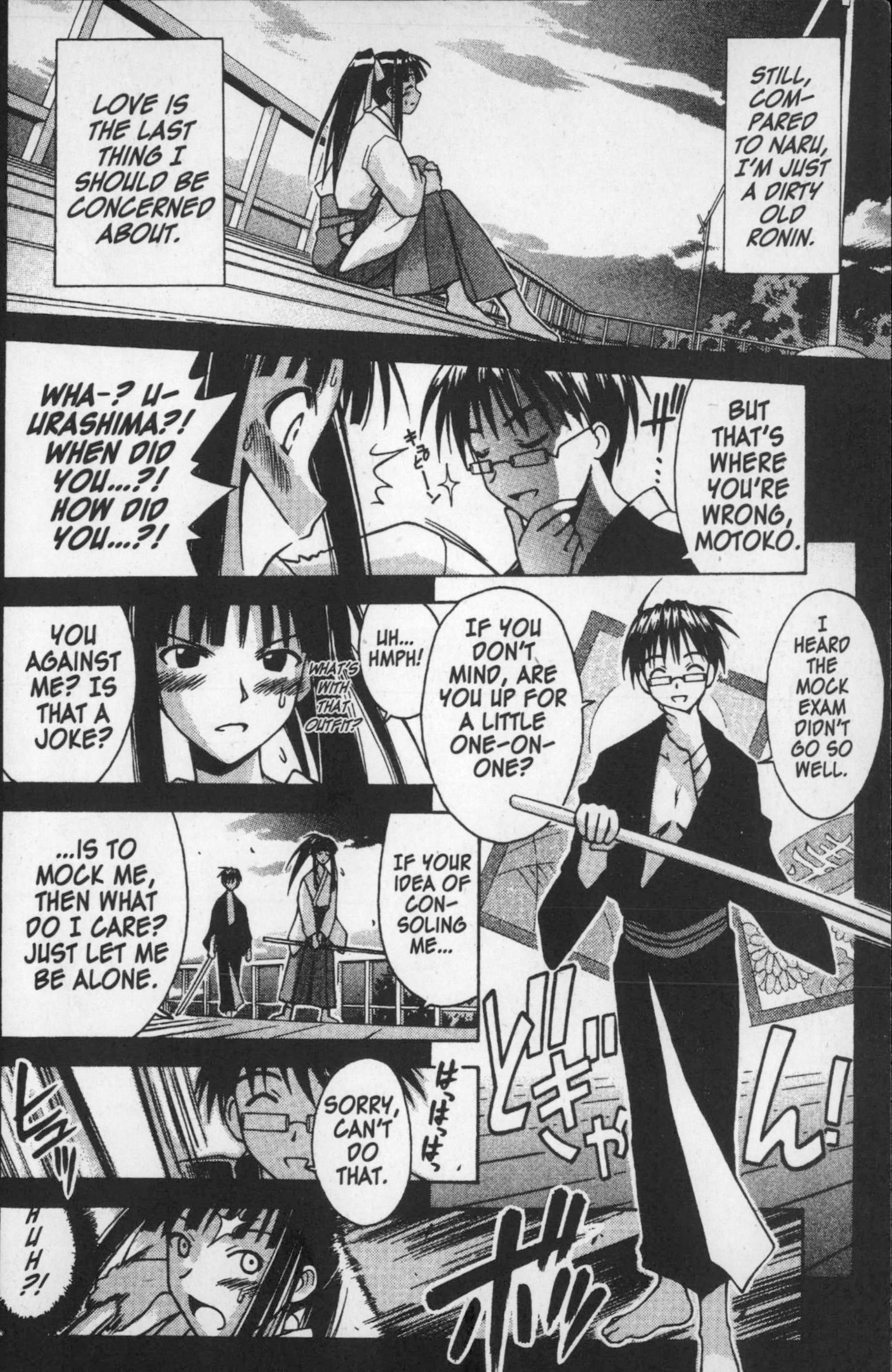
STILL, COMPARED TO NARU, I'M JUST A DIRTY OLD RONIN.
LOVE IS THE LAST THING I SHOULD BE CONCERNED ABOUT.
BUT THAT'S WHERE YOU'RE WRONG, MOTOKO.
WHA-? U-URASHIMA?! WHEN DID YOU...?! HOW DID YOU...?!
I HEARD THE MOCK EXAM DIDN'T GO SO WELL.
IF YOU DON'T MIND, ARE YOU UP FOR A LITTLE ONE-ON-ONE?
UH... HMPH!
WHAT'S WITH THAT OUTFIT?
YOU AGAINST ME? IS THAT A JOKE?
IF YOUR IDEA OF CONSOLING ME...
...IS TO MOCK ME, THEN WHAT DO I CARE? JUST LET ME BE ALONE.
SORRY, CAN'T DO THAT.
HUH?!

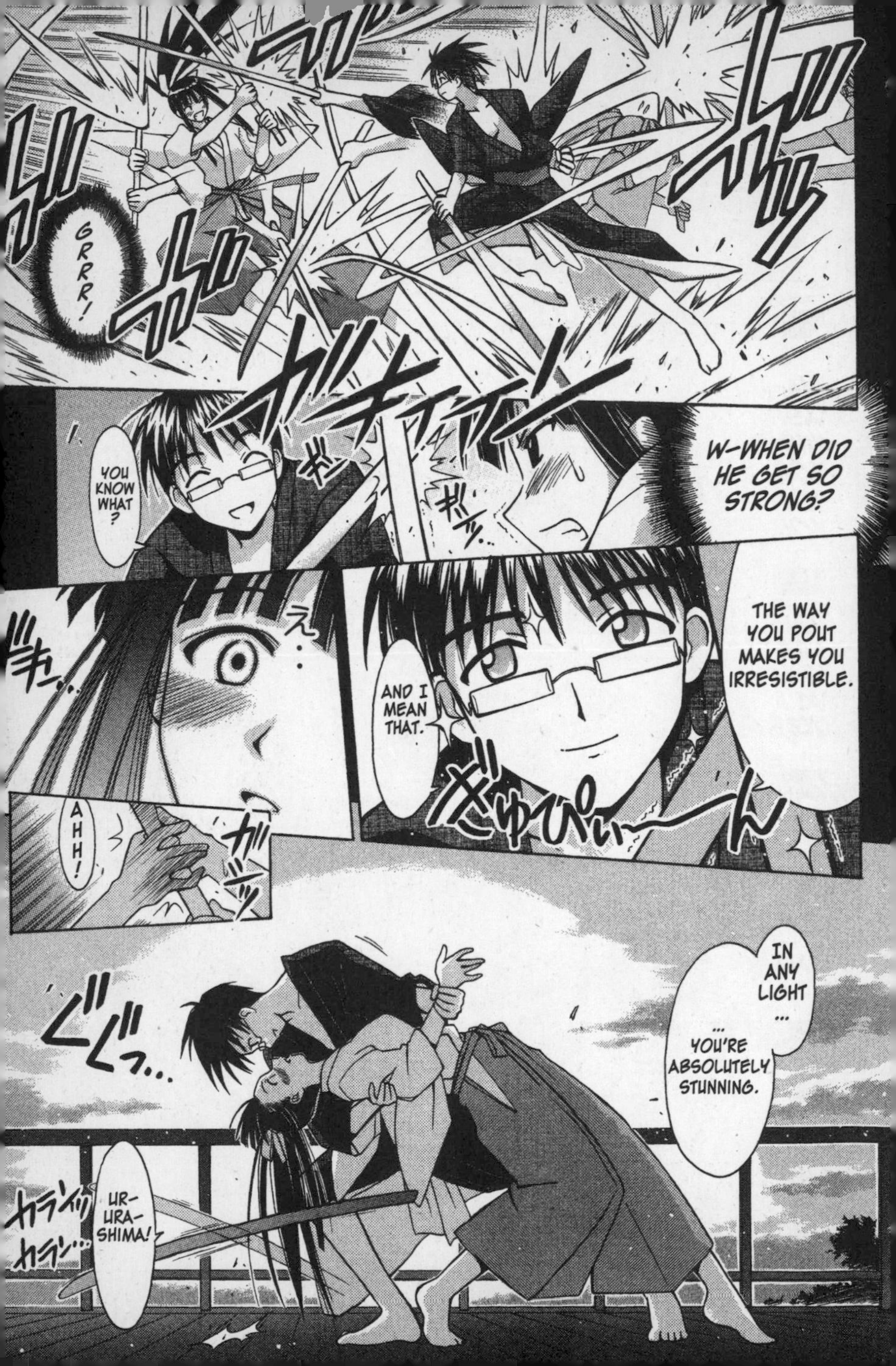
GRRR!
W-WHEN DID HE GET SO STRONG?
YOU KNOW WHAT?
THE WAY YOU POUT MAKES YOU IRRESISTIBLE.
AND I MEAN THAT.
え…
AHH!
IN ANY LIGHT ... YOU'RE ABSOLUTELY STUNNING.
UR-URA-SHIMA!

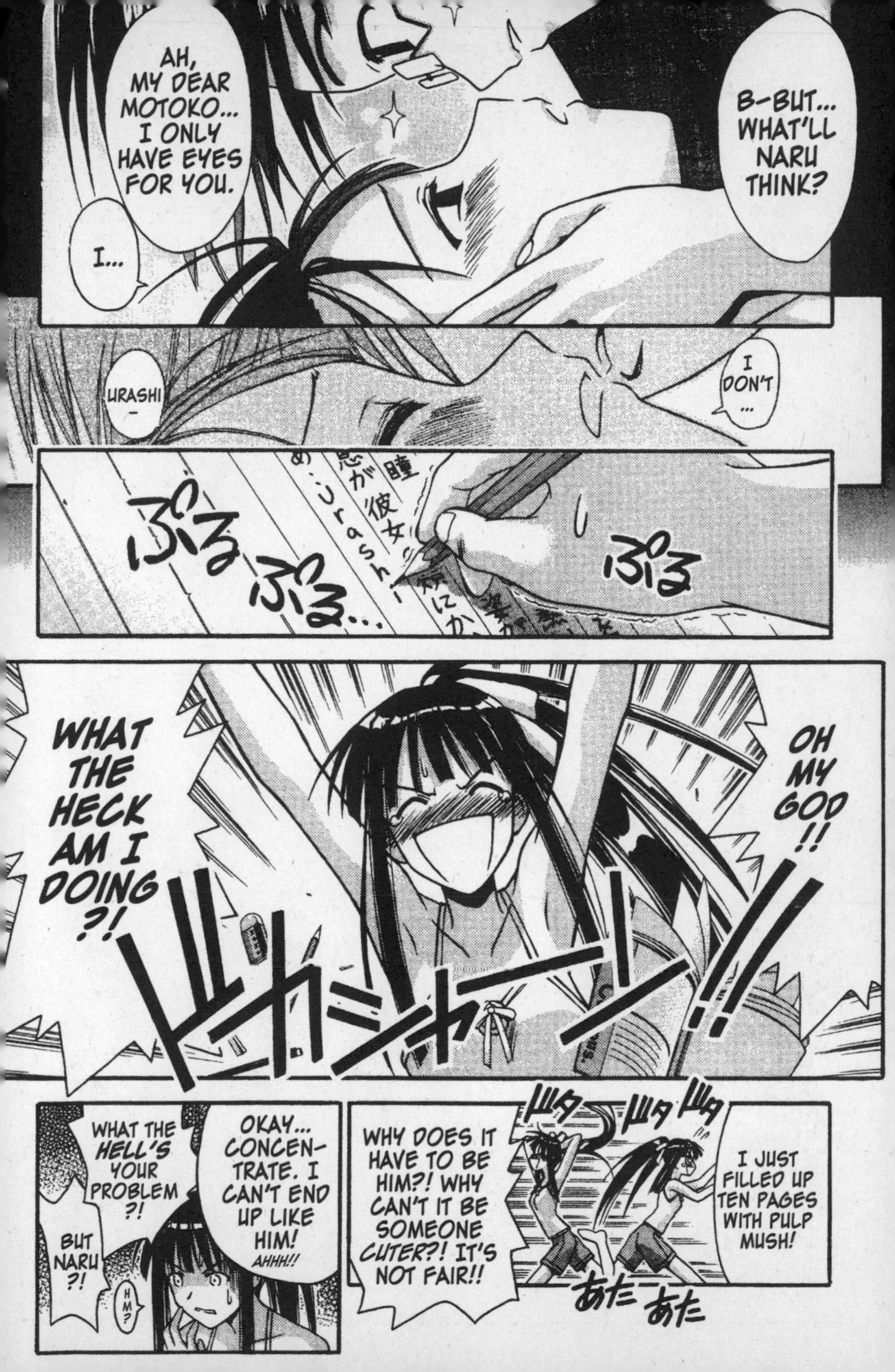
B-BUT... WHAT'LL NARU THINK?
AH, MY DEAR MOTOKO... I ONLY HAVE EYES FOR YOU.
I...
I DON'T ...
URASHI-
ぷる
ぷる ぷる...
OH MY GOD!!
WHAT THE HECK AM I DOING?!
ドガシャーン!!
ジタ ジタ ジタ
I JUST FILLED UP TEN PAGES WITH PULP MUSH!
WHY DOES IT HAVE TO BE HIM?! WHY CAN'T IT BE SOMEONE CUTER?! IT'S NOT FAIR!!
あた あた
OKAY... CONCENTRATE. I CAN'T END UP LIKE HIM! AHHH!!
WHAT THE HELL'S YOUR PROBLEM?!
BUT NARU?!
HM?

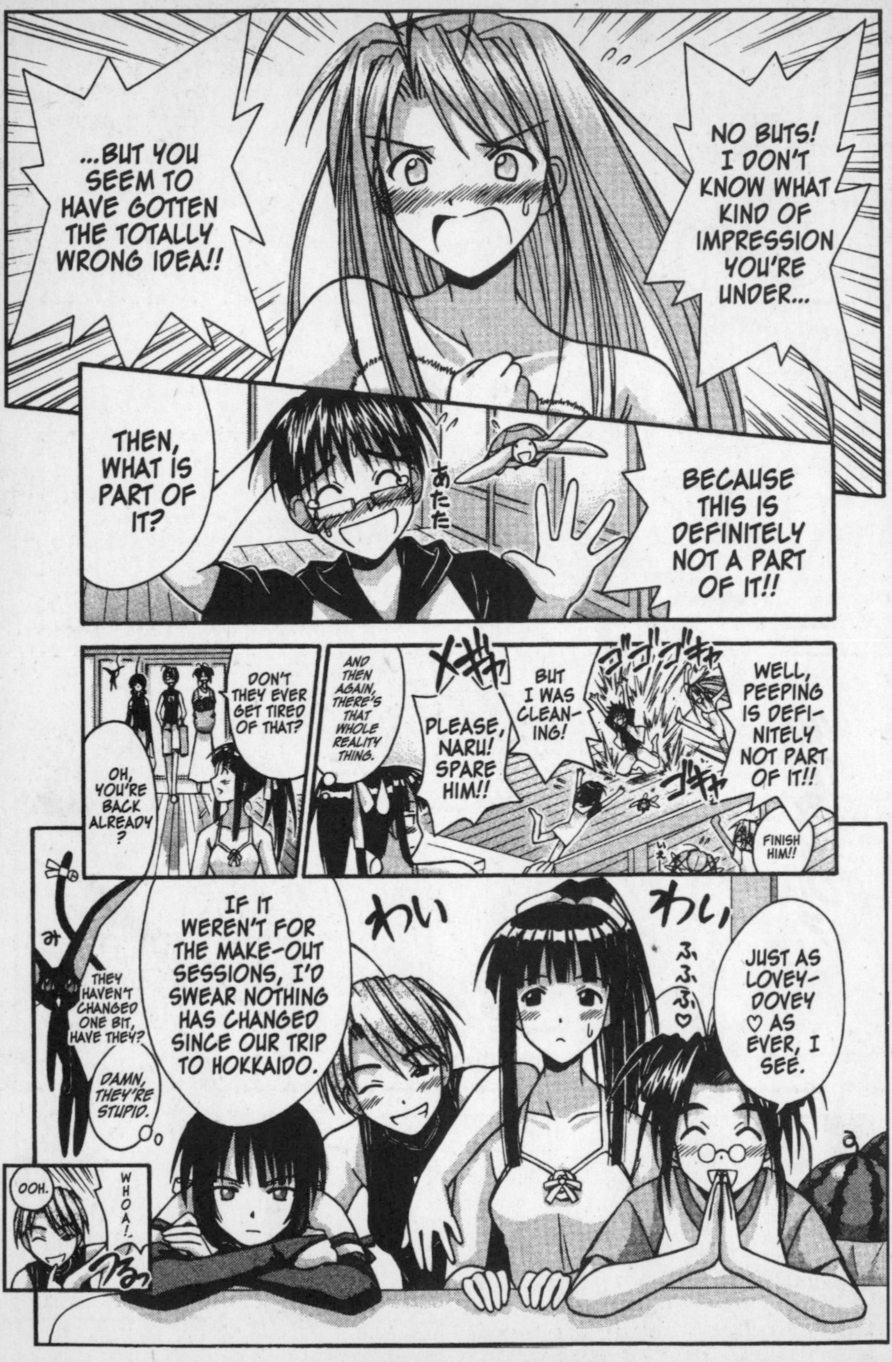
NO BUTS! I DON'T KNOW WHAT KIND OF IMPRESSION YOU'RE UNDER...
...BUT YOU SEEM TO HAVE GOTTEN THE TOTALLY WRONG IDEA!!
BECAUSE THIS IS DEFINITELY NOT A PART OF IT!!
あたた
THEN, WHAT IS PART OF IT?
WELL, PEEPING IS DEFI-NITELY NOT PART OF IT!!
ゴゴゴキャ
BUT I WAS CLEAN-ING!
メギャ
PLEASE, NARU! SPARE HIM!!
AND THEN AGAIN, THERE'S THAT WHOLE REALITY THING.
ゴキャ
FINISH HIM!!
DON'T THEY EVER GET TIRED OF THAT?
OH, YOU'RE BACK ALREADY?
JUST AS LOVEY-DOVEY ♡ AS EVER, I SEE.
ふふふ♡
わい
わい
IF IT WEREN'T FOR THE MAKE-OUT SESSIONS, I'D SWEAR NOTHING HAS CHANGED SINCE OUR TRIP TO HOKKAIDO.
み
THEY HAVEN'T CHANGED ONE BIT, HAVE THEY?
DAMN, THEY'RE STUPID.
WHOA!
OOH.

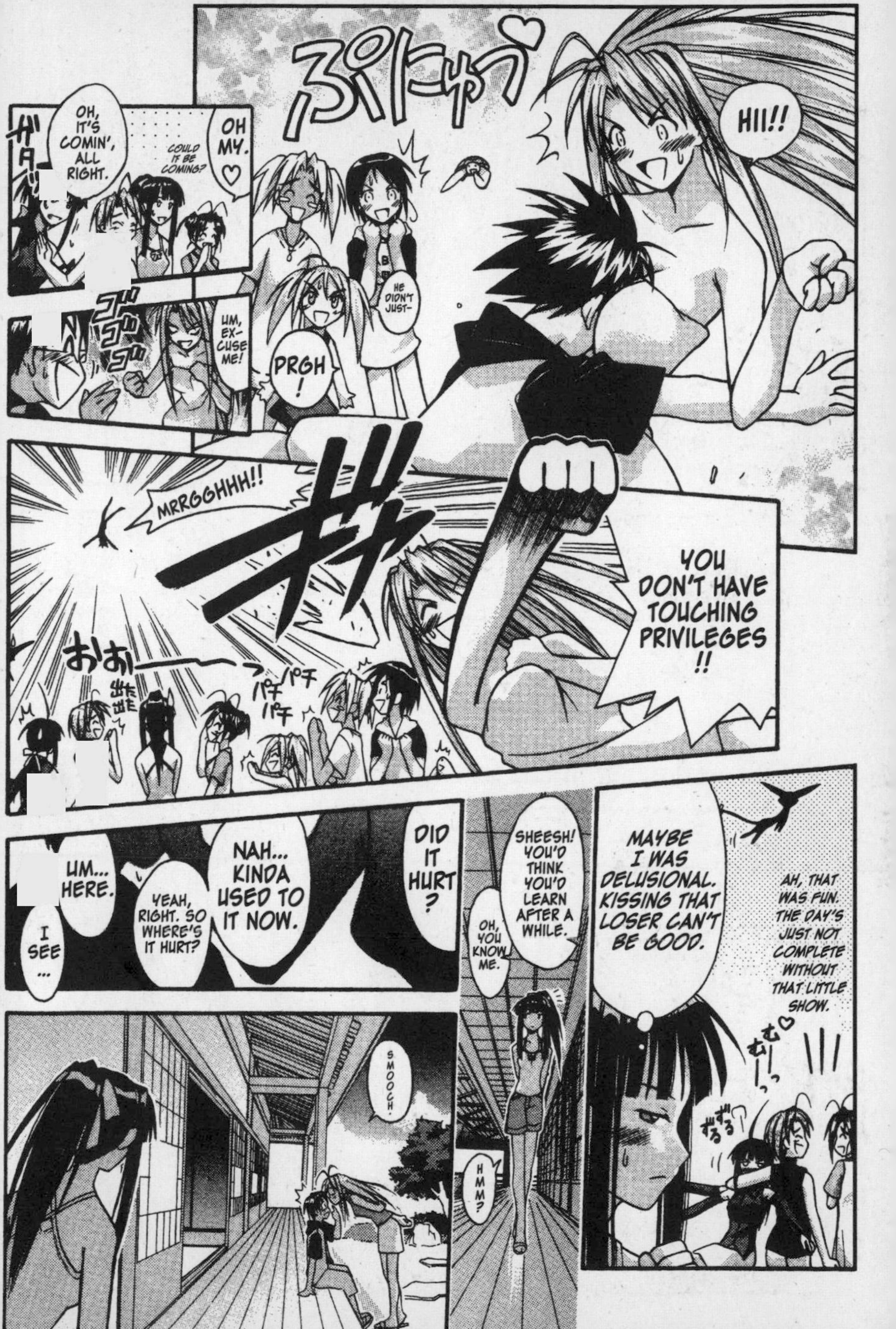
ぷにゅっ♡
HII!!
HE DIDN'T JUST-
PRGH!
OH MY. ♡
COULD IT BE COMING?
OH, IT'S COMIN', ALL RIGHT.
UM, EXCUSE ME!
MRRGGHHH!!
YOU DON'T HAVE TOUCHING PRIVILEGES!!
おお～～
パチパチパチ
AH, THAT WAS FUN. THE DAY'S JUST NOT COMPLETE WITHOUT THAT LITTLE SHOW.
MAYBE I WAS DELUSIONAL. KISSING THAT LOSER CAN'T BE GOOD.
SHEESH! YOU'D THINK YOU'D LEARN AFTER A WHILE.
OH, YOU KNOW ME.
HMM?
DID IT HURT?
NAH... KINDA USED TO IT NOW.
YEAH, RIGHT. SO WHERE'S IT HURT?
UM... HERE.
I SEE...
SMOOCH.

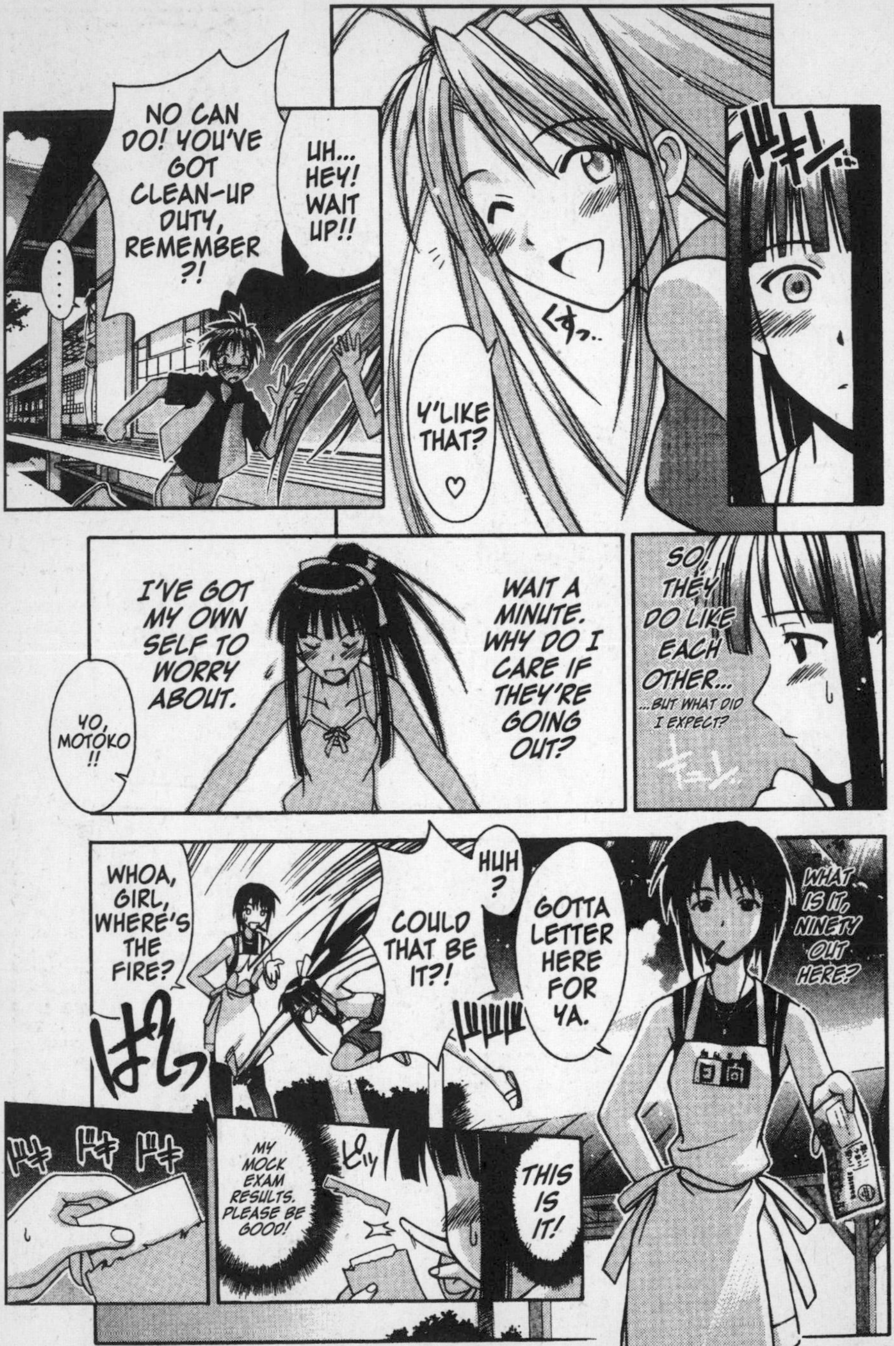
ドキン
くすっ..
Y'LIKE THAT?
♡
UH... HEY! WAIT UP!!
NO CAN DO! YOU'VE GOT CLEAN-UP DUTY, REMEMBER?!
......
SO, THEY DO LIKE EACH OTHER...
...BUT WHAT DID I EXPECT?
キュン
WAIT A MINUTE. WHY DO I CARE IF THEY'RE GOING OUT?
I'VE GOT MY OWN SELF TO WORRY ABOUT.
YO, MOTOKO!!
WHAT IS IT, NINETY OUT HERE?
GOTTA LETTER HERE FOR YA.
HUH?
COULD THAT BE IT?!
WHOA, GIRL, WHERE'S THE FIRE?
ぱっ
THIS IS IT!
ピッ
MY MOCK EXAM RESULTS. PLEASE BE GOOD!
ドキ ドキ ドキ

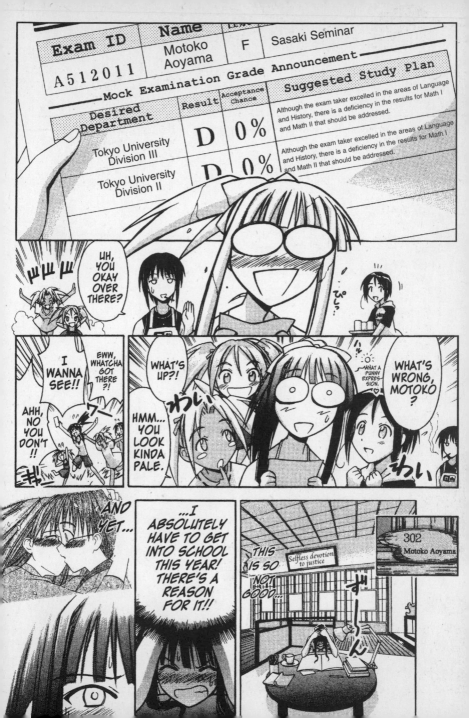

Exam ID	Name		Sasaki Seminar
A512011	Motoko Aoyama	F	

Mock Examination Grade Announcement

Desired Department	Result	Acceptance Chance	Suggested Study Plan
Tokyo University Division III	D	0%	Although the exam taker excelled in the areas of Language and History, there is a deficiency in the results for Math I and Math II that should be addressed.
Tokyo University Division II	D	0%	Although the exam taker excelled in the areas of Language and History, there is a deficiency in the results for Math I and Math II that should be addressed.

UH, YOU OKAY OVER THERE?

I WANNA SEE!!

AHH, NO YOU DON'T!!

EWW, WHATCHA GOT THERE?!

WHAT'S UP?!

HMM... YOU LOOK KINDA PALE.

WHAT A FUNNY EXPRESSION.

WHAT'S WRONG, MOTOKO?

AND YET...

...I ABSOLUTELY HAVE TO GET INTO SCHOOL THIS YEAR! THERE'S A REASON FOR IT!!

THIS IS SO NOT GOOD...

Selfless devotion to justice

302
Motoko Aoyama

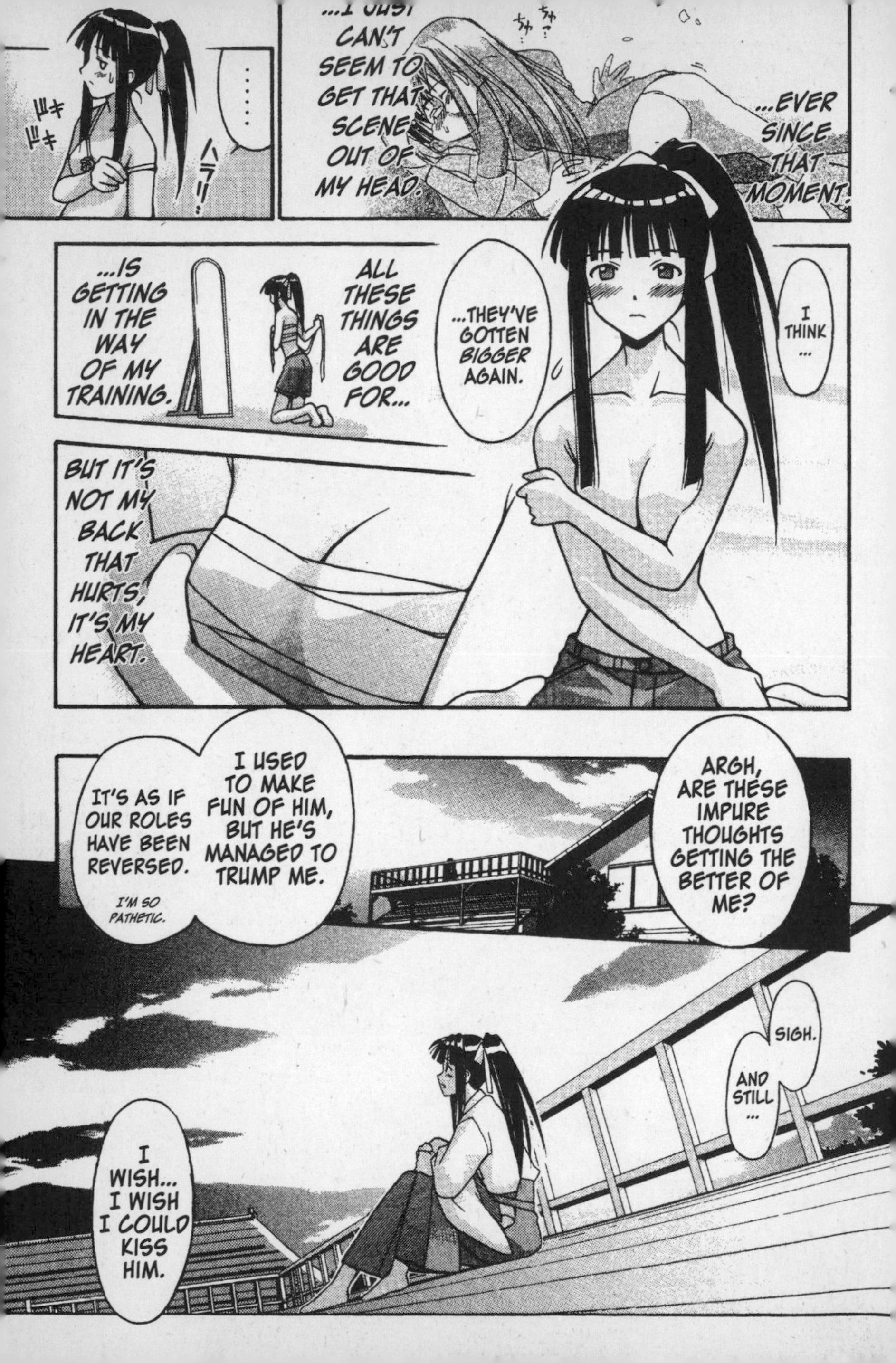
...I JUST CAN'T SEEM TO GET THAT SCENE OUT OF MY HEAD.
...EVER SINCE THAT MOMENT.
......
ドキドキ
I THINK...
...THEY'VE GOTTEN BIGGER AGAIN.
ALL THESE THINGS ARE GOOD FOR...
...IS GETTING IN THE WAY OF MY TRAINING.
BUT IT'S NOT MY BACK THAT HURTS, IT'S MY HEART.
ARGH, ARE THESE IMPURE THOUGHTS GETTING THE BETTER OF ME?
I USED TO MAKE FUN OF HIM, BUT HE'S MANAGED TO TRUMP ME.
IT'S AS IF OUR ROLES HAVE BEEN REVERSED.
I'M SO PATHETIC.
SIGH.
AND STILL...
I WISH... I WISH I COULD KISS HIM.

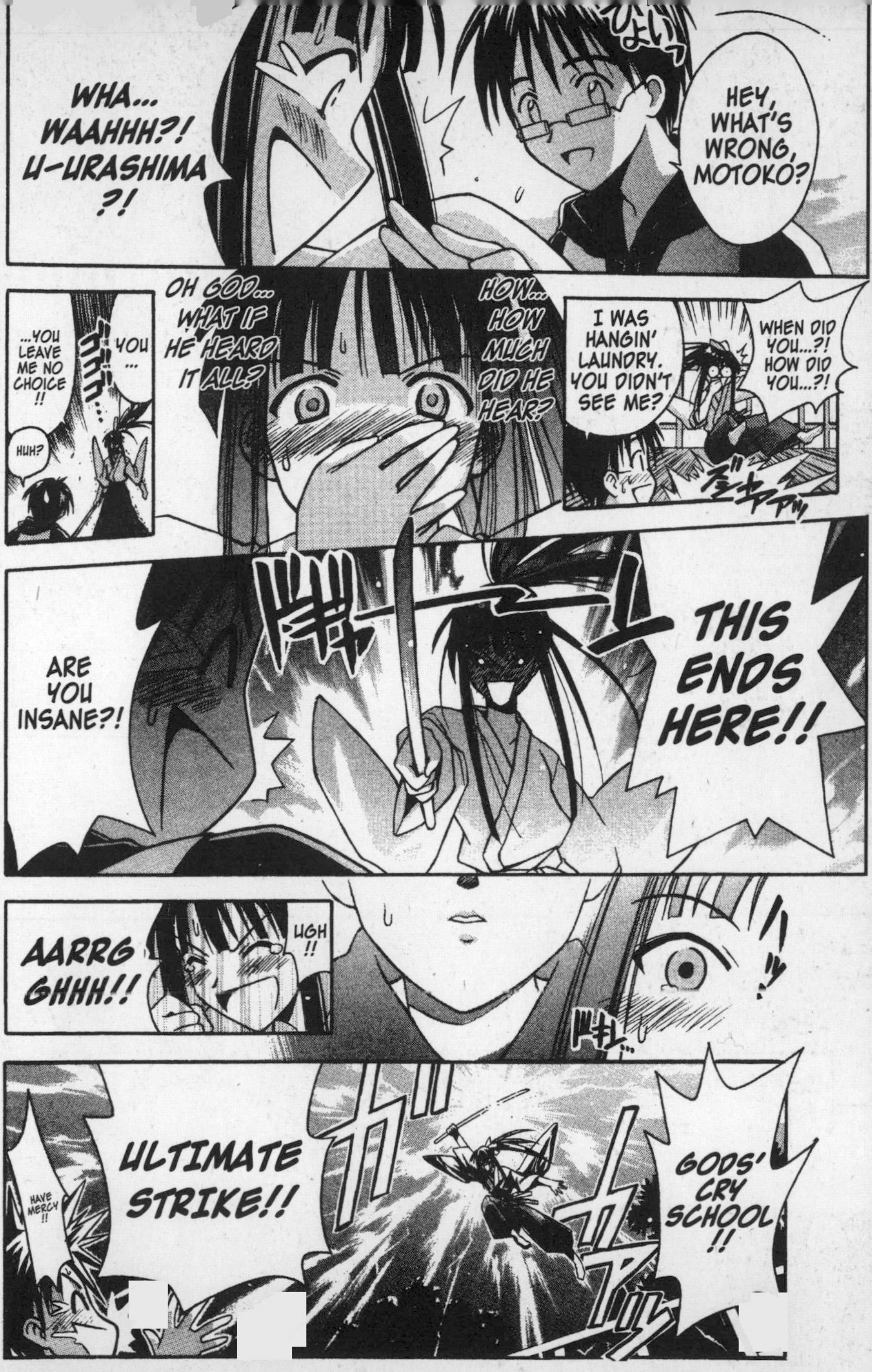

HEY, WHAT'S WRONG, MOTOKO?
WHA... WAAHHH?! U-URASHIMA ?!
WHEN DID YOU...?! HOW DID YOU...?!
I WAS HANGIN' LAUNDRY. YOU DIDN'T SEE ME?
HOW... HOW MUCH DID HE HEAR?
OH GOD... WHAT IF HE HEARD IT ALL?
YOU ...
...YOU LEAVE ME NO CHOICE !!
HUH?
THIS ENDS HERE!!
ARE YOU INSANE?!
UGH !!
AARRG GHHH!!
GODS' CRY SCHOOL !!
ULTIMATE STRIKE!!
HAVE MERCY !!

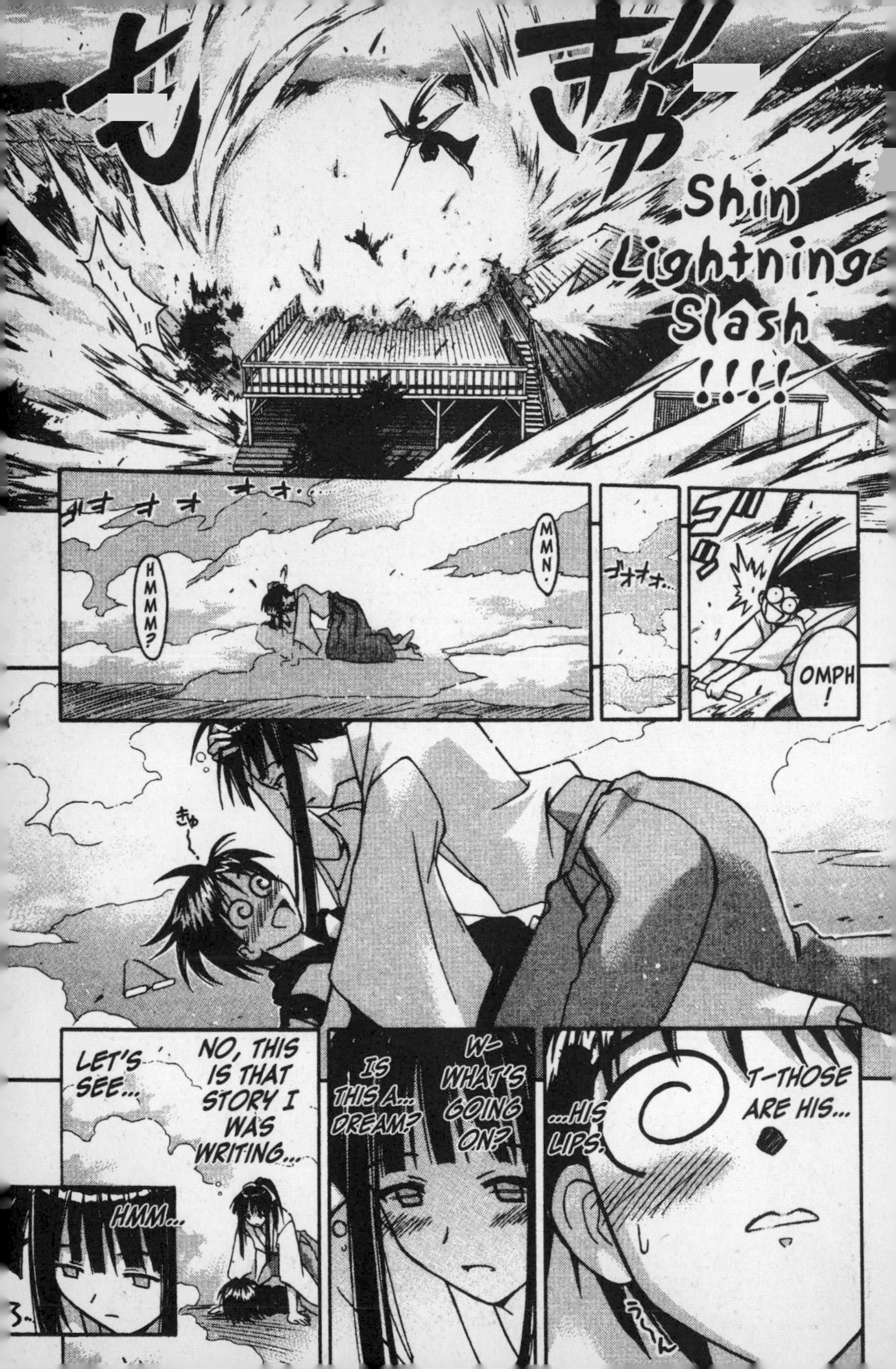

Shin Lightning Slash !!!!
H------!!
OMPH!
MMN.
HMMM?
T-THOSE ARE HIS...
...HIS LIPS.
W-WHAT'S GOING ON?
IS THIS A... DREAM?
NO, THIS IS THAT STORY I WAS WRITING...
LET'S SEE...
HMM...

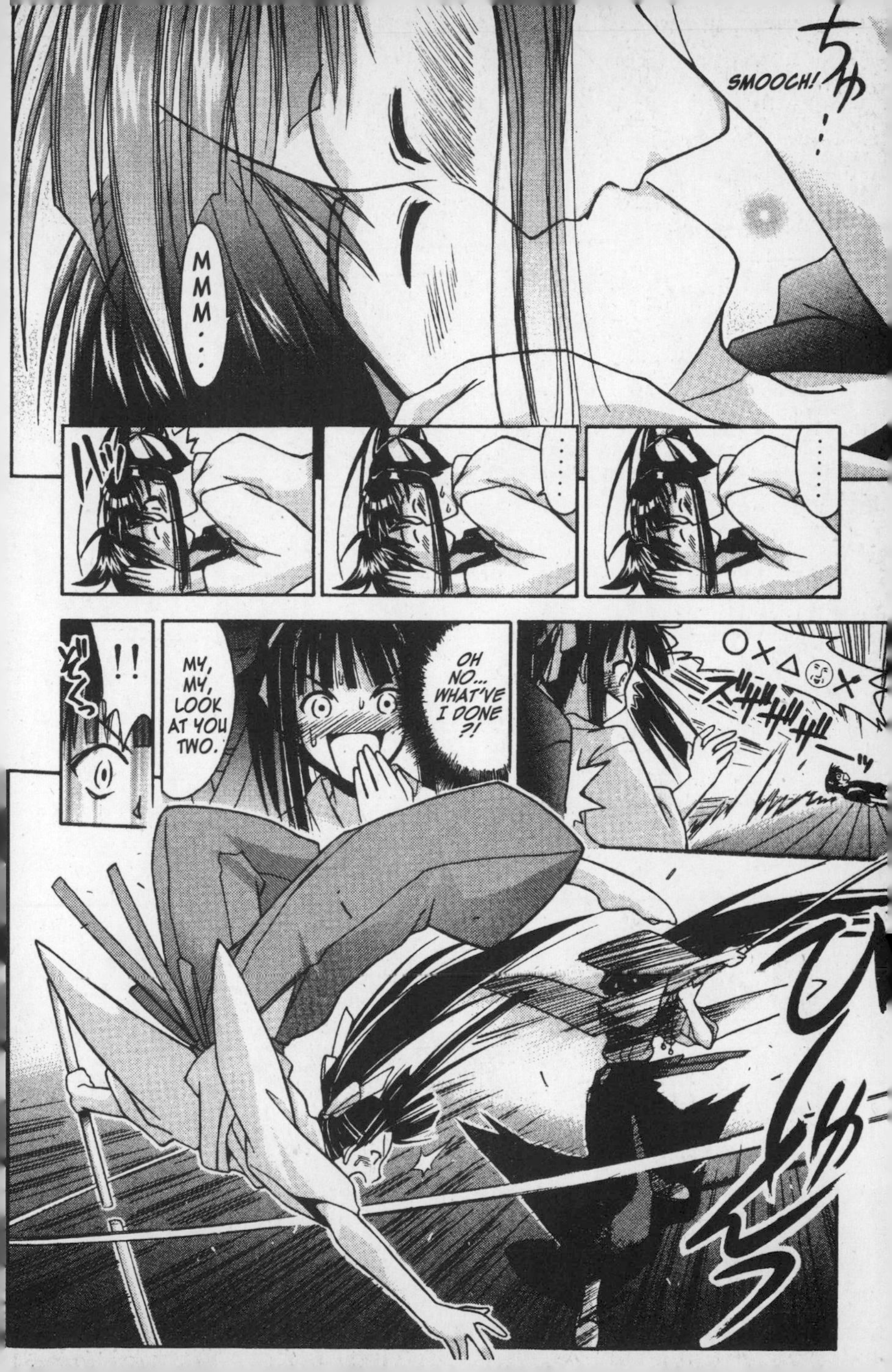
SMOOCH!
MMM...
OH NO... WHAT'VE I DONE?!
MY, MY, LOOK AT YOU TWO.
!!

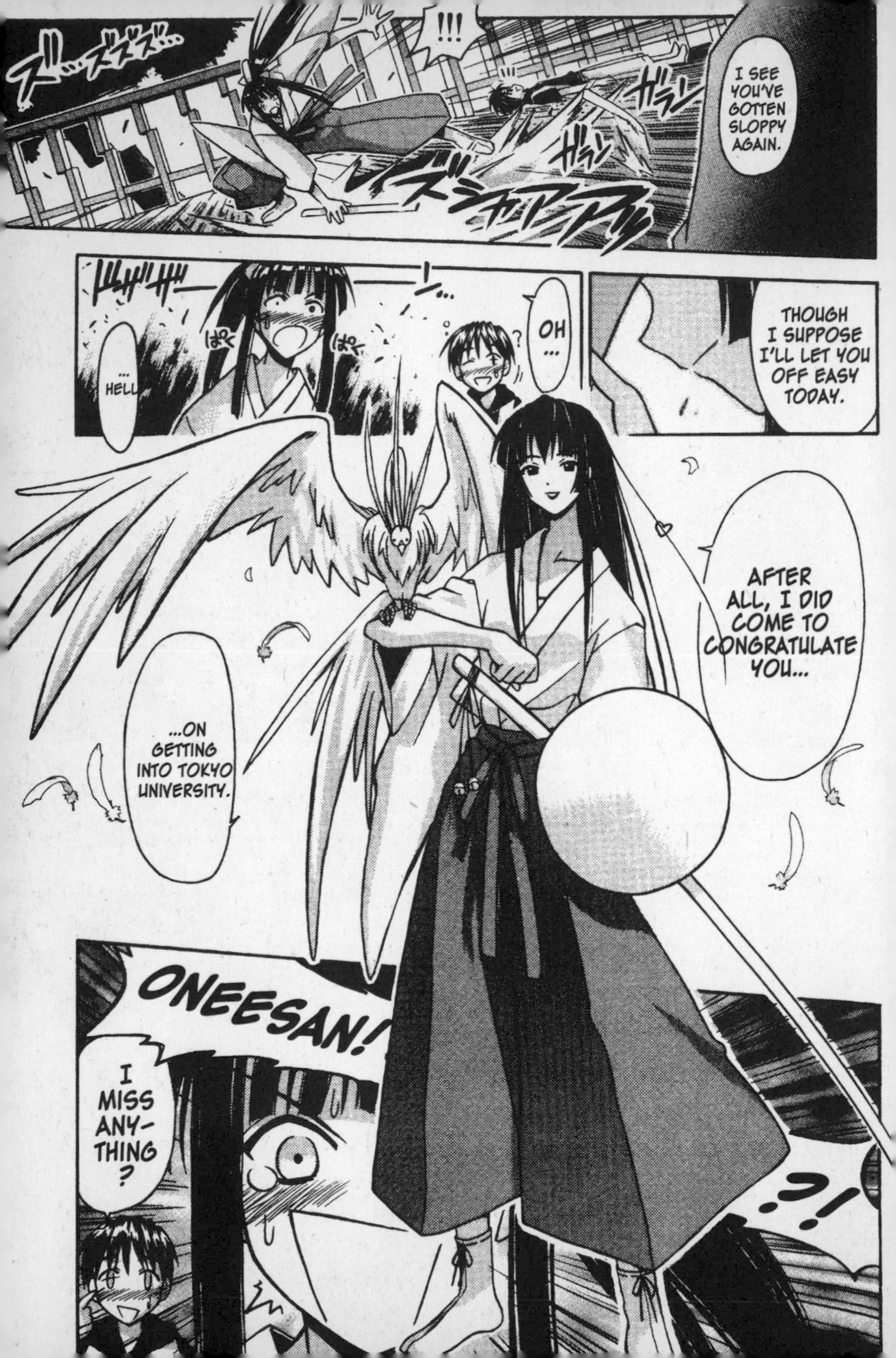

!!!
I SEE YOU'VE GOTTEN SLOPPY AGAIN.
THOUGH I SUPPOSE I'LL LET YOU OFF EASY TODAY.
OH ...
...HELL
AFTER ALL, I DID COME TO CONGRATULATE YOU...
...ON GETTING INTO TOKYO UNIVERSITY.
ONEESAN!
I MISS ANYTHING?
?!

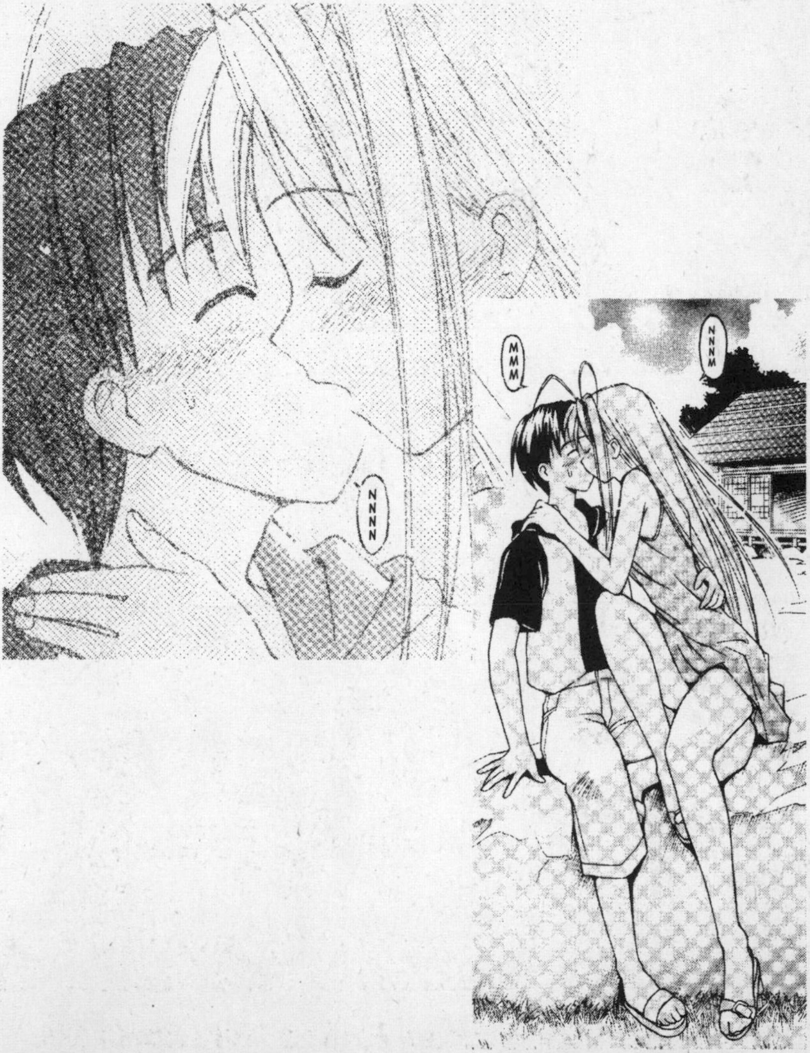
NNNN
MMM
NNNN

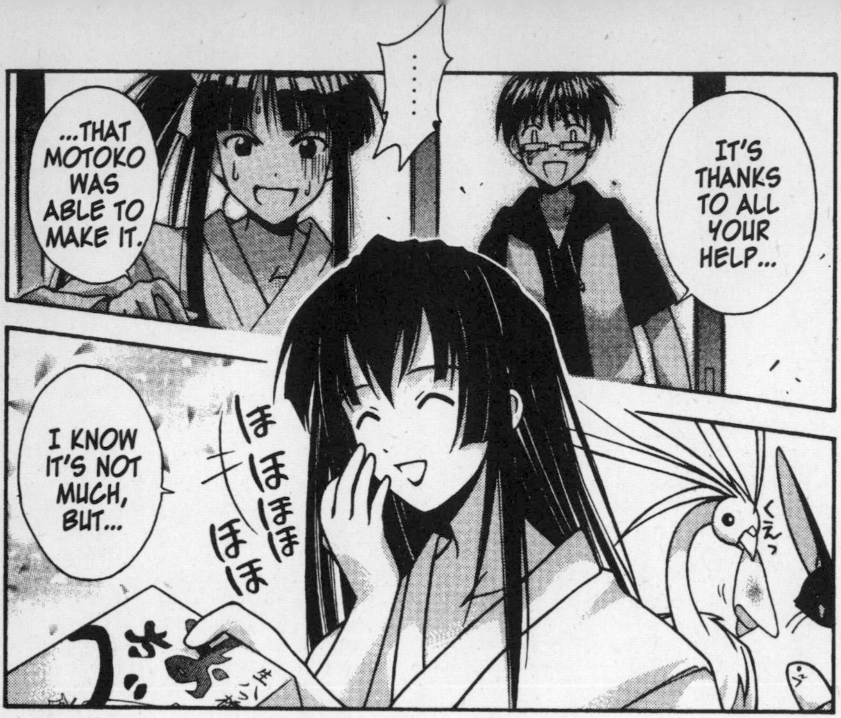
IT'S THANKS TO ALL YOUR HELP...
...
...THAT MOTOKO WAS ABLE TO MAKE IT.
ほほほほほほほ
I KNOW IT'S NOT MUCH, BUT...

Love Hina

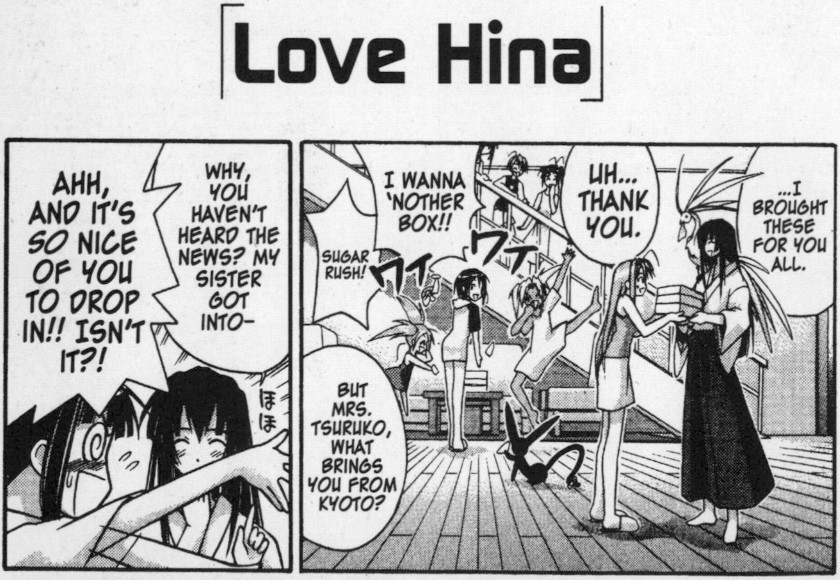
...I BROUGHT THESE FOR YOU ALL.
UH... THANK YOU.
I WANNA 'NOTHER BOX!!
ワイワイ
SUGAR RUSH!
BUT MRS. TSURUKO, WHAT BRINGS YOU FROM KYOTO?
WHY, YOU HAVEN'T HEARD THE NEWS? MY SISTER GOT INTO-
AHH, AND IT'S SO NICE OF YOU TO DROP IN!! ISN'T IT?!
ほほ

HINATA. 107 Big Troubles For the Little Ronin Girl.

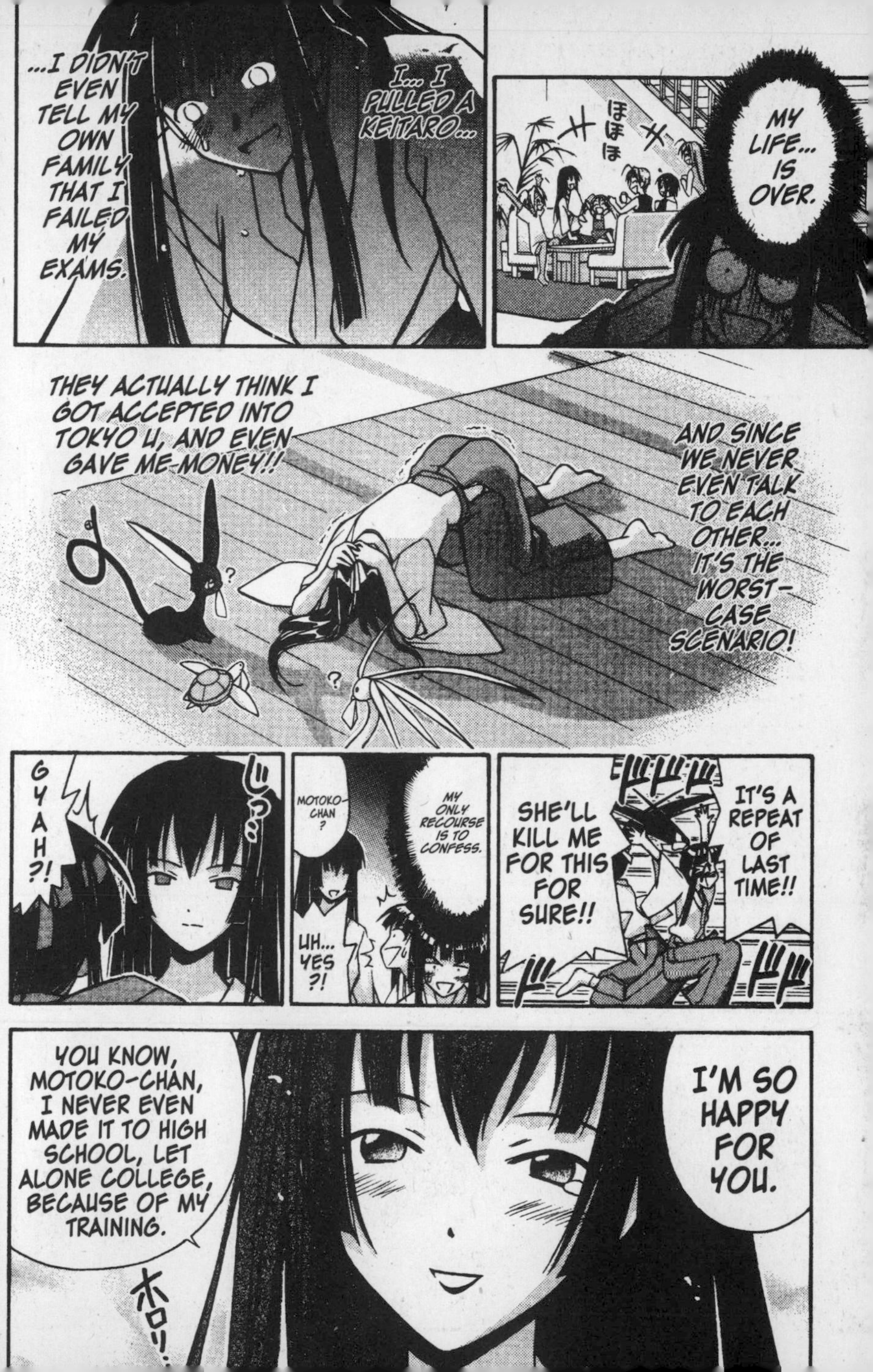
MY LIFE... IS OVER.
ほほほ
I... I PULLED A KEITARO...
...I DIDN'T EVEN TELL MY OWN FAMILY THAT I FAILED MY EXAMS.
THEY ACTUALLY THINK I GOT ACCEPTED INTO TOKYO U, AND EVEN GAVE ME MONEY!!
AND SINCE WE NEVER EVEN TALK TO EACH OTHER... IT'S THE WORST-CASE SCENARIO!
IT'S A REPEAT OF LAST TIME!!
SHE'LL KILL ME FOR THIS FOR SURE!!
MY ONLY RECOURSE IS TO CONFESS.
MOTOKO-CHAN?
UH... YES?!
じっ
GYAH?!
I'M SO HAPPY FOR YOU.
YOU KNOW, MOTOKO-CHAN, I NEVER EVEN MADE IT TO HIGH SCHOOL, LET ALONE COLLEGE, BECAUSE OF MY TRAINING.
ホロリ

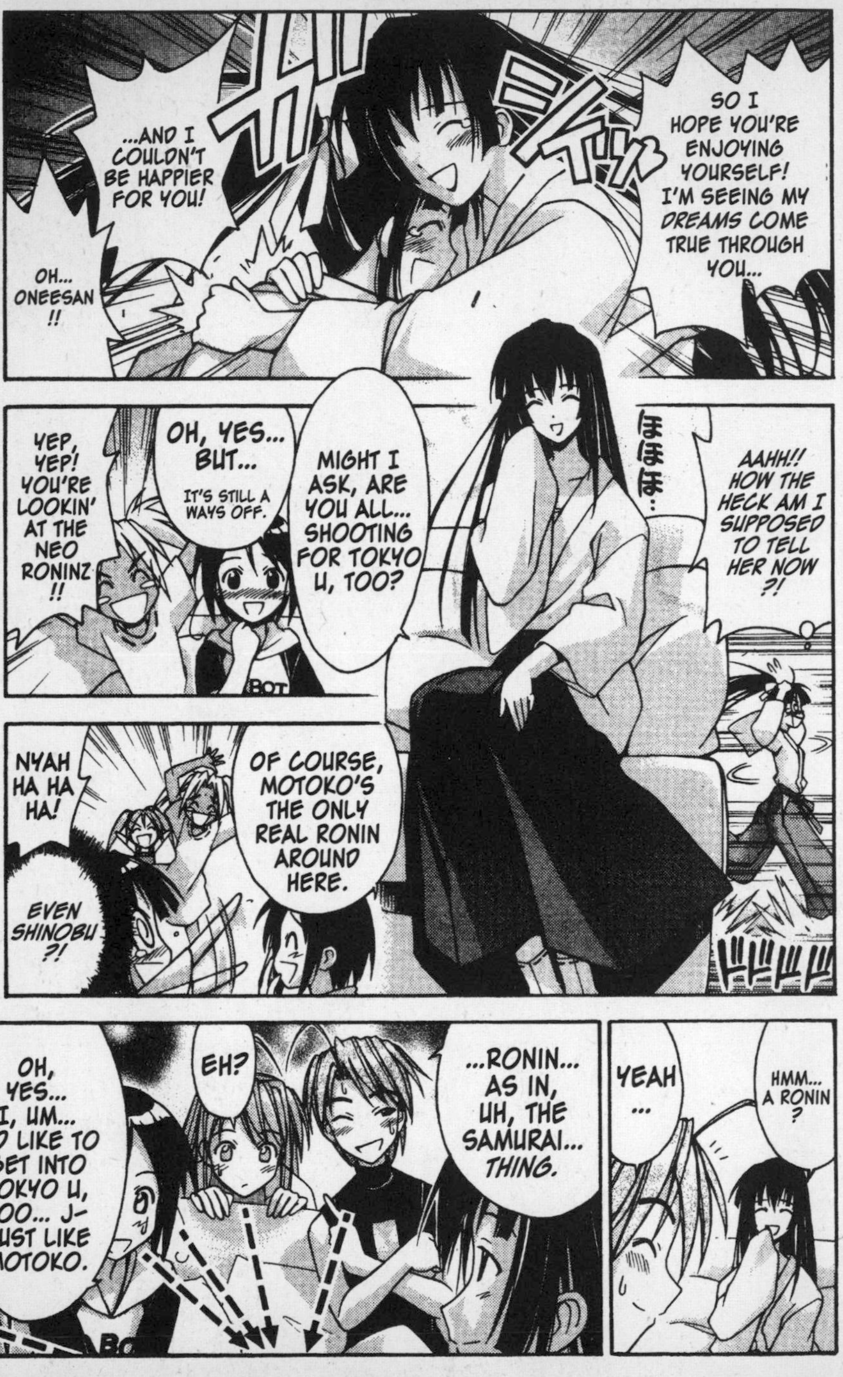

SO I HOPE YOU'RE ENJOYING YOURSELF! I'M SEEING MY DREAMS COME TRUE THROUGH YOU...
...AND I COULDN'T BE HAPPIER FOR YOU!
OH... ONEESAN !!
AAHH!! HOW THE HECK AM I SUPPOSED TO TELL HER NOW ?!
ほほほ…
MIGHT I ASK, ARE YOU ALL... SHOOTING FOR TOKYO U, TOO?
OH, YES... BUT...
IT'S STILL A WAYS OFF.
YEP, YEP! YOU'RE LOOKIN' AT THE NEO RONINZ !!
ドドドド
OF COURSE, MOTOKO'S THE ONLY REAL RONIN AROUND HERE.
NYAH HA HA HA!
EVEN SHINOBU ?!
HMM... A RONIN ?
YEAH ...
...RONIN... AS IN, UH, THE SAMURAI... THING.
EH?
OH, YES... I, UM... I'D LIKE TO GET INTO TOKYO U, TOO... J-JUST LIKE MOTOKO.

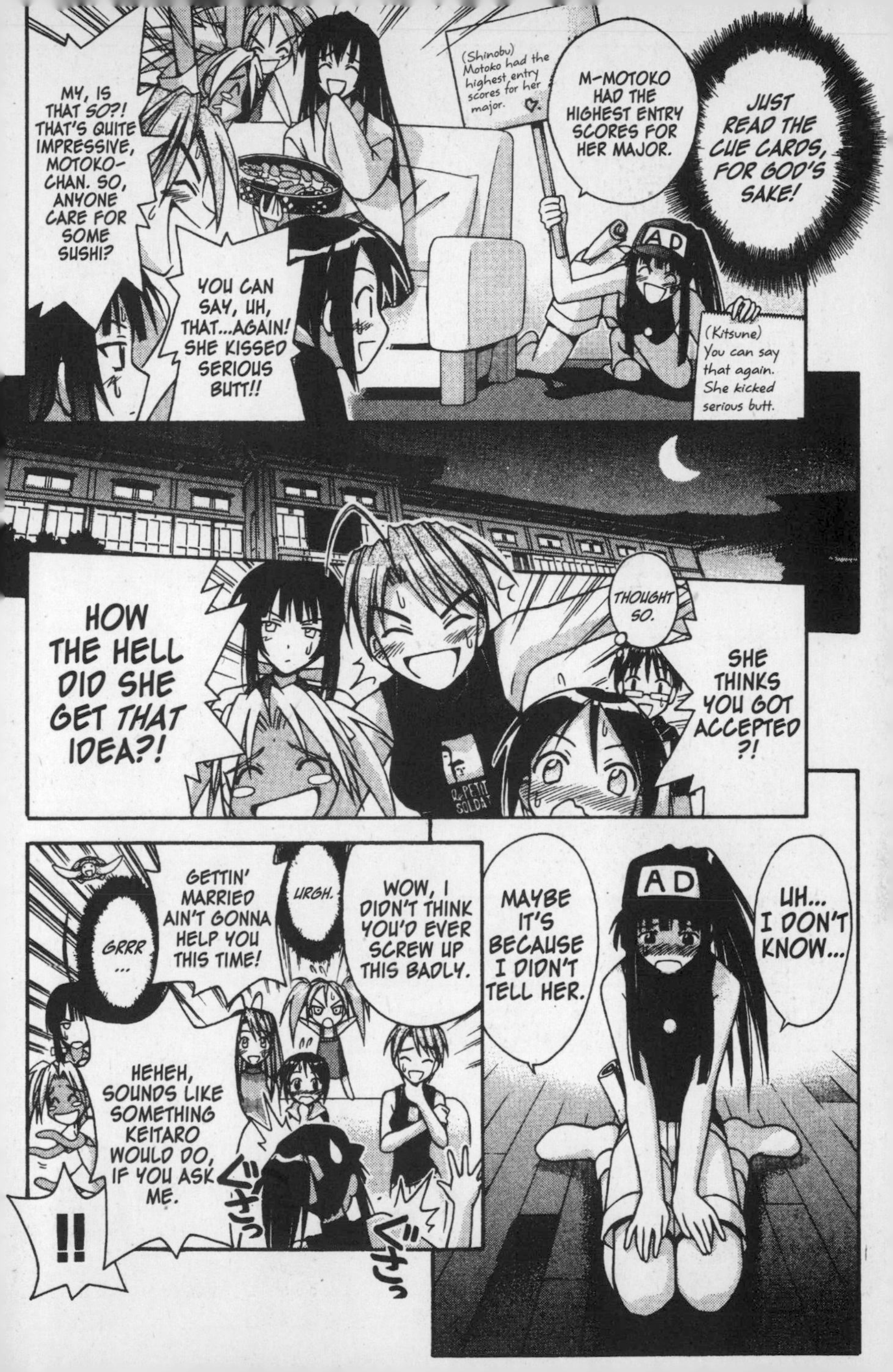

M-MOTOKO HAD THE HIGHEST ENTRY SCORES FOR HER MAJOR.
(Shinobu) Motoko had the highest entry scores for her major.
JUST READ THE CUE CARDS, FOR GOD'S SAKE!
MY, IS THAT SO?! THAT'S QUITE IMPRESSIVE, MOTOKO-CHAN. SO, ANYONE CARE FOR SOME SUSHI?
(Kitsune) You can say that again. She kicked serious butt.
YOU CAN SAY, UH, THAT...AGAIN! SHE KISSED SERIOUS BUTT!!
THOUGHT SO.
SHE THINKS YOU GOT ACCEPTED?!
HOW THE HELL DID SHE GET THAT IDEA?!
UH... I DON'T KNOW...
MAYBE IT'S BECAUSE I DIDN'T TELL HER.
WOW, I DIDN'T THINK YOU'D EVER SCREW UP THIS BADLY.
URGH.
GETTIN' MARRIED AIN'T GONNA HELP YOU THIS TIME!
GRRR...
HEHEH, SOUNDS LIKE SOMETHING KEITARO WOULD DO, IF YOU ASK ME.
!!

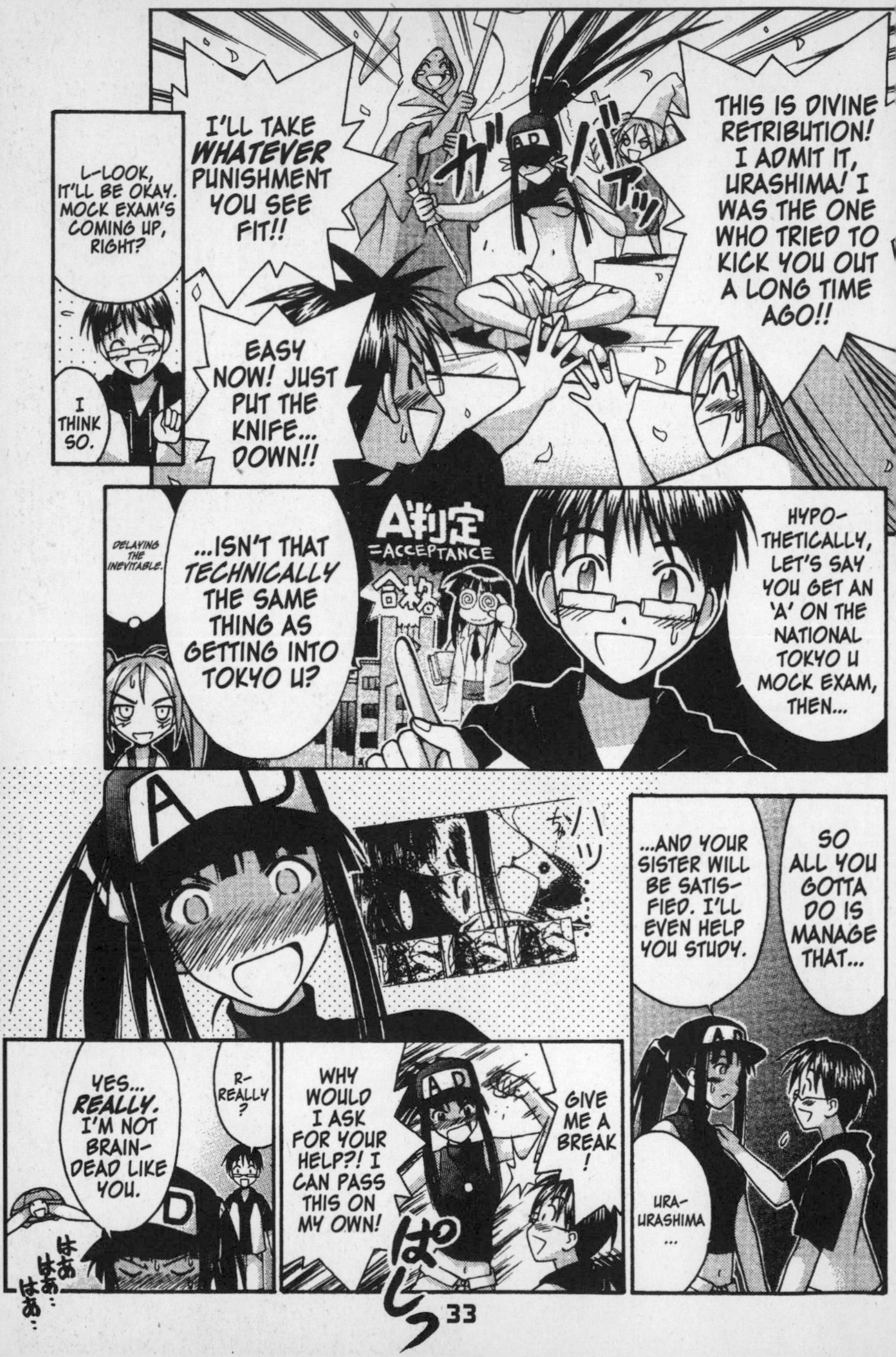

THIS IS DIVINE RETRIBUTION! I ADMIT IT, URASHIMA! I WAS THE ONE WHO TRIED TO KICK YOU OUT A LONG TIME AGO!!
ガバァッ
I'LL TAKE WHATEVER PUNISHMENT YOU SEE FIT!!
EASY NOW! JUST PUT THE KNIFE... DOWN!!
L-LOOK, IT'LL BE OKAY. MOCK EXAM'S COMING UP, RIGHT?
I THINK SO.
HYPO-THETICALLY, LET'S SAY YOU GET AN 'A' ON THE NATIONAL TOKYO U MOCK EXAM, THEN...
A判定
=ACCEPTANCE
合格
...ISN'T THAT TECHNICALLY THE SAME THING AS GETTING INTO TOKYO U?
DELAYING THE INEVITABLE.
SO ALL YOU GOTTA DO IS MANAGE THAT...
...AND YOUR SISTER WILL BE SATIS-FIED. I'LL EVEN HELP YOU STUDY.
URA-URASHIMA ...
GIVE ME A BREAK!
WHY WOULD I ASK FOR YOUR HELP?! I CAN PASS THIS ON MY OWN!
ぱしっ
R-REALLY?
YES... REALLY. I'M NOT BRAIN-DEAD LIKE YOU.
はあ はあ はあ

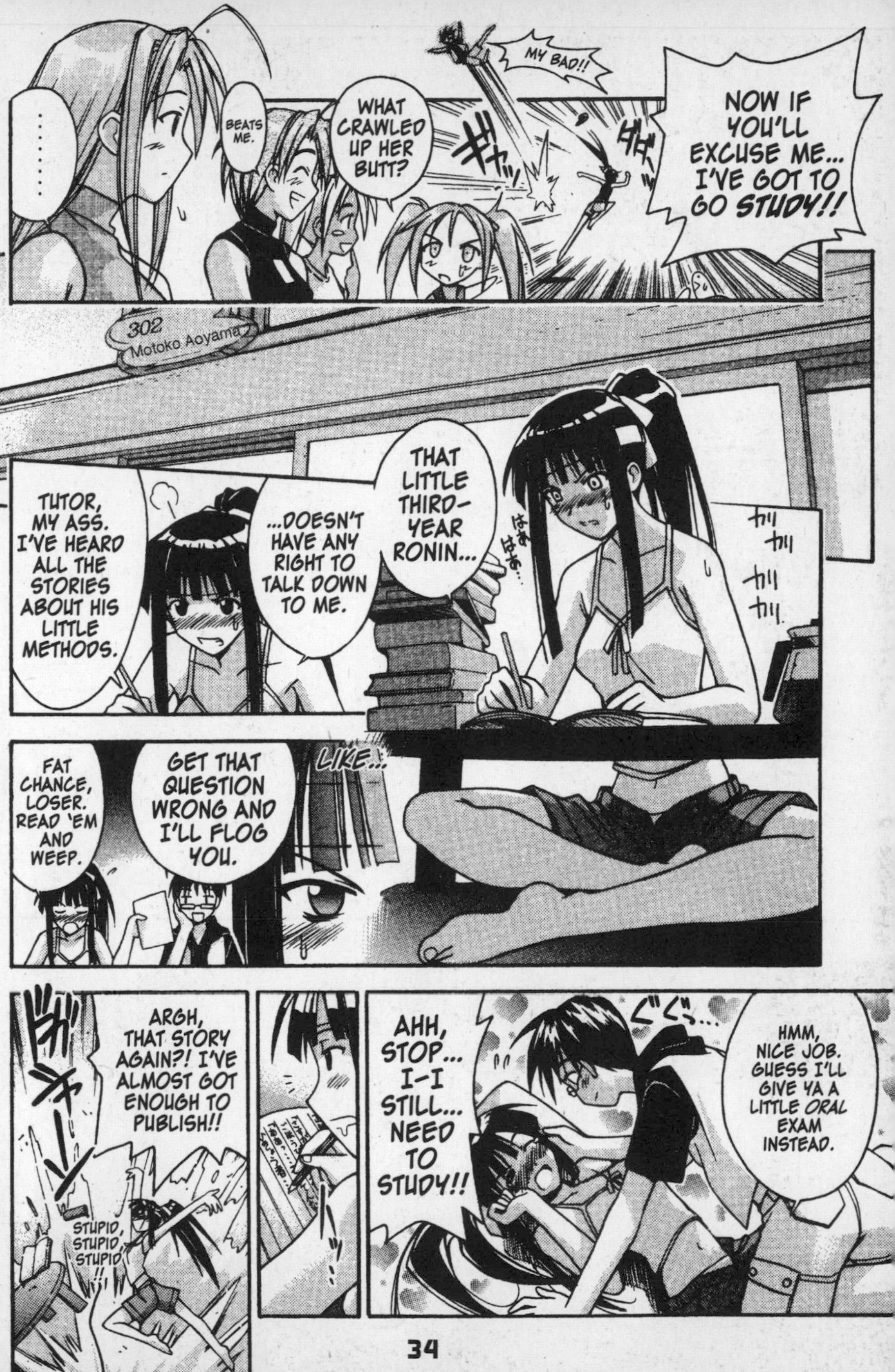
NOW IF YOU'LL EXCUSE ME... I'VE GOT TO GO STUDY!!
MY BAD!!
WHAT CRAWLED UP HER BUTT?
BEATS ME.
......
302
Motoko Aoyama
THAT LITTLE THIRD-YEAR RONIN...
...DOESN'T HAVE ANY RIGHT TO TALK DOWN TO ME.
TUTOR, MY ASS. I'VE HEARD ALL THE STORIES ABOUT HIS LITTLE METHODS.
LIKE...
GET THAT QUESTION WRONG AND I'LL FLOG YOU.
FAT CHANCE, LOSER. READ 'EM AND WEEP.
HMM, NICE JOB. GUESS I'LL GIVE YA A LITTLE ORAL EXAM INSTEAD.
AHH, STOP... I-I STILL... NEED TO STUDY!!
ARGH, THAT STORY AGAIN?! I'VE ALMOST GOT ENOUGH TO PUBLISH!!
STUPID, STUPID, STUPID!!

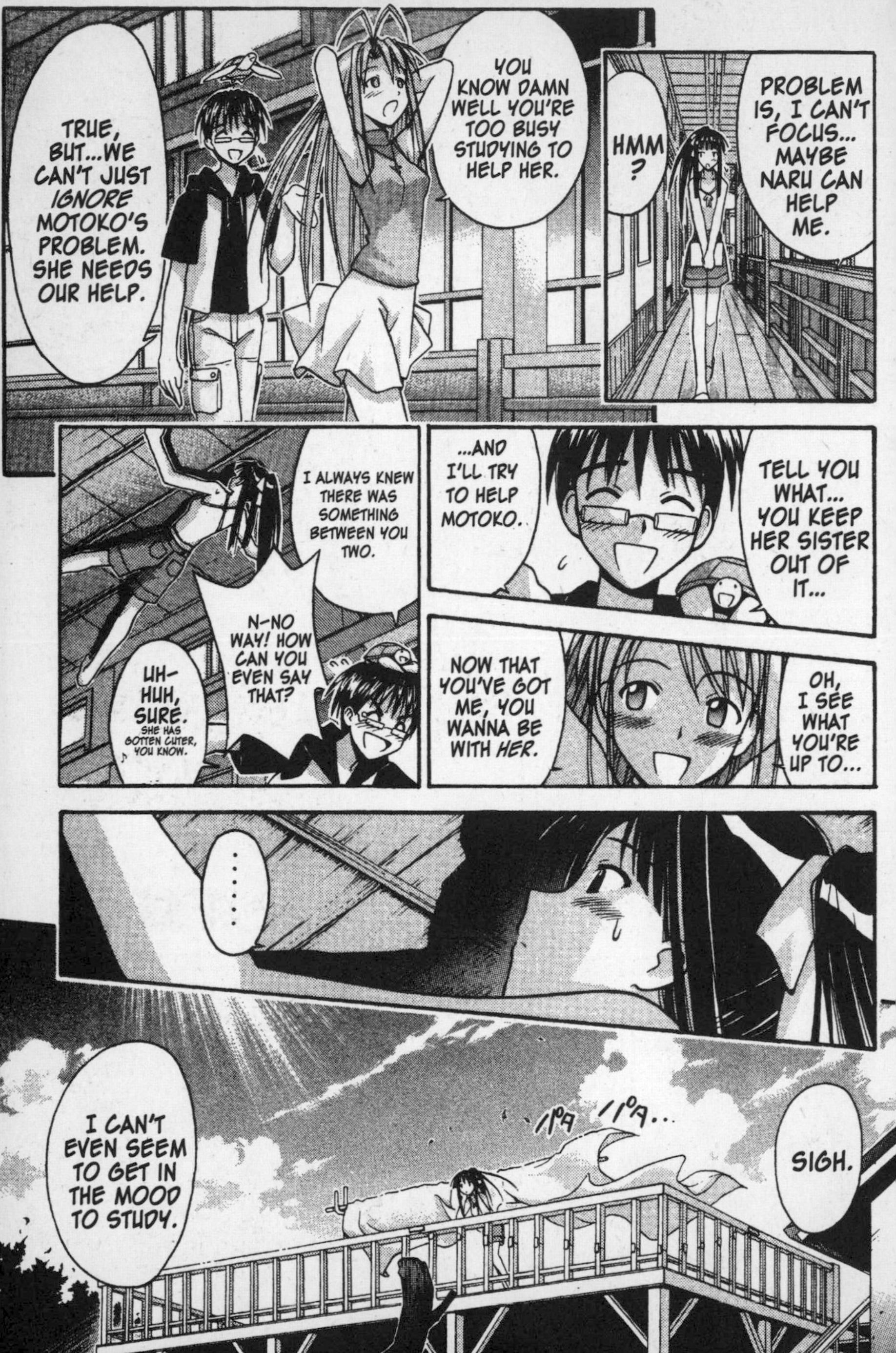
PROBLEM IS, I CAN'T FOCUS... MAYBE NARU CAN HELP ME.
HMM?
YOU KNOW DAMN WELL YOU'RE TOO BUSY STUDYING TO HELP HER.
TRUE, BUT...WE CAN'T JUST *IGNORE* MOTOKO'S PROBLEM. SHE NEEDS OUR HELP.
TELL YOU WHAT... YOU KEEP HER SISTER OUT OF IT...
...AND I'LL TRY TO HELP MOTOKO.
OH, I SEE WHAT YOU'RE UP TO...
NOW THAT YOU'VE GOT ME, YOU WANNA BE WITH *HER*.
I ALWAYS KNEW THERE WAS SOMETHING BETWEEN YOU TWO.
N-NO WAY! HOW CAN YOU EVEN SAY THAT?
UH-HUH, SURE.
SHE HAS GOTTEN CUTER, YOU KNOW.
......
SIGH.
パタ パタ...
I CAN'T EVEN SEEM TO GET IN THE MOOD TO STUDY.

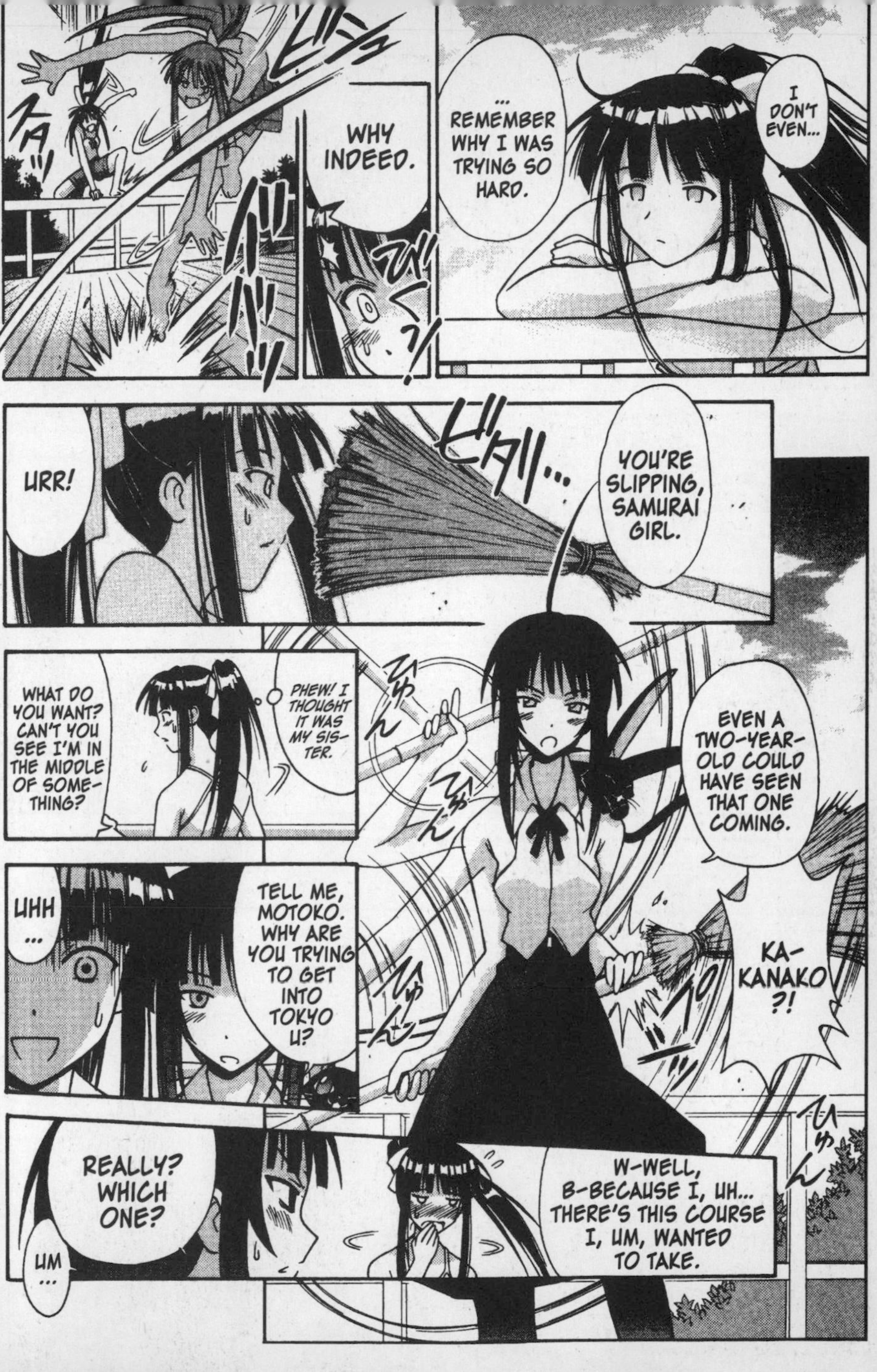
I DON'T EVEN...
...REMEMBER WHY I WAS TRYING SO HARD.
WHY INDEED.
YOU'RE SLIPPING, SAMURAI GIRL.
URR!
EVEN A TWO-YEAR-OLD COULD HAVE SEEN THAT ONE COMING.
KA-KANAKO?!
PHEW! I THOUGHT IT WAS MY SISTER.
WHAT DO YOU WANT? CAN'T YOU SEE I'M IN THE MIDDLE OF SOMETHING?
TELL ME, MOTOKO. WHY ARE YOU TRYING TO GET INTO TOKYO U?
UHH ...
W-WELL, B-BECAUSE I, UH... THERE'S THIS COURSE I, UM, WANTED TO TAKE.
REALLY? WHICH ONE?
UM ...

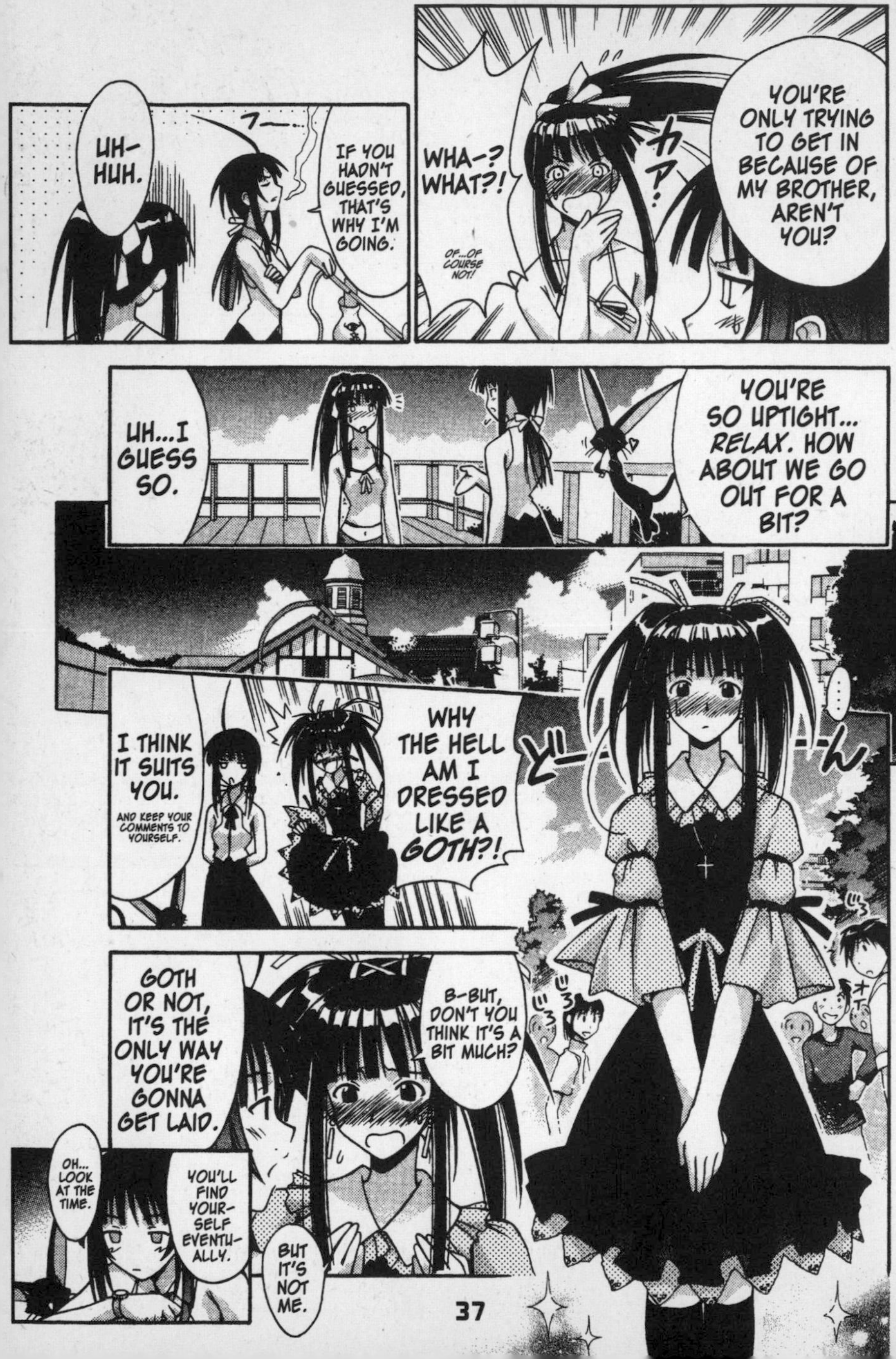

YOU'RE ONLY TRYING TO GET IN BECAUSE OF MY BROTHER, AREN'T YOU?
WHA-? WHAT?!
OF...OF COURSE NOT!
IF YOU HADN'T GUESSED, THAT'S WHY I'M GOING.
UH-HUH.
YOU'RE SO UPTIGHT... RELAX. HOW ABOUT WE GO OUT FOR A BIT?
UH...I GUESS SO.
...
WHY THE HELL AM I DRESSED LIKE A GOTH?!
I THINK IT SUITS YOU.
AND KEEP YOUR COMMENTS TO YOURSELF.
B-BUT, DON'T YOU THINK IT'S A BIT MUCH?
GOTH OR NOT, IT'S THE ONLY WAY YOU'RE GONNA GET LAID.
BUT IT'S NOT ME.
YOU'LL FIND YOURSELF EVENTUALLY.
OH... LOOK AT THE TIME.

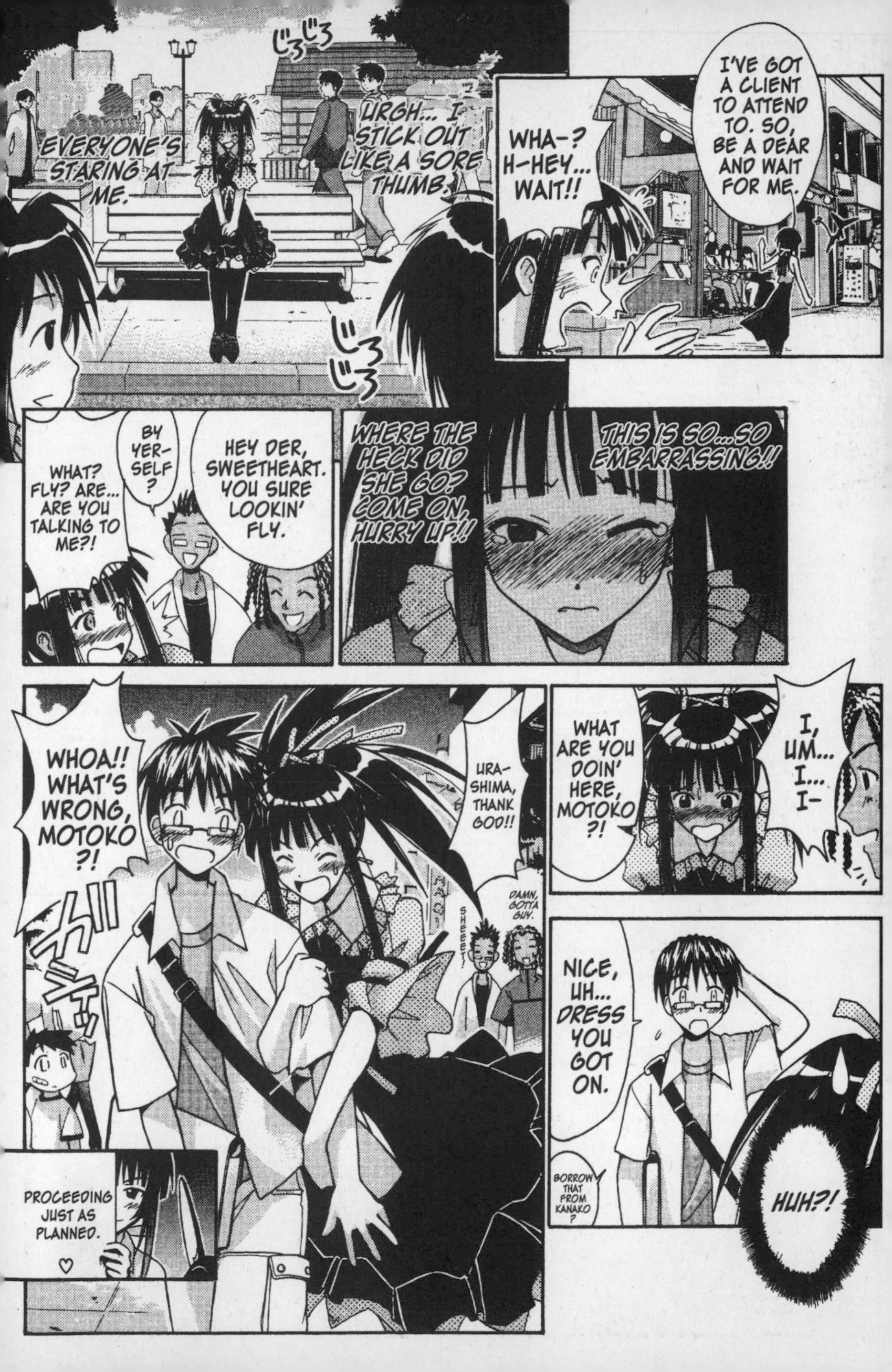
I'VE GOT A CLIENT TO ATTEND TO. SO, BE A DEAR AND WAIT FOR ME.
WHA-? H-HEY... WAIT!!
じろじろ
URGH... I STICK OUT LIKE A SORE THUMB.
EVERYONE'S STARING AT ME.
じろじろ
THIS IS SO...SO EMBARRASSING!!
WHERE THE HECK DID SHE GO? COME ON, HURRY UP!!
HEY DER, SWEETHEART. YOU SURE LOOKIN' FLY.
BY YER-SELF?
WHAT? FLY? ARE... ARE YOU TALKING TO ME?!
I, UM... I... I-
WHAT ARE YOU DOIN' HERE, MOTOKO?!
NICE, UH... DRESS YOU GOT ON.
HUH?!
BORROW THAT FROM KANAKO?
URA-SHIMA, THANK GOD!!
DAMN, GOTTA GUY.
SHEEET!
WHOA!! WHAT'S WRONG, MOTOKO?!
PROCEEDING JUST AS PLANNED.
♡

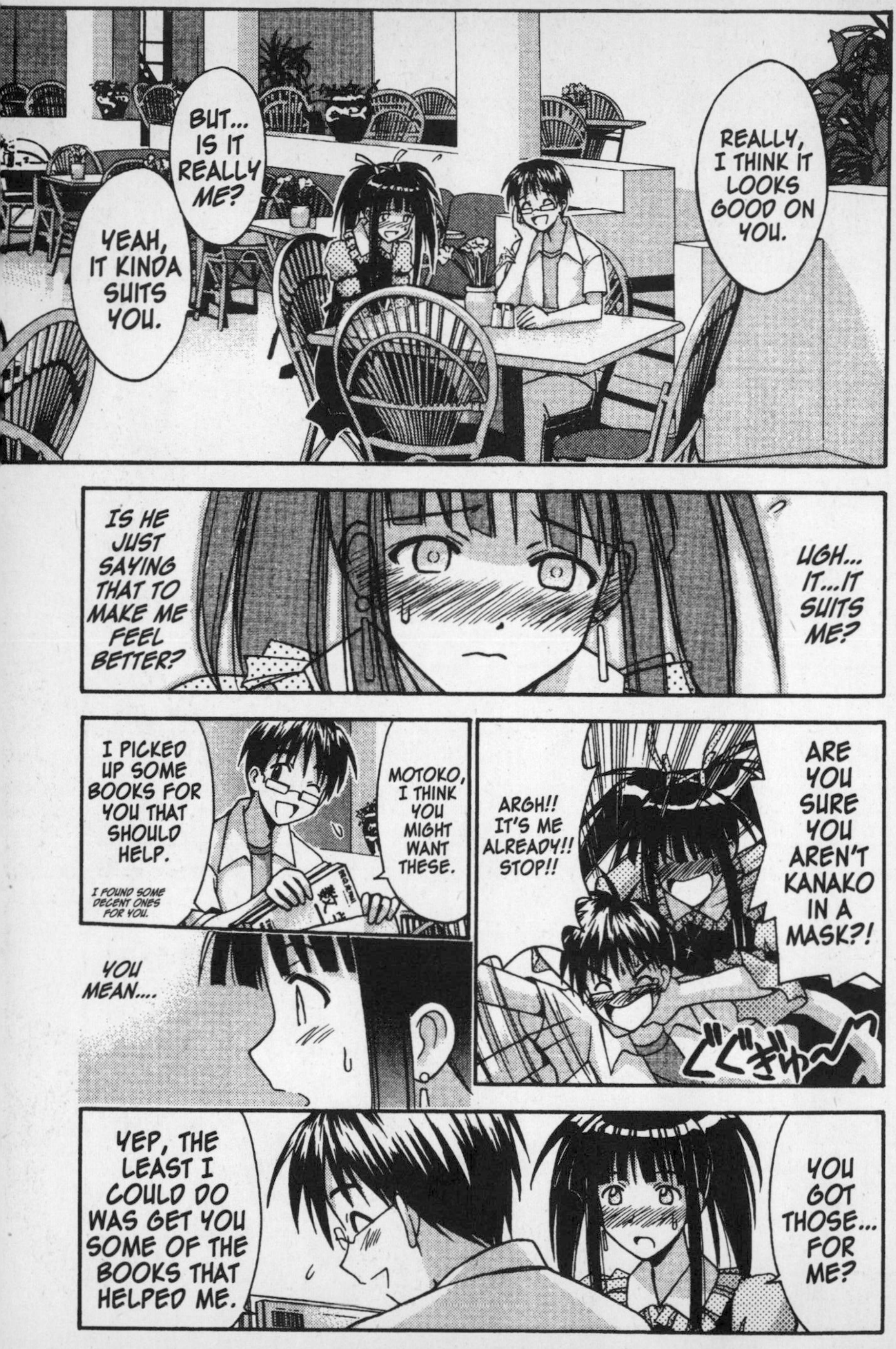
REALLY, I THINK IT LOOKS GOOD ON YOU.
BUT... IS IT REALLY ME?
YEAH, IT KINDA SUITS YOU.
UGH... IT...IT SUITS ME?
IS HE JUST SAYING THAT TO MAKE ME FEEL BETTER?
ARE YOU SURE YOU AREN'T KANAKO IN A MASK?!
ARGH!! IT'S ME ALREADY!! STOP!!
ぐぐぎゅ〜
MOTOKO, I THINK YOU MIGHT WANT THESE.
I PICKED UP SOME BOOKS FOR YOU THAT SHOULD HELP.
I FOUND SOME DECENT ONES FOR YOU.
YOU MEAN....
YOU GOT THOSE... FOR ME?
YEP, THE LEAST I COULD DO WAS GET YOU SOME OF THE BOOKS THAT HELPED ME.

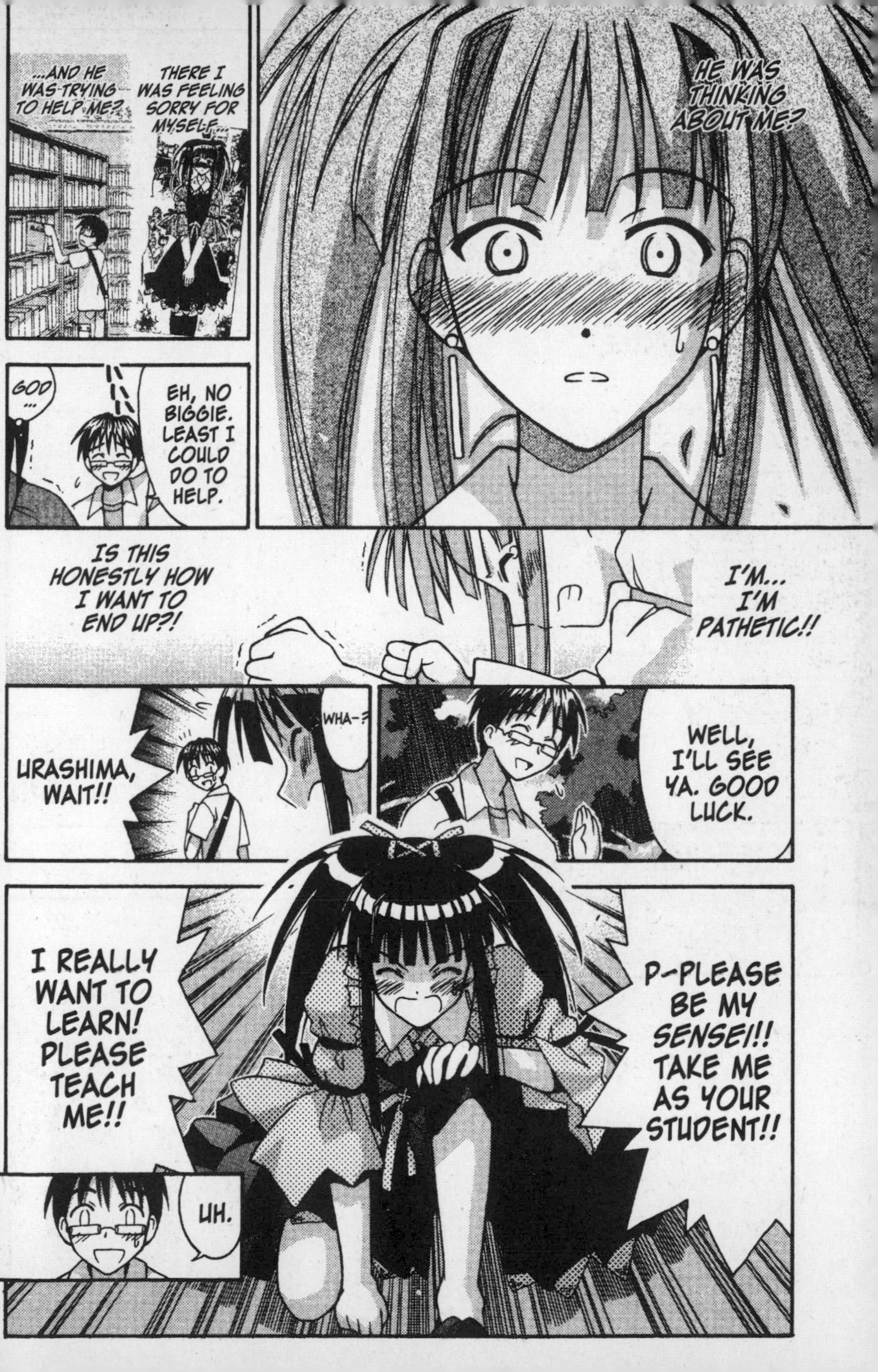
HE WAS THINKING ABOUT ME?
THERE I WAS FEELING SORRY FOR MYSELF...
...AND HE WAS TRYING TO HELP ME?
EH, NO BIGGIE. LEAST I COULD DO TO HELP.
GOD...
I'M... I'M PATHETIC!!
IS THIS HONESTLY HOW I WANT TO END UP?!
WELL, I'LL SEE YA. GOOD LUCK.
WHA-?
URASHIMA, WAIT!!
P-PLEASE BE MY SENSEI!! TAKE ME AS YOUR STUDENT!!
I REALLY WANT TO LEARN! PLEASE TEACH ME!!
UH.

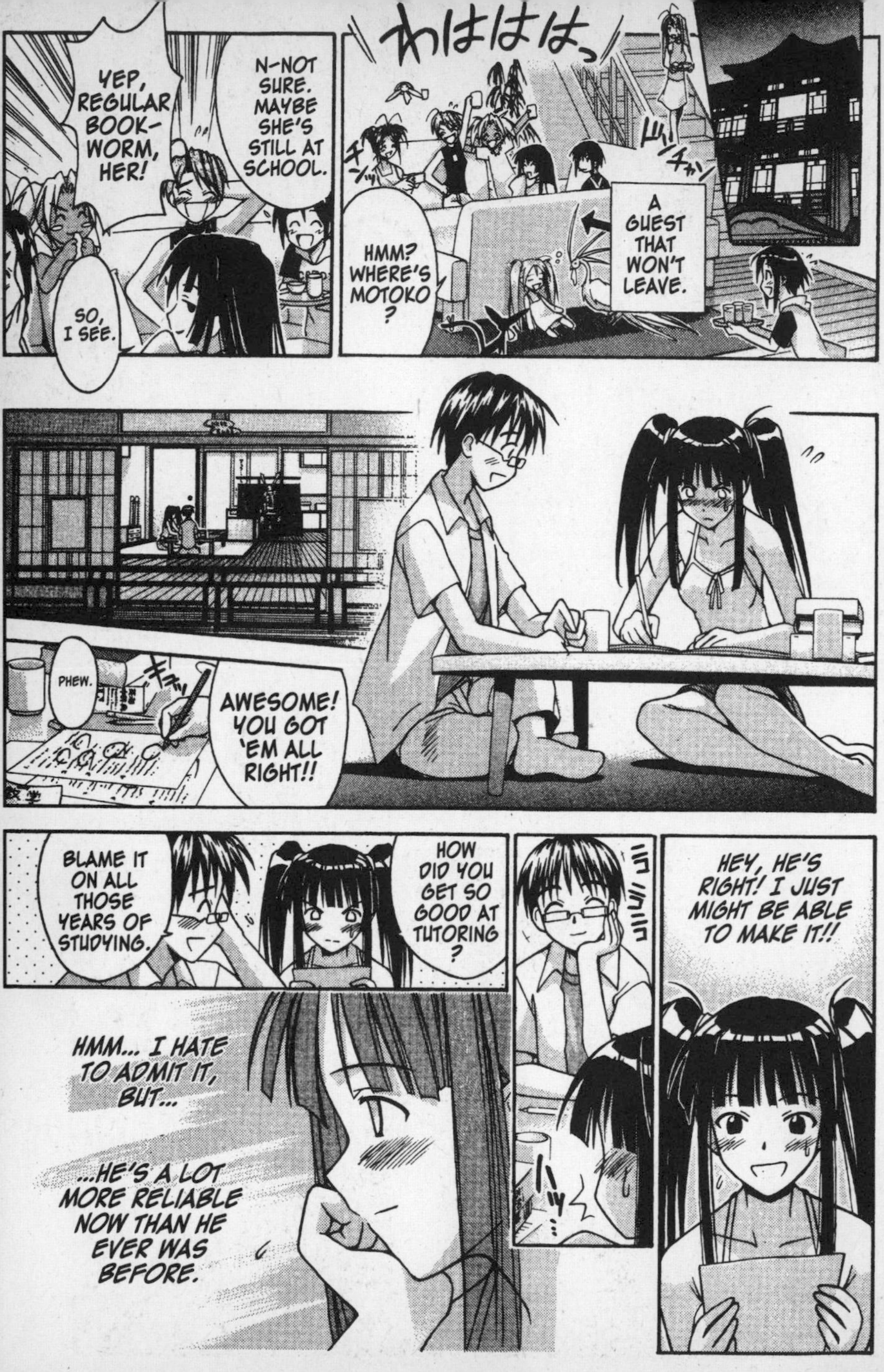
わははは
A GUEST THAT WON'T LEAVE.
HMM? WHERE'S MOTOKO?
N-NOT SURE. MAYBE SHE'S STILL AT SCHOOL.
YEP, REGULAR BOOK-WORM, HER!
SO, I SEE.
AWESOME! YOU GOT 'EM ALL RIGHT!!
PHEW.
HEY, HE'S RIGHT! I JUST MIGHT BE ABLE TO MAKE IT!!
ニコ ニコ
ハッ
HOW DID YOU GET SO GOOD AT TUTORING?
BLAME IT ON ALL THOSE YEARS OF STUDYING.
HMM... I HATE TO ADMIT IT, BUT...
...HE'S A LOT MORE RELIABLE NOW THAN HE EVER WAS BEFORE.

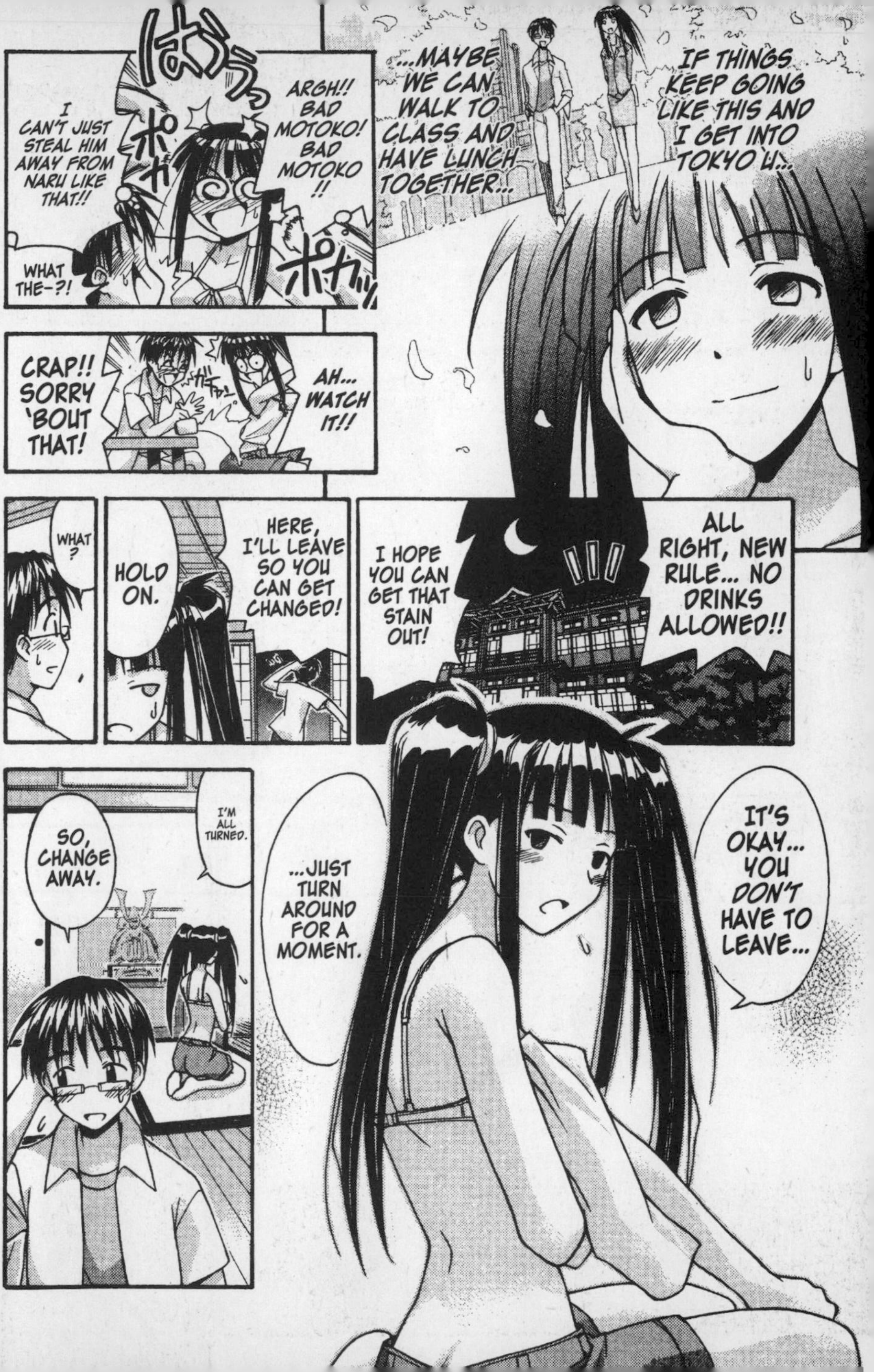
IF THINGS KEEP GOING LIKE THIS AND I GET INTO TOKYO U...
...MAYBE WE CAN WALK TO CLASS AND HAVE LUNCH TOGETHER...
ARGH!! BAD MOTOKO! BAD MOTOKO !!
I CAN'T JUST STEAL HIM AWAY FROM NARU LIKE THAT!!
WHAT THE-?!
AH... WATCH IT!!
CRAP!! SORRY 'BOUT THAT!
ALL RIGHT, NEW RULE... NO DRINKS ALLOWED!!
I HOPE YOU CAN GET THAT STAIN OUT!
HERE, I'LL LEAVE SO YOU CAN GET CHANGED!
HOLD ON.
WHAT ?
IT'S OKAY... YOU DON'T HAVE TO LEAVE...
...JUST TURN AROUND FOR A MOMENT.
I'M ALL TURNED.
SO, CHANGE AWAY.

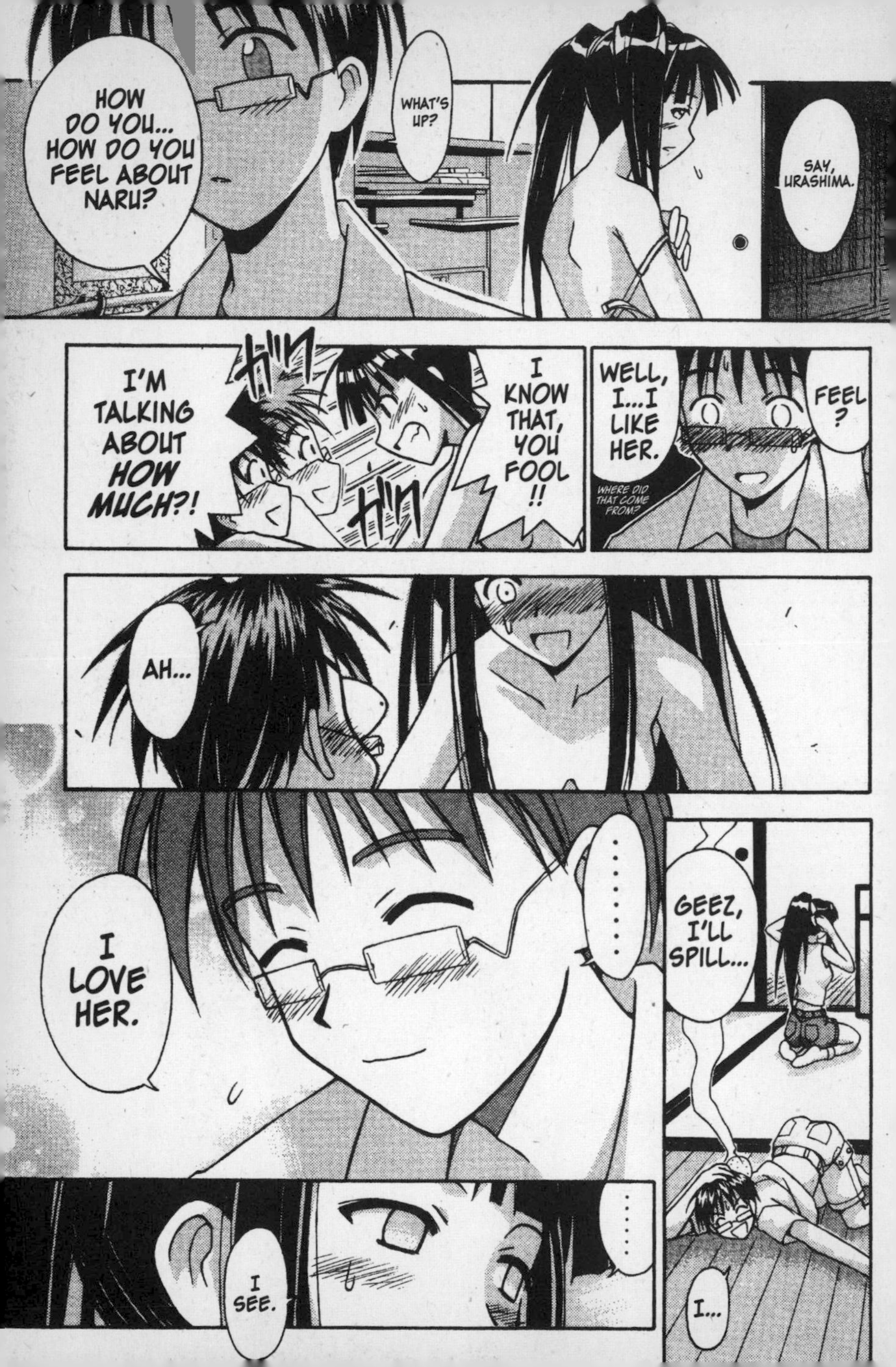
SAY, URASHIMA.
WHAT'S UP?
HOW DO YOU... HOW DO YOU FEEL ABOUT NARU?
FEEL?
WELL, I...I LIKE HER.
WHERE DID THAT COME FROM?
I KNOW THAT, YOU FOOL!!
I'M TALKING ABOUT *HOW MUCH*?!
AH...
GEEZ, I'LL SPILL...
I...
......
I LOVE HER.
......
I SEE.

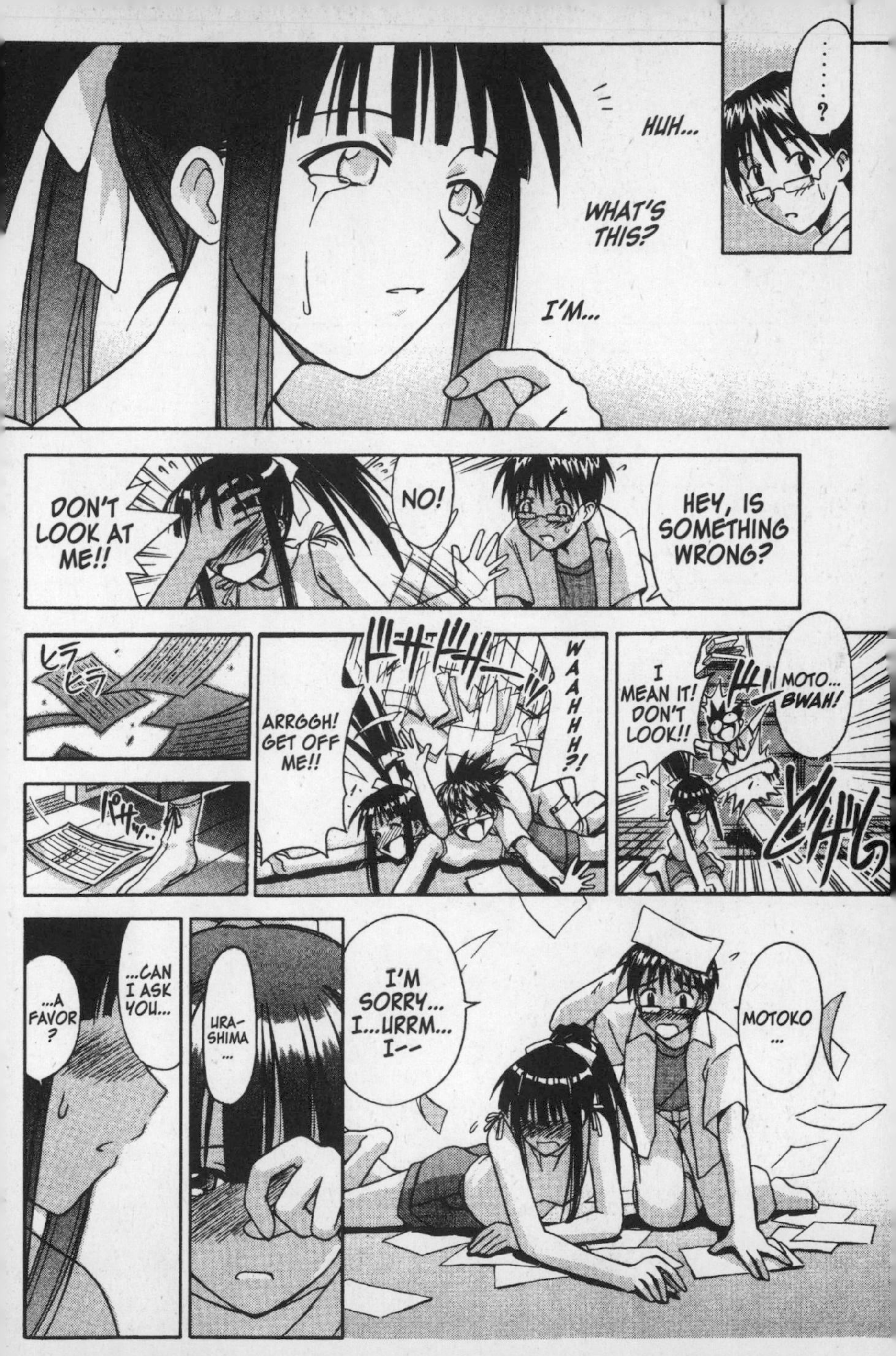

......?
HUH...
WHAT'S THIS?
I'M...
HEY, IS SOMETHING WRONG?
NO!
DON'T LOOK AT ME!!
MOTO... BWAH!
I MEAN IT! DON'T LOOK!!
WAAHHHH?!
ARRGGH! GET OFF ME!!
ヒラ ヒラ
MOTOKO ...
I'M SORRY... I...URRM... I--
URA-SHIMA ...
...CAN I ASK YOU...
...A FAVOR ?

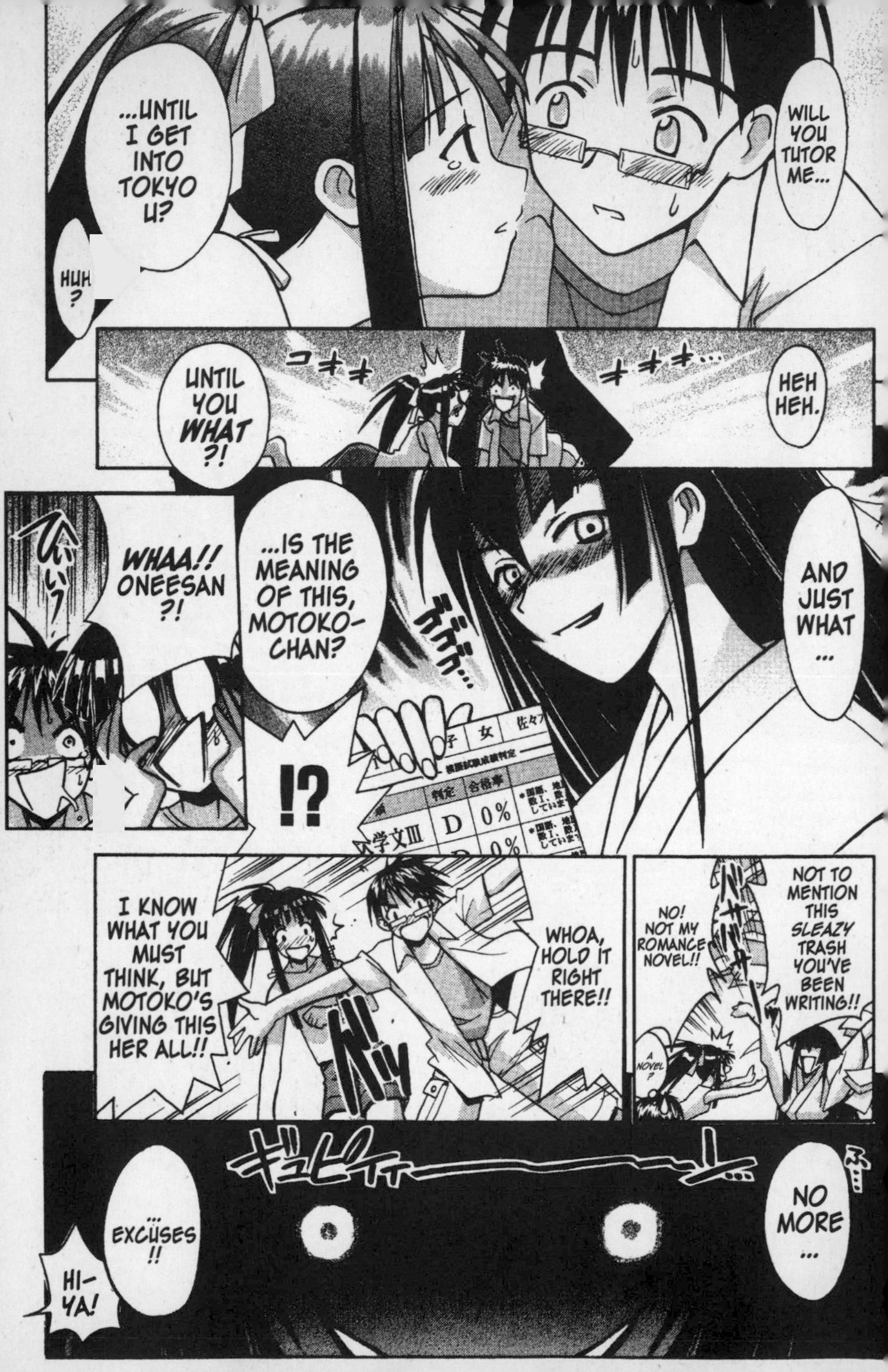
WILL YOU TUTOR ME...
...UNTIL I GET INTO TOKYO U?
HUH?
HEH HEH.
UNTIL YOU WHAT?!
AND JUST WHAT...
...IS THE MEANING OF THIS, MOTOKO-CHAN?
!?
WHAA!! ONEESAN?!
NOT TO MENTION THIS SLEAZY TRASH YOU'VE BEEN WRITING!!
NO! NOT MY ROMANCE NOVEL!!
A NOVEL?
WHOA, HOLD IT RIGHT THERE!!
I KNOW WHAT YOU MUST THINK, BUT MOTOKO'S GIVING THIS HER ALL!!
NO MORE...
...EXCUSES!!
HI-YA!

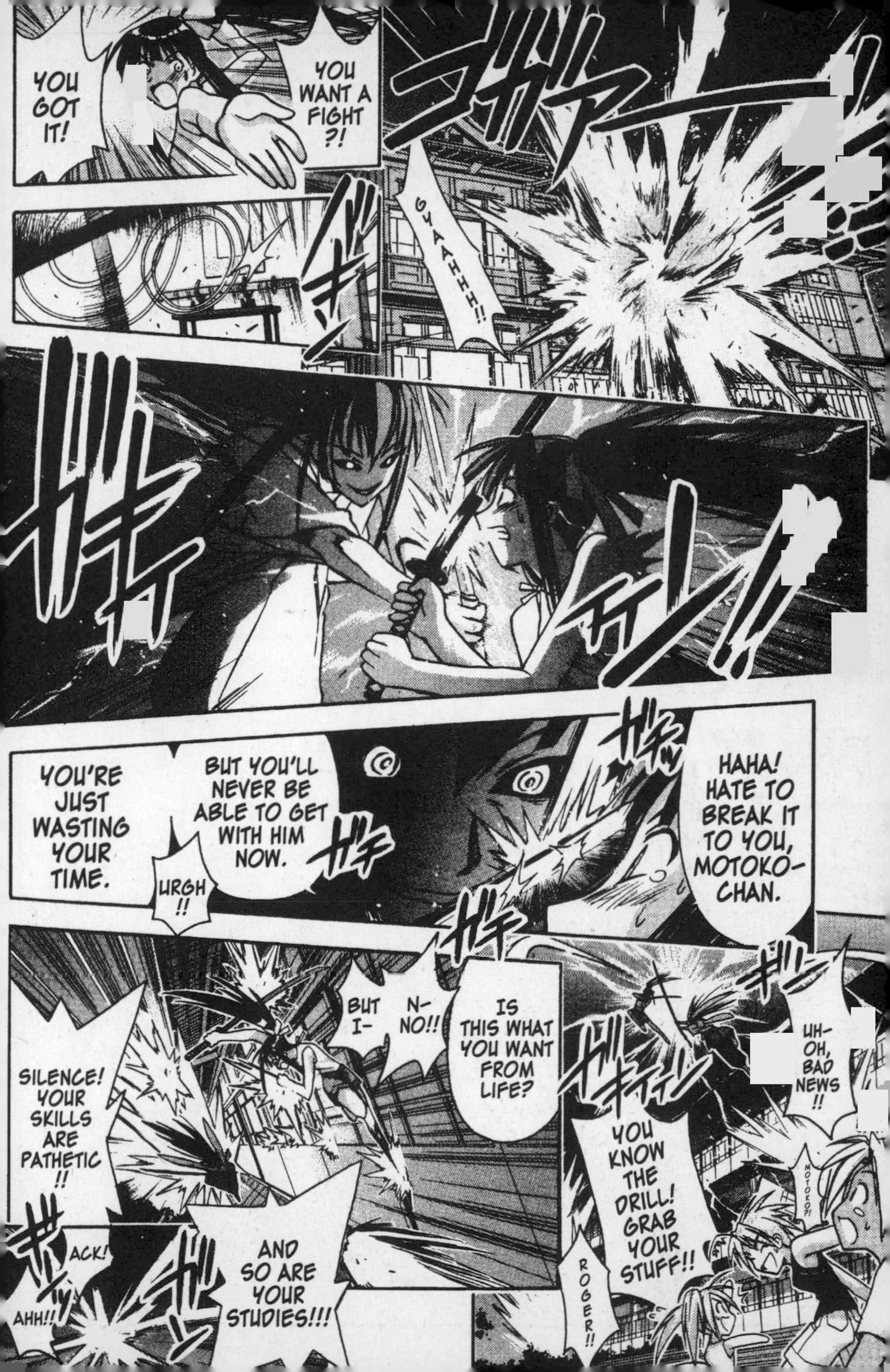
GYAAHHH!!
YOU WANT A FIGHT ?!
YOU GOT IT!
HAHA! HATE TO BREAK IT TO YOU, MOTOKO-CHAN.
BUT YOU'LL NEVER BE ABLE TO GET WITH HIM NOW.
URGH !!
YOU'RE JUST WASTING YOUR TIME.
UH-OH, BAD NEWS !!
MOTOKO?!
YOU KNOW THE DRILL! GRAB YOUR STUFF!!
ROGER!!
IS THIS WHAT YOU WANT FROM LIFE?
N-NO!!
BUT I-
SILENCE! YOUR SKILLS ARE PATHETIC !!
AND SO ARE YOUR STUDIES!!!
ACK!
AHH!!

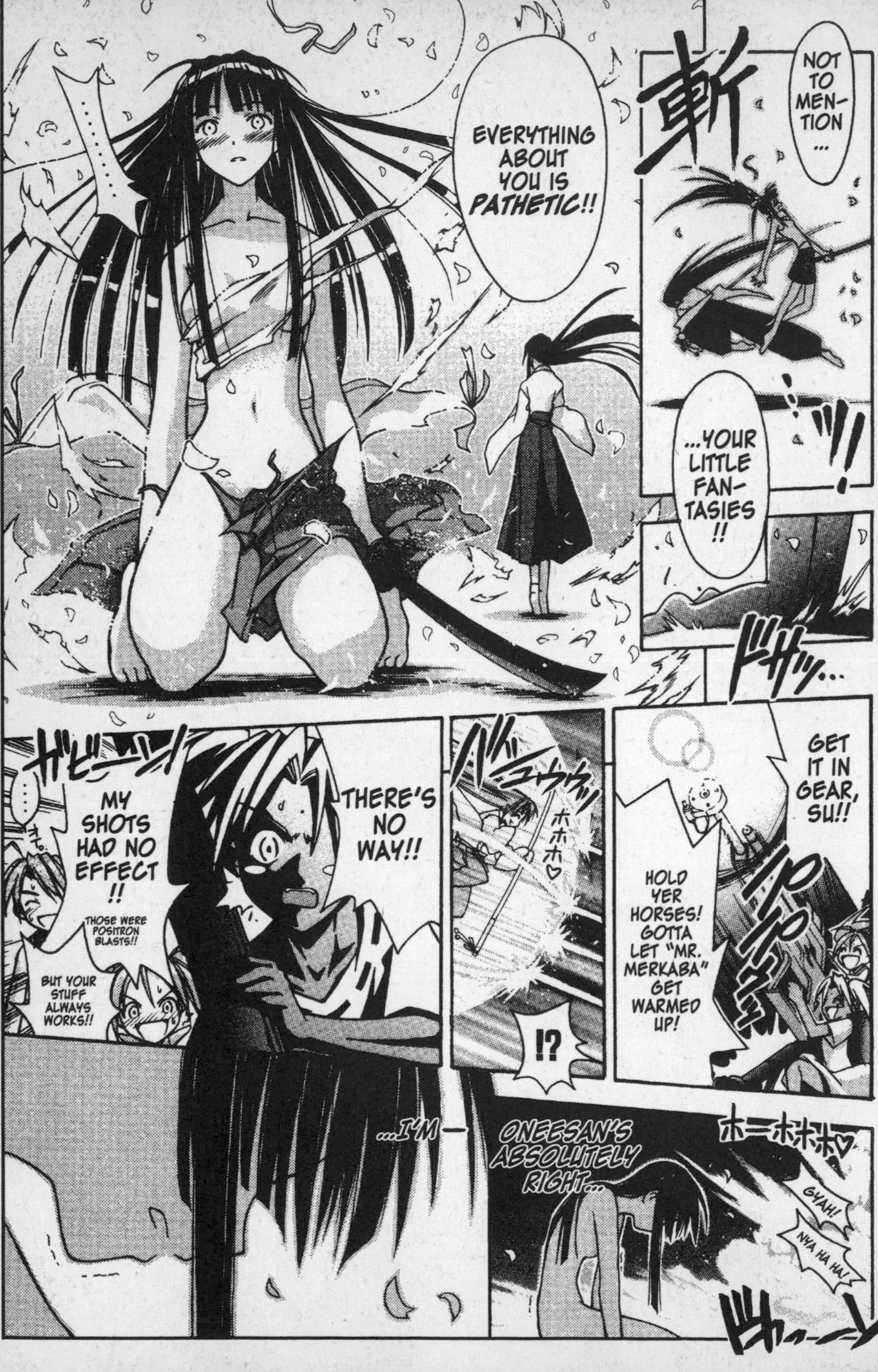
斬
NOT TO MEN-TION ...
...YOUR LITTLE FAN-TASIES !!
EVERYTHING ABOUT YOU IS PATHETIC!!
GET IT IN GEAR, SU!!
HOLD YER HORSES! GOTTA LET "MR. MERKABA" GET WARMED UP!
!?
THERE'S NO WAY!!
MY SHOTS HAD NO EFFECT !!
THOSE WERE POSITRON BLASTS!!
BUT YOUR STUFF ALWAYS WORKS!!
ホーホホホ♡
GYAH!
NYA HA HA!
ONEESAN'S ABSOLUTELY RIGHT...
...I'M—

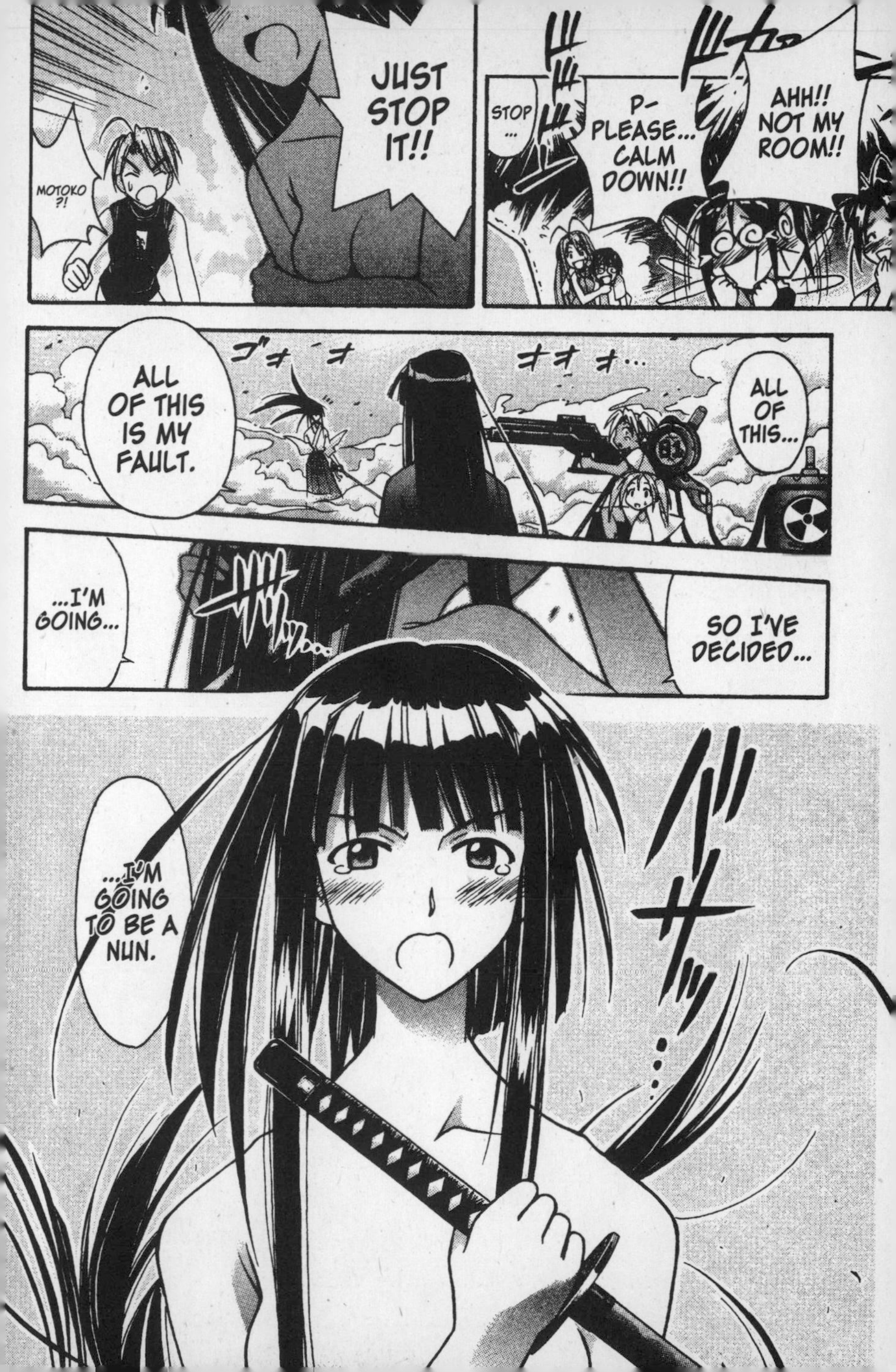
AHH!! NOT MY ROOM!!
P- PLEASE... CALM DOWN!!
STOP ...
JUST STOP IT!!
MOTOKO ?!
ALL OF THIS...
ALL OF THIS IS MY FAULT.
SO I'VE DECIDED...
...I'M GOING...
...I'M GOING TO BE A NUN.

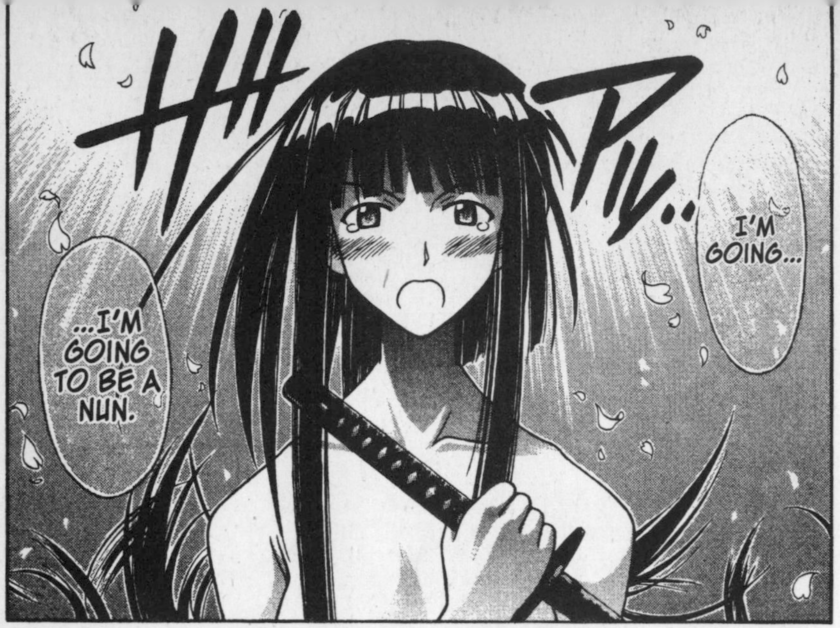
I'M GOING...
...I'M GOING TO BE A NUN.

Love Hina

HINATA.108 The Sword, Exams, and Love...

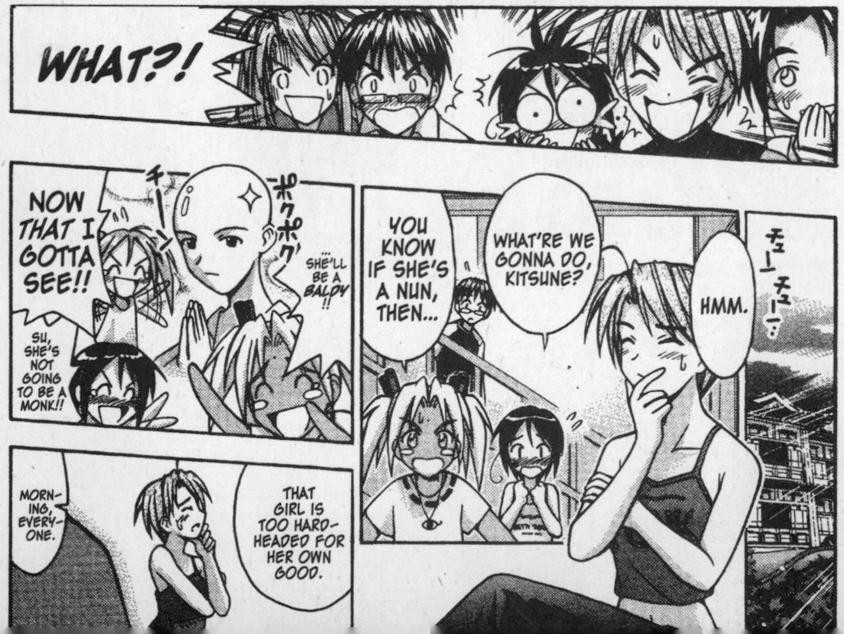
WHAT?!
HMM.
WHAT'RE WE GONNA DO, KITSUNE?
YOU KNOW IF SHE'S A NUN, THEN...
...SHE'LL BE A BALDY!!
NOW THAT I GOTTA SEE!!
SU, SHE'S NOT GOING TO BE A MONK!!
THAT GIRL IS TOO HARD-HEADED FOR HER OWN GOOD.
MORNING, EVERYONE.

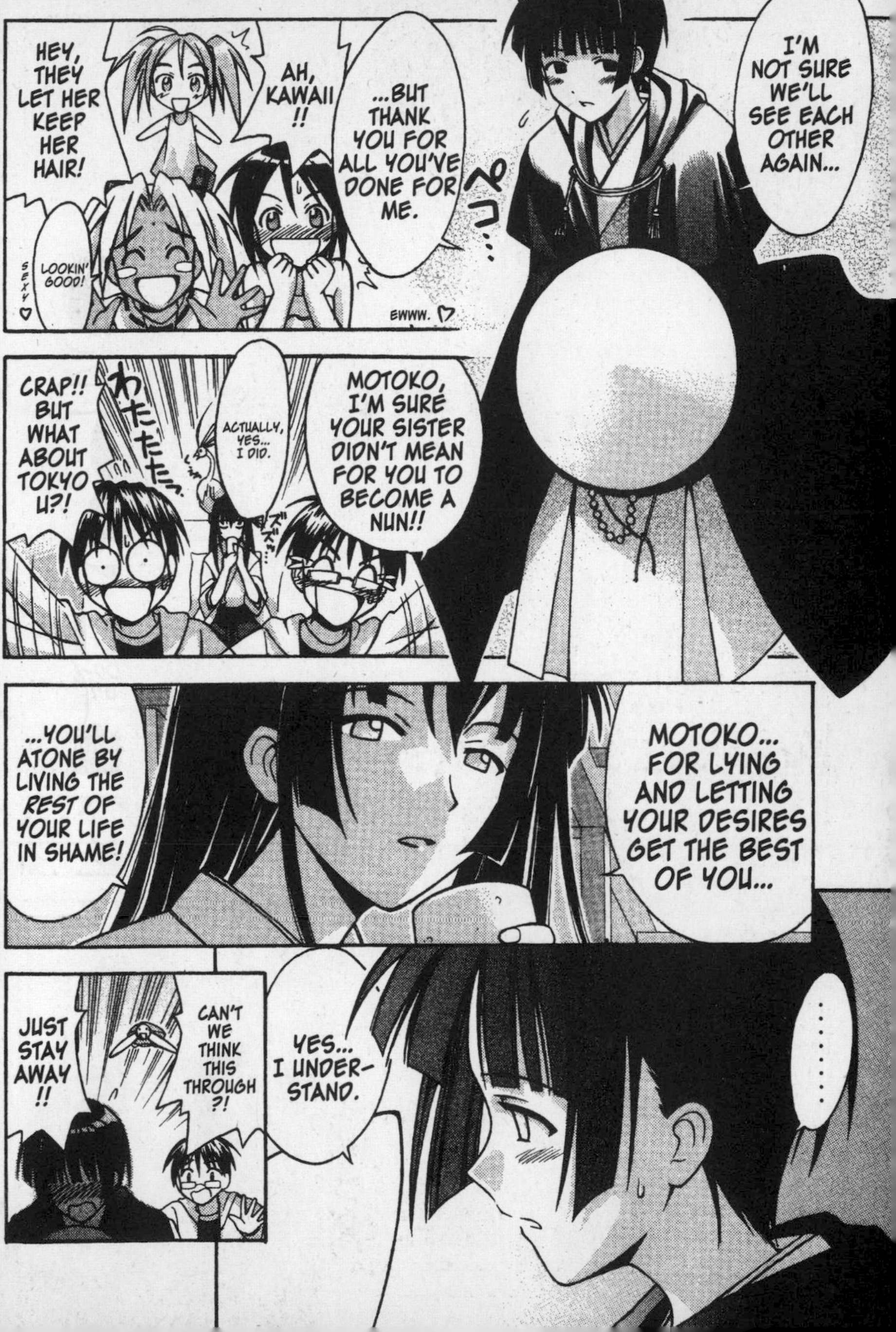
I'M NOT SURE WE'LL SEE EACH OTHER AGAIN...
...BUT THANK YOU FOR ALL YOU'VE DONE FOR ME.
ペコ…
AH, KAWAII!!
HEY, THEY LET HER KEEP HER HAIR!
LOOKIN' GOOD!
SEXY ♡
EWWW. ♡
MOTOKO, I'M SURE YOUR SISTER DIDN'T MEAN FOR YOU TO BECOME A NUN!!
ACTUALLY, YES... I DID.
わたたたっ
CRAP!! BUT WHAT ABOUT TOKYO U?!
MOTOKO... FOR LYING AND LETTING YOUR DESIRES GET THE BEST OF YOU...
...YOU'LL ATONE BY LIVING THE *REST* OF YOUR LIFE IN SHAME!
......
YES... I UNDERSTAND.
CAN'T WE THINK THIS THROUGH?!
JUST STAY AWAY!!

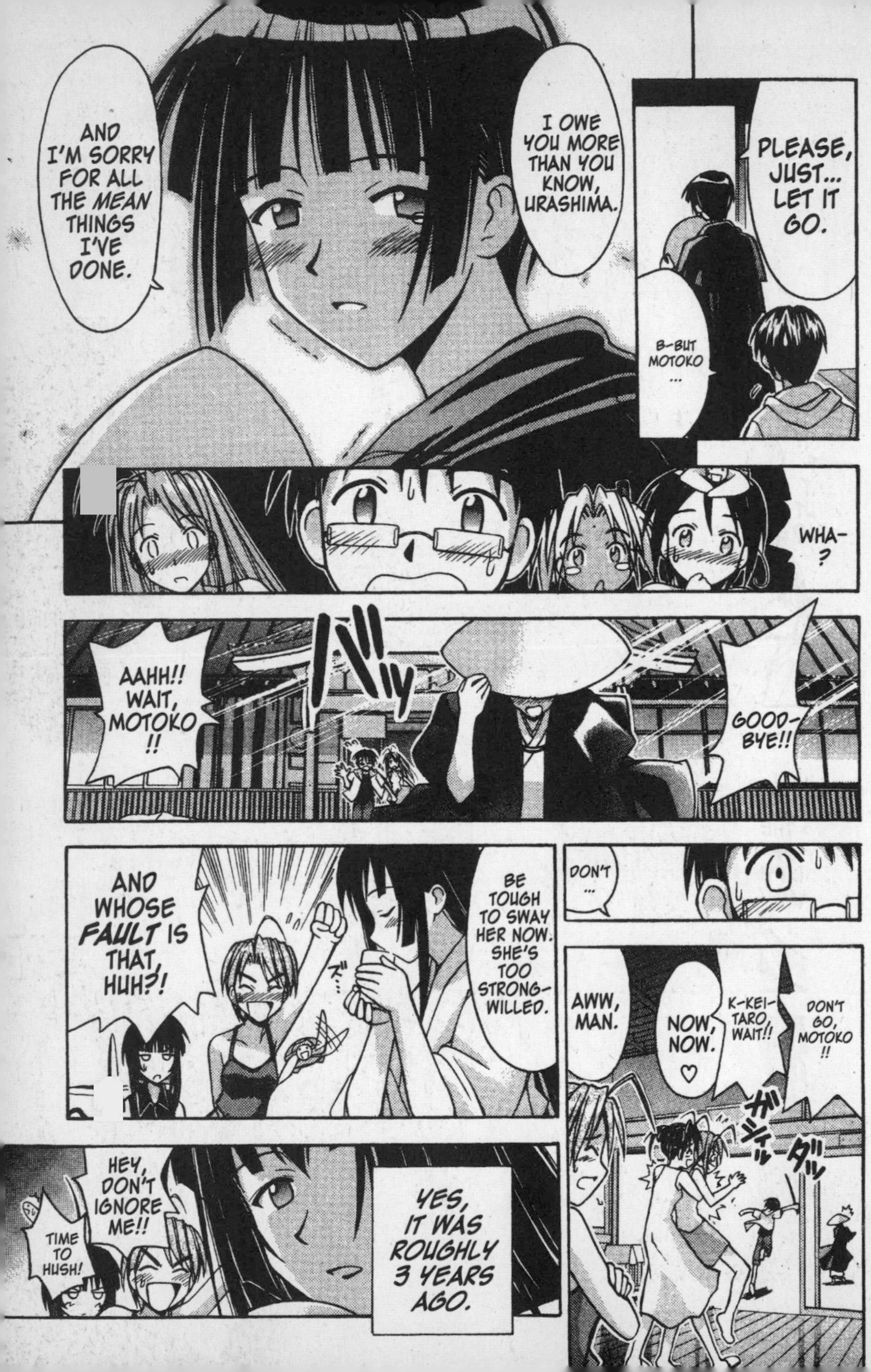

PLEASE, JUST... LET IT GO.
B-BUT MOTOKO...
I OWE YOU MORE THAN YOU KNOW, URASHIMA.
AND I'M SORRY FOR ALL THE *MEAN* THINGS I'VE DONE.
WHA-?
GOOD-BYE!!
AAHH!! WAIT, MOTOKO!!
DON'T...
DON'T GO, MOTOKO!!
K-KEI-TARO, WAIT!!
NOW, NOW. ♡
AWW, MAN.
BE TOUGH TO SWAY HER NOW. SHE'S TOO STRONG-WILLED.
AND WHOSE ***FAULT*** IS THAT, HUH?!
YES, IT WAS ROUGHLY 3 YEARS AGO.
HEY, DON'T IGNORE ME!!
TIME TO HUSH!

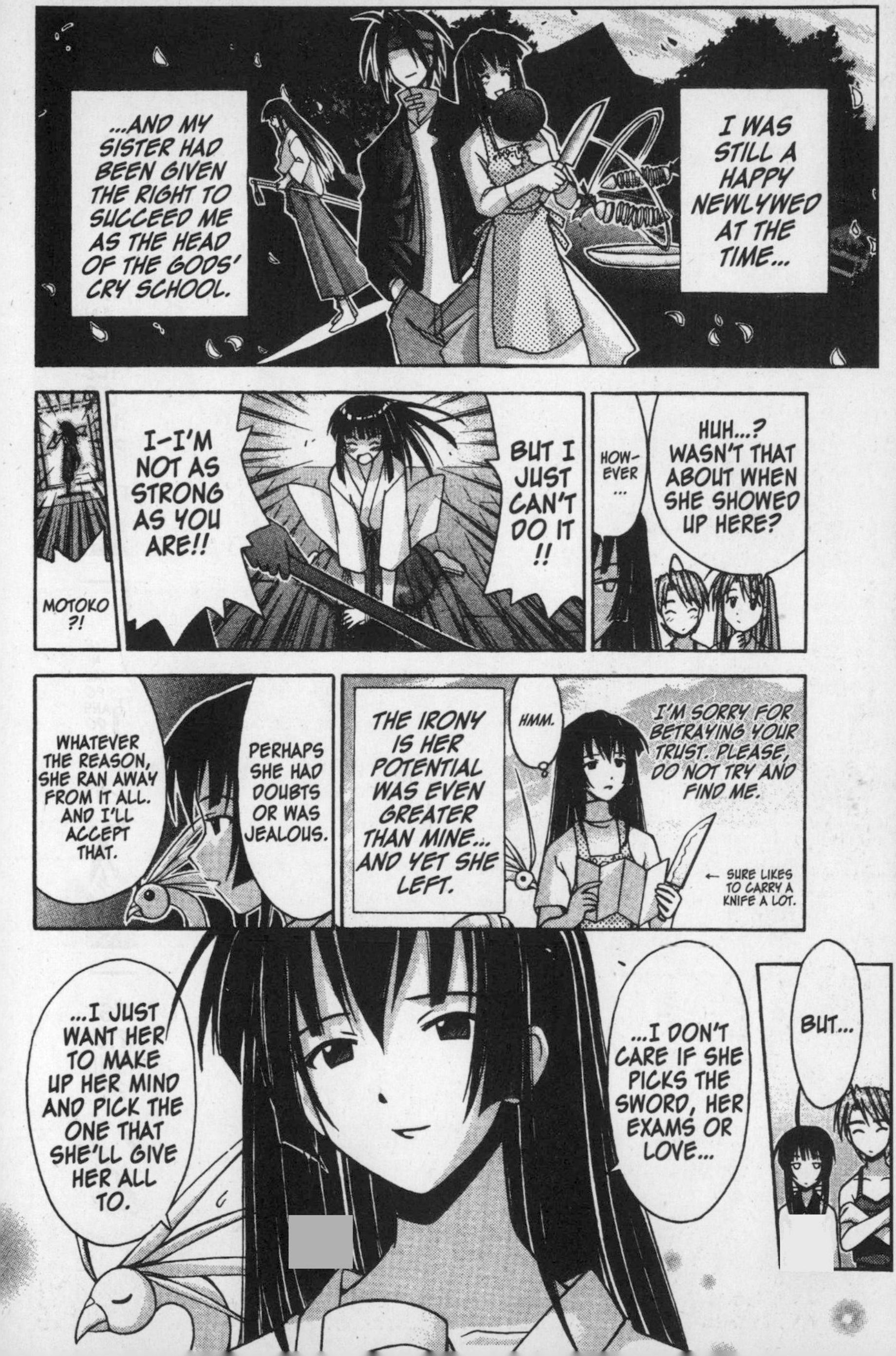
I WAS STILL A HAPPY NEWLYWED AT THE TIME...
...AND MY SISTER HAD BEEN GIVEN THE RIGHT TO SUCCEED ME AS THE HEAD OF THE GODS' CRY SCHOOL.
HUH...? WASN'T THAT ABOUT WHEN SHE SHOWED UP HERE?
HOW-EVER...
BUT I JUST CAN'T DO IT!!
I-I'M NOT AS STRONG AS YOU ARE!!
MOTOKO?!
I'M SORRY FOR BETRAYING YOUR TRUST. PLEASE, DO NOT TRY AND FIND ME.
HMM.
THE IRONY IS HER POTENTIAL WAS EVEN GREATER THAN MINE... AND YET SHE LEFT.
← SURE LIKES TO CARRY A KNIFE A LOT.
PERHAPS SHE HAD DOUBTS OR WAS JEALOUS.
WHATEVER THE REASON, SHE RAN AWAY FROM IT ALL. AND I'LL ACCEPT THAT.
BUT...
...I DON'T CARE IF SHE PICKS THE SWORD, HER EXAMS OR LOVE...
...I JUST WANT HER TO MAKE UP HER MIND AND PICK THE ONE THAT SHE'LL GIVE HER ALL TO.

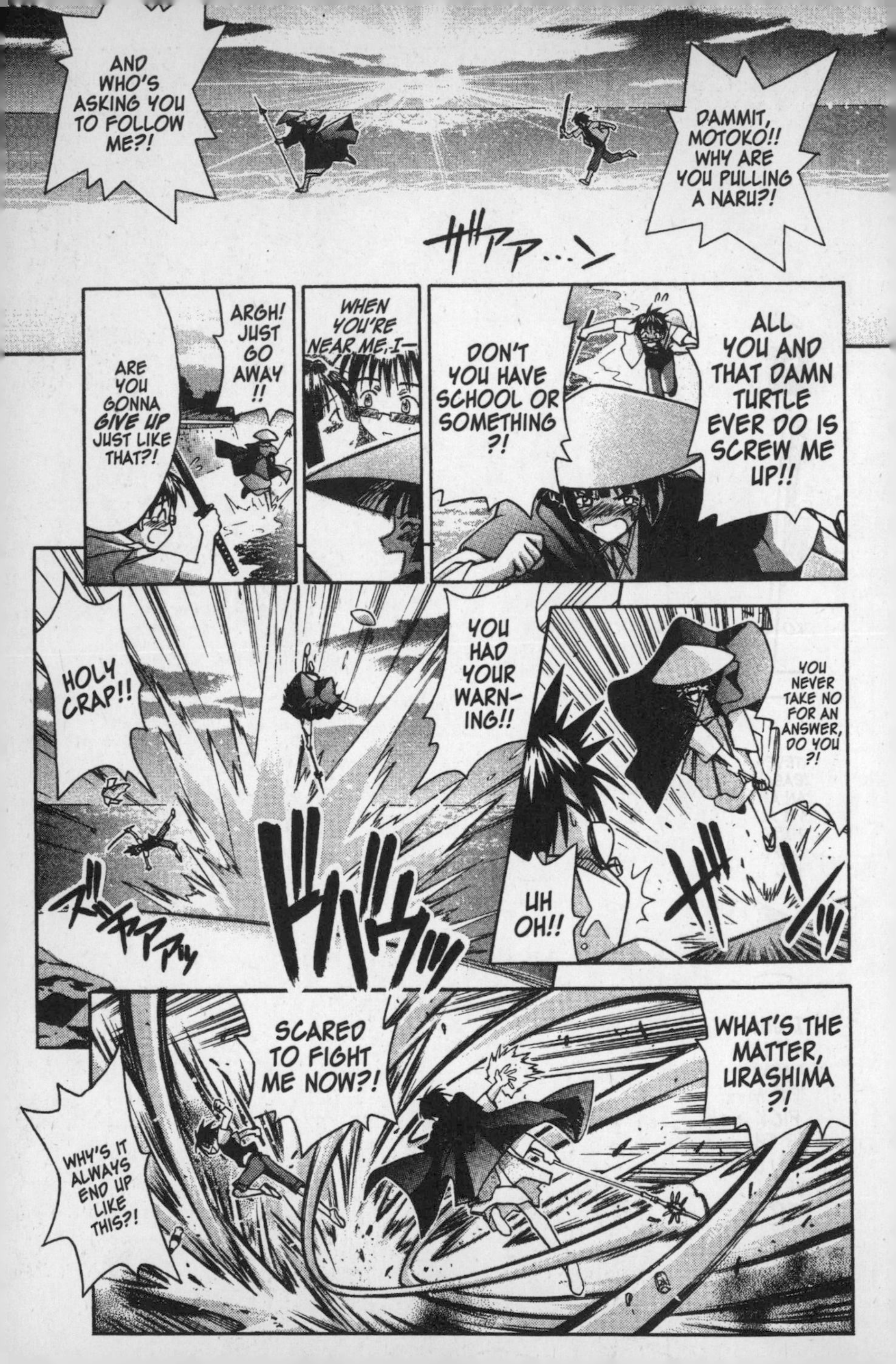
DAMMIT, MOTOKO!! WHY ARE YOU PULLING A NARU?!
AND WHO'S ASKING YOU TO FOLLOW ME?!
ALL YOU AND THAT DAMN TURTLE EVER DO IS SCREW ME UP!!
DON'T YOU HAVE SCHOOL OR SOMETHING?!
WHEN YOU'RE NEAR ME, I—
ARGH! JUST GO AWAY!!
ARE YOU GONNA *GIVE UP* JUST LIKE THAT?!
YOU NEVER TAKE NO FOR AN ANSWER, DO YOU?!
YOU HAD YOUR WARNING!!
UH OH!!
HOLY CRAP!!
WHAT'S THE MATTER, URASHIMA?!
SCARED TO FIGHT ME NOW?!
WHY'S IT ALWAYS END UP LIKE THIS?!

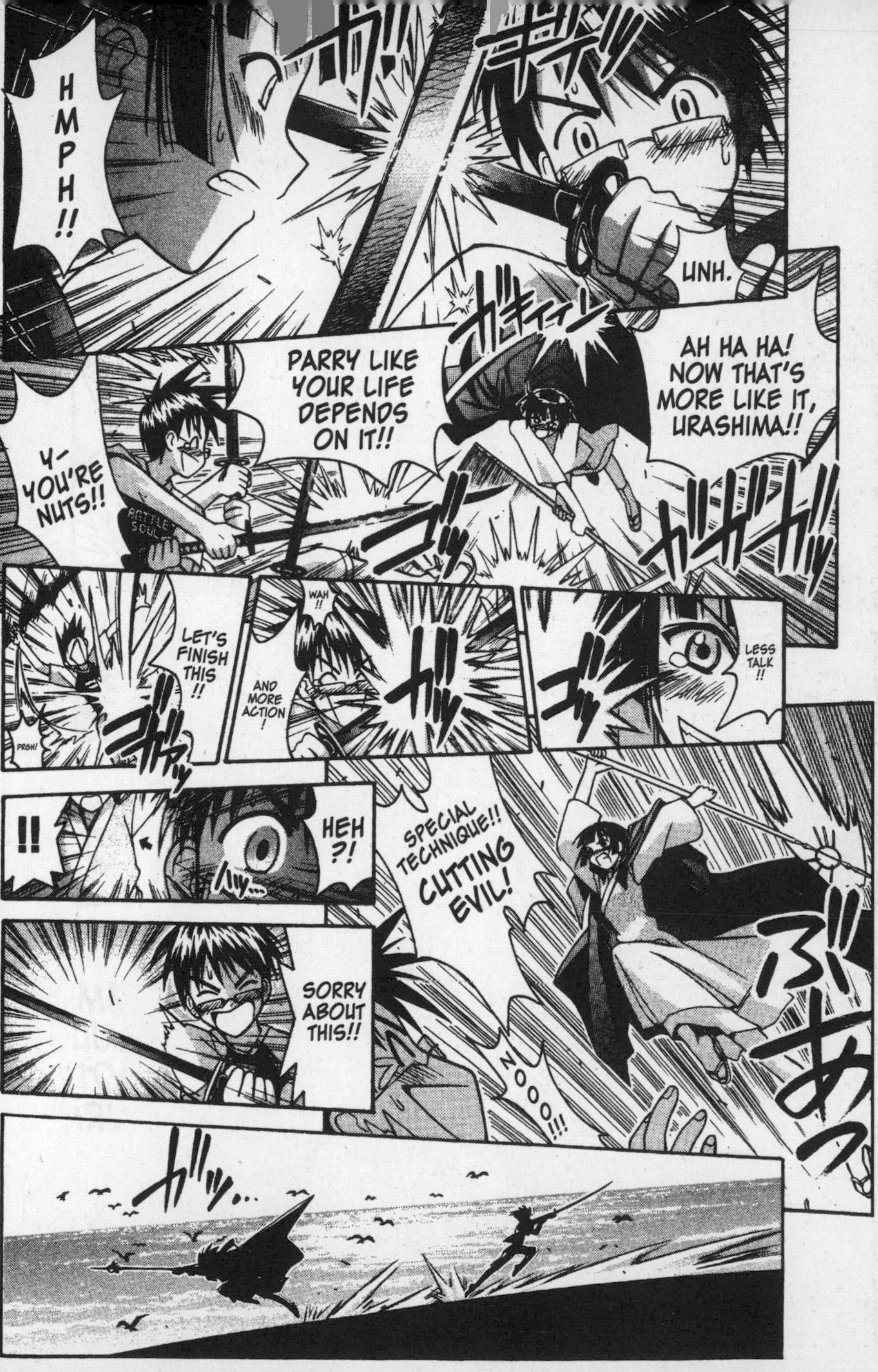
UNH.
HMPH!!
AH HA HA! NOW THAT'S MORE LIKE IT, URASHIMA!!
PARRY LIKE YOUR LIFE DEPENDS ON IT!!
Y-YOU'RE NUTS!!
LESS TALK!!
WAH!!
AND MORE ACTION!
LET'S FINISH THIS!!
PRGH!
SPECIAL TECHNIQUE!! CUTTING EVIL!
NOOOO!!!
!!
HEH?!
SORRY ABOUT THIS!!

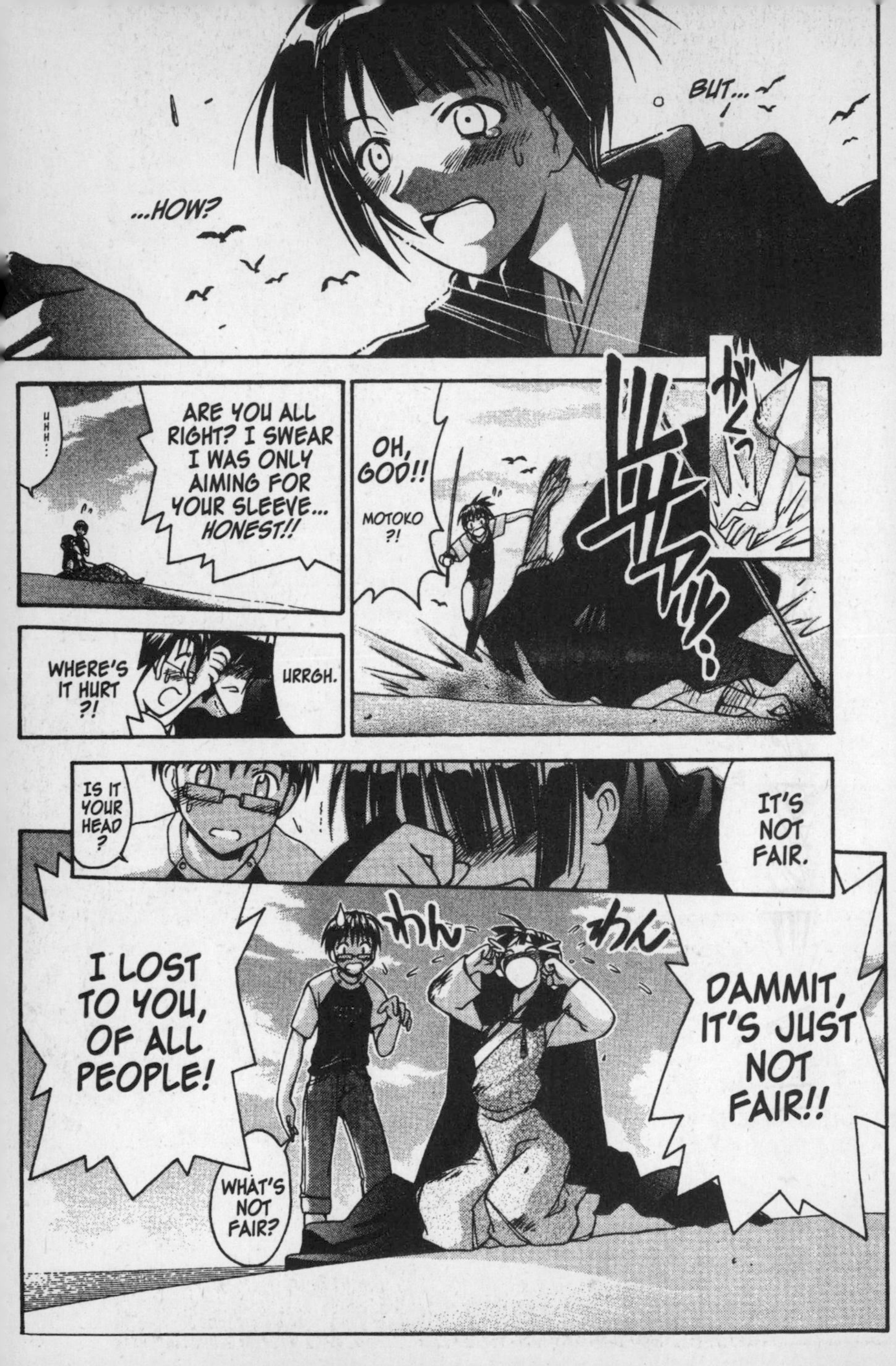
BUT...
...HOW?
がくっ
OH, GOD!!
MOTOKO ?!
ARE YOU ALL RIGHT? I SWEAR I WAS ONLY AIMING FOR YOUR SLEEVE... HONEST!!
UHH...
URRGH.
WHERE'S IT HURT ?!
IT'S NOT FAIR.
IS IT YOUR HEAD ?
DAMMIT, IT'S JUST NOT FAIR!!
わん
わん
I LOST TO YOU, OF ALL PEOPLE!
WHAT'S NOT FAIR?

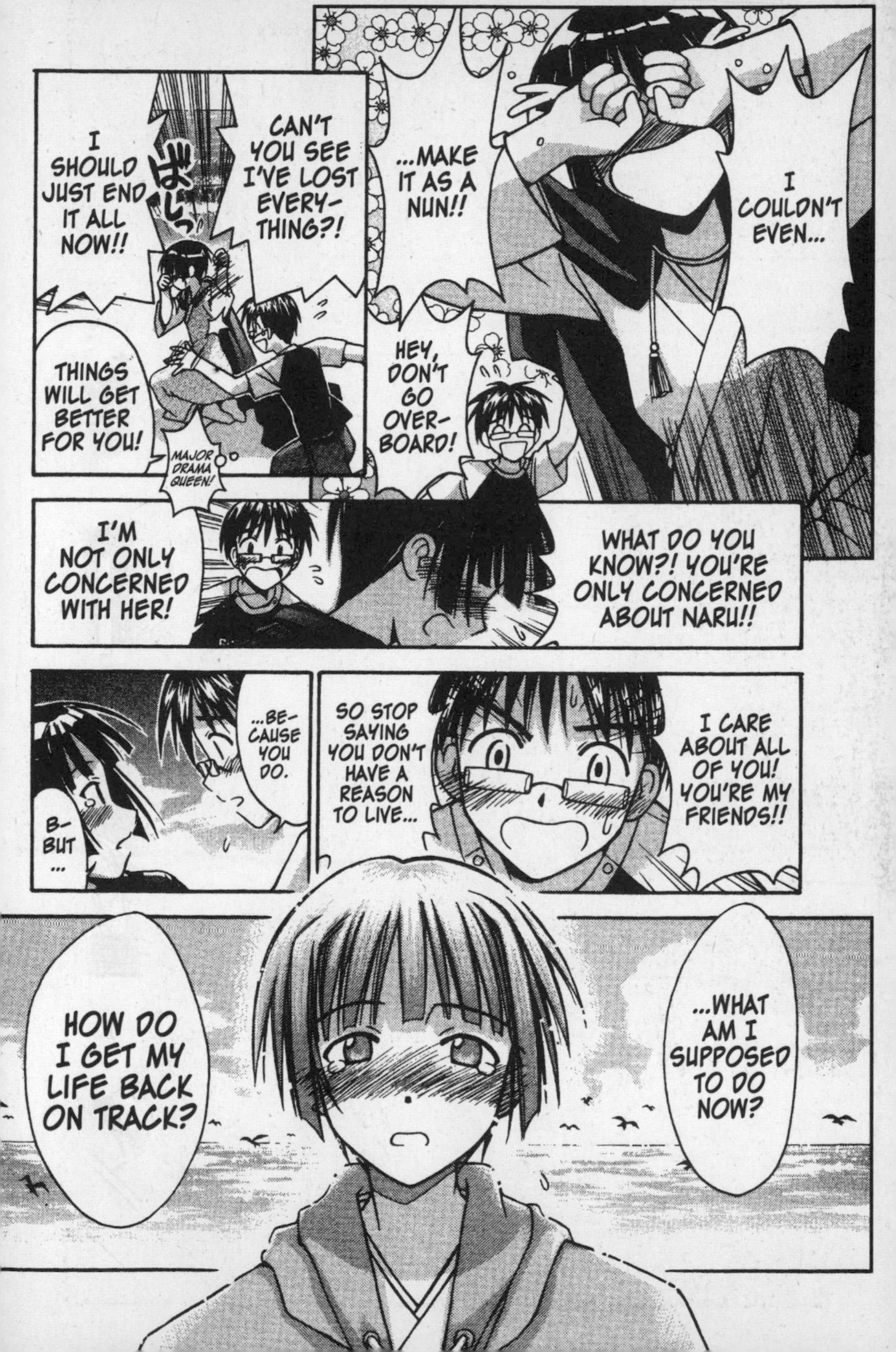
I COULDN'T EVEN...
...MAKE IT AS A NUN!!
HEY, DON'T GO OVERBOARD!
CAN'T YOU SEE I'VE LOST EVERYTHING?!
I SHOULD JUST END IT ALL NOW!!
ばしっ
THINGS WILL GET BETTER FOR YOU!
MAJOR DRAMA QUEEN!
WHAT DO YOU KNOW?! YOU'RE ONLY CONCERNED ABOUT NARU!!
I'M NOT ONLY CONCERNED WITH HER!
I CARE ABOUT ALL OF YOU! YOU'RE MY FRIENDS!!
SO STOP SAYING YOU DON'T HAVE A REASON TO LIVE...
...BECAUSE YOU DO.
B-BUT...
...WHAT AM I SUPPOSED TO DO NOW?
HOW DO I GET MY LIFE BACK ON TRACK?

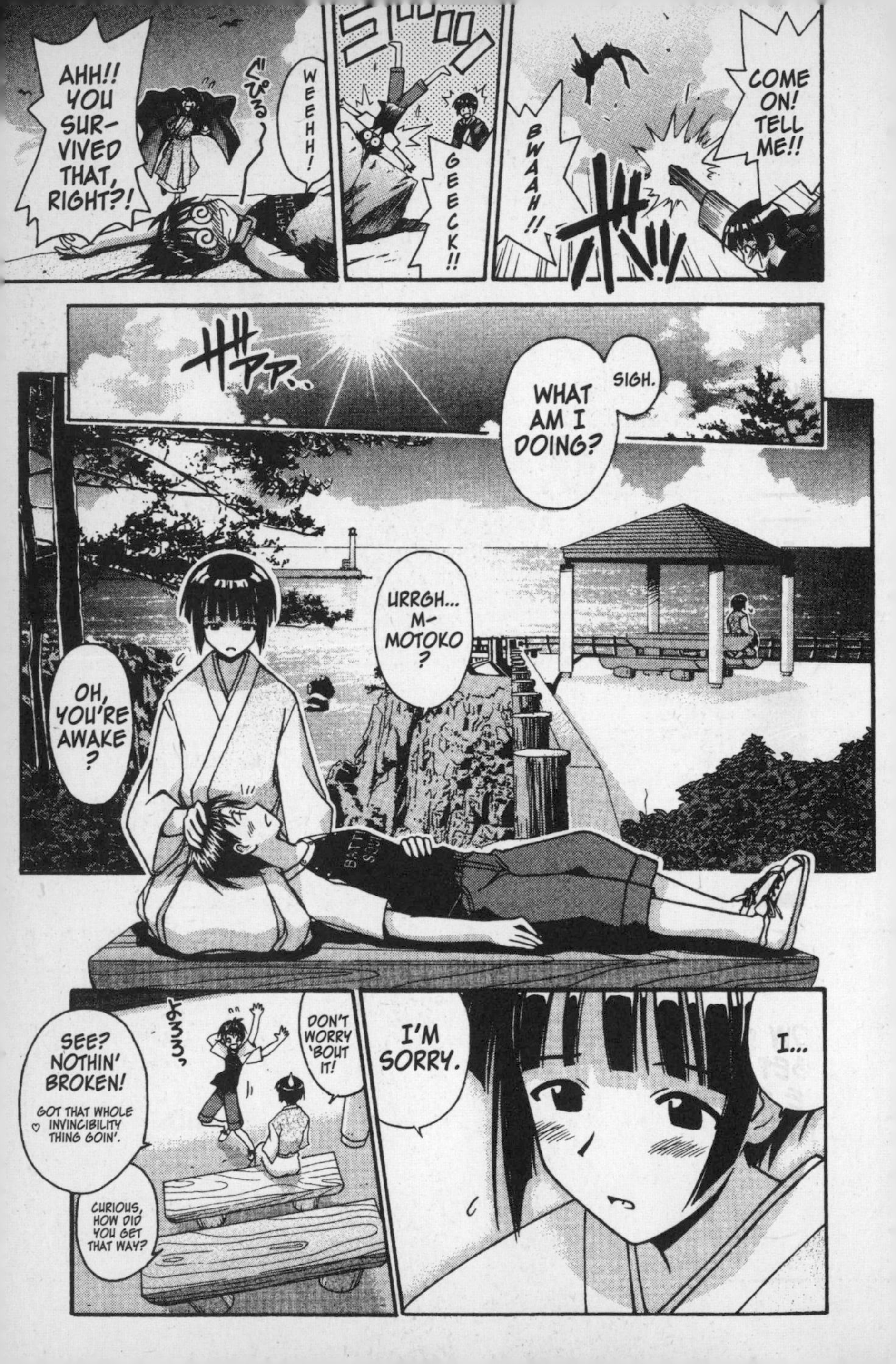
COME ON! TELL ME!!
BWAAH!!
GEEECK!!
WEEHH!
AHH!! YOU SURVIVED THAT, RIGHT?!
SIGH.
WHAT AM I DOING?
URRGH... M-MOTOKO?
OH, YOU'RE AWAKE?
I...
I'M SORRY.
DON'T WORRY 'BOUT IT!
SEE? NOTHIN' BROKEN!
GOT THAT WHOLE INVINCIBILITY THING GOIN'.
CURIOUS, HOW DID YOU GET THAT WAY?

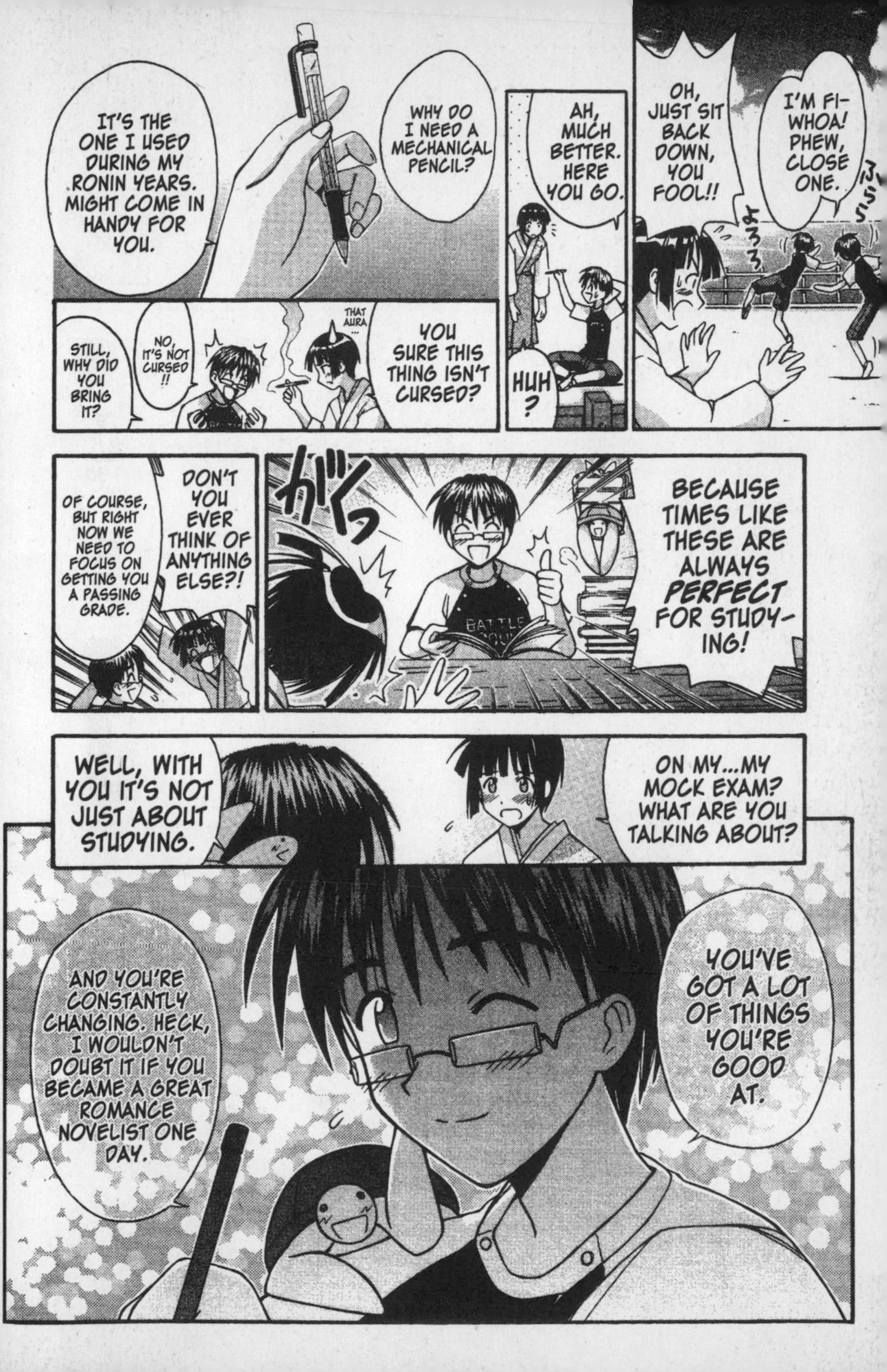
I'M FI- WHOA! PHEW, CLOSE ONE.
よろろ
OH, JUST SIT BACK DOWN, YOU FOOL!!
AH, MUCH BETTER. HERE YOU GO.
HUH?
WHY DO I NEED A MECHANICAL PENCIL?
IT'S THE ONE I USED DURING MY RONIN YEARS. MIGHT COME IN HANDY FOR YOU.
YOU SURE THIS THING ISN'T CURSED?
THAT AURA...
NO, IT'S NOT CURSED!!
STILL, WHY DID YOU BRING IT?
BECAUSE TIMES LIKE THESE ARE ALWAYS PERFECT FOR STUDYING!
がくっ
DON'T YOU EVER THINK OF ANYTHING ELSE?!
OF COURSE, BUT RIGHT NOW WE NEED TO FOCUS ON GETTING YOU A PASSING GRADE.
ON MY...MY MOCK EXAM? WHAT ARE YOU TALKING ABOUT?
WELL, WITH YOU IT'S NOT JUST ABOUT STUDYING.
YOU'VE GOT A LOT OF THINGS YOU'RE GOOD AT.
AND YOU'RE CONSTANTLY CHANGING. HECK, I WOULDN'T DOUBT IT IF YOU BECAME A GREAT ROMANCE NOVELIST ONE DAY.

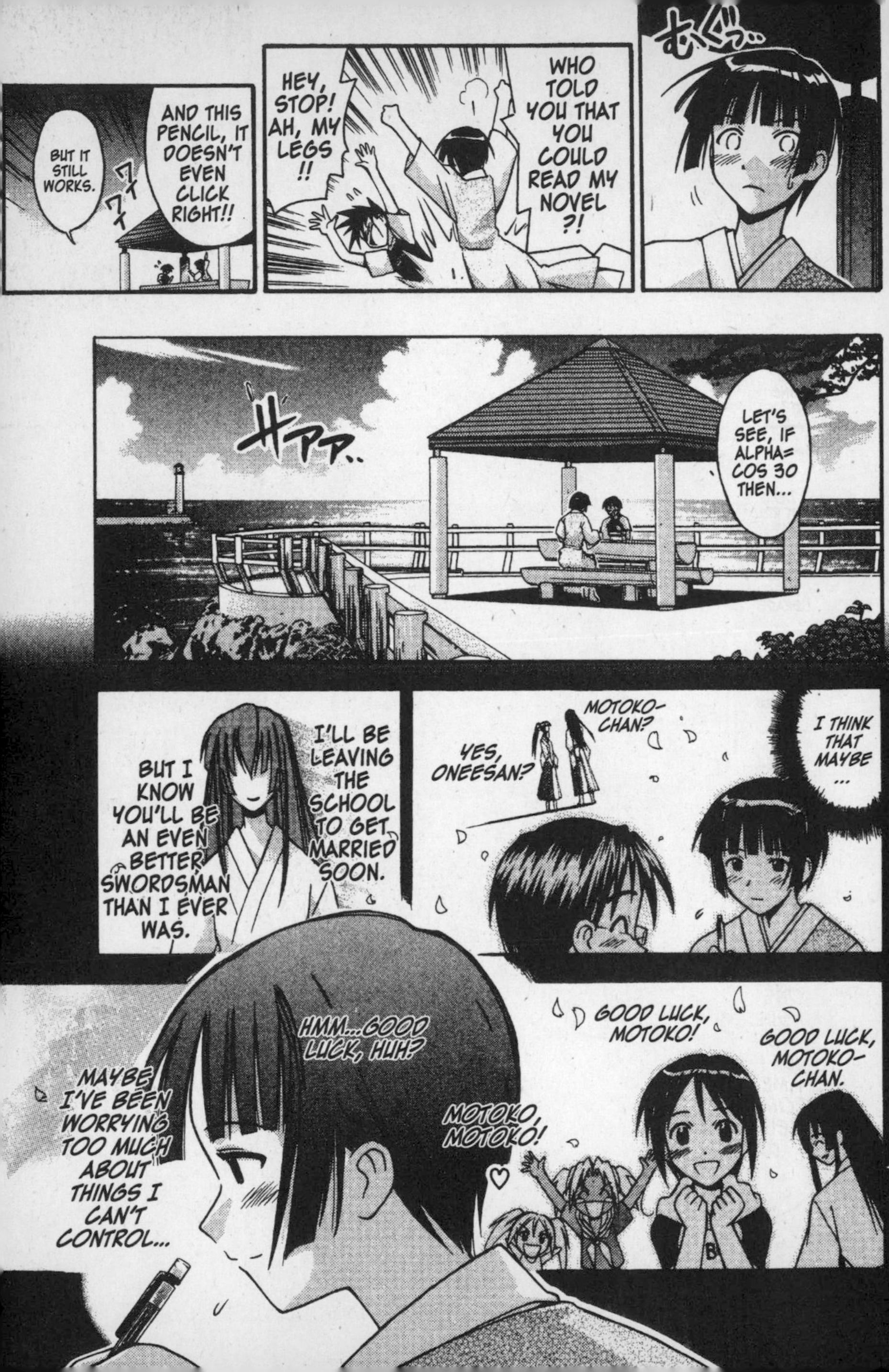
むぐっ..
WHO TOLD YOU THAT YOU COULD READ MY NOVEL ?!
HEY, STOP! AH, MY LEGS !!
AND THIS PENCIL, IT DOESN'T EVEN CLICK RIGHT!!
ワイワイ
BUT IT STILL WORKS.
LET'S SEE, IF ALPHA= COS 30 THEN...
ハァァ..
I THINK THAT MAYBE ...
MOTOKO-CHAN?
YES, ONEESAN?
I'LL BE LEAVING THE SCHOOL TO GET MARRIED SOON.
BUT I KNOW YOU'LL BE AN EVEN BETTER SWORDSMAN THAN I EVER WAS.
GOOD LUCK, MOTOKO-CHAN.
GOOD LUCK, MOTOKO!
MOTOKO, MOTOKO!
HMM...GOOD LUCK, HUH?
MAYBE I'VE BEEN WORRYING TOO MUCH ABOUT THINGS I CAN'T CONTROL...

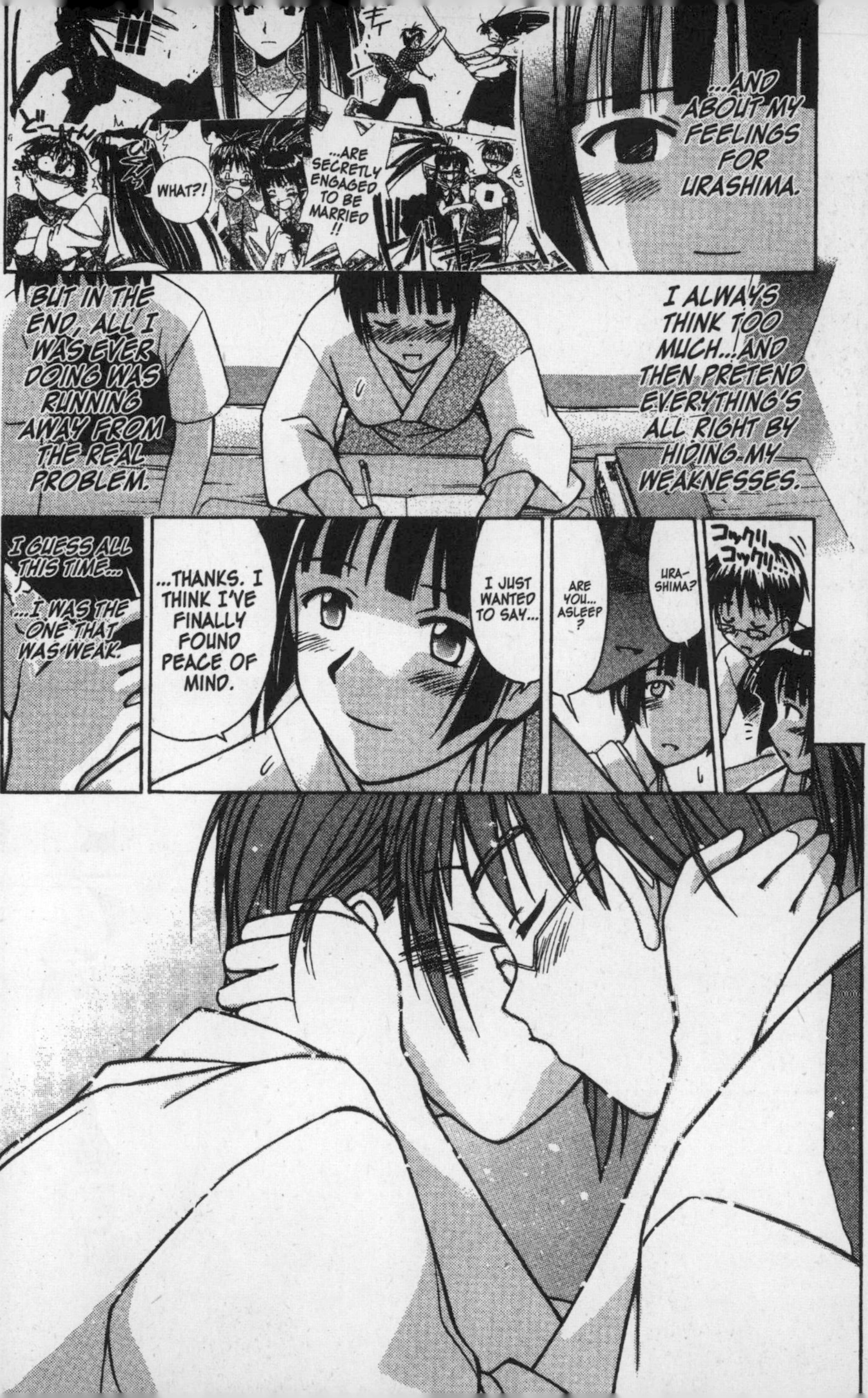
...AND ABOUT MY FEELINGS FOR URASHIMA.
...ARE SECRETLY ENGAGED TO BE MARRIED!!
WHAT?!
I ALWAYS THINK TOO MUCH... AND THEN PRETEND EVERYTHING'S ALL RIGHT BY HIDING MY WEAKNESSES.
BUT IN THE END, ALL I WAS EVER DOING WAS RUNNING AWAY FROM THE REAL PROBLEM.
コックリ コックリ
URA-SHIMA?
ARE YOU... ASLEEP?
I JUST WANTED TO SAY...
...THANKS. I THINK I'VE FINALLY FOUND PEACE OF MIND.
I GUESS ALL THIS TIME...
...I WAS THE ONE THAT WAS WEAK.

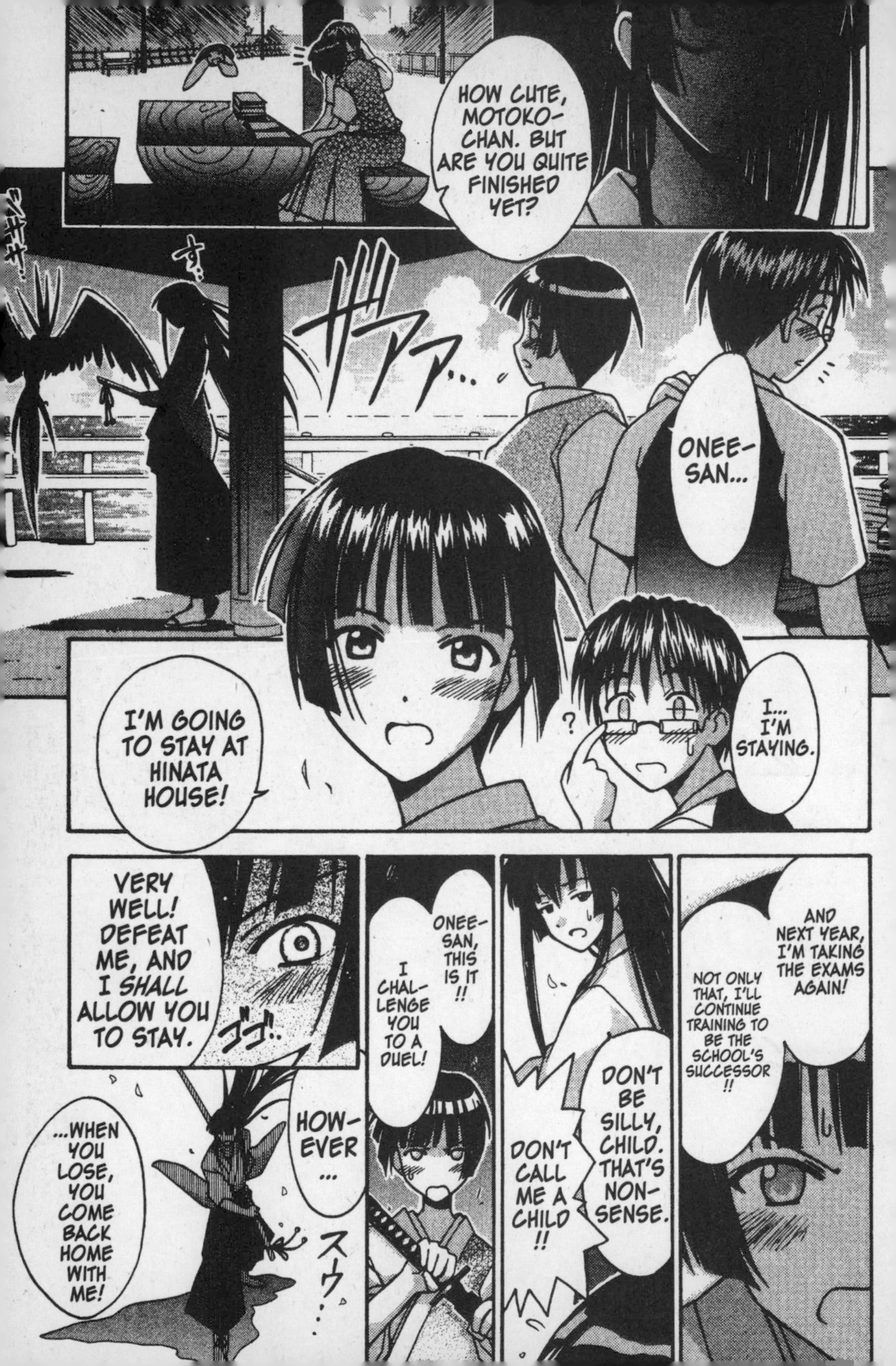
HOW CUTE, MOTOKO-CHAN. BUT ARE YOU QUITE FINISHED YET?
ザァァ...
ONEE-SAN...
I... I'M STAYING.
I'M GOING TO STAY AT HINATA HOUSE!
AND NEXT YEAR, I'M TAKING THE EXAMS AGAIN!
NOT ONLY THAT, I'LL CONTINUE TRAINING TO BE THE SCHOOL'S SUCCESSOR!!
DON'T BE SILLY, CHILD. THAT'S NONSENSE.
DON'T CALL ME A CHILD!!
ONEE-SAN, THIS IS IT!!
I CHALLENGE YOU TO A DUEL!
HOW-EVER...
スゥ...
VERY WELL! DEFEAT ME, AND I SHALL ALLOW YOU TO STAY.
ゴゴ..
...WHEN YOU LOSE, YOU COME BACK HOME WITH ME!

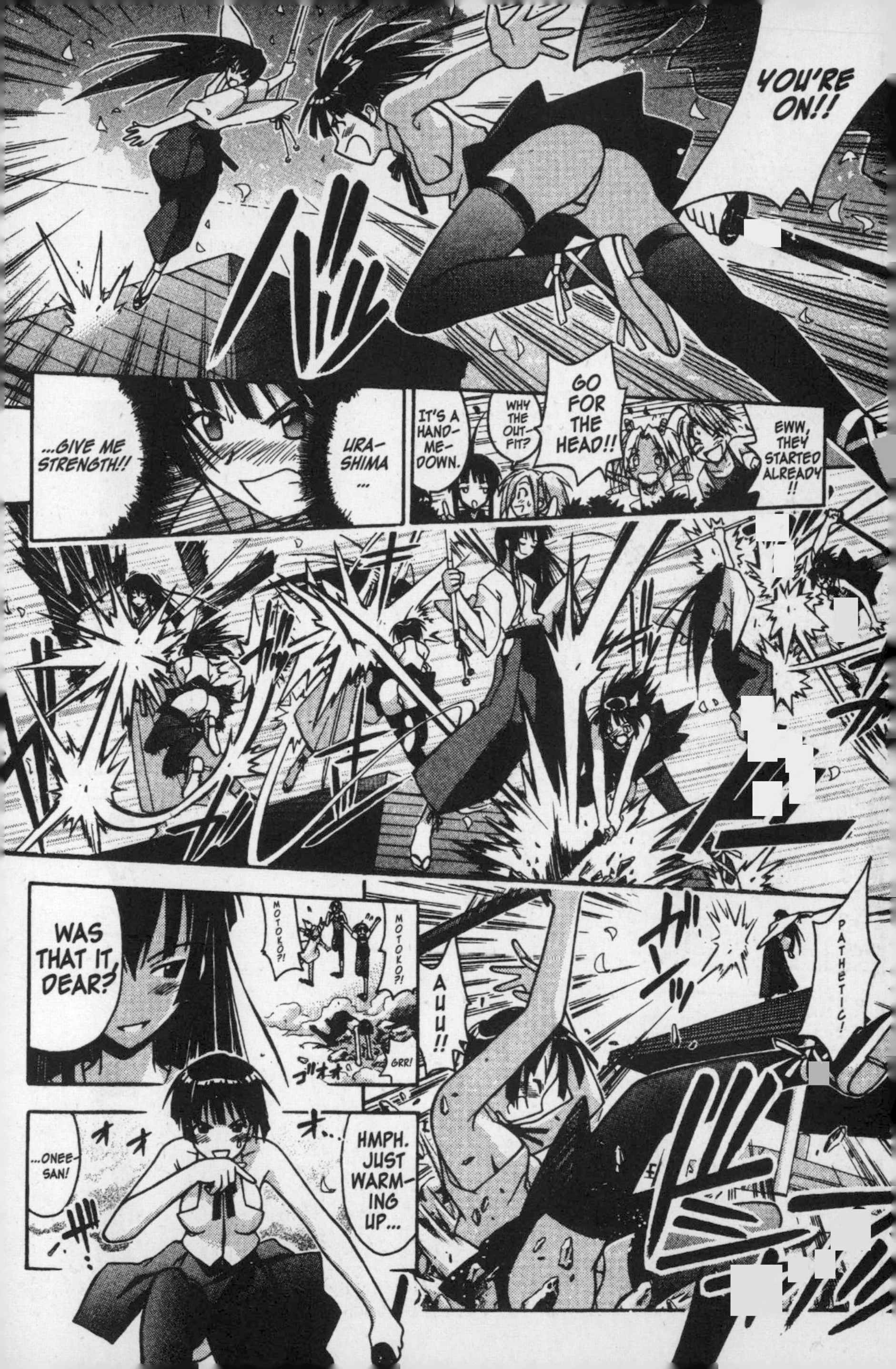

YOU'RE ON!!
EWW, THEY STARTED ALREADY!!
GO FOR THE HEAD!!
WHY THE OUT-FIT?
IT'S A HAND-ME-DOWN.
URA-SHIMA...
...GIVE ME STRENGTH!!
PATHETIC!
AUUU!!
MOTOKO?!
MOTOKO?!
GRR!
WAS THAT IT, DEAR?
HMPH. JUST WARMING UP...
...ONEE-SAN!

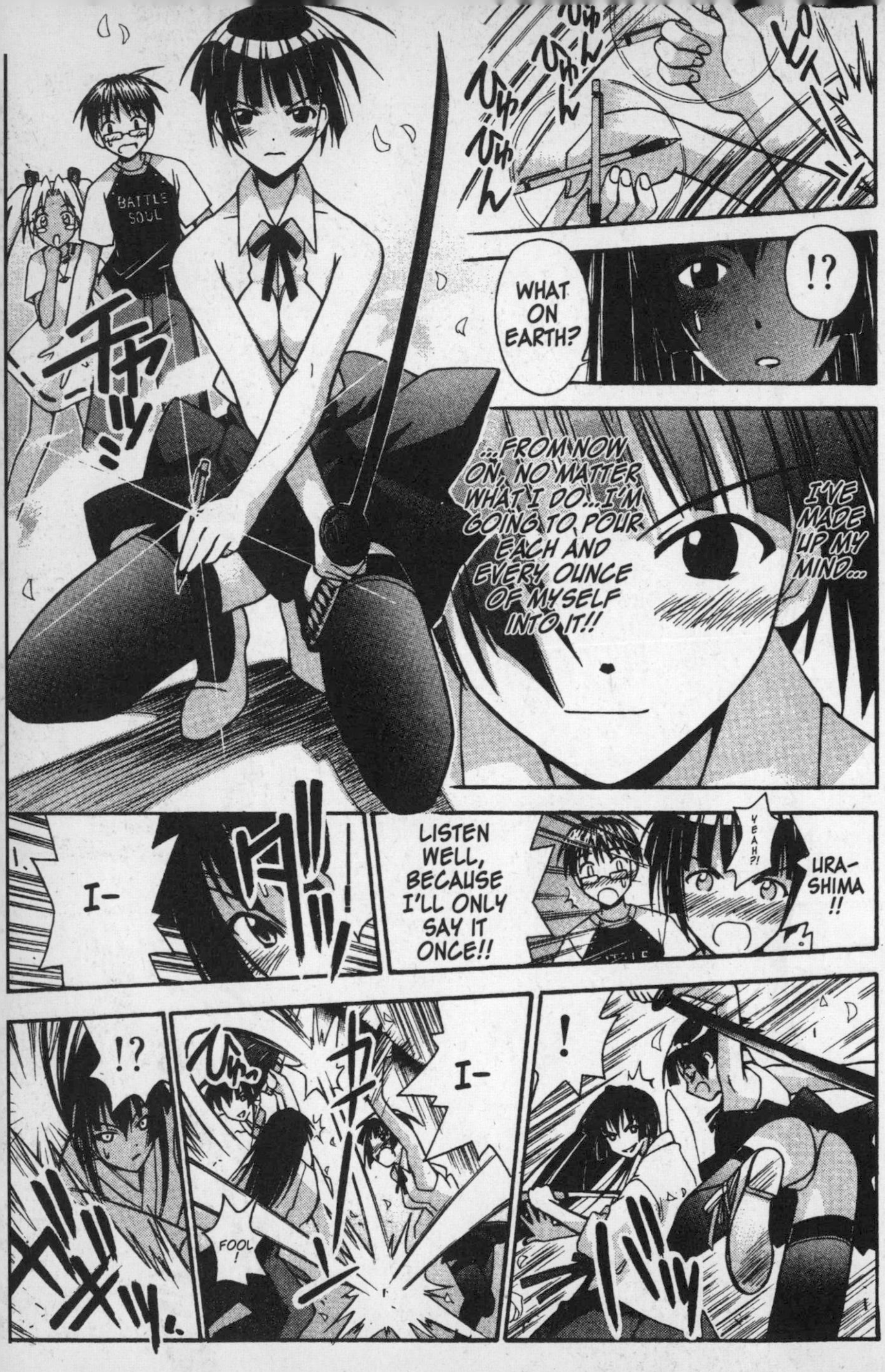
!?
WHAT ON EARTH?
I'VE MADE UP MY MIND...
...FROM NOW ON, NO MATTER WHAT I DO...I'M GOING TO POUR EACH AND EVERY OUNCE OF MYSELF INTO IT!!
URA-SHIMA!!
YEAH?!
LISTEN WELL, BECAUSE I'LL ONLY SAY IT ONCE!!
I-
!
I-
FOOL!
!?

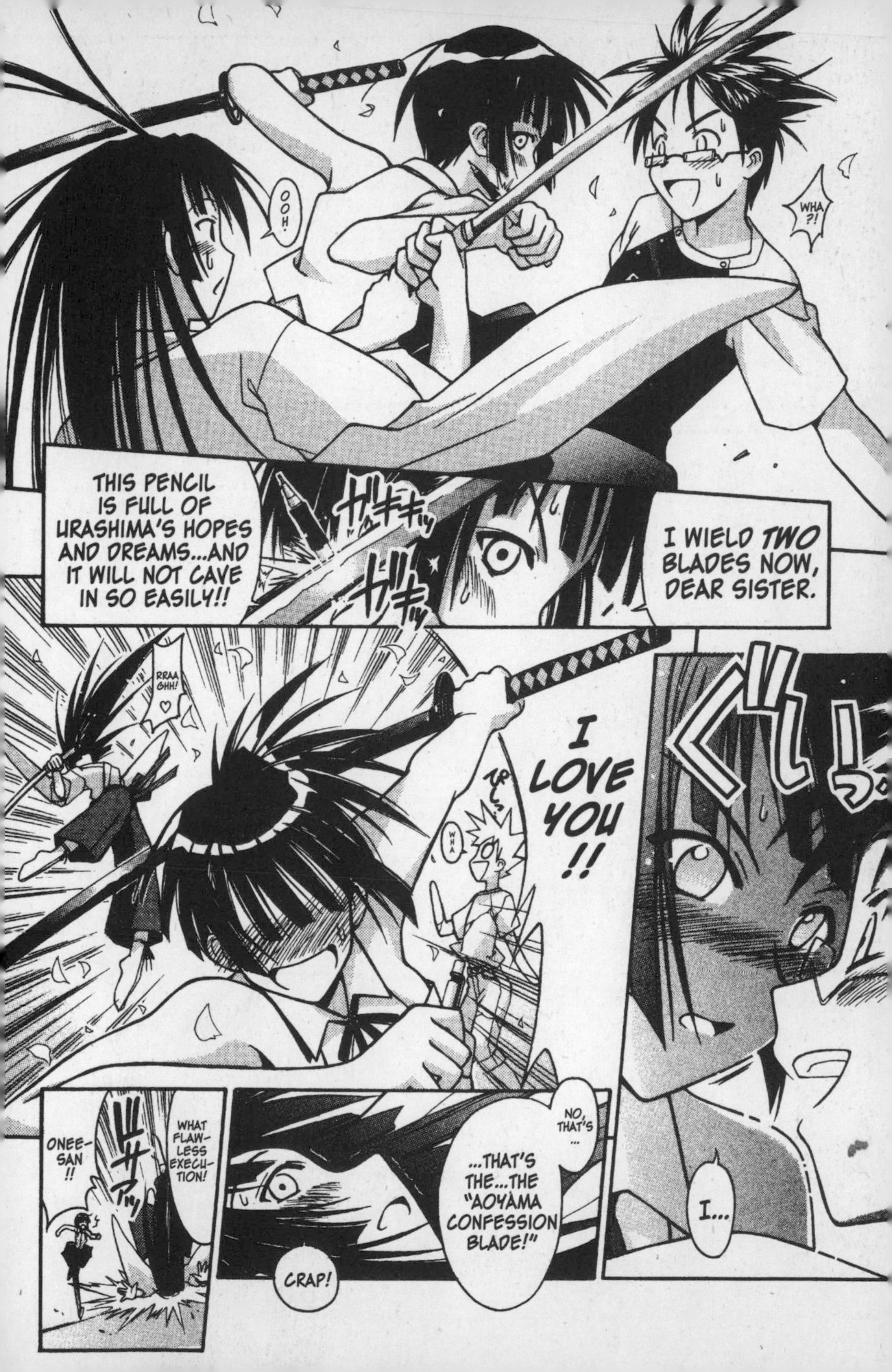

WHA ?!
OOH!
I WIELD TWO BLADES NOW, DEAR SISTER.
THIS PENCIL IS FULL OF URASHIMA'S HOPES AND DREAMS...AND IT WILL NOT CAVE IN SO EASILY!!
I...
I LOVE YOU !!
WHA
RRAAGHH! ♡
NO, THAT'S ...
...THAT'S THE...THE "AOYAMA CONFESSION BLADE!"
CRAP!
WHAT FLAWLESS EXECUTION!
ONEE-SAN !!

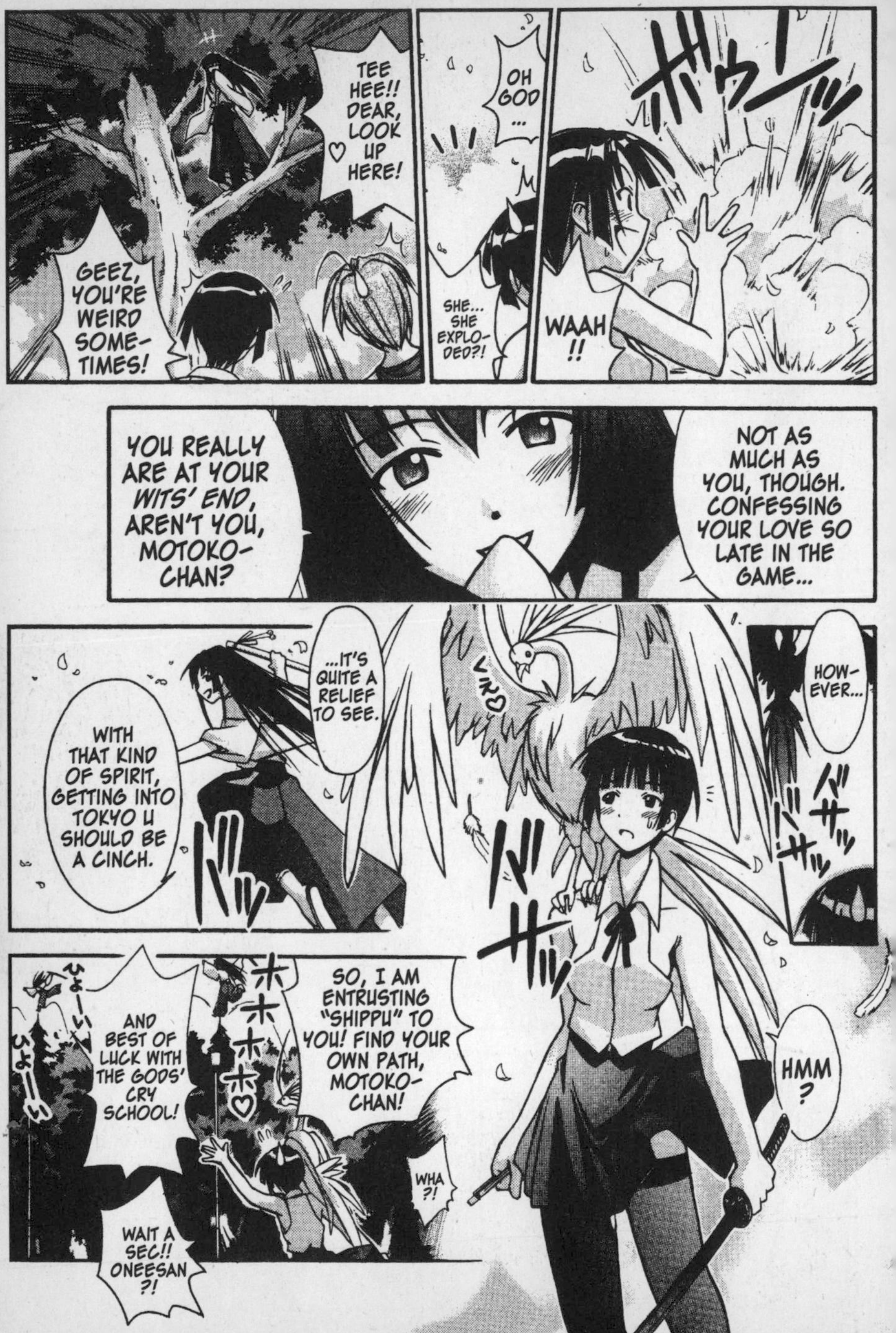
WAAH!!
OH GOD...
SHE... SHE EXPLODED?!
TEE HEE!! DEAR, LOOK UP HERE! ♡
GEEZ, YOU'RE WEIRD SOME-TIMES!
NOT AS MUCH AS YOU, THOUGH. CONFESSING YOUR LOVE SO LATE IN THE GAME...
YOU REALLY ARE AT YOUR WITS' END, AREN'T YOU, MOTOKO-CHAN?
HOW-EVER...
HMM?
...IT'S QUITE A RELIEF TO SEE.
WITH THAT KIND OF SPIRIT, GETTING INTO TOKYO U SHOULD BE A CINCH.
SO, I AM ENTRUSTING "SHIPPU" TO YOU! FIND YOUR OWN PATH, MOTOKO-CHAN!
ホホホホ♡
AND BEST OF LUCK WITH THE GODS' CRY SCHOOL!
ひょーい
ひょーい
WHA?!
WAIT A SEC!! ONEESAN?!

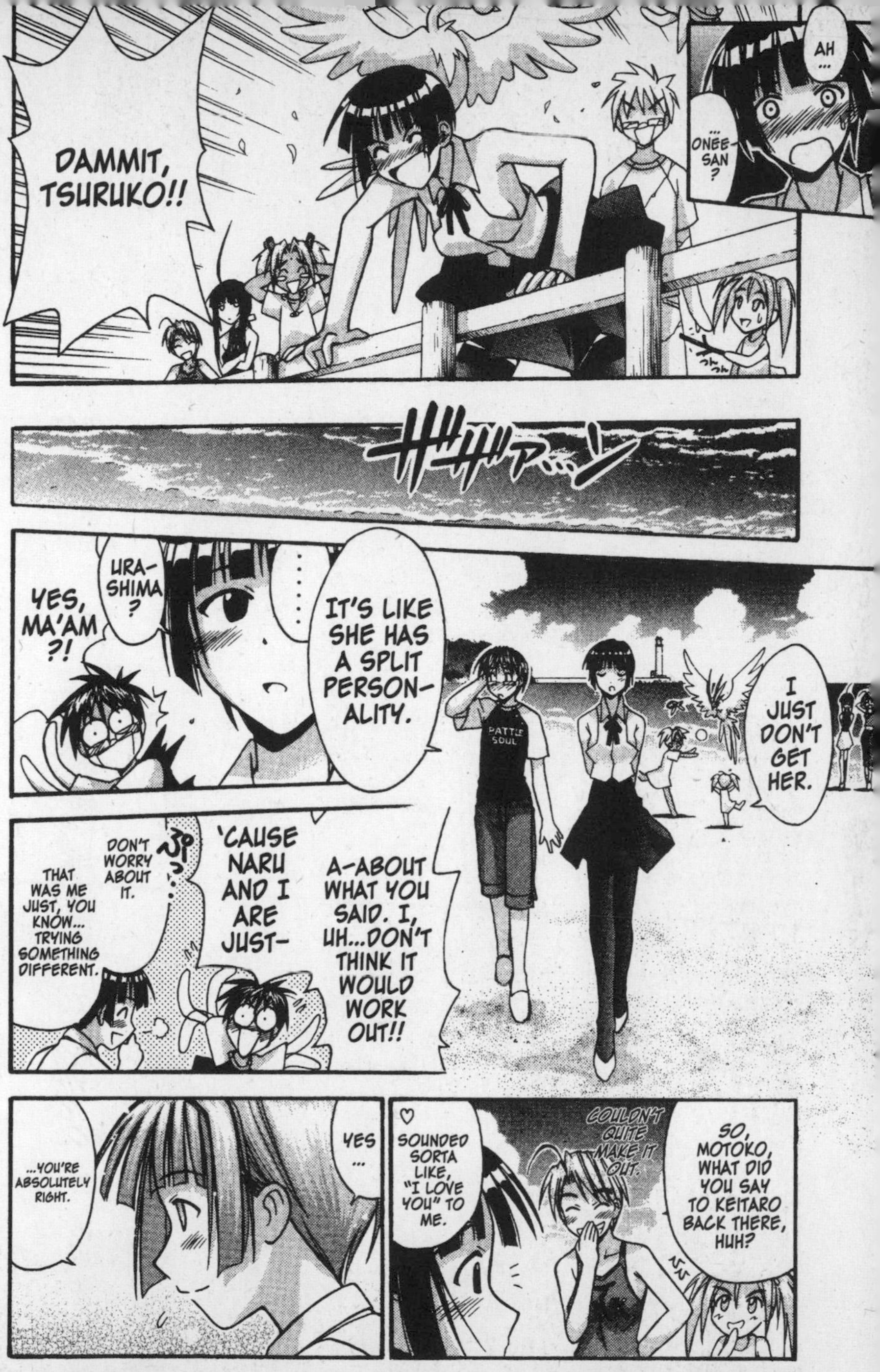
AH ...
... ONEE-SAN ?
DAMMIT, TSURUKO!!
ザザザァ…ン
I JUST DON'T GET HER.
IT'S LIKE SHE HAS A SPLIT PERSONALITY.
....
URA-SHIMA ?
YES, MA'AM ?!
A-ABOUT WHAT YOU SAID. I, UH...DON'T THINK IT WOULD WORK OUT!!
'CAUSE NARU AND I ARE JUST-
DON'T WORRY ABOUT IT.
THAT WAS ME JUST, YOU KNOW... TRYING SOMETHING DIFFERENT.
SO, MOTOKO, WHAT DID YOU SAY TO KEITARO BACK THERE, HUH?
COULDN'T QUITE MAKE IT OUT.
SOUNDED SORTA LIKE, "I LOVE YOU" TO ME.
YES ...
...YOU'RE ABSOLUTELY RIGHT.

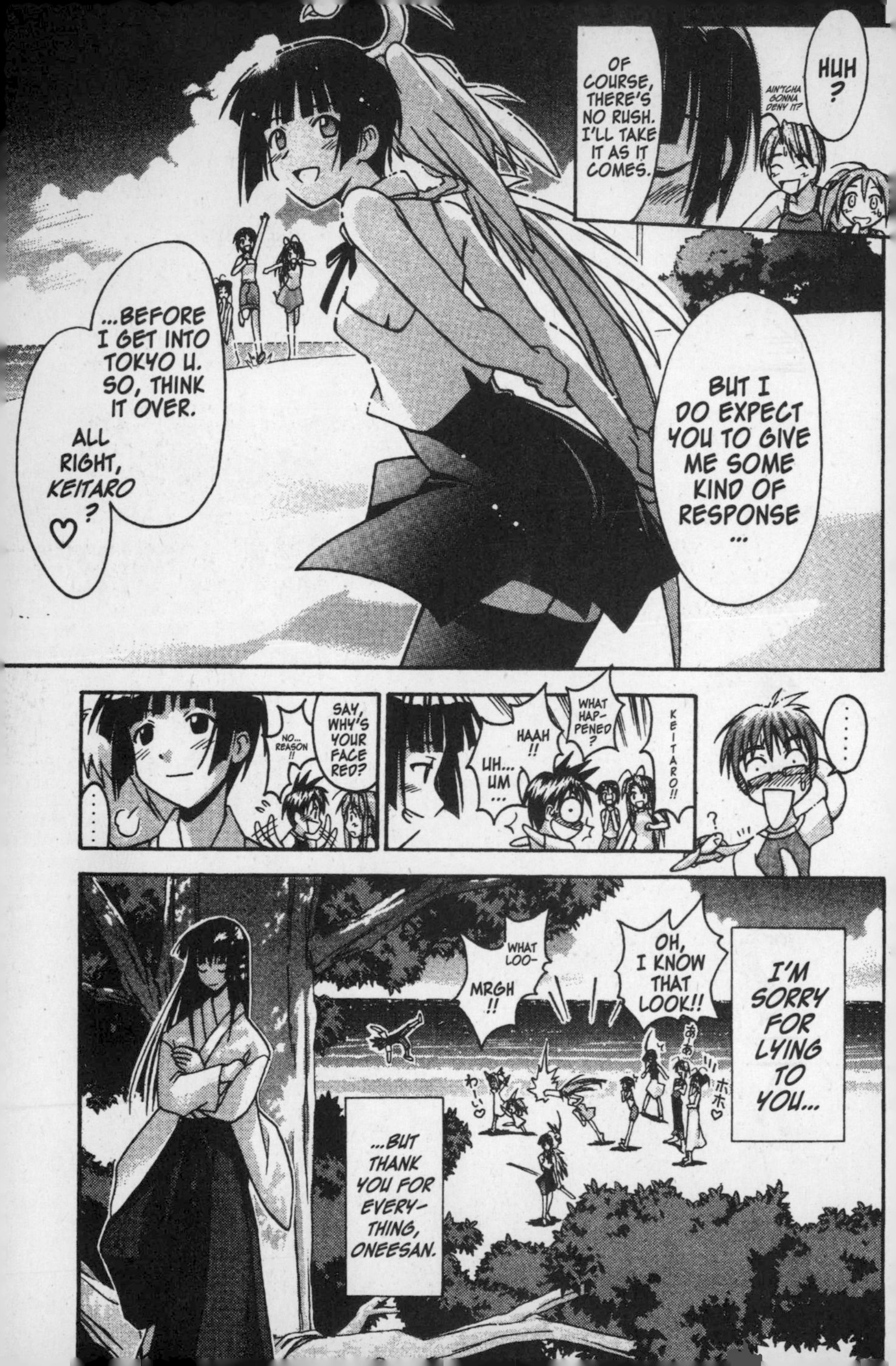
HUH ?
AIN'TCHA GONNA DENY IT?
OF COURSE, THERE'S NO RUSH. I'LL TAKE IT AS IT COMES.
BUT I DO EXPECT YOU TO GIVE ME SOME KIND OF RESPONSE ...
...BEFORE I GET INTO TOKYO U. SO, THINK IT OVER.
ALL RIGHT, KEITARO ? ♡
......
KEITARO!!
WHAT HAPPENED ?
HAAH !!
UH... UM ...
SAY, WHY'S YOUR FACE RED?
NO... REASON !!
......
I'M SORRY FOR LYING TO YOU...
あぁ
ホホ♡
OH, I KNOW THAT LOOK!!
WHAT LOO-
MRGH !!
わーい♡
...BUT THANK YOU FOR EVERYTHING, ONEESAN.

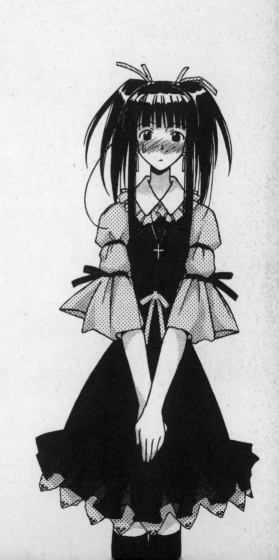

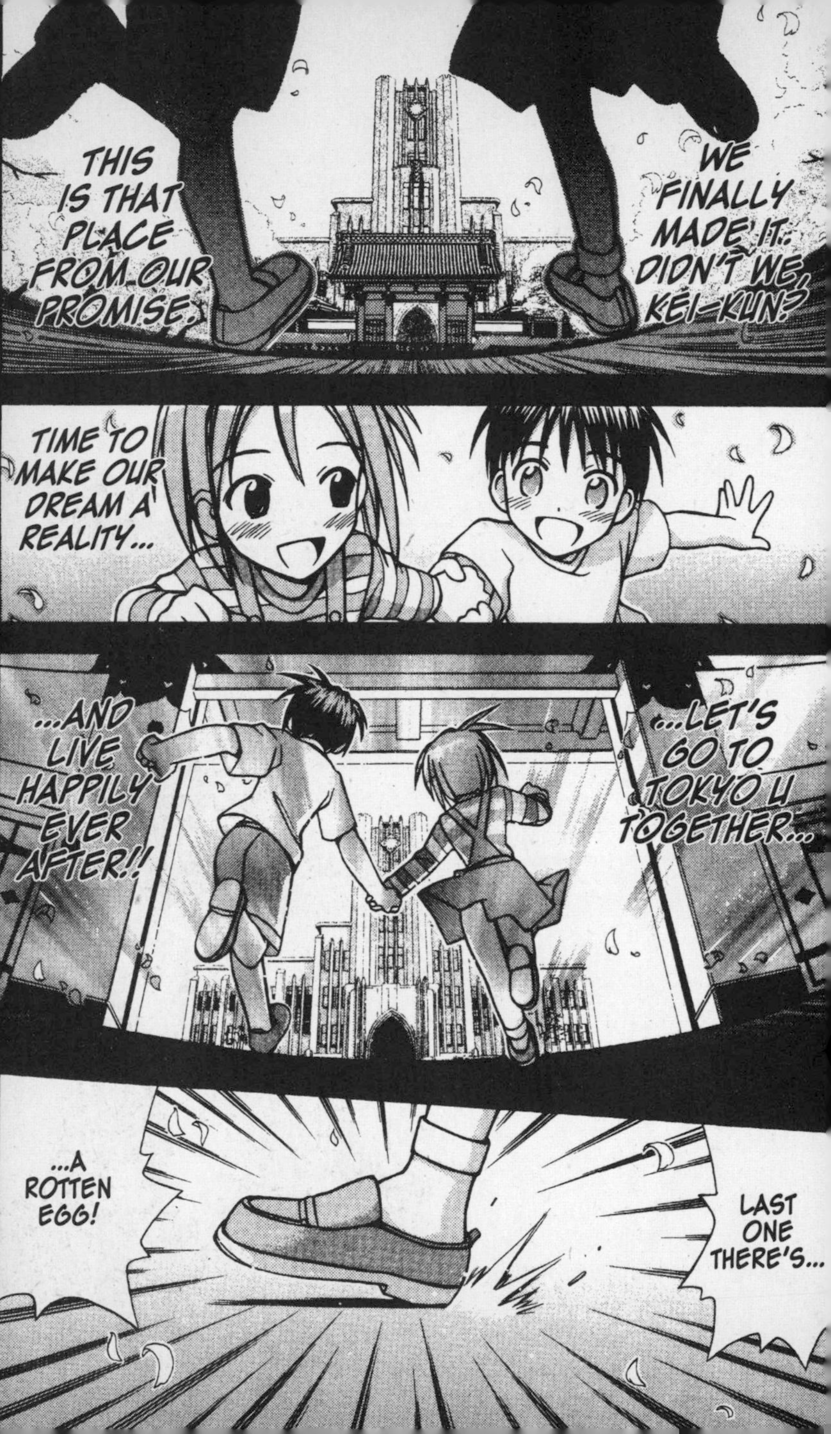
WE FINALLY MADE IT. DIDN'T WE, KEI-KUN?
THIS IS THAT PLACE FROM OUR PROMISE.
TIME TO MAKE OUR DREAM A REALITY...
...LET'S GO TO TOKYO U TOGETHER...
...AND LIVE HAPPILY EVER AFTER!!
LAST ONE THERE'S...
...A ROTTEN EGG!

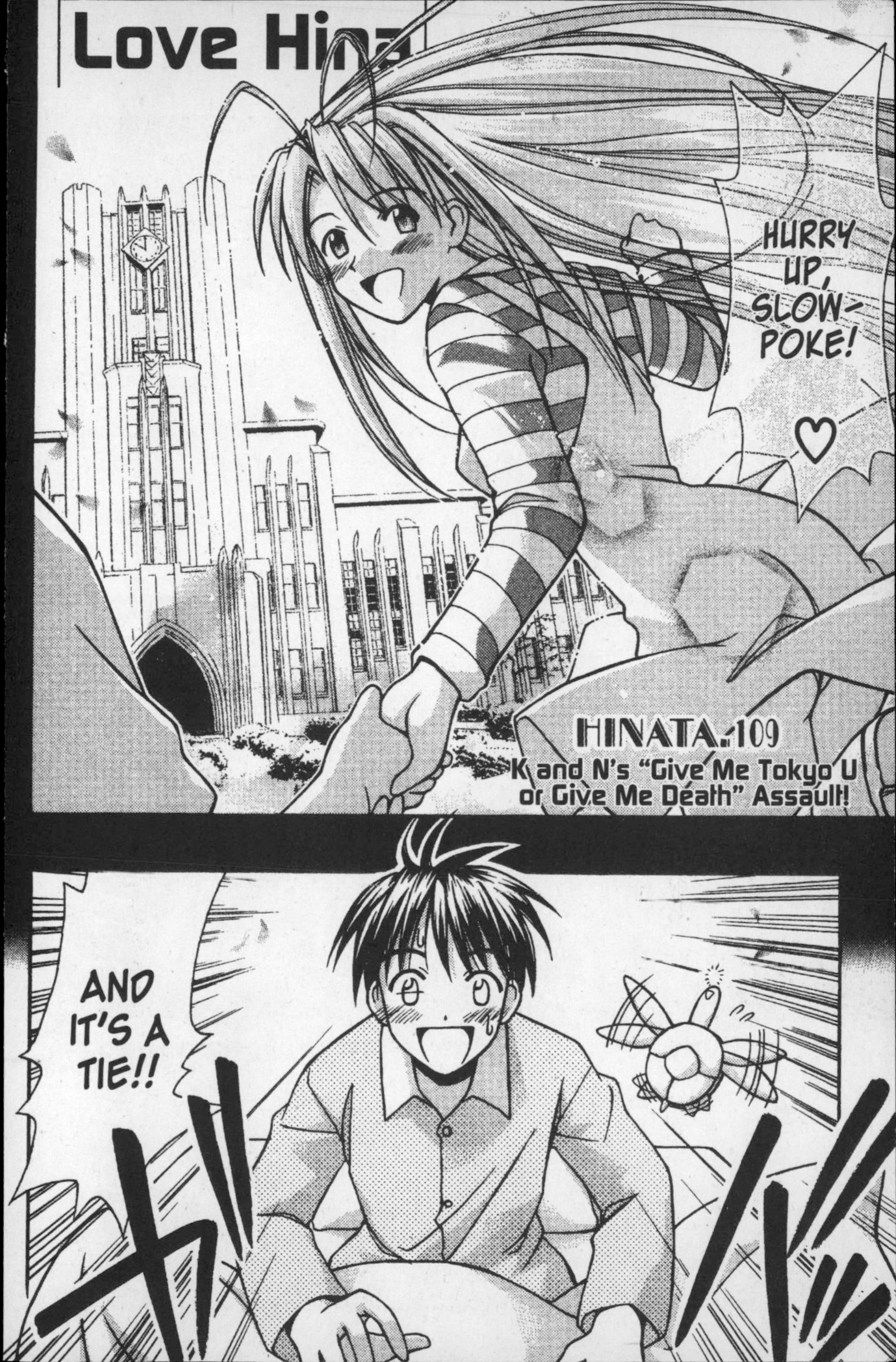
Love Hina
HURRY UP, SLOW-POKE! ♡
HINATA. 109
K and N's "Give Me Tokyo U or Give Me Death" Assault!
AND IT'S A TIE!!

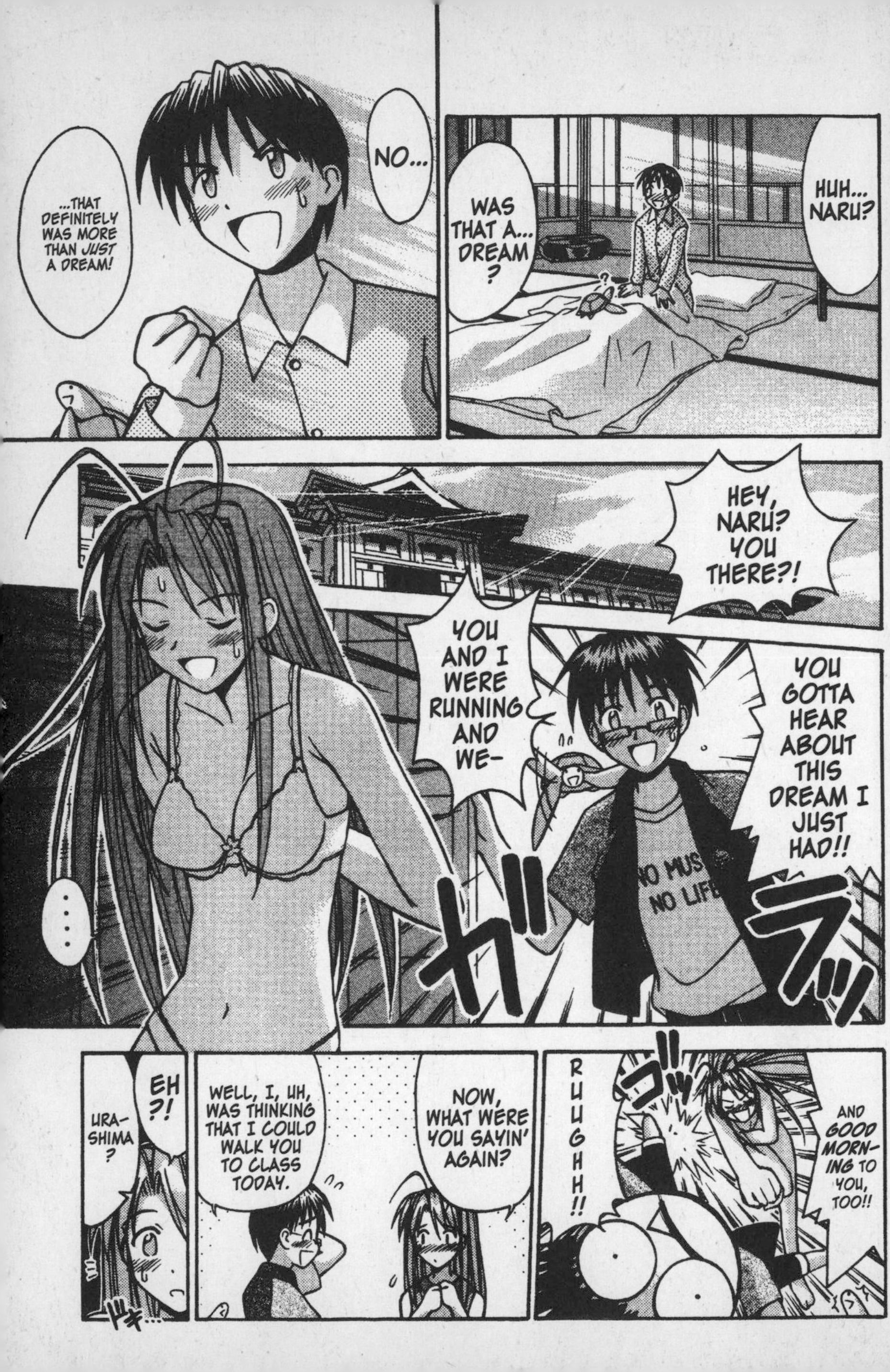
HUH... NARU?
WAS THAT A... DREAM?
NO...
...THAT DEFINITELY WAS MORE THAN JUST A DREAM!
HEY, NARU? YOU THERE?!
YOU GOTTA HEAR ABOUT THIS DREAM I JUST HAD!!
YOU AND I WERE RUNNING AND WE-
NO MUS NO LIFE
ガラッ
....
RUUGHH!!
AND GOOD MORNING TO YOU, TOO!!
NOW, WHAT WERE YOU SAYIN' AGAIN?
WELL, I, UH, WAS THINKING THAT I COULD WALK YOU TO CLASS TODAY.
EH?!
URA-SHIMA?

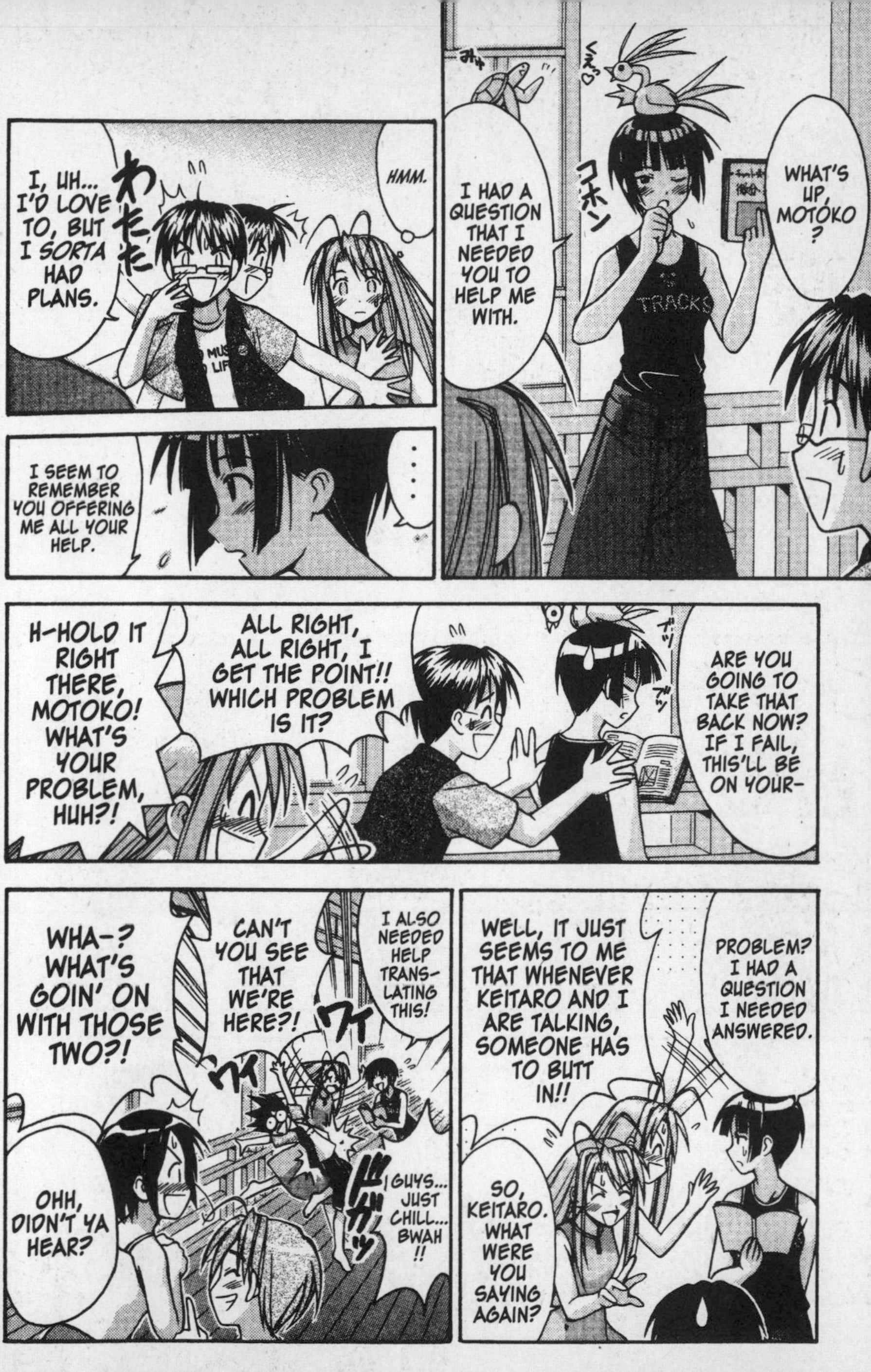
みゅ
くえっ♡
WHAT'S UP, MOTOKO?
コホン
I HAD A QUESTION THAT I NEEDED YOU TO HELP ME WITH.
TRACKS
HMM.
I, UH... I'D LOVE TO, BUT I SORTA HAD PLANS.
わたた
....
I SEEM TO REMEMBER YOU OFFERING ME ALL YOUR HELP.
ARE YOU GOING TO TAKE THAT BACK NOW? IF I FAIL, THIS'LL BE ON YOUR-
ブツ
ブツ
ALL RIGHT, ALL RIGHT, I GET THE POINT!! WHICH PROBLEM IS IT?
H-HOLD IT RIGHT THERE, MOTOKO! WHAT'S YOUR PROBLEM, HUH?!
PROBLEM? I HAD A QUESTION I NEEDED ANSWERED.
WELL, IT JUST SEEMS TO ME THAT WHENEVER KEITARO AND I ARE TALKING, SOMEONE HAS TO BUTT IN!!
SO, KEITARO. WHAT WERE YOU SAYING AGAIN?
I ALSO NEEDED HELP TRANS-LATING THIS!
CAN'T YOU SEE THAT WE'RE HERE?!
ワイ
ワイ
WHA-? WHAT'S GOIN' ON WITH THOSE TWO?!
GUYS... JUST CHILL... BWAH!!
ドガッ
OHH, DIDN'T YA HEAR?

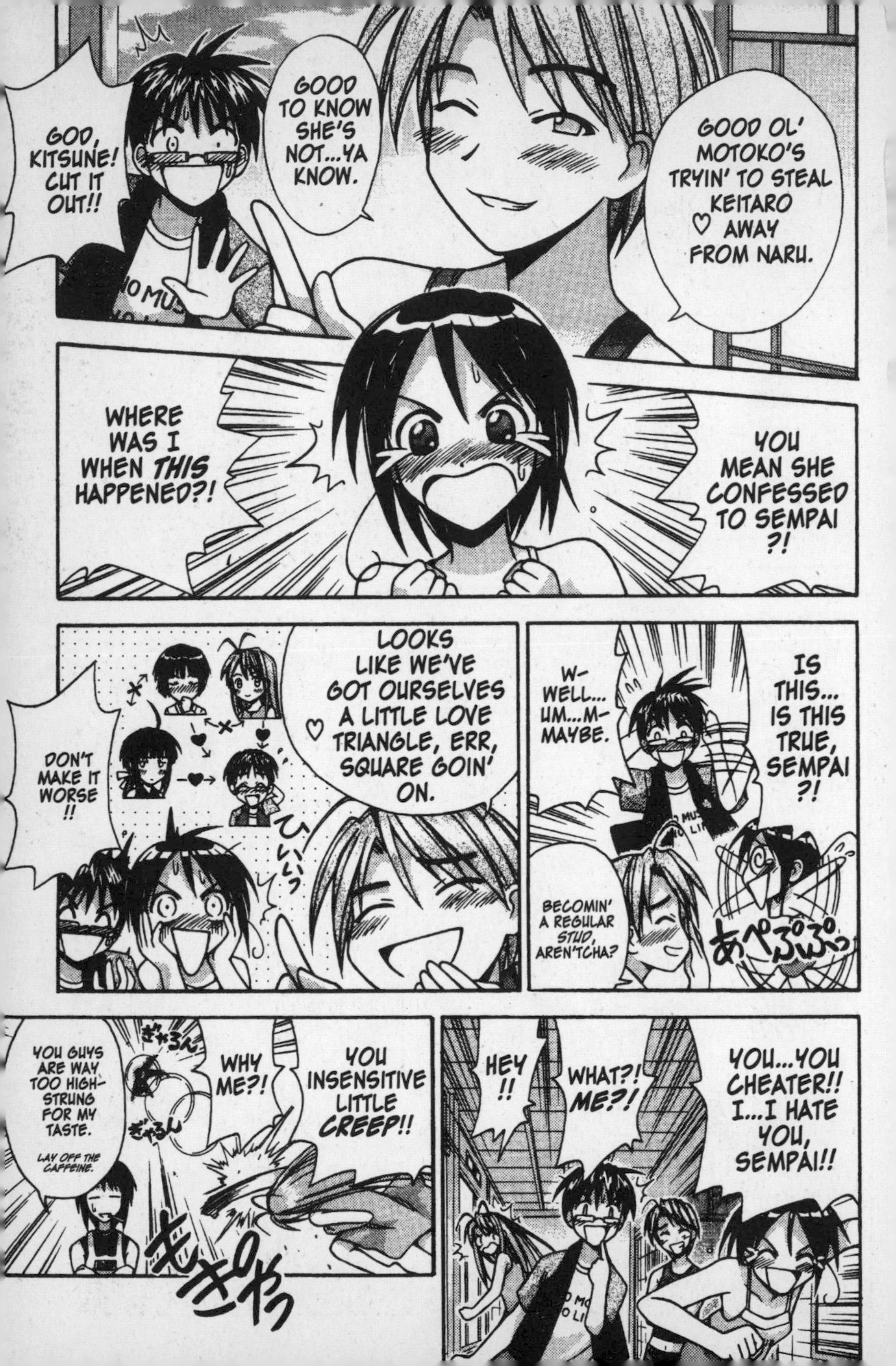
GOOD OL' MOTOKO'S TRYIN' TO STEAL KEITARO ♡ AWAY FROM NARU.
GOOD TO KNOW SHE'S NOT...YA KNOW.
GOD, KITSUNE! CUT IT OUT!!
YOU MEAN SHE CONFESSED TO SEMPAI?!
WHERE WAS I WHEN *THIS* HAPPENED?!
IS THIS... IS THIS TRUE, SEMPAI?!
W-WELL... UM...M-MAYBE.
BECOMIN' A REGULAR STUD, AREN'TCHA?
あぺぷぷっ
LOOKS LIKE WE'VE GOT OURSELVES A LITTLE LOVE ♡ TRIANGLE, ERR, SQUARE GOIN' ON.
ひいいっ
DON'T MAKE IT WORSE!!
YOU...YOU CHEATER!! I...I HATE YOU, SEMPAI!!
WHAT?! *ME?!*
HEY!!
YOU INSENSITIVE LITTLE *CREEP!!*
WHY ME?!
ぎゃるん
ぎゃるん
YOU GUYS ARE WAY TOO HIGH-STRUNG FOR MY TASTE.
LAY OFF THE CAFFEINE.

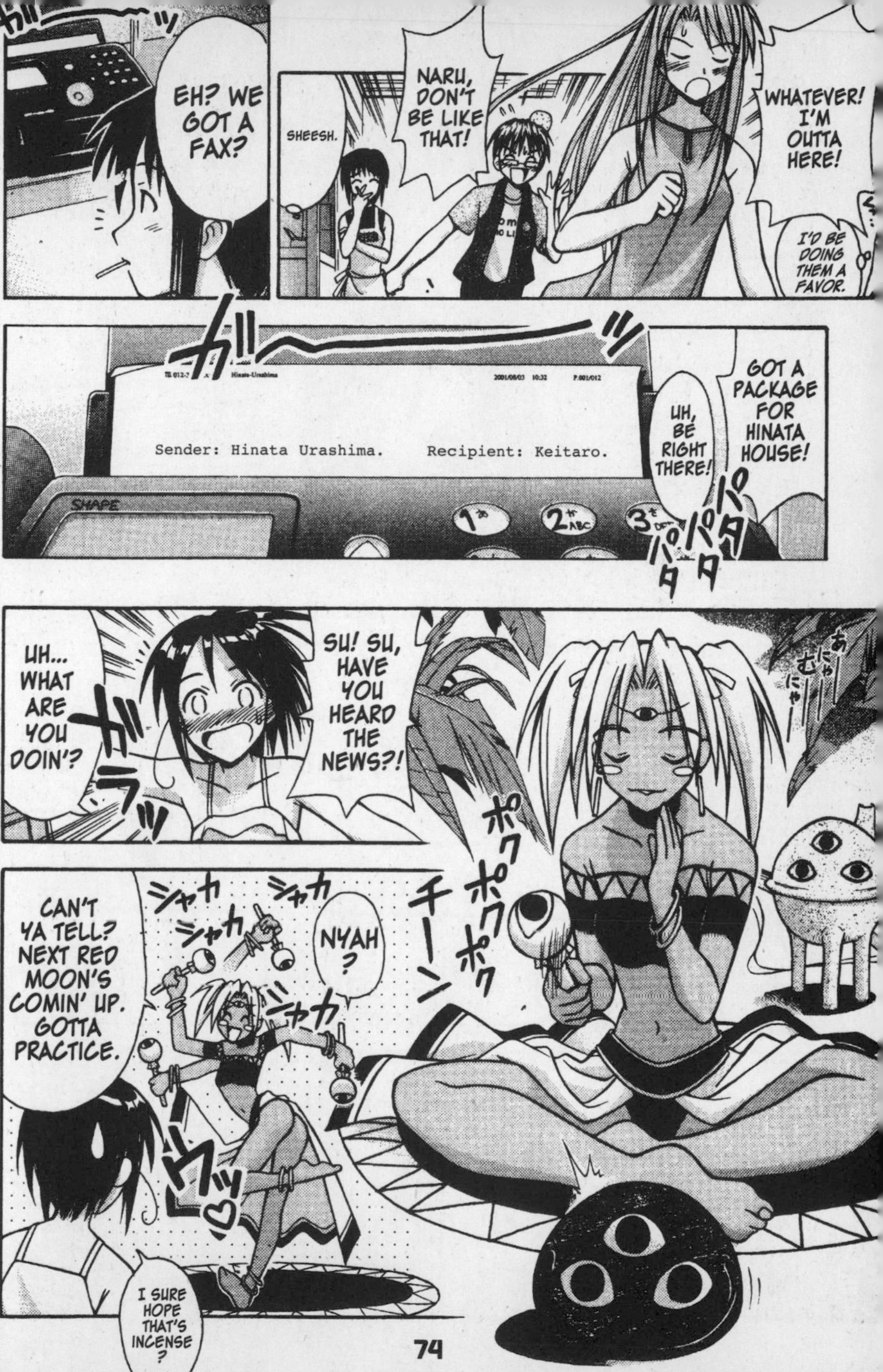
WHATEVER! I'M OUTTA HERE!
NARU, DON'T BE LIKE THAT!
SHEESH.
I'D BE DOING THEM A FAVOR.
EH? WE GOT A FAX?
GOT A PACKAGE FOR HINATA HOUSE!
UH, BE RIGHT THERE!
パタパタパタ
Sender: Hinata Urashima. Recipient: Keitaro.
SHAPE
あにゃーむにゃー
SU! SU, HAVE YOU HEARD THE NEWS?!
UH... WHAT ARE YOU DOIN'?
ガラッ
ポクポクポクポクチーン
NYAH?
シャカ シャカ シャカ シャカ
CAN'T YA TELL? NEXT RED MOON'S COMIN' UP. GOTTA PRACTICE.
I SURE HOPE THAT'S INCENSE?

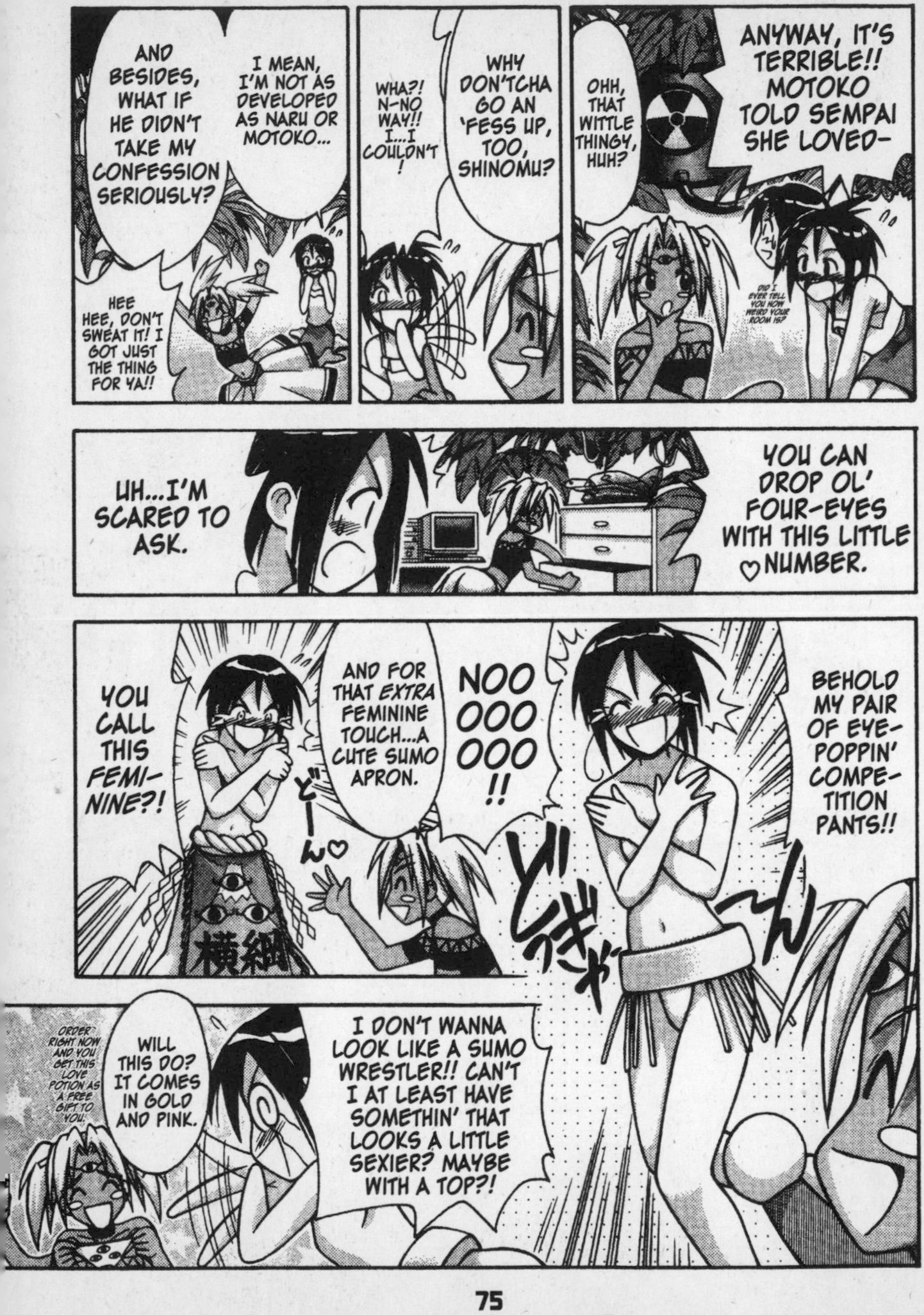
ANYWAY, IT'S TERRIBLE!! MOTOKO TOLD SEMPAI SHE LOVED-
OHH, THAT WITTLE THINGY, HUH?
DID I EVER TELL YOU HOW WEIRD YOUR ROOM IS?
WHY DON'TCHA GO AN 'FESS UP, TOO, SHINOMU?
WHA?! N-NO WAY!! I...I COULDN'T!
I MEAN, I'M NOT AS DEVELOPED AS NARU OR MOTOKO...
AND BESIDES, WHAT IF HE DIDN'T TAKE MY CONFESSION SERIOUSLY?
HEE HEE, DON'T SWEAT IT! I GOT JUST THE THING FOR YA!!
YOU CAN DROP OL' FOUR-EYES WITH THIS LITTLE ♡ NUMBER.
UH...I'M SCARED TO ASK.
BEHOLD MY PAIR OF EYE-POPPIN' COMPETITION PANTS!!
NOOOOOOOOO!!
AND FOR THAT *EXTRA* FEMININE TOUCH...A CUTE SUMO APRON.
どーん♡
YOU CALL THIS *FEMININE*?!
横綱
I DON'T WANNA LOOK LIKE A SUMO WRESTLER!! CAN'T I AT LEAST HAVE SOMETHIN' THAT LOOKS A LITTLE SEXIER? MAYBE WITH A TOP?!
WILL THIS DO? IT COMES IN GOLD AND PINK.
ORDER RIGHT NOW AND YOU GET THIS LOVE POTION AS A FREE GIFT TO YOU.

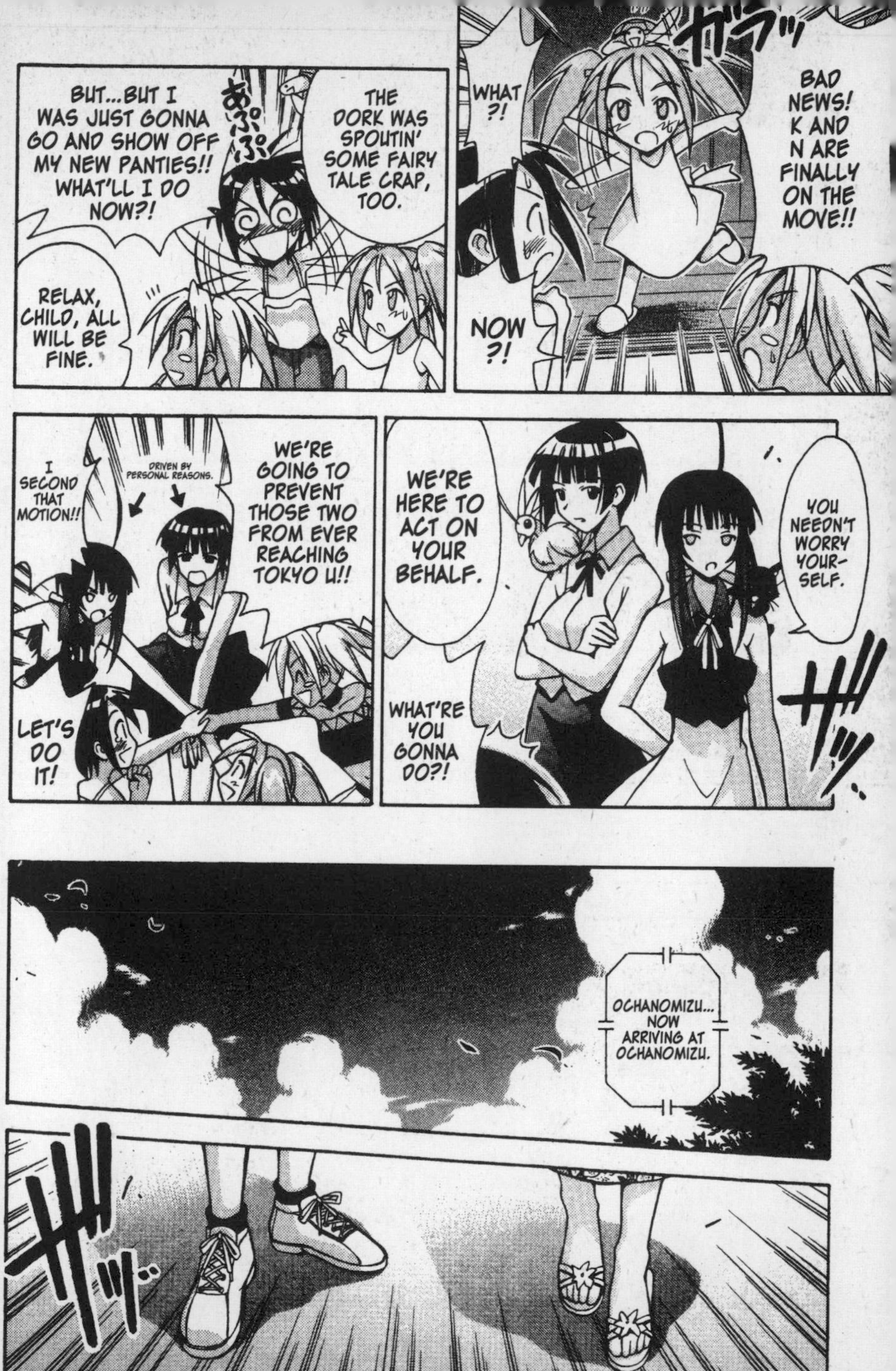
ガラッ
BAD NEWS! K AND N ARE FINALLY ON THE MOVE!!
WHAT?!
NOW?!
THE DORK WAS SPOUTIN' SOME FAIRY TALE CRAP, TOO.
BUT...BUT I WAS JUST GONNA GO AND SHOW OFF MY NEW PANTIES!! WHAT'LL I DO NOW?!
あぷぷ
RELAX, CHILD, ALL WILL BE FINE.
YOU NEEDN'T WORRY YOURSELF.
WE'RE HERE TO ACT ON YOUR BEHALF.
WHAT'RE YOU GONNA DO?!
WE'RE GOING TO PREVENT THOSE TWO FROM EVER REACHING TOKYO U!!
DRIVEN BY PERSONAL REASONS.
I SECOND THAT MOTION!!
LET'S DO IT!
OCHANOMIZU... NOW ARRIVING AT OCHANOMIZU.

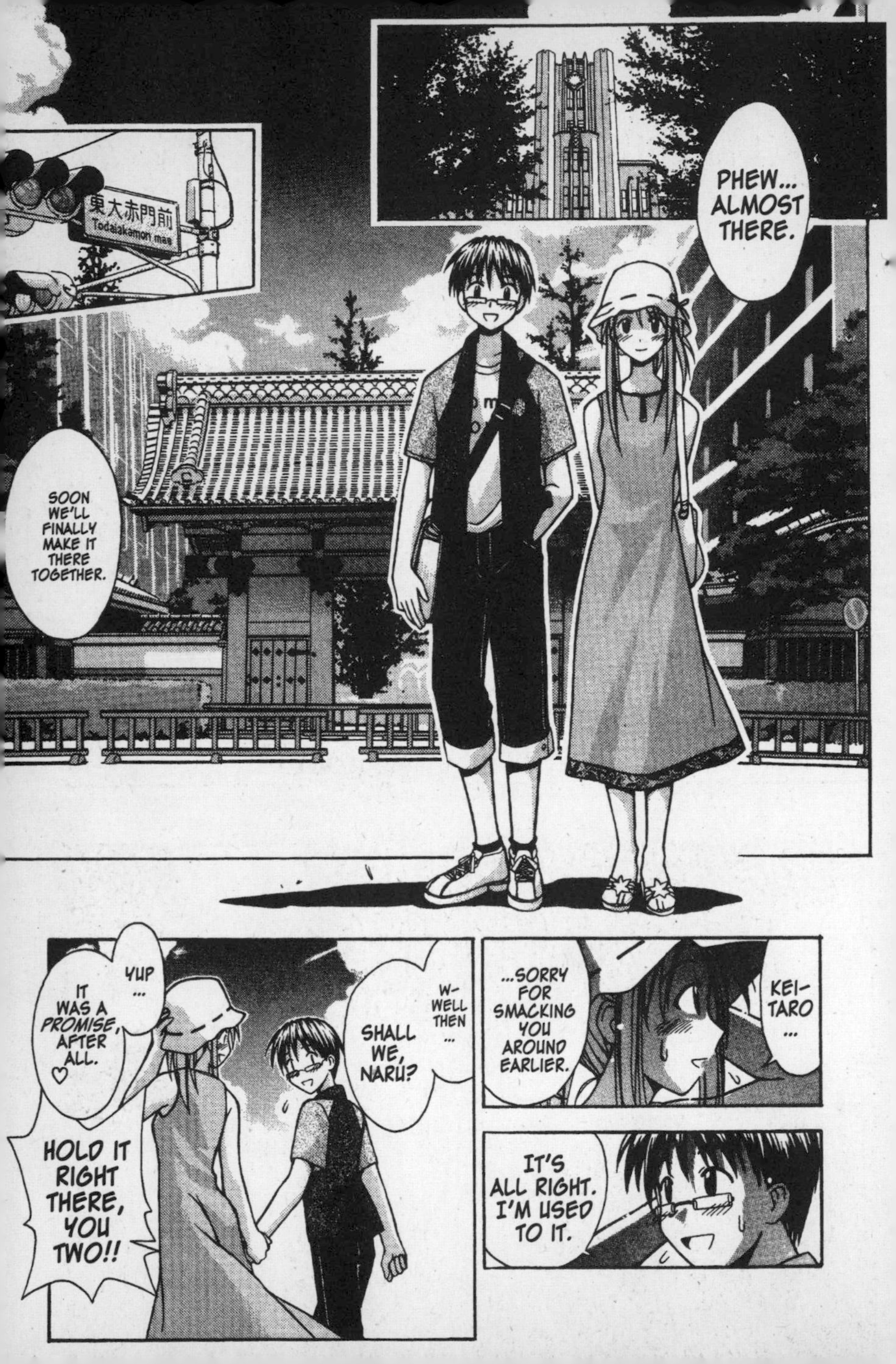
PHEW... ALMOST THERE.
東大赤門前
Todaiakamon mae
SOON WE'LL FINALLY MAKE IT THERE TOGETHER.
KEI-TARO...
...SORRY FOR SMACKING YOU AROUND EARLIER.
IT'S ALL RIGHT. I'M USED TO IT.
W-WELL THEN...
SHALL WE, NARU?
YUP...
IT WAS A *PROMISE*, AFTER ALL. ♡
HOLD IT RIGHT THERE, YOU TWO!!

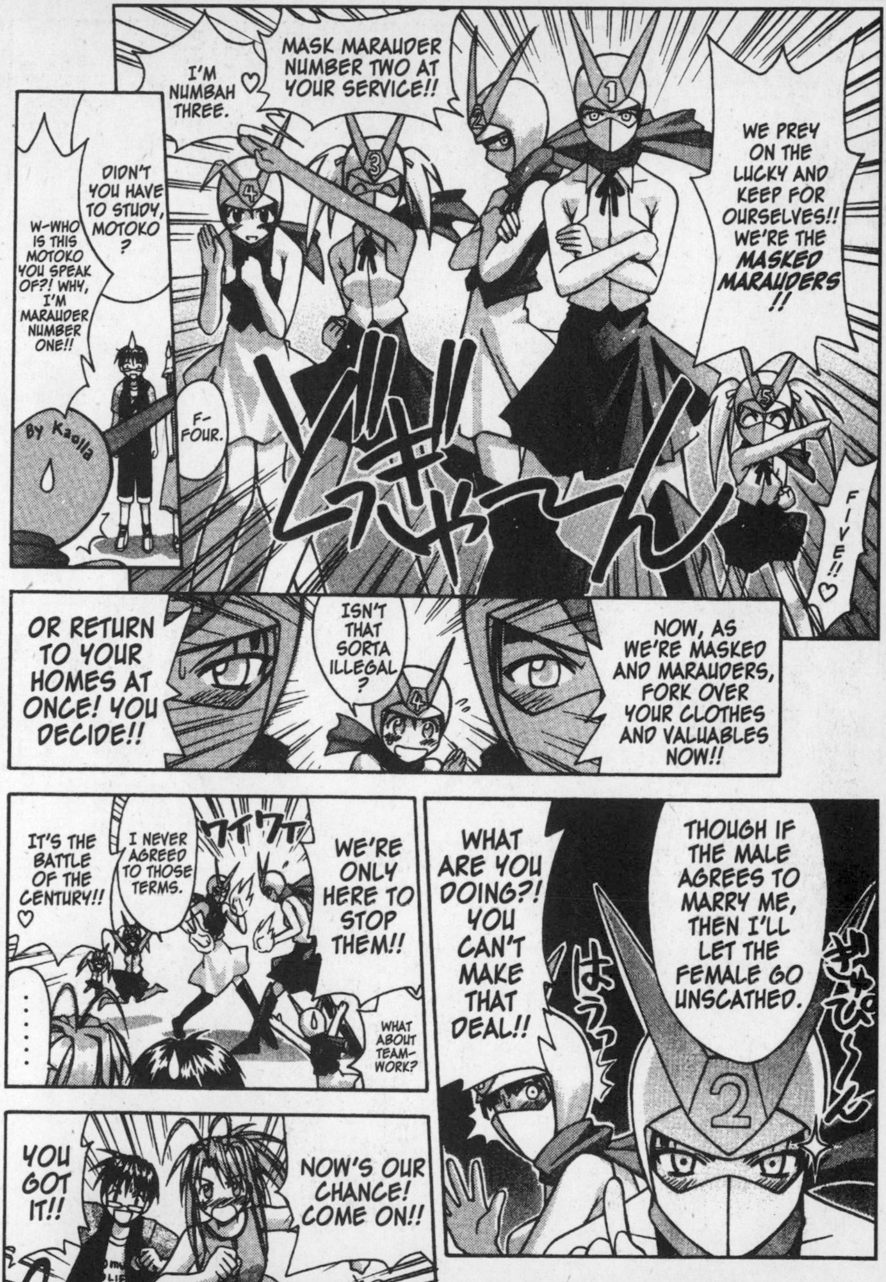
WE PREY ON THE LUCKY AND KEEP FOR OURSELVES!! WE'RE THE MASKED MARAUDERS!!
MASK MARAUDER NUMBER TWO AT YOUR SERVICE!!
I'M NUMBAH THREE. ♡
FIVE!! ♡
F-FOUR.
DIDN'T YOU HAVE TO STUDY, MOTOKO?
W-WHO IS THIS MOTOKO YOU SPEAK OF?! WHY, I'M MARAUDER NUMBER ONE!!
By Kaolla
NOW, AS WE'RE MASKED AND MARAUDERS, FORK OVER YOUR CLOTHES AND VALUABLES NOW!!
ISN'T THAT SORTA ILLEGAL?
OR RETURN TO YOUR HOMES AT ONCE! YOU DECIDE!!
THOUGH IF THE MALE AGREES TO MARRY ME, THEN I'LL LET THE FEMALE GO UNSCATHED.
WHAT ARE YOU DOING?! YOU CAN'T MAKE THAT DEAL!!
WE'RE ONLY HERE TO STOP THEM!!
ワイワイ
I NEVER AGREED TO THOSE TERMS.
IT'S THE BATTLE OF THE CENTURY!! ♡
WHAT ABOUT TEAM-WORK?
......
NOW'S OUR CHANCE! COME ON!!
YOU GOT IT!!

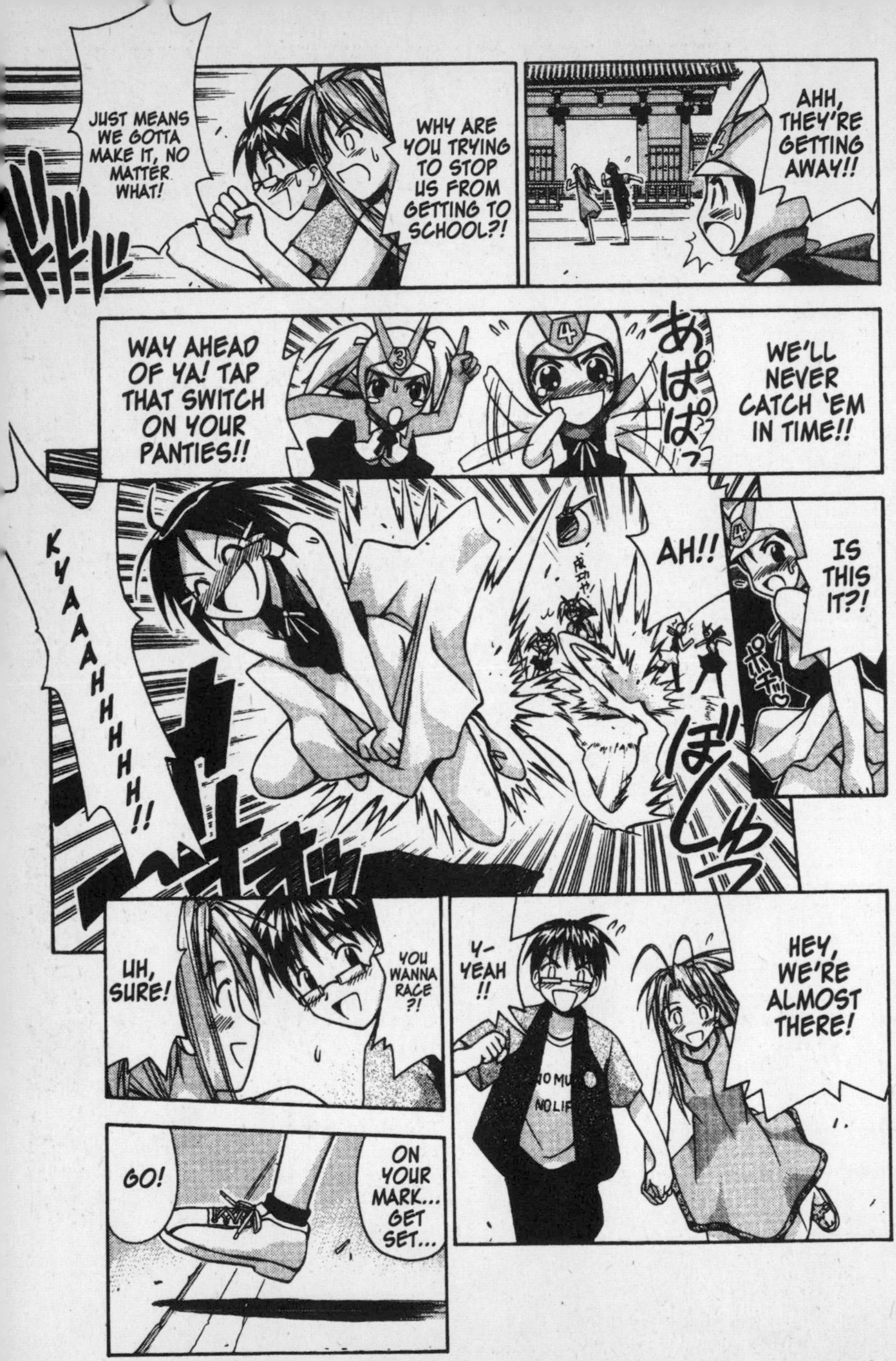
AHH, THEY'RE GETTING AWAY!!
WHY ARE YOU TRYING TO STOP US FROM GETTING TO SCHOOL?!
JUST MEANS WE GOTTA MAKE IT, NO MATTER WHAT!
WE'LL NEVER CATCH 'EM IN TIME!!
あぱぱっ
WAY AHEAD OF YA! TAP THAT SWITCH ON YOUR PANTIES!!
IS THIS IT?!
AH!!
ぼしゅっ
KYAAAAHHHHHH!!
HEY, WE'RE ALMOST THERE!
Y-YEAH!!
YOU WANNA RACE?!
UH, SURE!
ON YOUR MARK... GET SET...
GO!

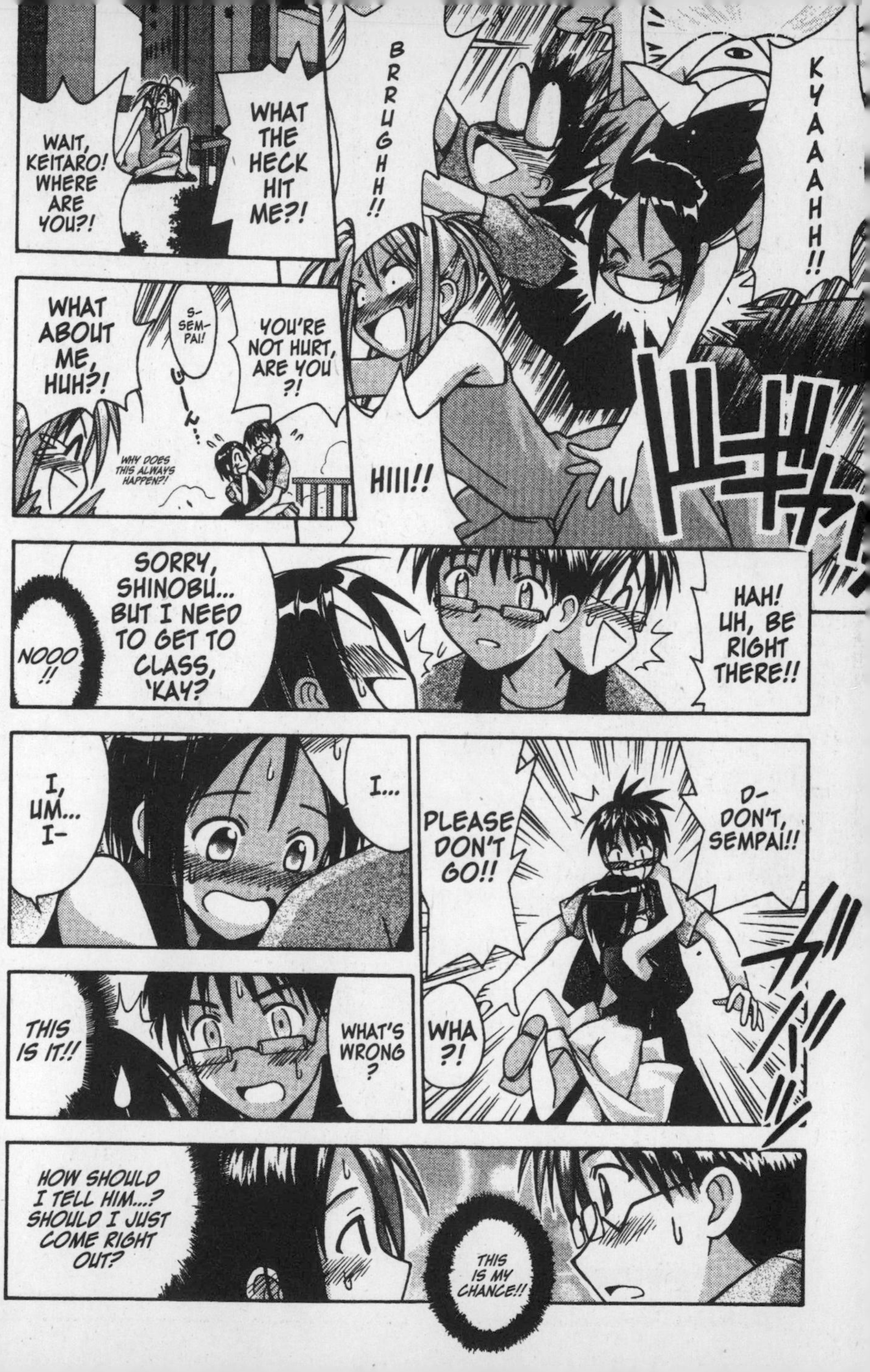
KYAAAAHH!!
BRRUGHH!!
HIII!!
WHAT THE HECK HIT ME?!
WAIT, KEITARO! WHERE ARE YOU?!
YOU'RE NOT HURT, ARE YOU?!
S-SEMPAI!
WHAT ABOUT ME, HUH?!
WHY DOES THIS ALWAYS HAPPEN?!
HAH! UH, BE RIGHT THERE!!
SORRY, SHINOBU... BUT I NEED TO GET TO CLASS, 'KAY?
NOOO!!
D-DON'T, SEMPAI!!
PLEASE DON'T GO!!
WHA?!
I...
I, UM... I-
WHAT'S WRONG?
THIS IS IT!!
THIS IS MY CHANCE!!
HOW SHOULD I TELL HIM...? SHOULD I JUST COME RIGHT OUT?

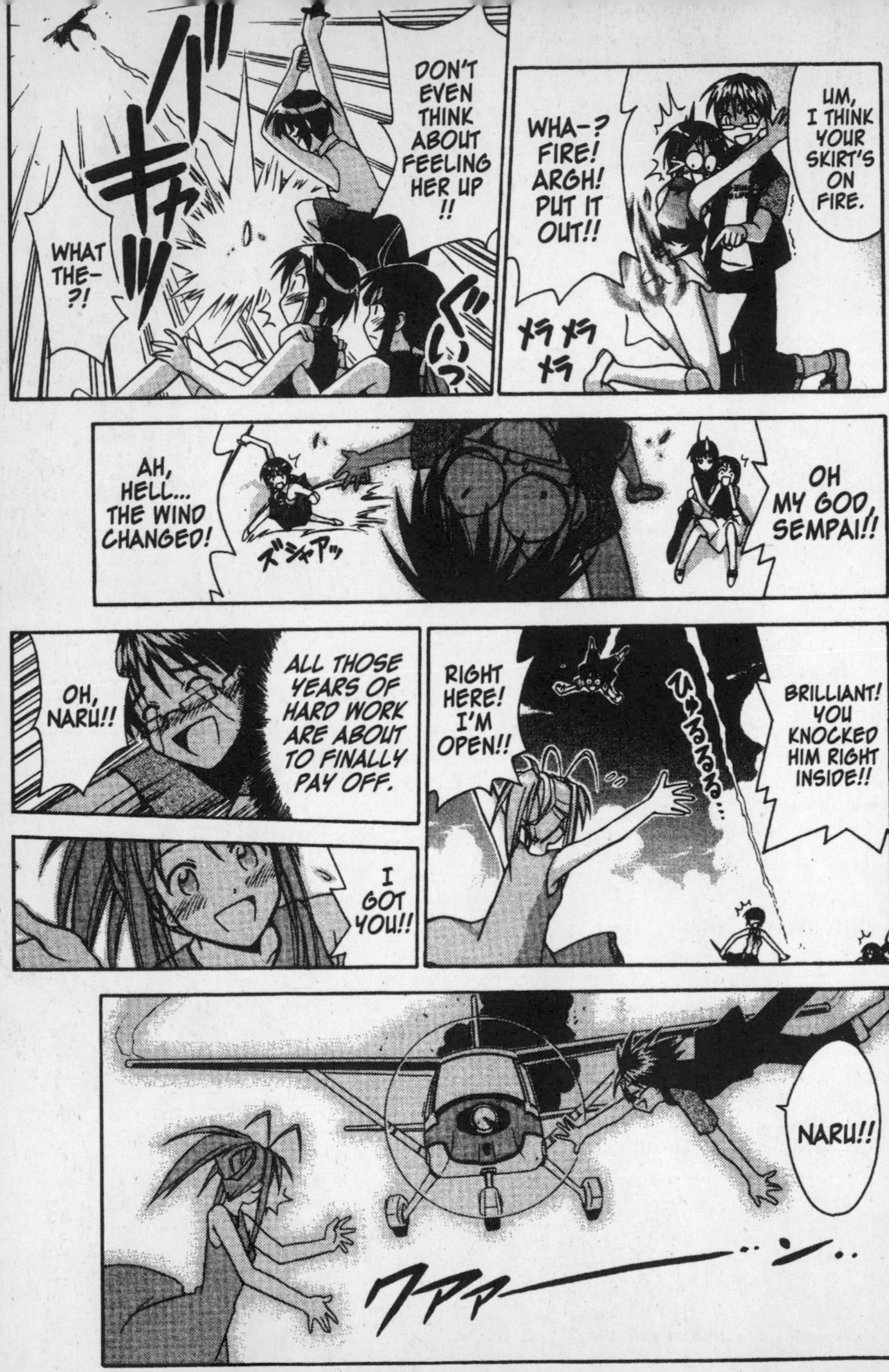
UM, I THINK YOUR SKIRT'S ON FIRE.
WHA-? FIRE! ARGH! PUT IT OUT!!
メラ メラ メラ
DON'T EVEN THINK ABOUT FEELING HER UP !!
ブギャッ
ぐいっ
WHAT THE-?!
OH MY GOD, SEMPAI!!
AH, HELL... THE WIND CHANGED!
ズシャアッ
BRILLIANT! YOU KNOCKED HIM RIGHT INSIDE!!
ひゅるるる...
RIGHT HERE! I'M OPEN!!
ALL THOSE YEARS OF HARD WORK ARE ABOUT TO FINALLY PAY OFF.
OH, NARU!!
I GOT YOU!!
NARU!!

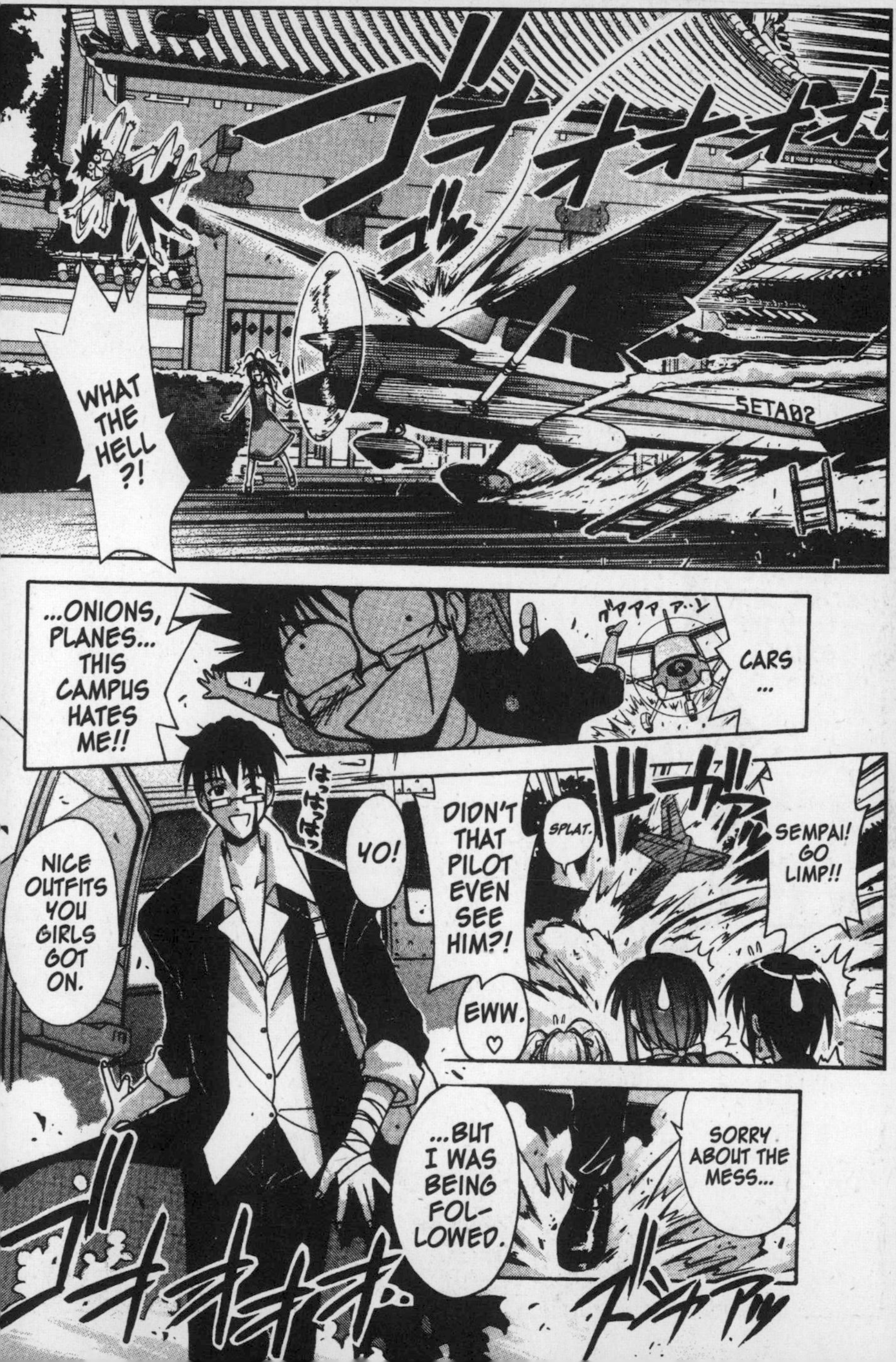
WHAT THE HELL ?!
CARS ...
...ONIONS, PLANES... THIS CAMPUS HATES ME!!
SEMPAI! GO LIMP!!
SPLAT.
DIDN'T THAT PILOT EVEN SEE HIM?!
YO!
NICE OUTFITS YOU GIRLS GOT ON.
EWW. ♡
SORRY ABOUT THE MESS...
...BUT I WAS BEING FOL-LOWED.

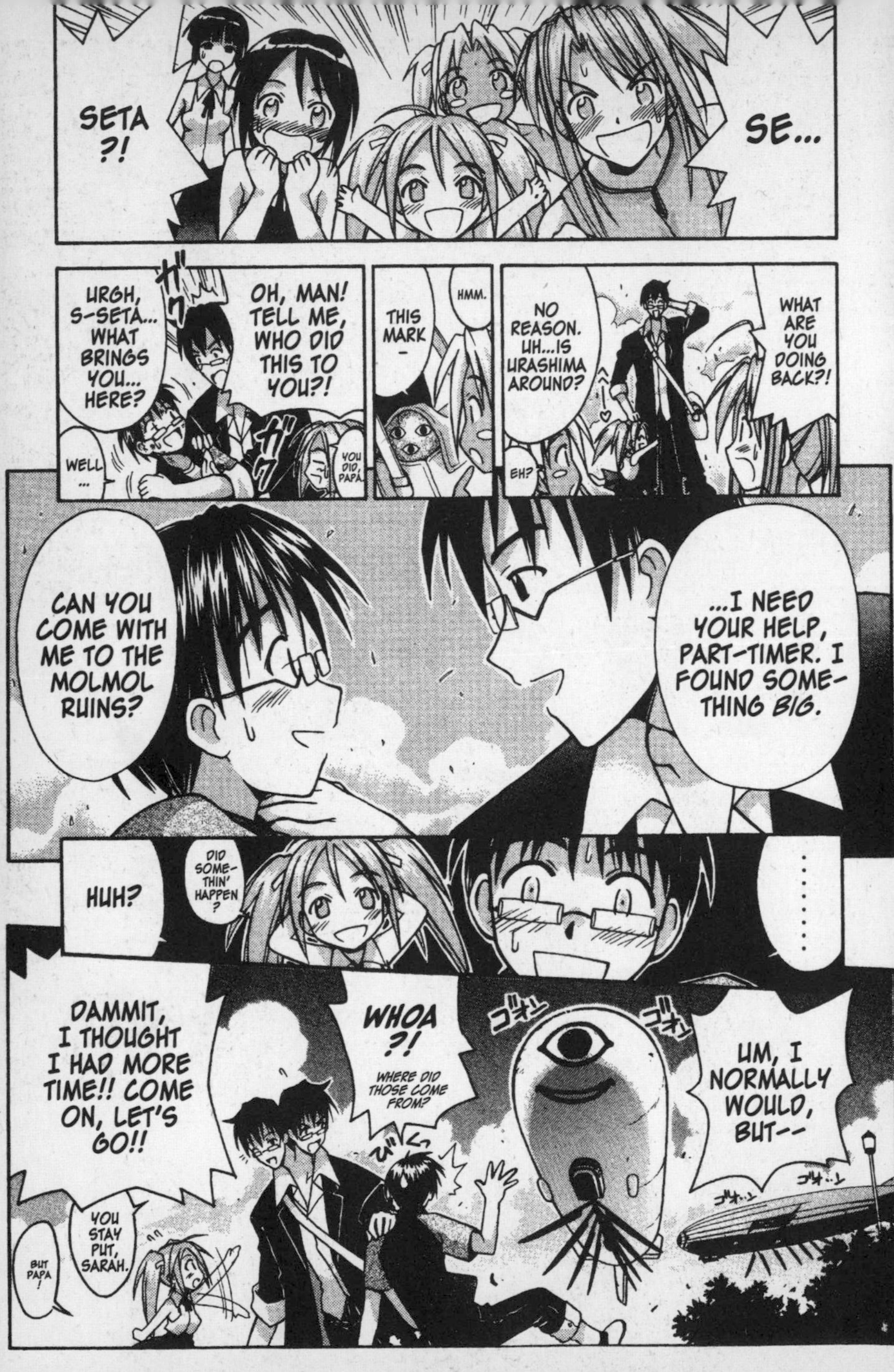
SE...
SETA ?!
WHAT ARE YOU DOING BACK?!
NO REASON. UH...IS URASHIMA AROUND?
EH?
HMM.
THIS MARK—
YOU DID, PAPA.
OH, MAN! TELL ME, WHO DID THIS TO YOU?!
URGH, S-SETA... WHAT BRINGS YOU... HERE?
WELL...
...I NEED YOUR HELP, PART-TIMER. I FOUND SOME-THING *BIG*.
CAN YOU COME WITH ME TO THE MOLMOL RUINS?
......
DID SOME-THIN' HAPPEN?
HUH?
UM, I NORMALLY WOULD, BUT--
ゴオン
ゴオン
WHOA ?!
WHERE DID THOSE COME FROM?
DAMMIT, I THOUGHT I HAD MORE TIME!! COME ON, LET'S GO!!
YOU STAY PUT, SARAH.
BUT PAPA!

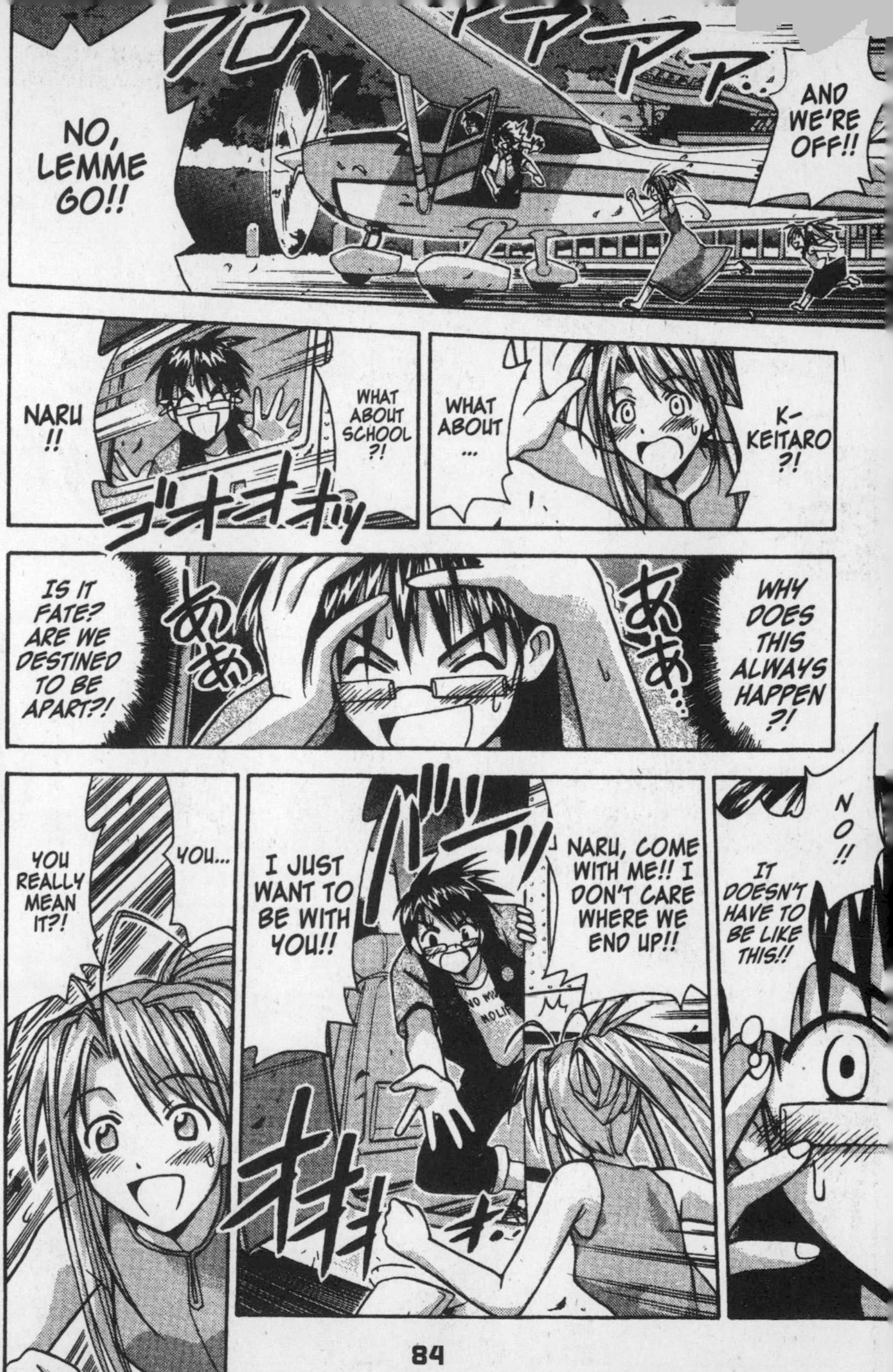
AND WE'RE OFF!!
NO, LEMME GO!!
K-KEITARO?!
WHAT ABOUT ...
WHAT ABOUT SCHOOL?!
NARU!!
ああ...
WHY DOES THIS ALWAYS HAPPEN?!
ああ
IS IT FATE? ARE WE DESTINED TO BE APART?!
NO!!
IT DOESN'T HAVE TO BE LIKE THIS!!
NARU, COME WITH ME!! I DON'T CARE WHERE WE END UP!!
I JUST WANT TO BE WITH YOU!!
YOU...
YOU REALLY MEAN IT?!

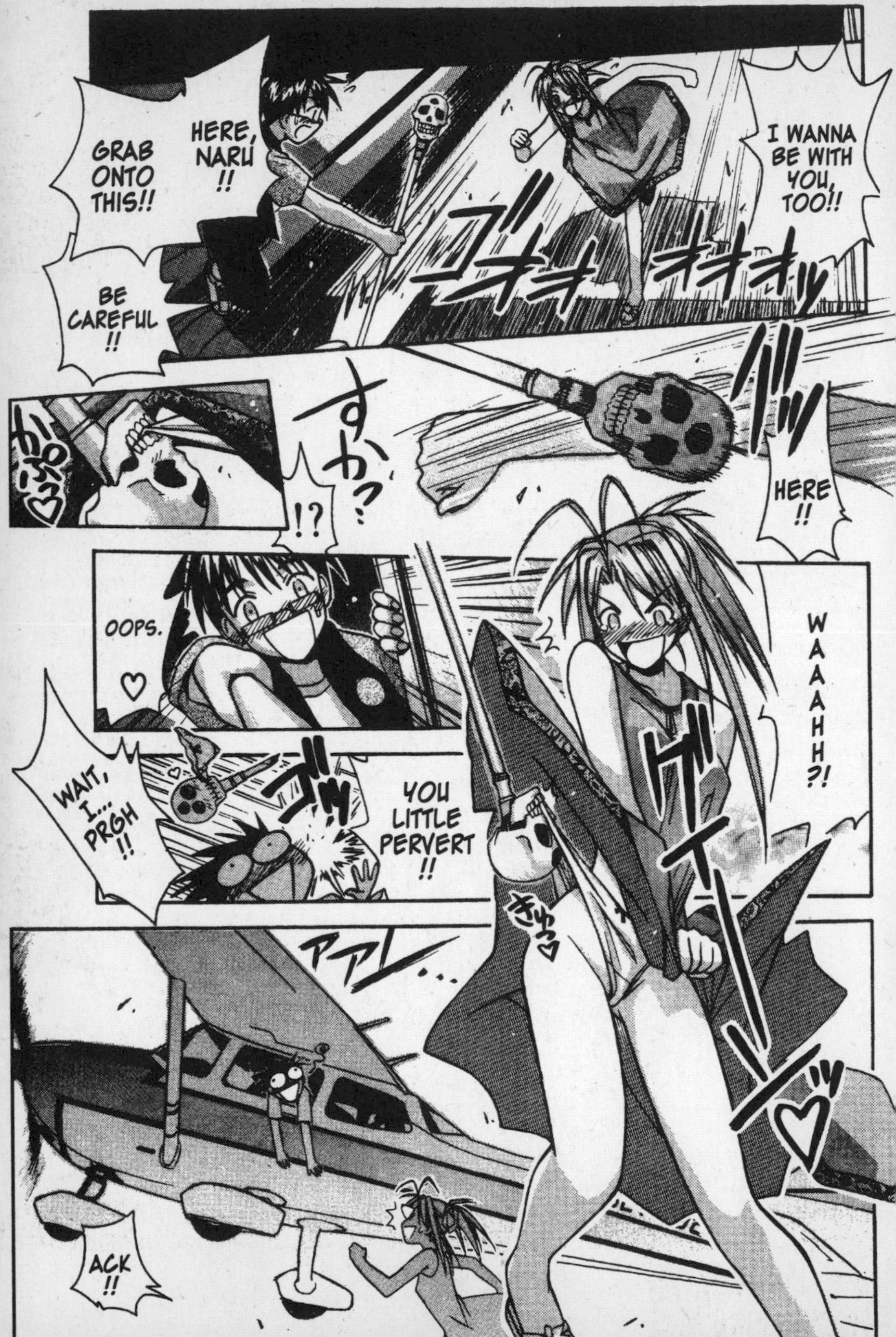
I WANNA BE WITH YOU, TOO!!
HERE, NARU!!
GRAB ONTO THIS!!
BE CAREFUL!!
HERE!!
!?
WAAAAHH?!
OOPS. ♡
YOU LITTLE PERVERT!!
WAIT, I... PRGH!!
ACK!!

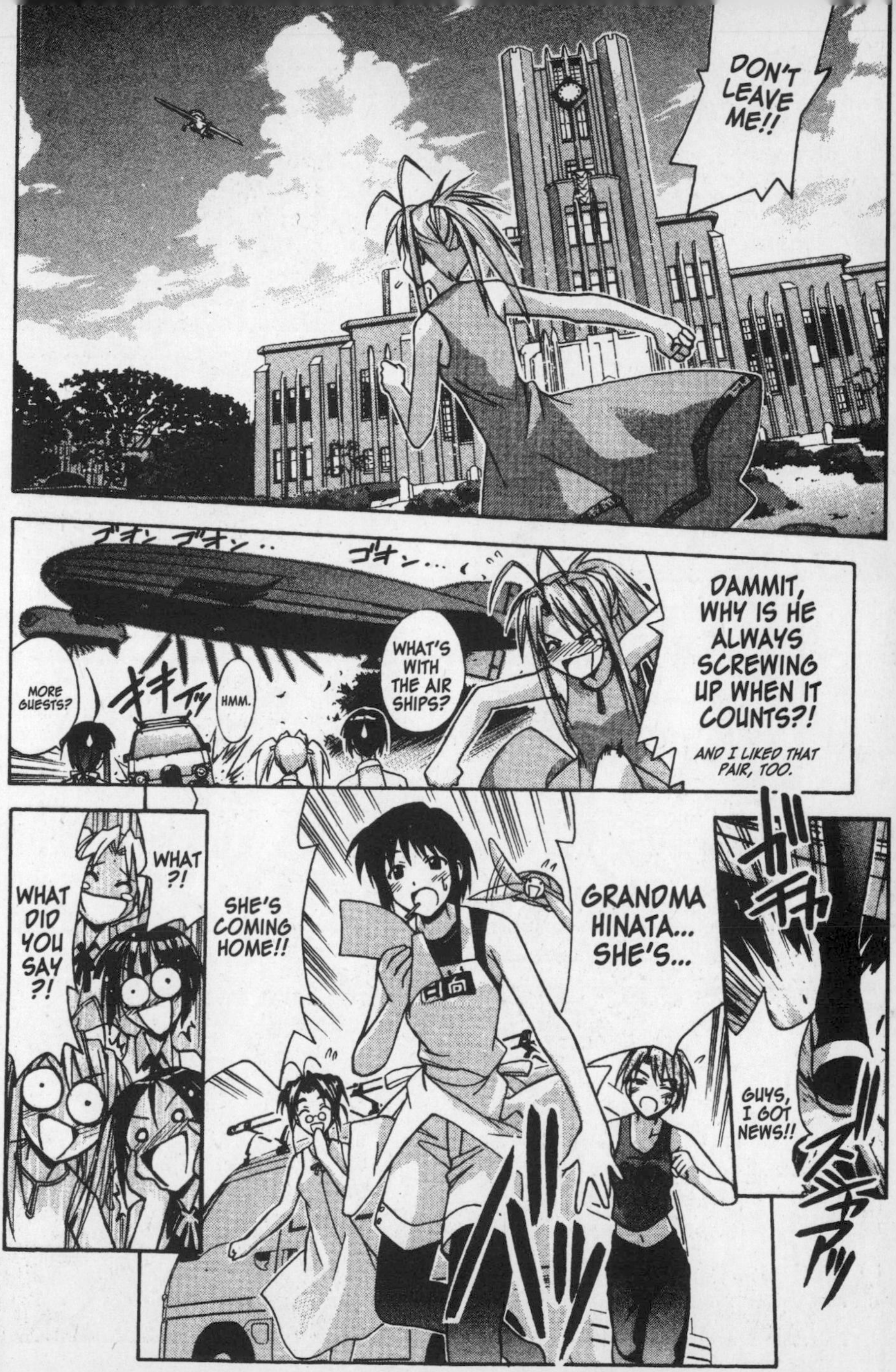
DON'T LEAVE ME!!
DAMMIT, WHY IS HE ALWAYS SCREWING UP WHEN IT COUNTS?!
AND I LIKED THAT PAIR, TOO.
WHAT'S WITH THE AIR SHIPS?
HMM.
MORE GUESTS?
GUYS, I GOT NEWS!!
GRANDMA HINATA... SHE'S...
SHE'S COMING HOME!!
WHAT ?!
WHAT DID YOU SAY ?!

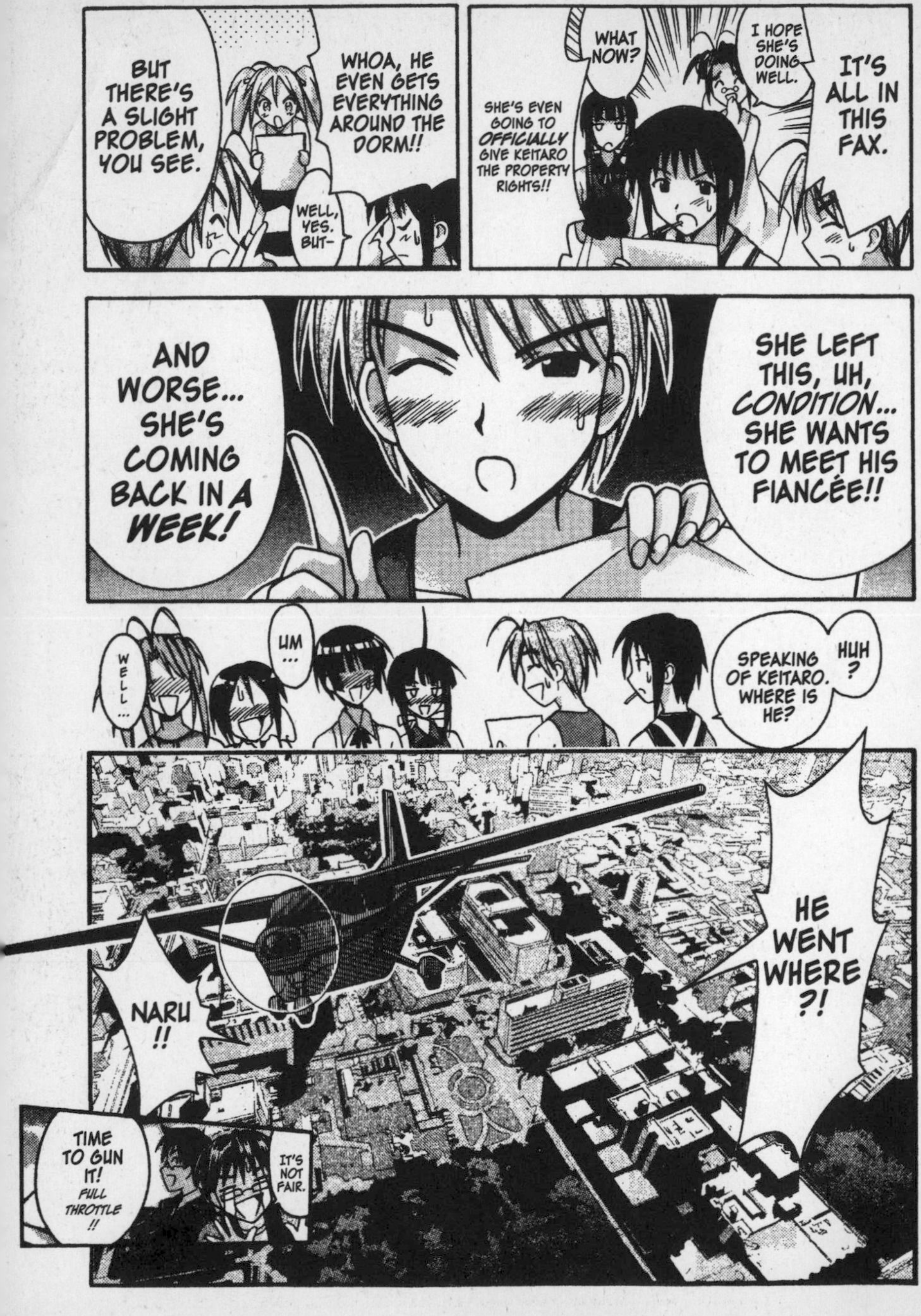
IT'S ALL IN THIS FAX.
I HOPE SHE'S DOING WELL.
WHAT NOW?
SHE'S EVEN GOING TO OFFICIALLY GIVE KEITARO THE PROPERTY RIGHTS!!
WHOA, HE EVEN GETS EVERYTHING AROUND THE DORM!!
WELL, YES. BUT-
BUT THERE'S A SLIGHT PROBLEM, YOU SEE.
SHE LEFT THIS, UH, CONDITION... SHE WANTS TO MEET HIS FIANCÉE!!
AND WORSE... SHE'S COMING BACK IN A WEEK!
HUH?
SPEAKING OF KEITARO. WHERE IS HE?
UM...
WELL...
HE WENT WHERE?!
NARU!!
IT'S NOT FAIR.
TIME TO GUN IT!
FULL THROTTLE!!

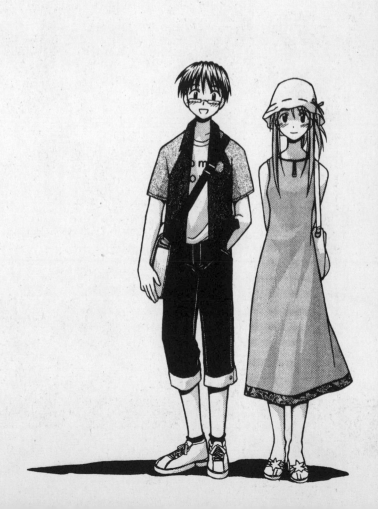

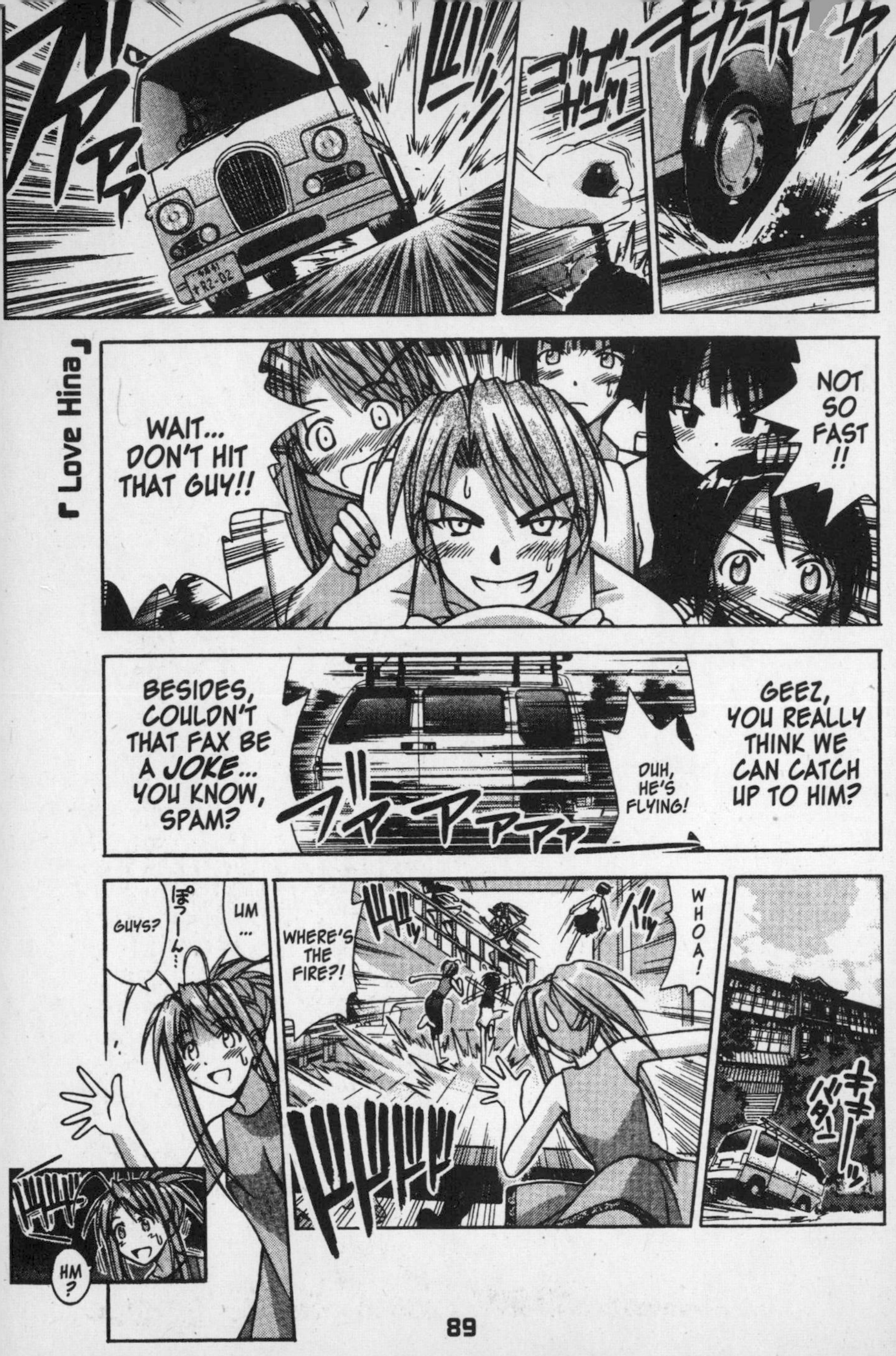
NOT SO FAST!!
WAIT... DON'T HIT THAT GUY!!
GEEZ, YOU REALLY THINK WE CAN CATCH UP TO HIM?
DUH, HE'S FLYING!
BESIDES, COULDN'T THAT FAX BE A *JOKE*... YOU KNOW, SPAM?
WHOA!
WHERE'S THE FIRE?!
UM...
ぽつーん...
GUYS?
HM?

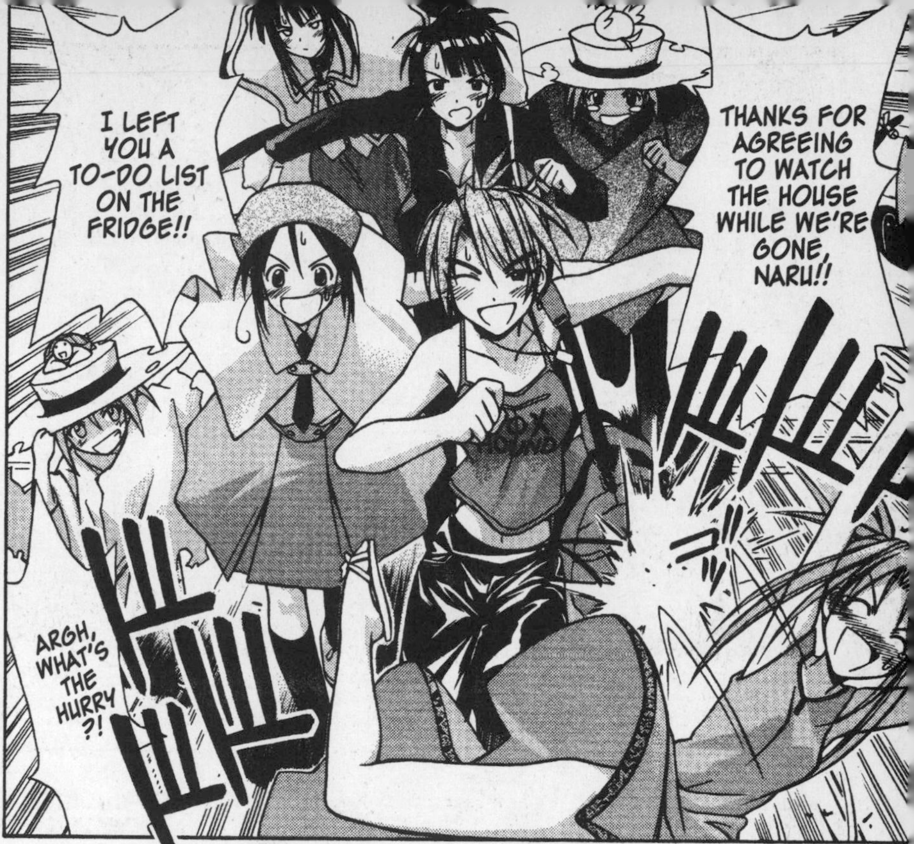
THANKS FOR AGREEING TO WATCH THE HOUSE WHILE WE'RE GONE, NARU!!
I LEFT YOU A TO-DO LIST ON THE FRIDGE!!
ARGH, WHAT'S THE HURRY?!

Love Hina

HINATA. 110 Set a Course For the Kingdom of Molmol.

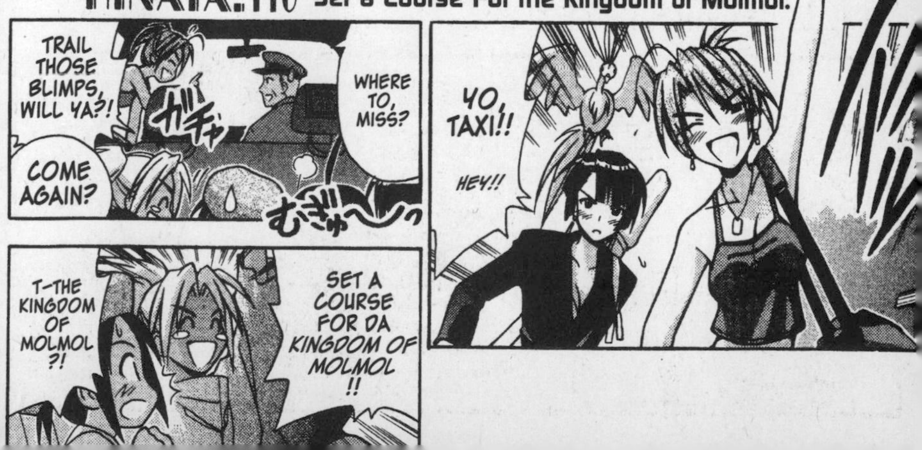
YO, TAXI!!
HEY!!
WHERE TO, MISS?
TRAIL THOSE BLIMPS, WILL YA?!
ガチャ
COME AGAIN?
むぎゅ〜〜っ
SET A COURSE FOR DA KINGDOM OF MOLMOL!!
T-THE KINGDOM OF MOLMOL?!

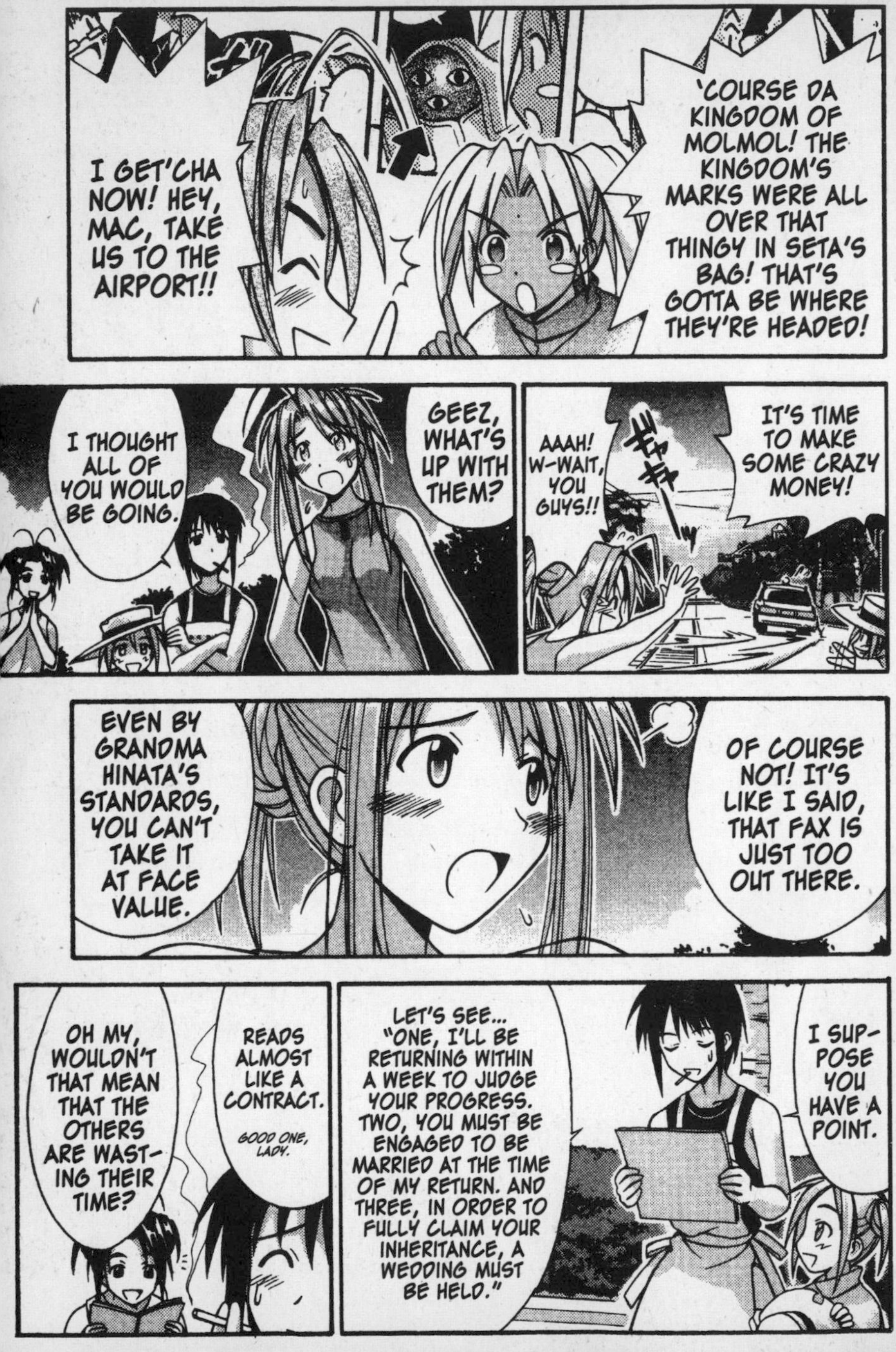
'COURSE DA KINGDOM OF MOLMOL! THE KINGDOM'S MARKS WERE ALL OVER THAT THINGY IN SETA'S BAG! THAT'S GOTTA BE WHERE THEY'RE HEADED!
I GET'CHA NOW! HEY, MAC, TAKE US TO THE AIRPORT!!
IT'S TIME TO MAKE SOME CRAZY MONEY!
AAAH! W-WAIT, YOU GUYS!!
GEEZ, WHAT'S UP WITH THEM?
I THOUGHT ALL OF YOU WOULD BE GOING.
OF COURSE NOT! IT'S LIKE I SAID, THAT FAX IS JUST TOO OUT THERE.
EVEN BY GRANDMA HINATA'S STANDARDS, YOU CAN'T TAKE IT AT FACE VALUE.
I SUP-POSE YOU HAVE A POINT.
LET'S SEE... "ONE, I'LL BE RETURNING WITHIN A WEEK TO JUDGE YOUR PROGRESS. TWO, YOU MUST BE ENGAGED TO BE MARRIED AT THE TIME OF MY RETURN. AND THREE, IN ORDER TO FULLY CLAIM YOUR INHERITANCE, A WEDDING MUST BE HELD."
READS ALMOST LIKE A CONTRACT.
GOOD ONE, LADY.
OH MY, WOULDN'T THAT MEAN THAT THE OTHERS ARE WAST-ING THEIR TIME?

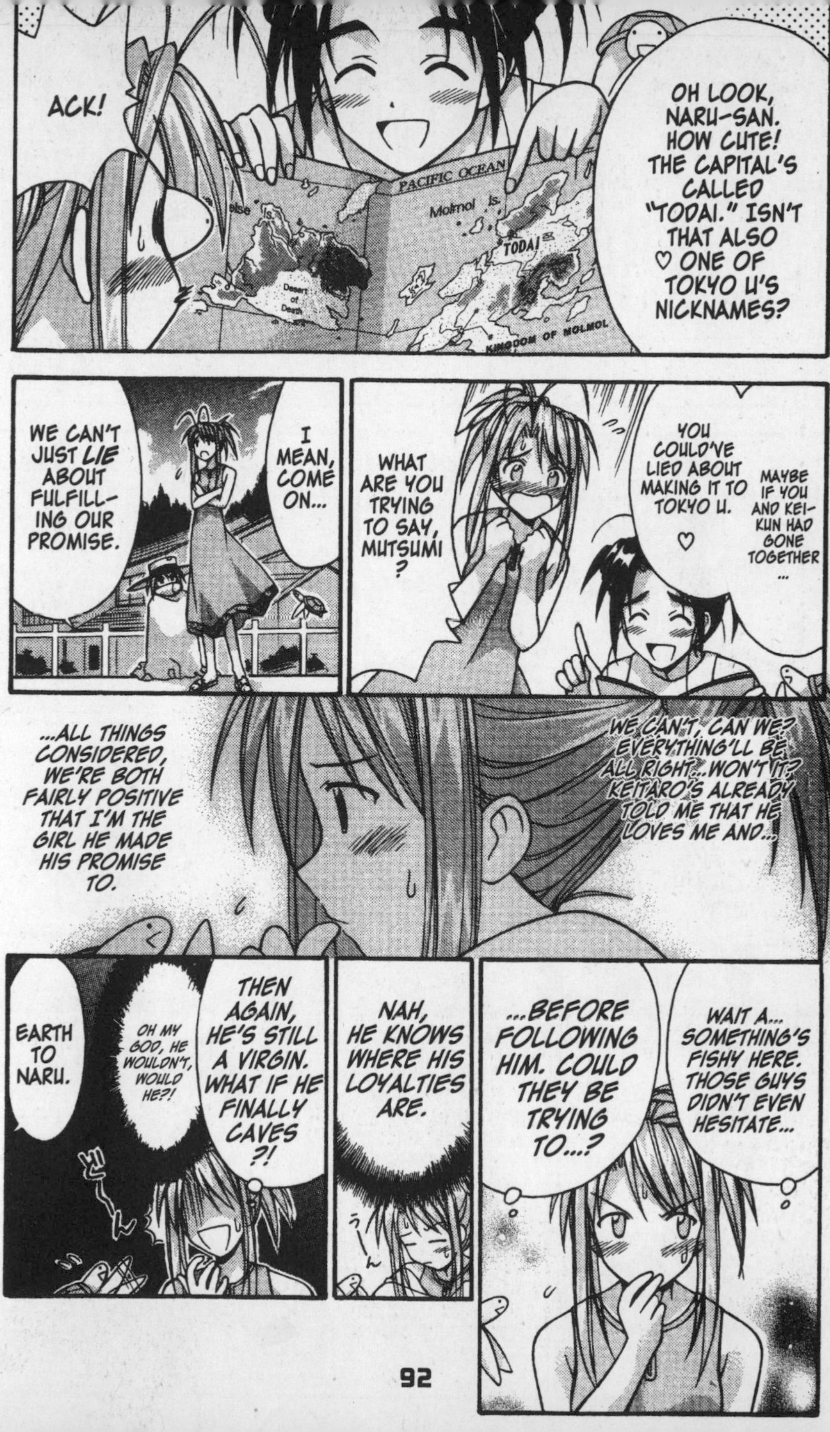
OH LOOK, NARU-SAN. HOW CUTE! THE CAPITAL'S CALLED "TODAI." ISN'T THAT ALSO ♡ ONE OF TOKYO U'S NICKNAMES?
ACK!
PACIFIC OCEAN
Molmol Is.
TODAI
Desert of Death
KINGDOM OF MOLMOL
YOU COULD'VE LIED ABOUT MAKING IT TO TOKYO U. ♡
MAYBE IF YOU AND KEI-KUN HAD GONE TOGETHER...
WHAT ARE YOU TRYING TO SAY, MUTSUMI?
I MEAN, COME ON...
WE CAN'T JUST LIE ABOUT FULFILL-ING OUR PROMISE.
WE CAN'T, CAN WE? EVERYTHING'LL BE ALL RIGHT...WON'T IT? KEITARO'S ALREADY TOLD ME THAT HE LOVES ME AND...
...ALL THINGS CONSIDERED, WE'RE BOTH FAIRLY POSITIVE THAT I'M THE GIRL HE MADE HIS PROMISE TO.
WAIT A... SOMETHING'S FISHY HERE. THOSE GUYS DIDN'T EVEN HESITATE...
...BEFORE FOLLOWING HIM. COULD THEY BE TRYING TO...?
NAH, HE KNOWS WHERE HIS LOYALTIES ARE.
THEN AGAIN, HE'S STILL A VIRGIN. WHAT IF HE FINALLY CAVES ?!
OH MY GOD, HE WOULDN'T, WOULD HE?!
EARTH TO NARU.

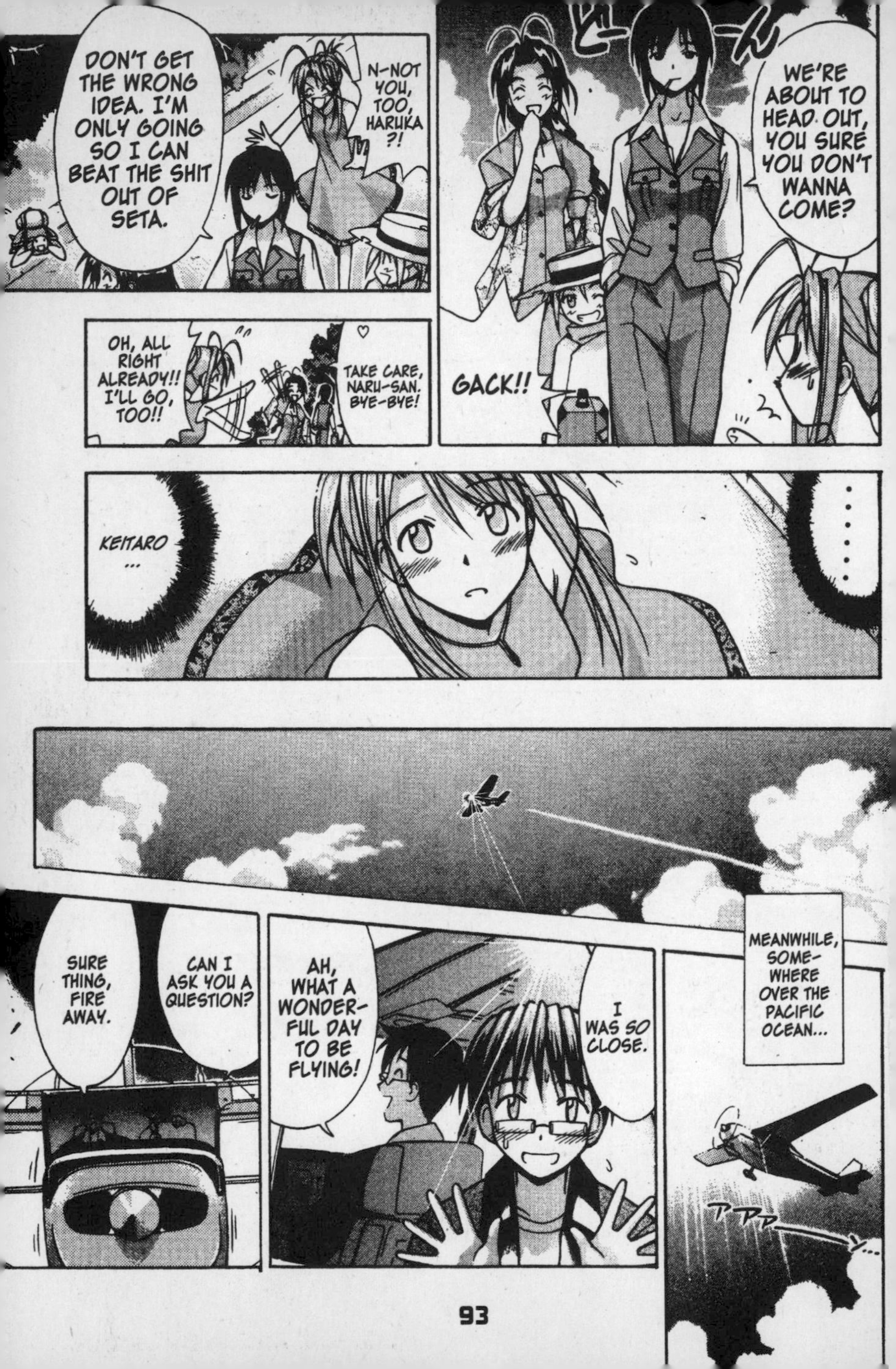
WE'RE ABOUT TO HEAD OUT, YOU SURE YOU DON'T WANNA COME?
GACK!!
N-NOT YOU, TOO, HARUKA ?!
DON'T GET THE WRONG IDEA. I'M ONLY GOING SO I CAN BEAT THE SHIT OUT OF SETA.
TAKE CARE, NARU-SAN. BYE-BYE!
OH, ALL RIGHT ALREADY!! I'LL GO, TOO!!
......
KEITARO ...
MEANWHILE, SOME-WHERE OVER THE PACIFIC OCEAN...
I WAS SO CLOSE.
AH, WHAT A WONDER-FUL DAY TO BE FLYING!
CAN I ASK YOU A QUESTION?
SURE THING, FIRE AWAY.

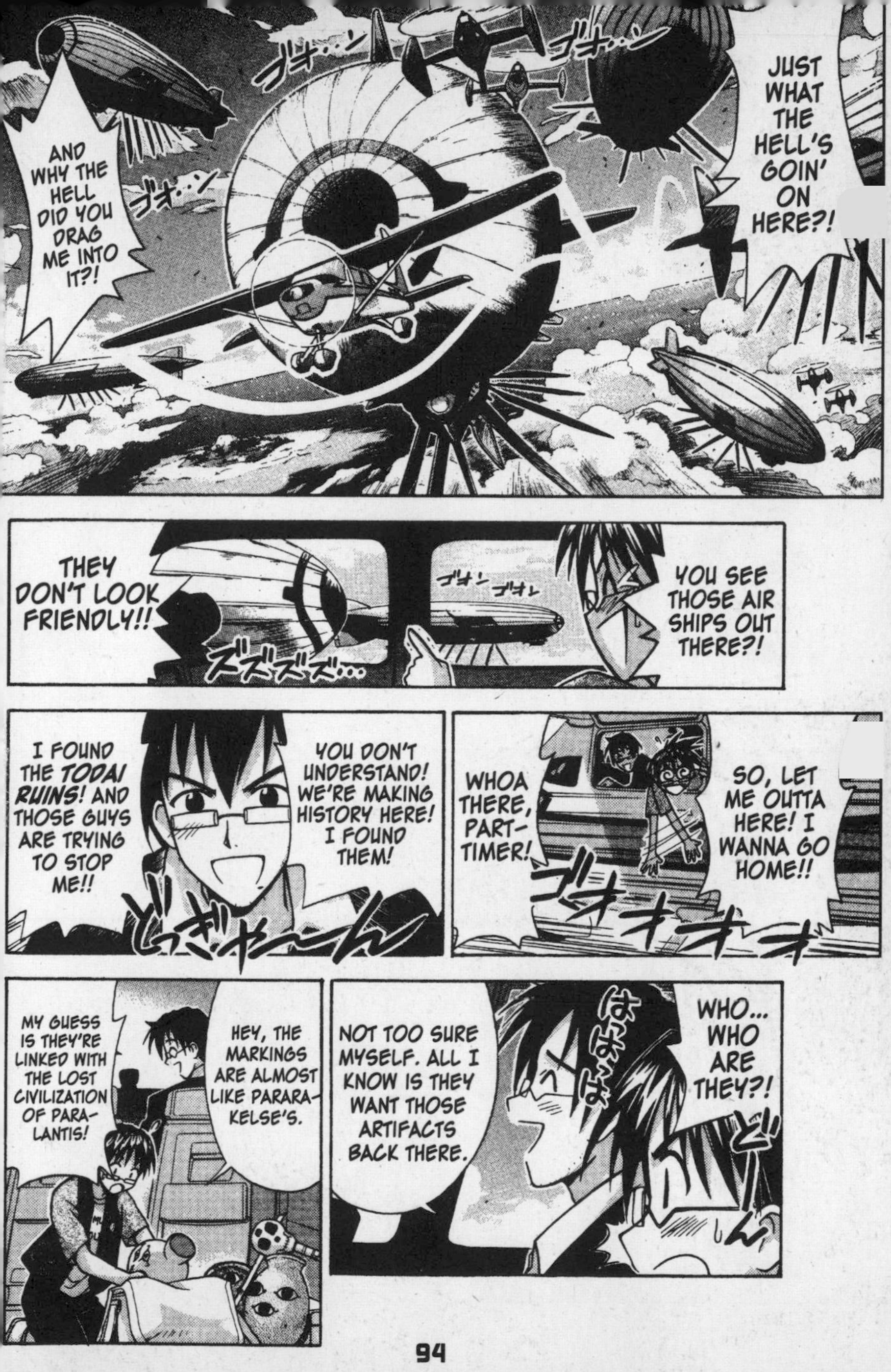
JUST WHAT THE HELL'S GOIN' ON HERE?!
AND WHY THE HELL DID YOU DRAG ME INTO IT?!
YOU SEE THOSE AIR SHIPS OUT THERE?!
THEY DON'T LOOK FRIENDLY!!
SO, LET ME OUTTA HERE! I WANNA GO HOME!!
WHOA THERE, PART-TIMER!
YOU DON'T UNDERSTAND! WE'RE MAKING HISTORY HERE! I FOUND THEM!
I FOUND THE *TODAI RUINS*! AND THOSE GUYS ARE TRYING TO STOP ME!!
WHO... WHO ARE THEY?!
NOT TOO SURE MYSELF. ALL I KNOW IS THEY WANT THOSE ARTIFACTS BACK THERE.
HEY, THE MARKINGS ARE ALMOST LIKE PARARA-KELSE'S.
MY GUESS IS THEY'RE LINKED WITH THE LOST CIVILIZATION OF PARA-LANTIS!

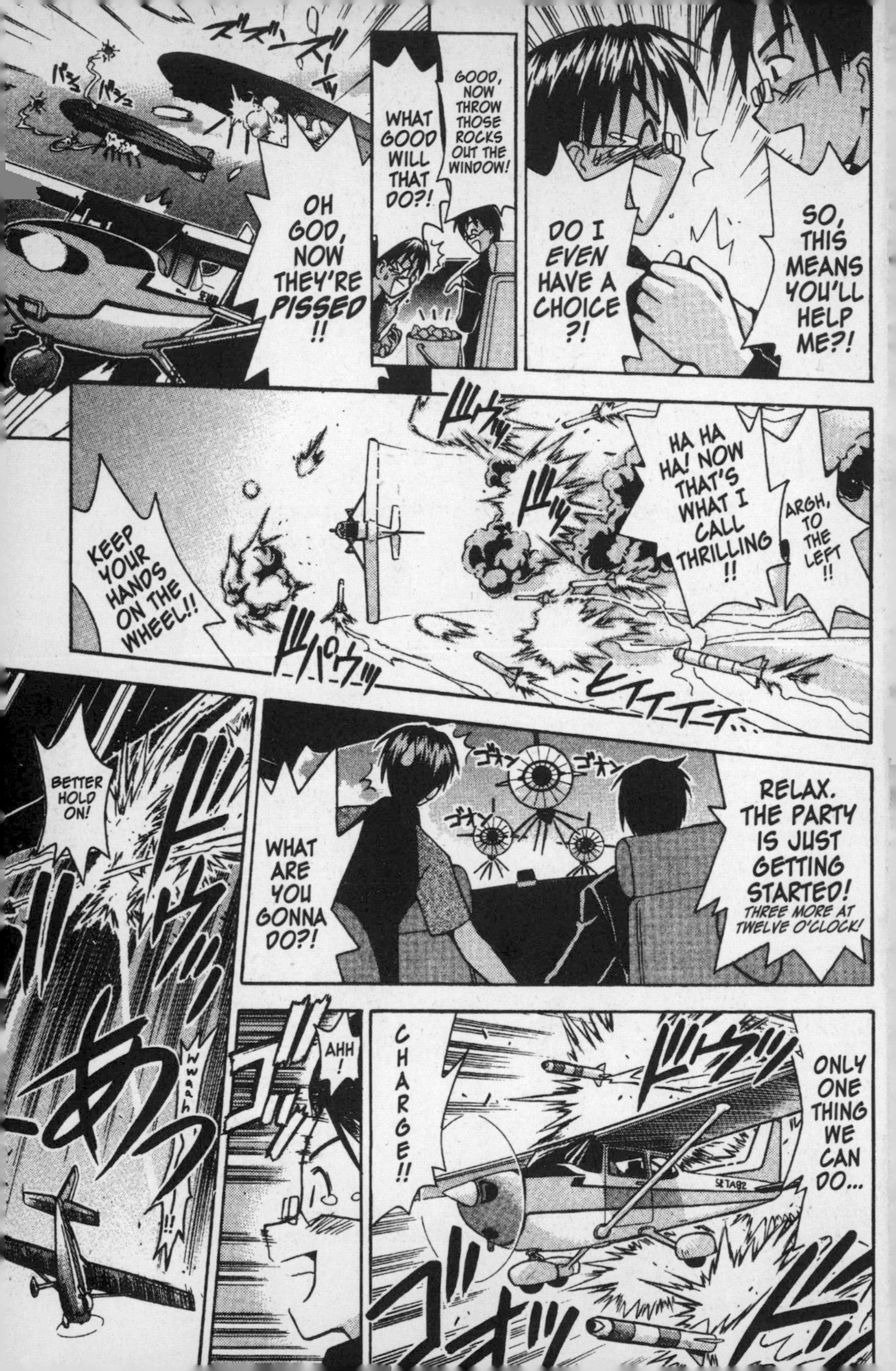
SO, THIS MEANS YOU'LL HELP ME?!
DO I EVEN HAVE A CHOICE?!
GOOD, NOW THROW THOSE ROCKS OUT THE WINDOW!
WHAT GOOD WILL THAT DO?!
OH GOD, NOW THEY'RE PISSED!!
HA HA HA! NOW THAT'S WHAT I CALL THRILLING!!
ARGH, TO THE LEFT!!
KEEP YOUR HANDS ON THE WHEEL!!
RELAX. THE PARTY IS JUST GETTING STARTED!
THREE MORE AT TWELVE O'CLOCK!
WHAT ARE YOU GONNA DO?!
ONLY ONE THING WE CAN DO...
CHARGE!!
AHH!
BETTER HOLD ON!
WWaah

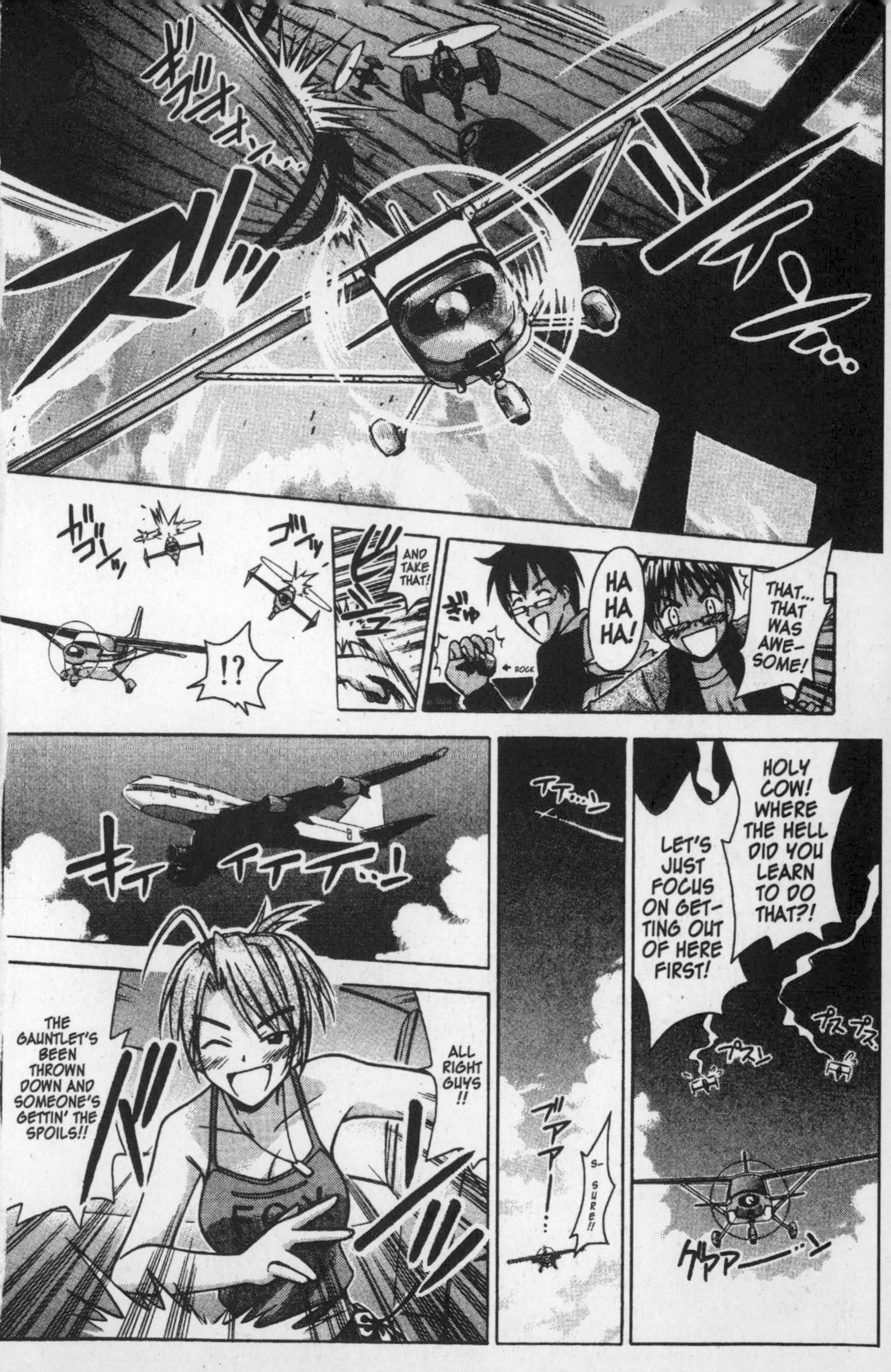

THAT... THAT WAS AWE-SOME!
HA HA HA!
ROCK
AND TAKE THAT!
!?
HOLY COW! WHERE THE HELL DID YOU LEARN TO DO THAT?!
LET'S JUST FOCUS ON GET-TING OUT OF HERE FIRST!
S-SURE!!
ALL RIGHT GUYS!!
THE GAUNTLET'S BEEN THROWN DOWN AND SOMEONE'S GETTIN' THE SPOILS!!

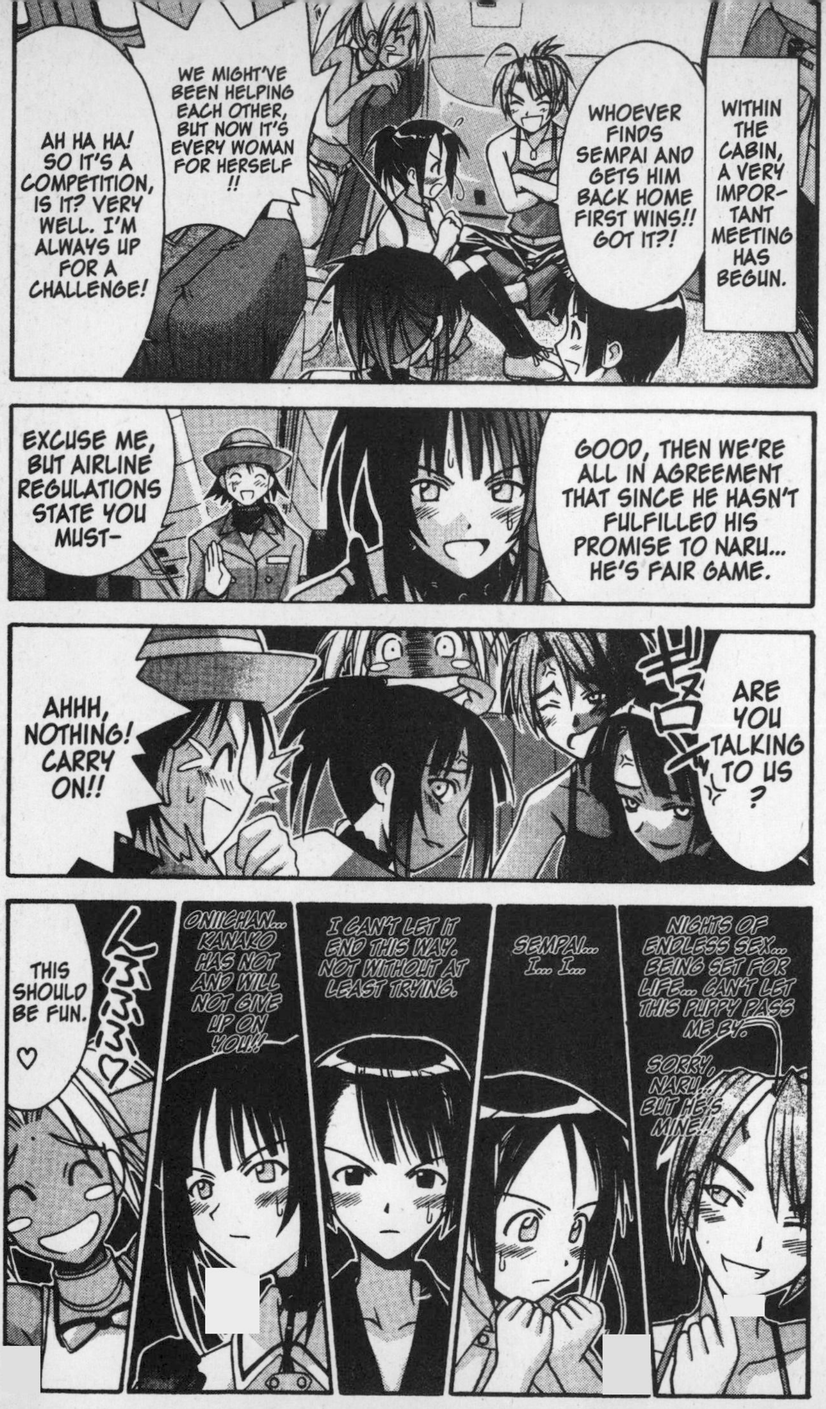

WITHIN THE CABIN, A VERY IMPORTANT MEETING HAS BEGUN.
WHOEVER FINDS SEMPAI AND GETS HIM BACK HOME FIRST WINS!! GOT IT?!
WE MIGHT'VE BEEN HELPING EACH OTHER, BUT NOW IT'S EVERY WOMAN FOR HERSELF!!
AH HA HA! SO IT'S A COMPETITION, IS IT? VERY WELL. I'M ALWAYS UP FOR A CHALLENGE!
GOOD, THEN WE'RE ALL IN AGREEMENT THAT SINCE HE HASN'T FULFILLED HIS PROMISE TO NARU... HE'S FAIR GAME.
EXCUSE ME, BUT AIRLINE REGULATIONS STATE YOU MUST-
ARE YOU TALKING TO US?
AHHH, NOTHING! CARRY ON!!
NIGHTS OF ENDLESS SEX... BEING SET FOR LIFE... CAN'T LET THIS PUPPY PASS ME BY.
SORRY, NARU... BUT HE'S MINE!!
SEMPAI... I... I...
I CAN'T LET IT END THIS WAY. NOT WITHOUT AT LEAST TRYING.
ONIICHAN... KANAKO HAS NOT AND WILL NOT GIVE UP ON YOU!!
THIS SHOULD BE FUN. ♡

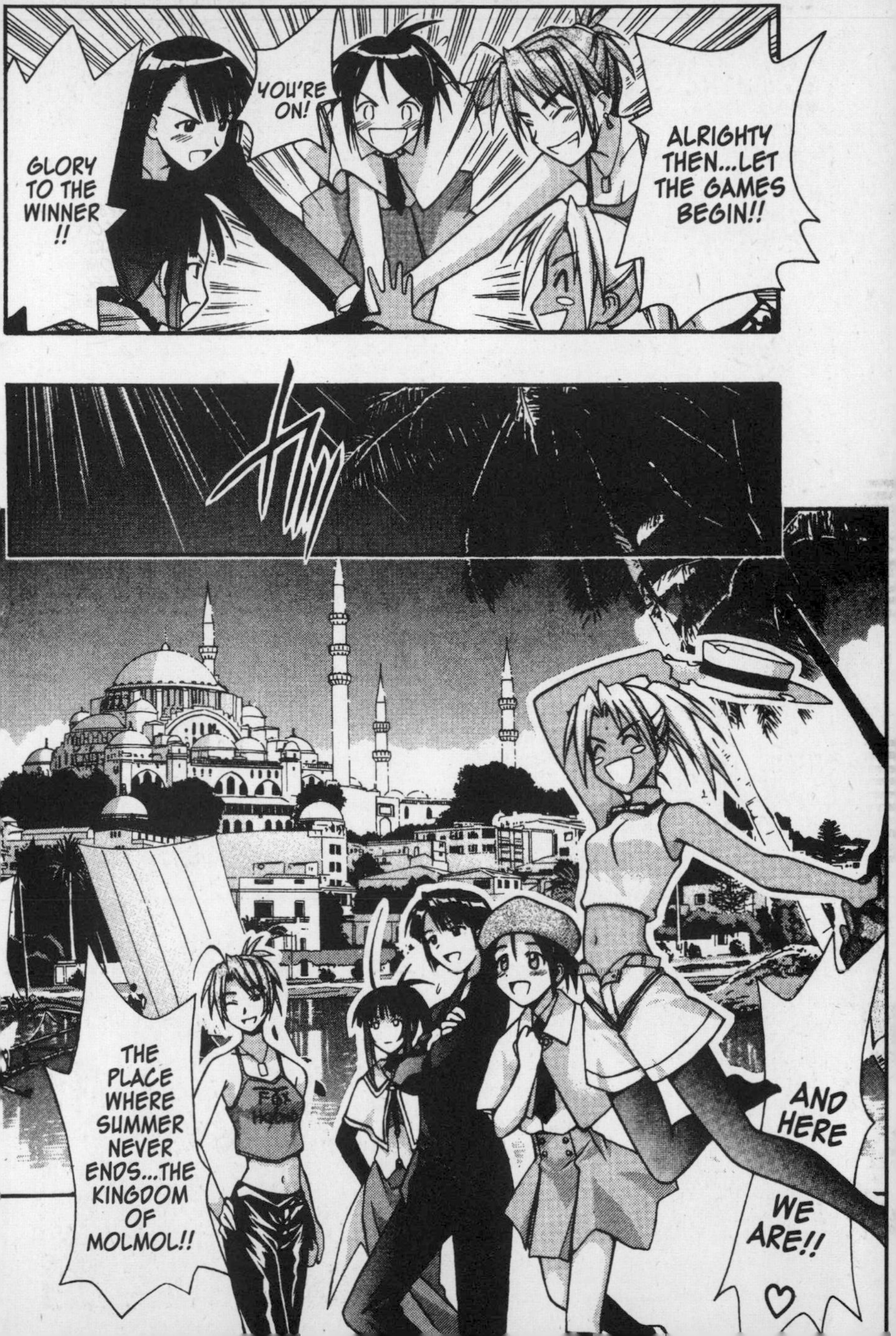
ALRIGHTY THEN...LET THE GAMES BEGIN!!
YOU'RE ON!
GLORY TO THE WINNER!!
AND HERE WE ARE!! ♡
THE PLACE WHERE SUMMER NEVER ENDS...THE KINGDOM OF MOLMOL!!

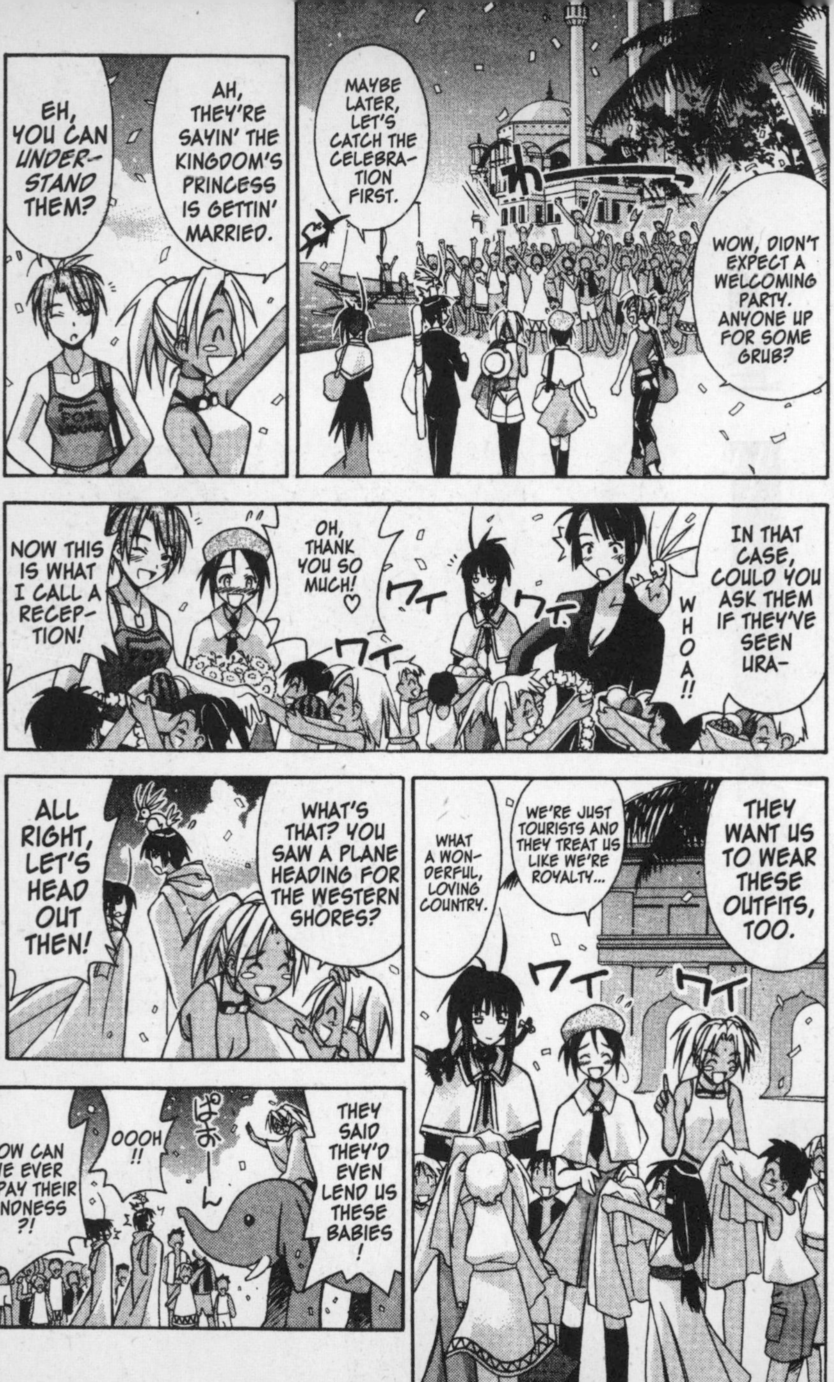
WOW, DIDN'T EXPECT A WELCOMING PARTY. ANYONE UP FOR SOME GRUB?
MAYBE LATER, LET'S CATCH THE CELEBRATION FIRST.
AH, THEY'RE SAYIN' THE KINGDOM'S PRINCESS IS GETTIN' MARRIED.
EH, YOU CAN UNDERSTAND THEM?
IN THAT CASE, COULD YOU ASK THEM IF THEY'VE SEEN URA-
WHOA!!
ワイ
ワイ
ワイ
OH, THANK YOU SO MUCH! ♡
NOW THIS IS WHAT I CALL A RECEPTION!
THEY WANT US TO WEAR THESE OUTFITS, TOO.
WE'RE JUST TOURISTS AND THEY TREAT US LIKE WE'RE ROYALTY...
WHAT A WONDERFUL, LOVING COUNTRY.
ワイ
ワイ
WHAT'S THAT? YOU SAW A PLANE HEADING FOR THE WESTERN SHORES?
ALL RIGHT, LET'S HEAD OUT THEN!
THEY SAID THEY'D EVEN LEND US THESE BABIES!
ぱおーん
OOOH!!
HOW CAN WE EVER REPAY THEIR KINDNESS?!

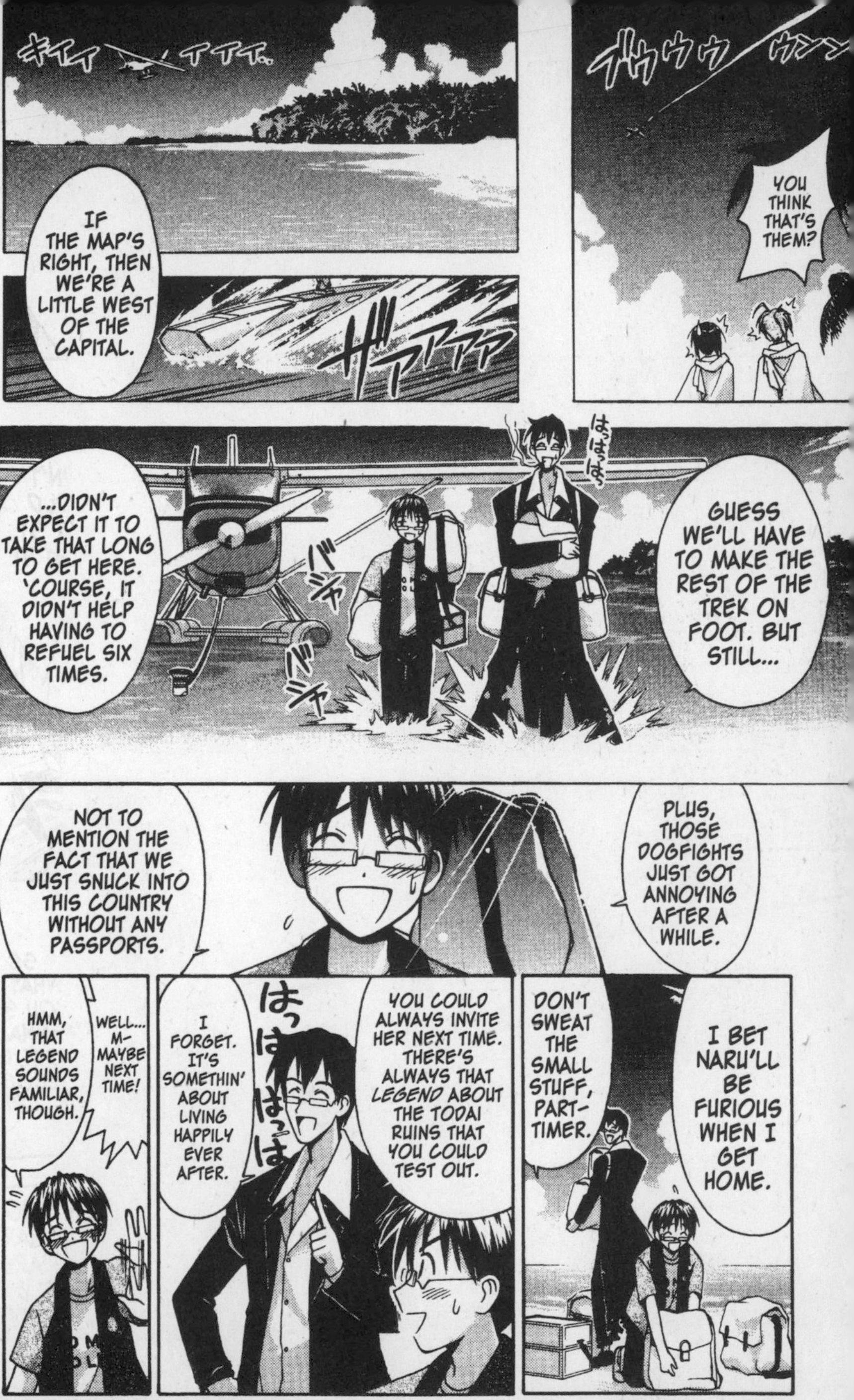
ブウウウ ウンン
YOU THINK THAT'S THEM?
キイイ イイイ
IF THE MAP'S RIGHT, THEN WE'RE A LITTLE WEST OF THE CAPITAL.
ザアアア
はっはっはっ
GUESS WE'LL HAVE TO MAKE THE REST OF THE TREK ON FOOT. BUT STILL...
...DIDN'T EXPECT IT TO TAKE THAT LONG TO GET HERE. 'COURSE, IT DIDN'T HELP HAVING TO REFUEL SIX TIMES.
バシャ
バシャ
PLUS, THOSE DOGFIGHTS JUST GOT ANNOYING AFTER A WHILE.
NOT TO MENTION THE FACT THAT WE JUST SNUCK INTO THIS COUNTRY WITHOUT ANY PASSPORTS.
I BET NARU'LL BE FURIOUS WHEN I GET HOME.
DON'T SWEAT THE SMALL STUFF, PART-TIMER.
YOU COULD ALWAYS INVITE HER NEXT TIME. THERE'S ALWAYS THAT LEGEND ABOUT THE TODAI RUINS THAT YOU COULD TEST OUT.
はっはっは
I FORGET. IT'S SOMETHIN' ABOUT LIVING HAPPILY EVER AFTER.
WELL... M-MAYBE NEXT TIME!
HMM, THAT LEGEND SOUNDS FAMILIAR, THOUGH.

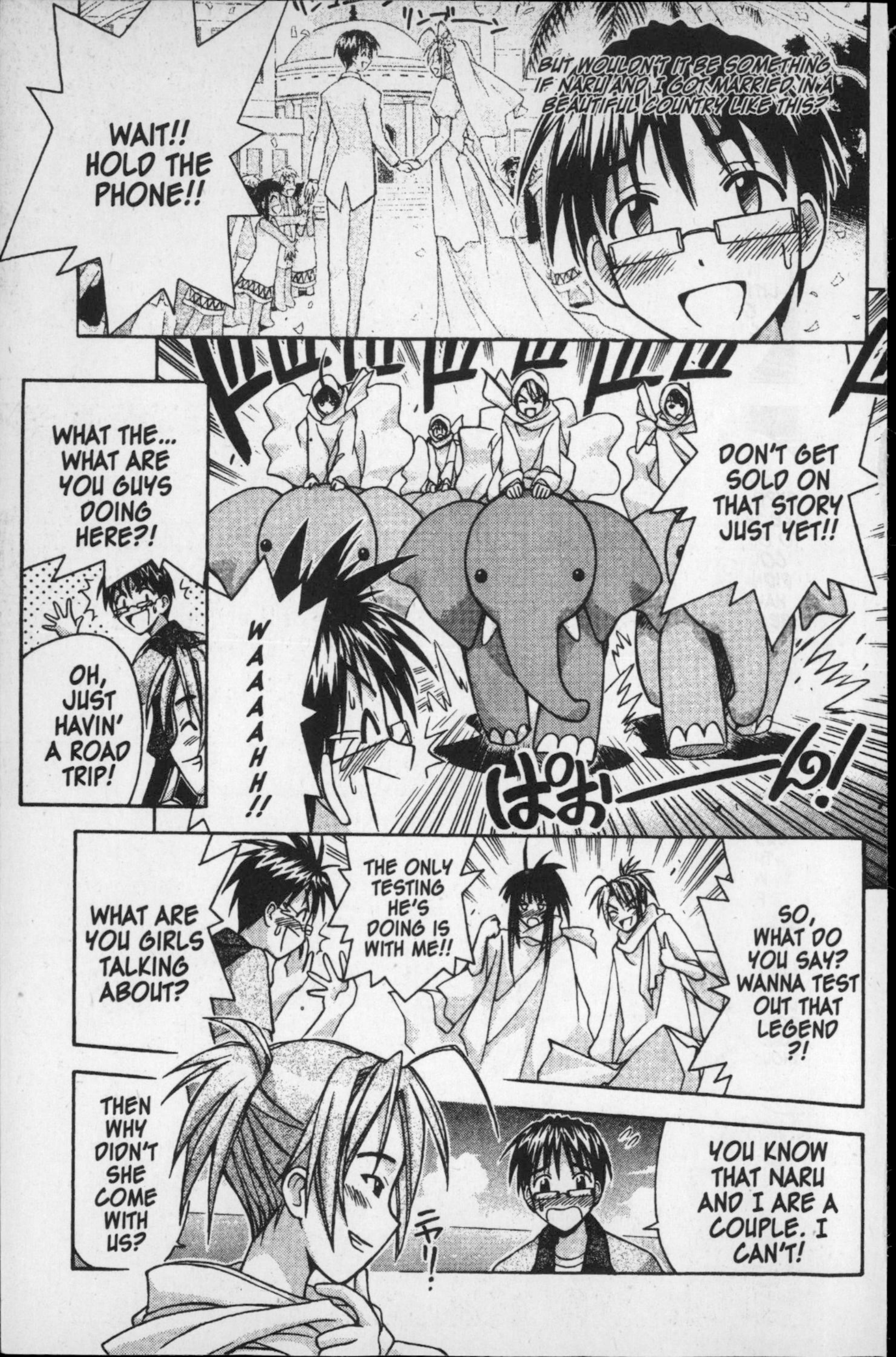
BUT WOULDN'T IT BE SOMETHING IF NARU AND I GOT MARRIED IN A BEAUTIFUL COUNTRY LIKE THIS?
WAIT!! HOLD THE PHONE!!
DON'T GET SOLD ON THAT STORY JUST YET!!
WAAAAAHH!!
ぱおーーん!
WHAT THE... WHAT ARE YOU GUYS DOING HERE?!
OH, JUST HAVIN' A ROAD TRIP!
SO, WHAT DO YOU SAY? WANNA TEST OUT THAT LEGEND?!
THE ONLY TESTING HE'S DOING IS WITH ME!!
WHAT ARE YOU GIRLS TALKING ABOUT?
YOU KNOW THAT NARU AND I ARE A COUPLE. I CAN'T!
ニヤ!
THEN WHY DIDN'T SHE COME WITH US?

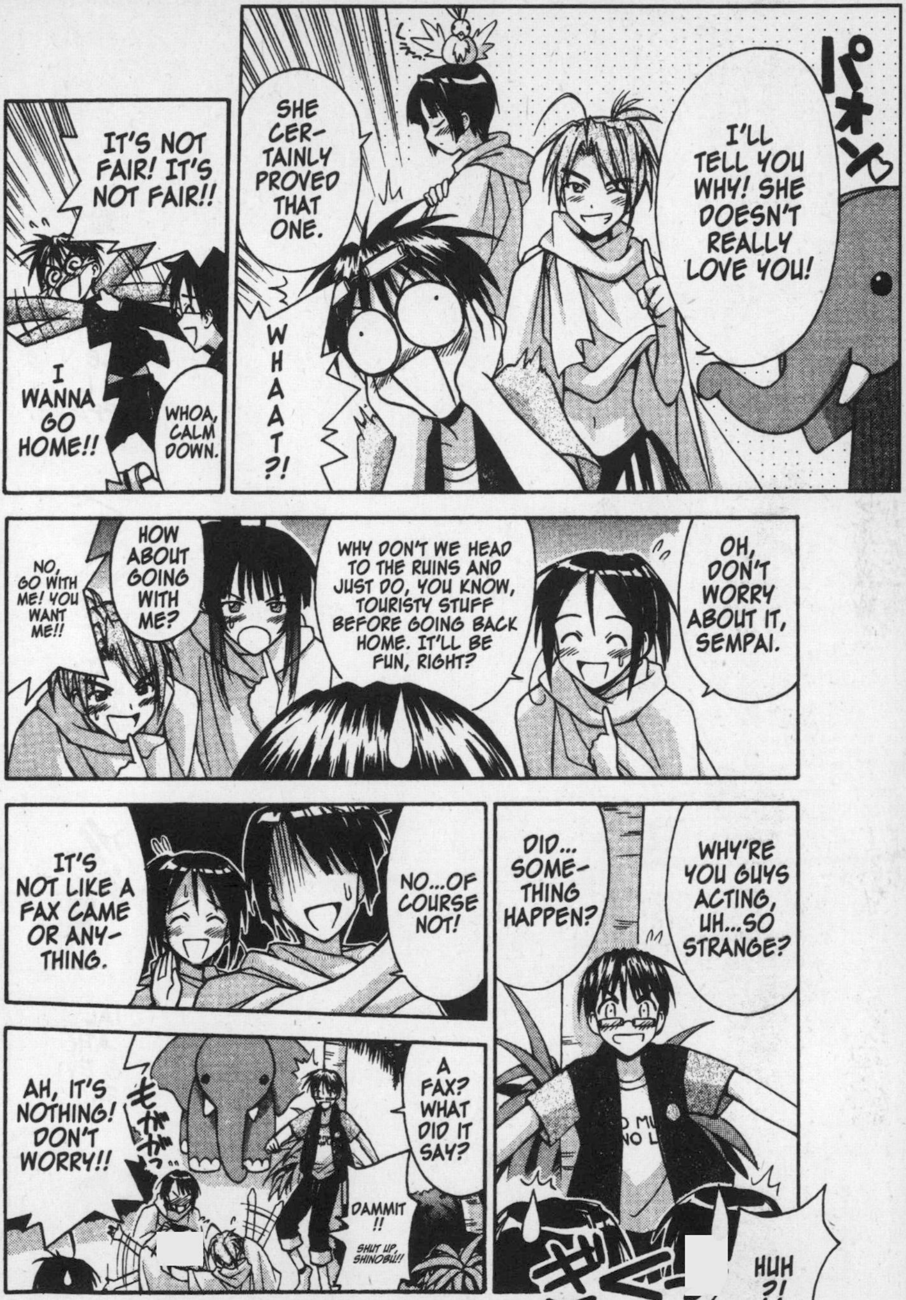
パオン
I'LL TELL YOU WHY! SHE DOESN'T REALLY LOVE YOU!
SHE CERTAINLY PROVED THAT ONE.
WHAAAT?!
IT'S NOT FAIR! IT'S NOT FAIR!!
WHOA, CALM DOWN.
I WANNA GO HOME!!
OH, DON'T WORRY ABOUT IT, SEMPAI.
WHY DON'T WE HEAD TO THE RUINS AND JUST DO, YOU KNOW, TOURISTY STUFF BEFORE GOING BACK HOME. IT'LL BE FUN, RIGHT?
HOW ABOUT GOING WITH ME?
NO, GO WITH ME! YOU WANT ME!!
WHY'RE YOU GUYS ACTING, UH...SO STRANGE?
DID... SOMETHING HAPPEN?
HUH?!
NO...OF COURSE NOT!
IT'S NOT LIKE A FAX CAME OR ANYTHING.
A FAX? WHAT DID IT SAY?
DAMMIT!!
SHUT UP, SHINOBU!!
AH, IT'S NOTHING! DON'T WORRY!!

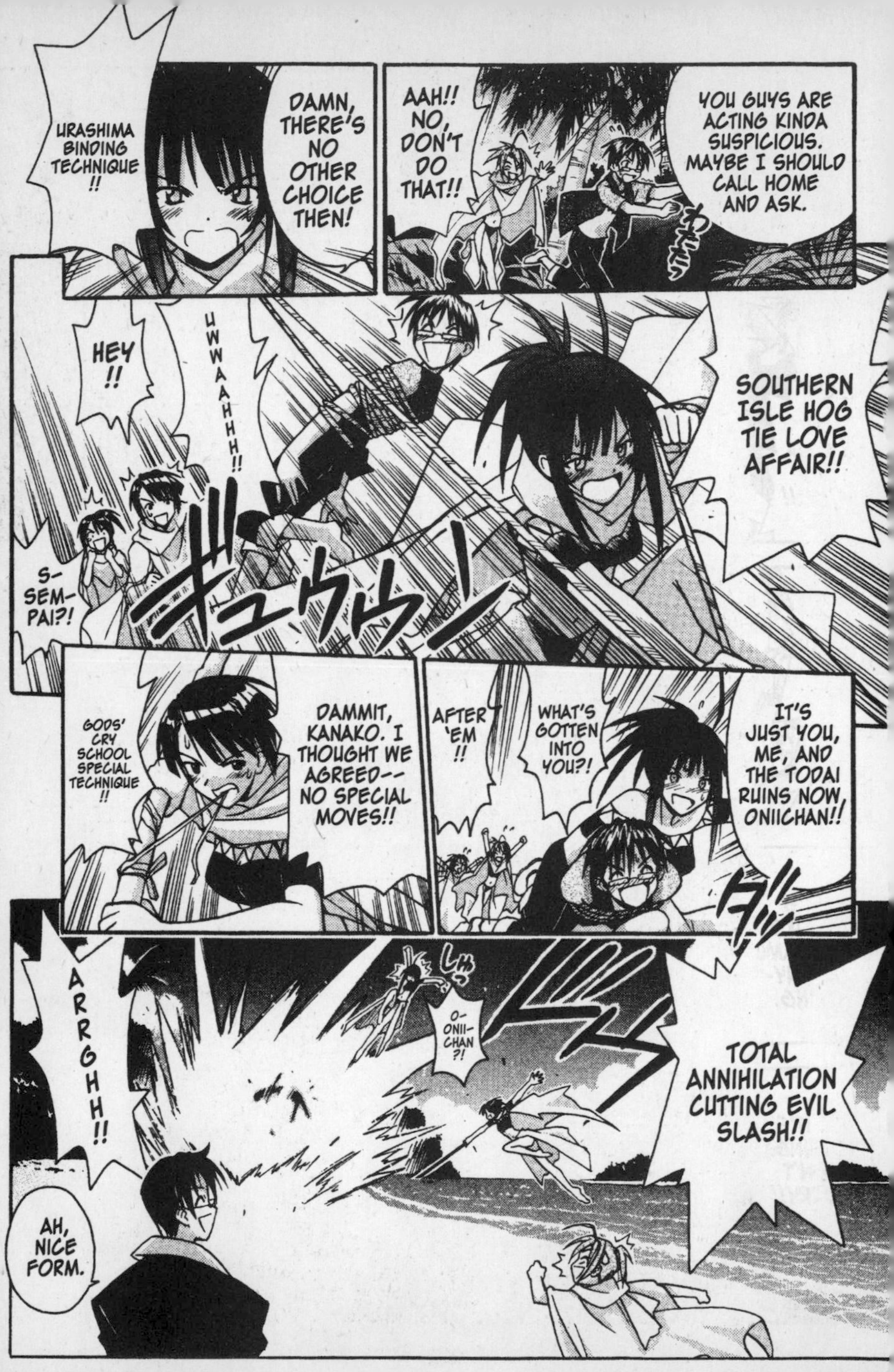
YOU GUYS ARE ACTING KINDA SUSPICIOUS. MAYBE I SHOULD CALL HOME AND ASK.
AAH!! NO, DON'T DO THAT!!
DAMN, THERE'S NO OTHER CHOICE THEN!
URASHIMA BINDING TECHNIQUE!!
SOUTHERN ISLE HOG TIE LOVE AFFAIR!!
UWWAAHHH!!
HEY!!
S-SEMPAI?!
IT'S JUST YOU, ME, AND THE TODAI RUINS NOW, ONIICHAN!!
WHAT'S GOTTEN INTO YOU?!
AFTER 'EM!!
DAMMIT, KANAKO. I THOUGHT WE AGREED-- NO SPECIAL MOVES!!
GODS' CRY SCHOOL SPECIAL TECHNIQUE!!
TOTAL ANNIHILATION CUTTING EVIL SLASH!!
O-ONIICHAN?!
ARRGHH!!
AH, NICE FORM.

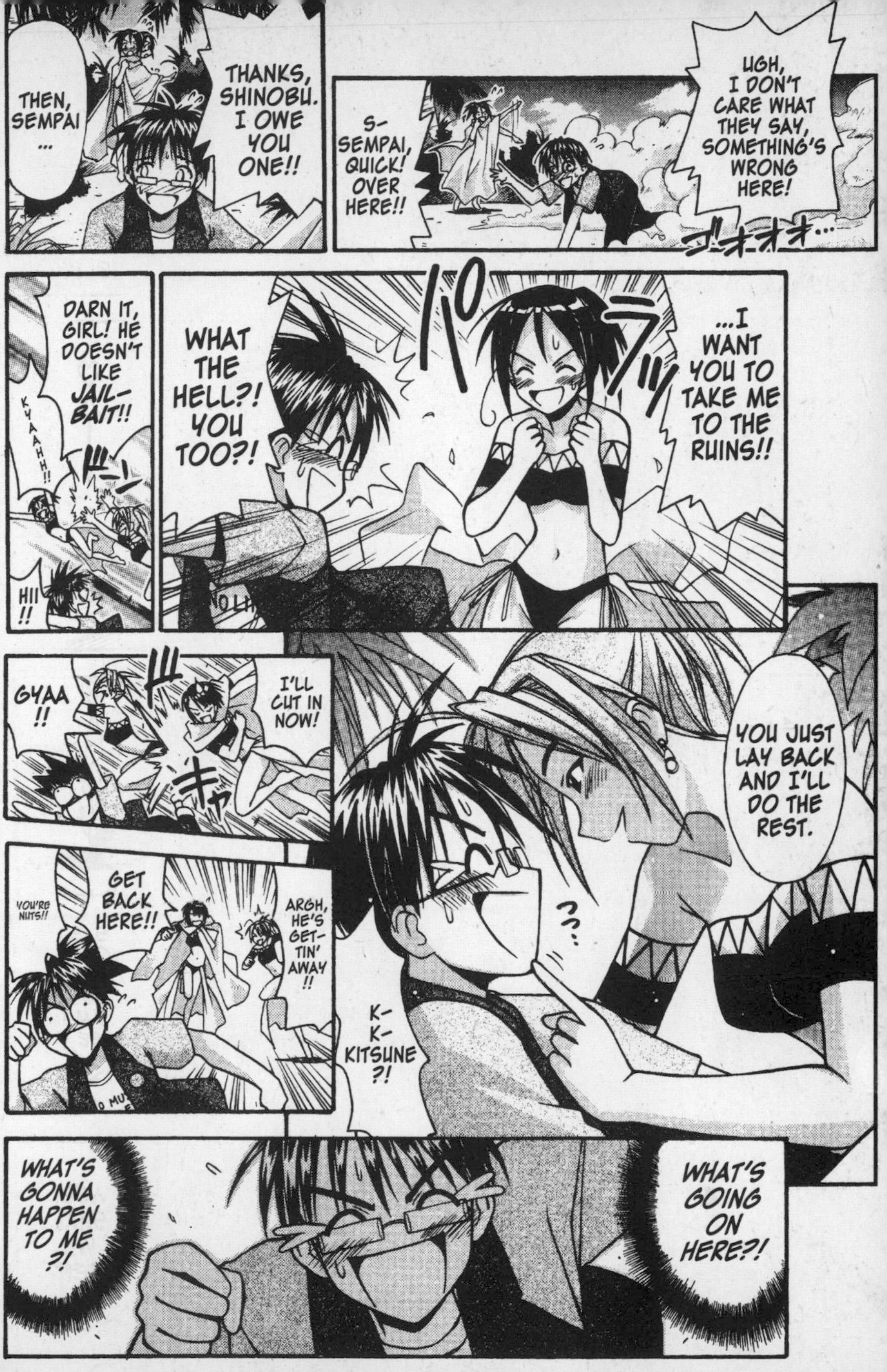
UGH, I DON'T CARE WHAT THEY SAY, SOMETHING'S WRONG HERE!
S-SEMPAI, QUICK! OVER HERE!!
ゴオオオ…
THANKS, SHINOBU. I OWE YOU ONE!!
THEN, SEMPAI ...
パラッ
...I WANT YOU TO TAKE ME TO THE RUINS!!
WHAT THE HELL?! YOU TOO?!
DARN IT, GIRL! HE DOESN'T LIKE JAIL-BAIT!!
KYAAHH!!
HII!!
YOU JUST LAY BACK AND I'LL DO THE REST.
K-K-KITSUNE?!
I'LL CUT IN NOW!
GYAA!!
ARGH, HE'S GET-TIN' AWAY!!
GET BACK HERE!!
YOU'RE NUTS!!
WHAT'S GOING ON HERE?!
WHAT'S GONNA HAPPEN TO ME?!

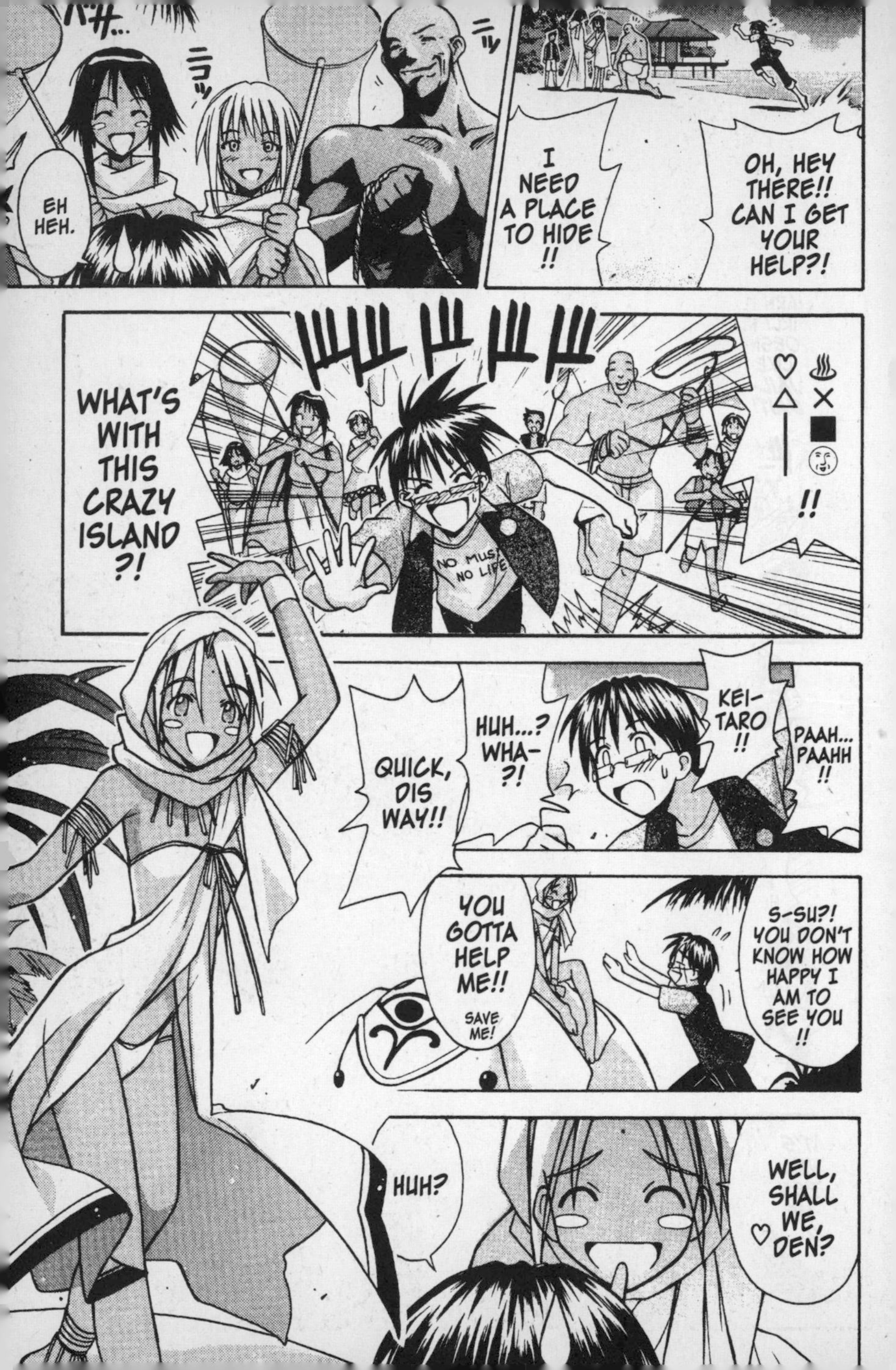

OH, HEY THERE!! CAN I GET YOUR HELP?!
I NEED A PLACE TO HIDE!!
ニッ
ニヤッ
バサ…
EH HEH.
WHAT'S WITH THIS CRAZY ISLAND?!
PAAH... PAAHH!!
KEI-TARO!!
HUH...? WHA-?!
QUICK, DIS WAY!!
S-SU?! YOU DON'T KNOW HOW HAPPY I AM TO SEE YOU!!
YOU GOTTA HELP ME!!
SAVE ME!
WELL, SHALL WE, DEN? ♡
HUH?

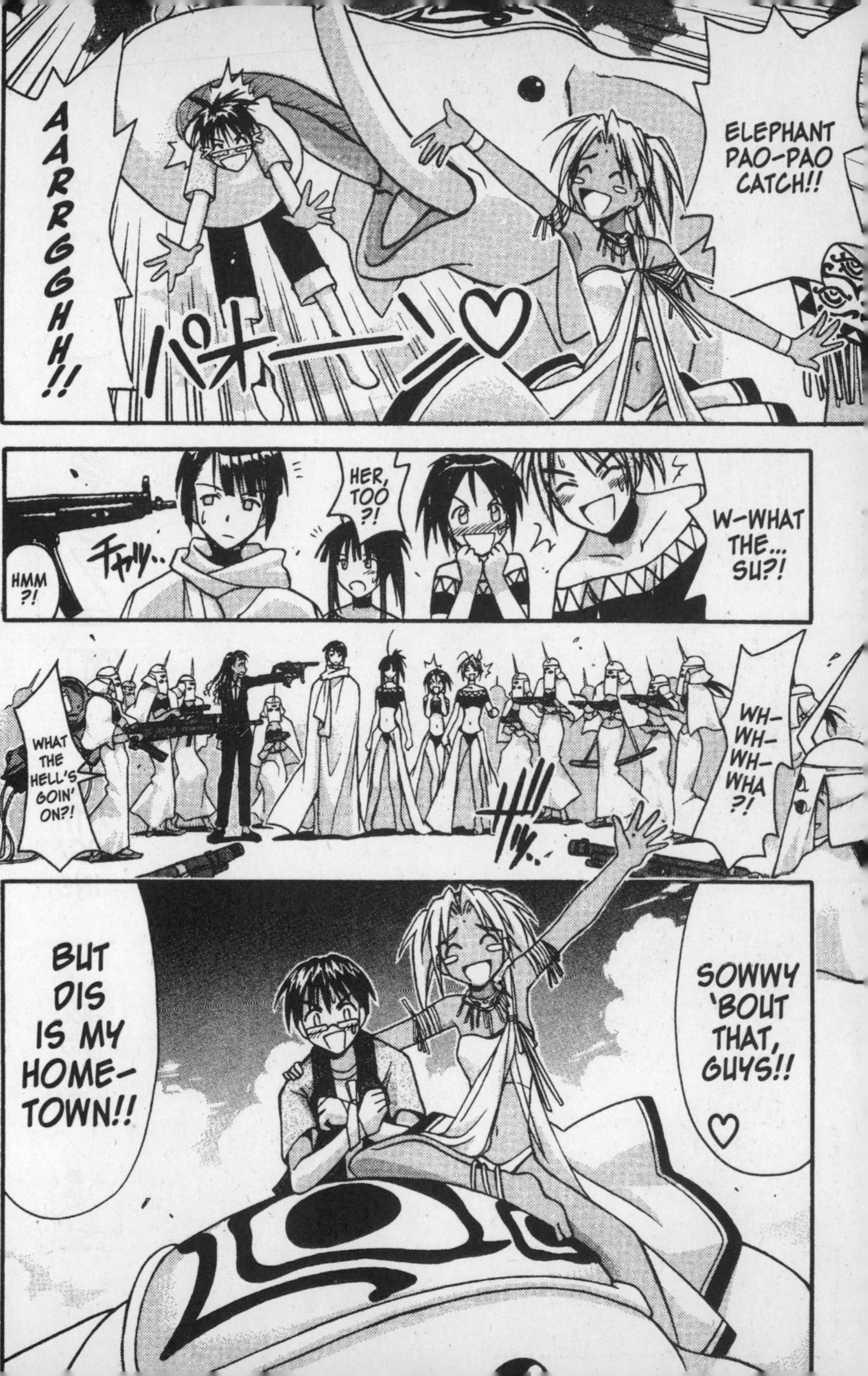
ELEPHANT PAO-PAO CATCH!!
AARRGGHH!!
パオーン♡
W-WHAT THE... SU?!
HER, TOO?!
チャリ..
HMM?!
WH-WH-WH-WHA?!
ザッ..
WHAT THE HELL'S GOIN' ON?!
SOWWY 'BOUT THAT, GUYS!! ♡
BUT DIS IS MY HOME-TOWN!!

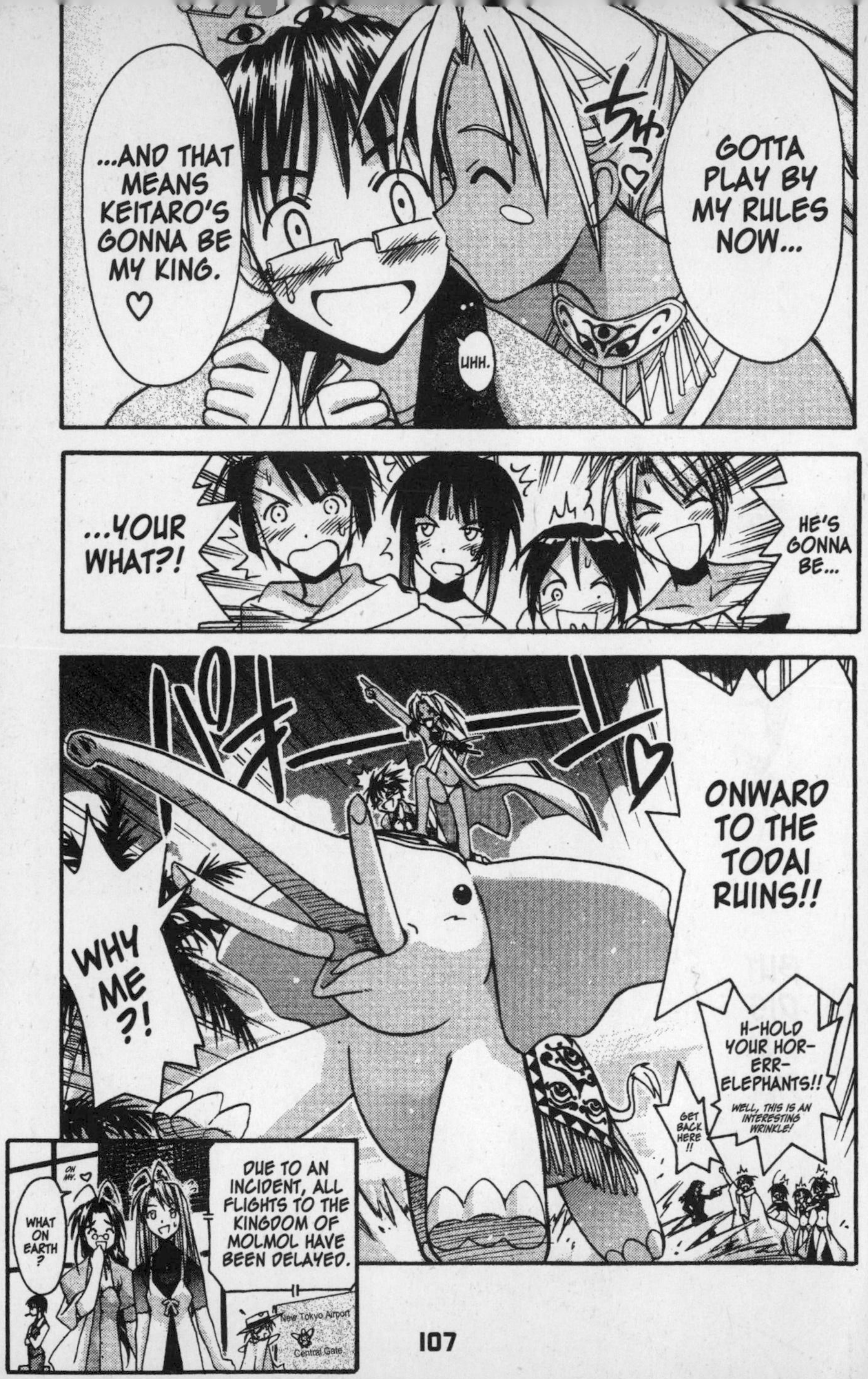
GOTTA PLAY BY MY RULES NOW...
ちゅっ ♡
...AND THAT MEANS KEITARO'S GONNA BE MY KING. ♡
UHH.
HE'S GONNA BE...
...YOUR WHAT?!
ONWARD TO THE TODAI RUINS!!
WHY ME?!
H-HOLD YOUR HOR-ERR-ELEPHANTS!!
WELL, THIS IS AN INTERESTING WRINKLE!
GET BACK HERE!!
DUE TO AN INCIDENT, ALL FLIGHTS TO THE KINGDOM OF MOLMOL HAVE BEEN DELAYED.
OH MY. ♡
WHAT ON EARTH?
New Tokyo Airport
Central Gate

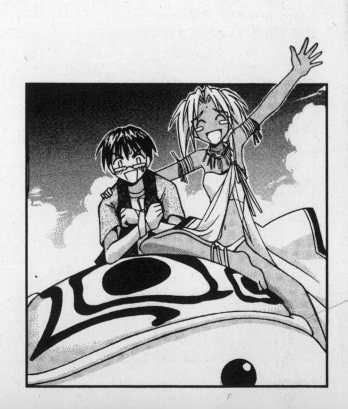

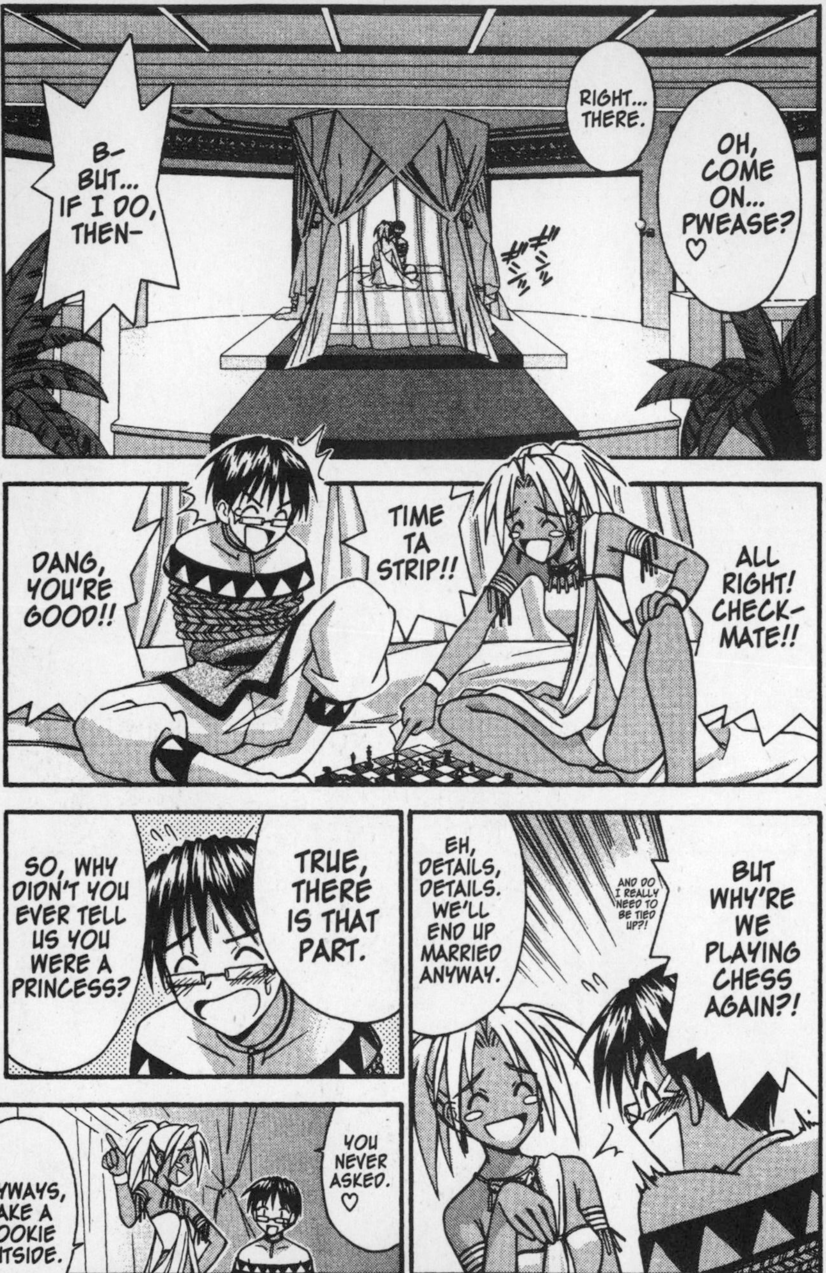
OH, COME ON... PWEASE? ♡
RIGHT... THERE.
B- BUT... IF I DO, THEN-
ALL RIGHT! CHECK-MATE!!
TIME TA STRIP!!
DANG, YOU'RE GOOD!!
BUT WHY'RE WE PLAYING CHESS AGAIN?!
AND DO I REALLY NEED TO BE TIED UP?!
EH, DETAILS, DETAILS. WE'LL END UP MARRIED ANYWAY.
TRUE, THERE IS THAT PART.
SO, WHY DIDN'T YOU EVER TELL US YOU WERE A PRINCESS?
YOU NEVER ASKED. ♡
ANYWAYS, TAKE A LOOKIE OUTSIDE.

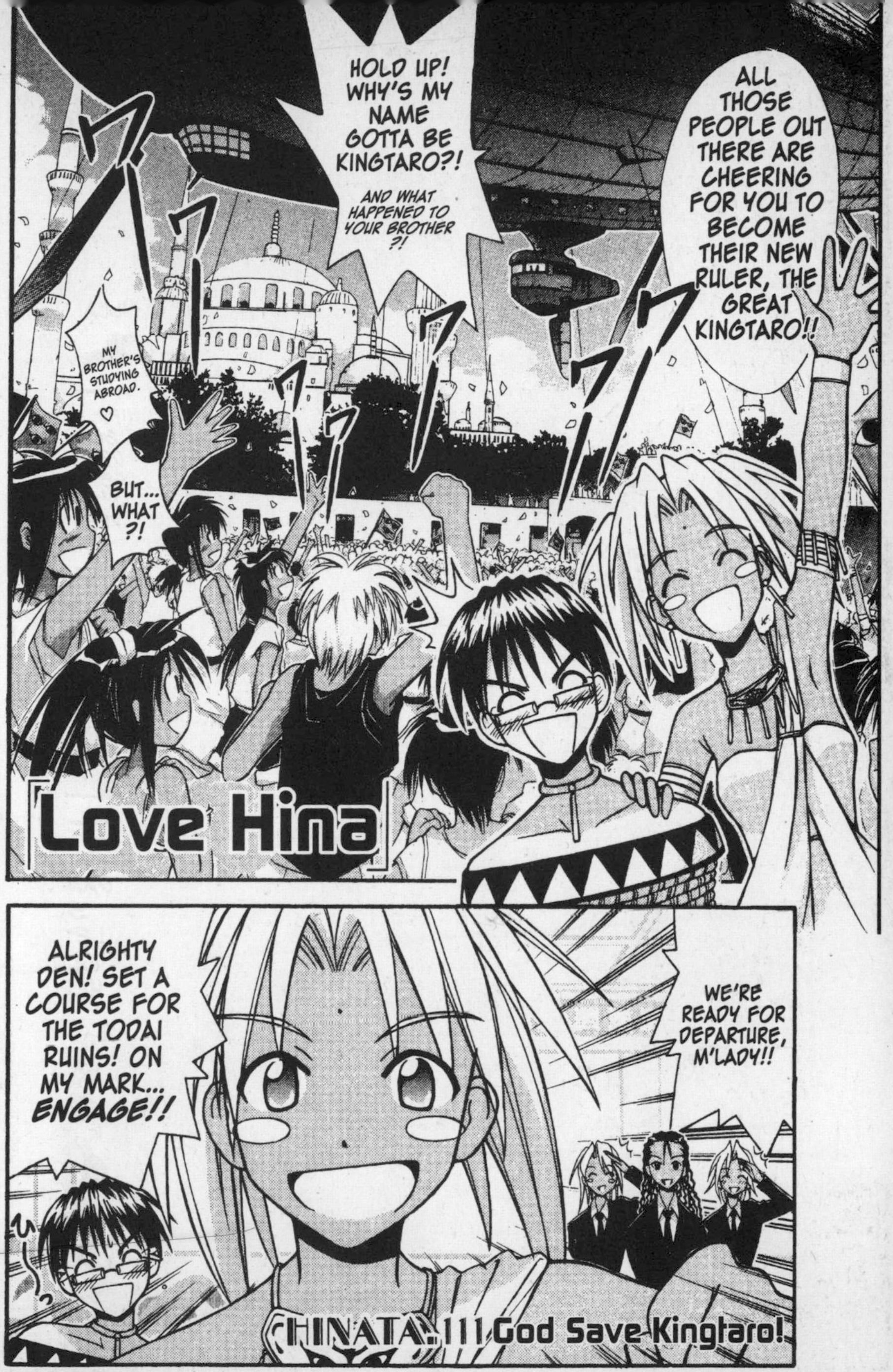
ALL THOSE PEOPLE OUT THERE ARE CHEERING FOR YOU TO BECOME THEIR NEW RULER, THE GREAT KINGTARO!!
HOLD UP! WHY'S MY NAME GOTTA BE KINGTARO?!
AND WHAT HAPPENED TO YOUR BROTHER?!
MY BROTHER'S STUDYING ABROAD. ♡
BUT... WHAT?!
Love Hina
WE'RE READY FOR DEPARTURE, M'LADY!!
ALRIGHTY DEN! SET A COURSE FOR THE TODAI RUINS! ON MY MARK... ENGAGE!!
HINATA. 111 God Save Kingtaro!

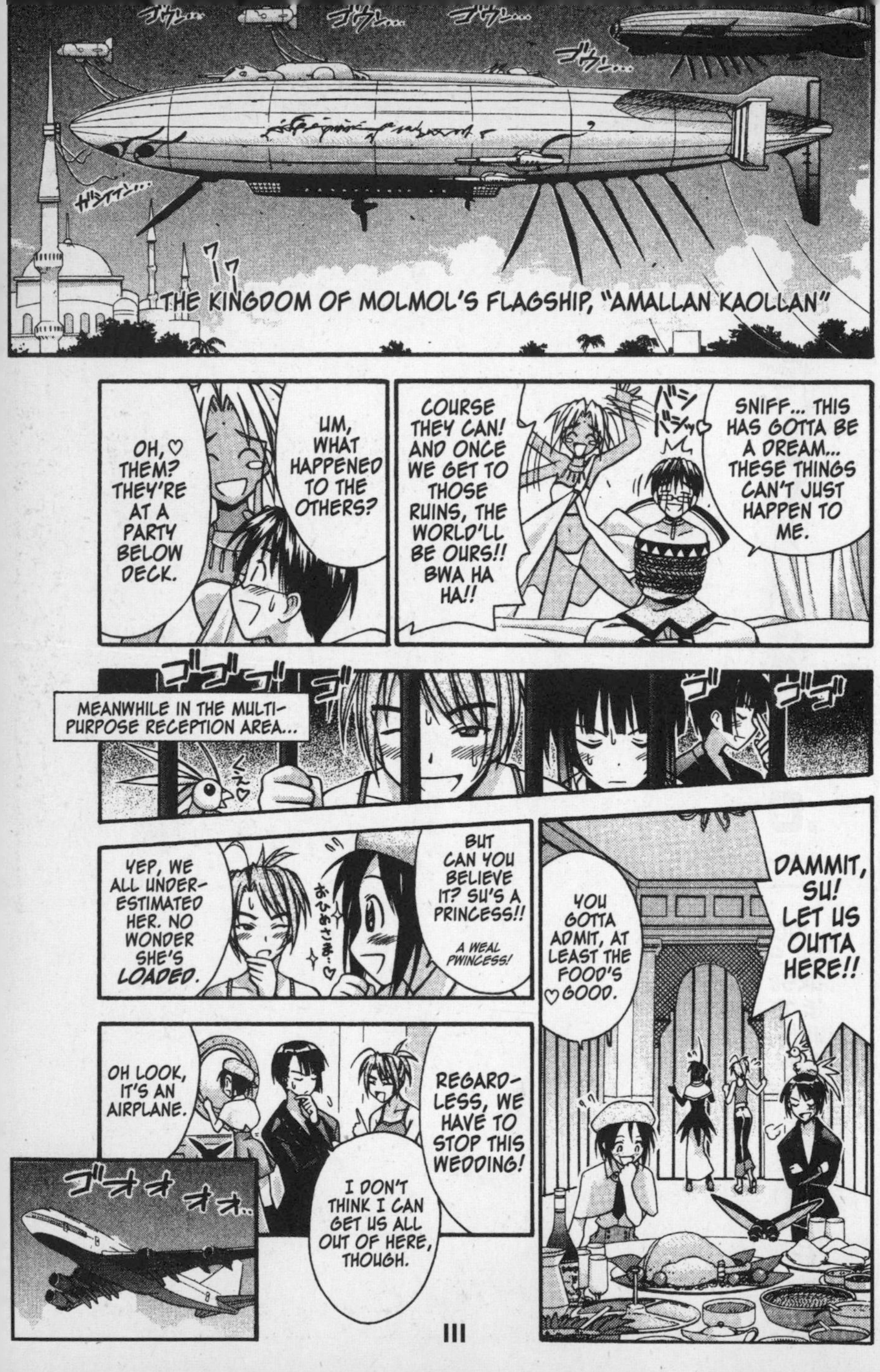
THE KINGDOM OF MOLMOL'S FLAGSHIP, "AMALLAN KAOLLAN"
SNIFF... THIS HAS GOTTA BE A DREAM... THESE THINGS CAN'T JUST HAPPEN TO ME.
COURSE THEY CAN! AND ONCE WE GET TO THOSE RUINS, THE WORLD'LL BE OURS!! BWA HA HA!!
UM, WHAT HAPPENED TO THE OTHERS?
OH, ♡ THEM? THEY'RE AT A PARTY BELOW DECK.
MEANWHILE IN THE MULTI-PURPOSE RECEPTION AREA...
DAMMIT, SU! LET US OUTTA HERE!!
YOU GOTTA ADMIT, AT LEAST THE FOOD'S ♡GOOD.
BUT CAN YOU BELIEVE IT? SU'S A PRINCESS!!
A WEAL PWINCESS!
YEP, WE ALL UNDER-ESTIMATED HER. NO WONDER SHE'S LOADED.
REGARD-LESS, WE HAVE TO STOP THIS WEDDING!
I DON'T THINK I CAN GET US ALL OUT OF HERE, THOUGH.
OH LOOK, IT'S AN AIRPLANE.

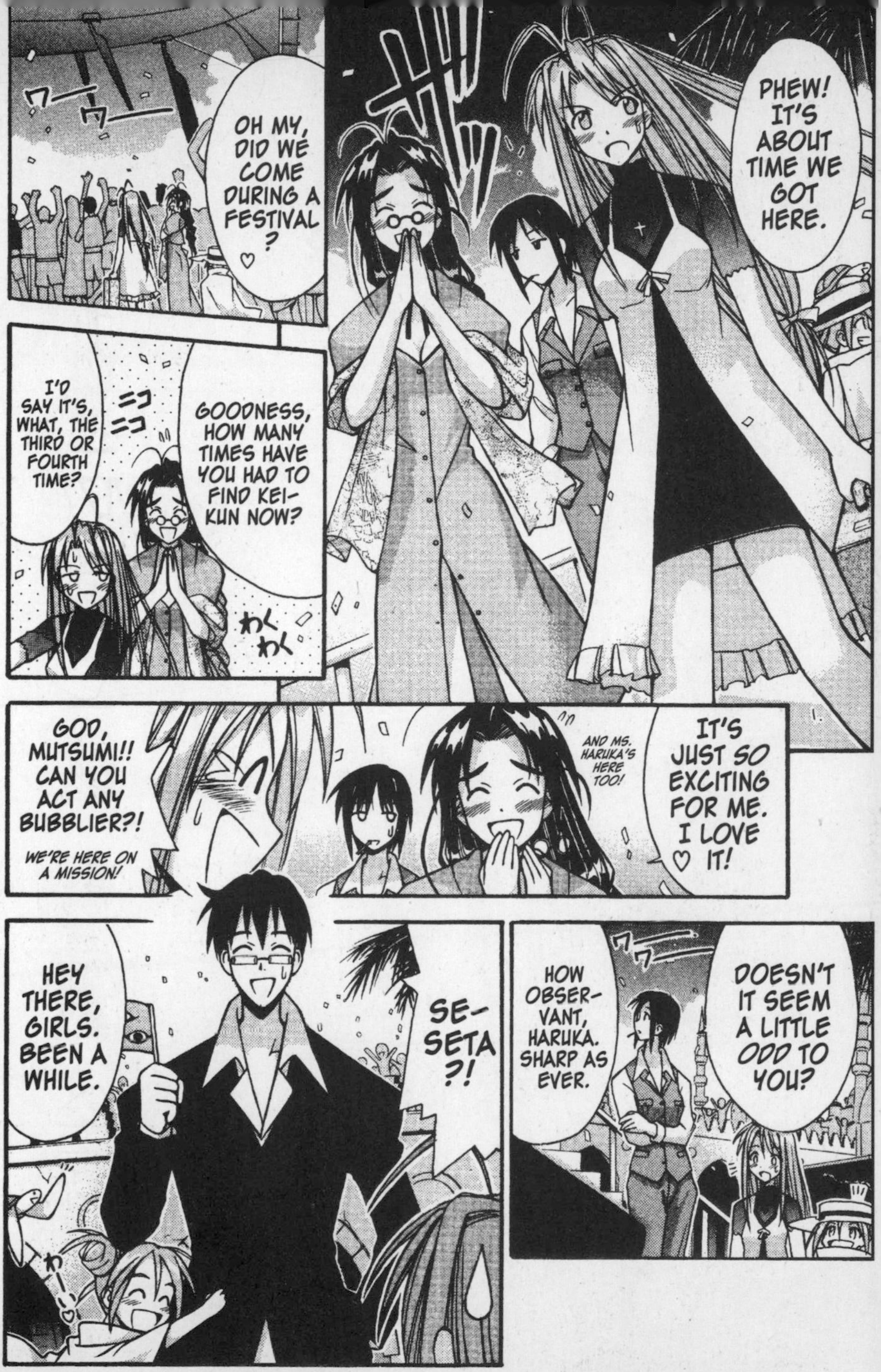
ザッ
PHEW! IT'S ABOUT TIME WE GOT HERE.
ワー ワー
OH MY, DID WE COME DURING A FESTIVAL? ♡
GOODNESS, HOW MANY TIMES HAVE YOU HAD TO FIND KEI-KUN NOW?
ニコ ニコ
I'D SAY IT'S, WHAT, THE THIRD OR FOURTH TIME?
わく わく
IT'S JUST SO EXCITING FOR ME. I LOVE ♡ IT!
AND MS. HARUKA'S HERE TOO!
GOD, MUTSUMI!! CAN YOU ACT ANY BUBBLIER?!
WE'RE HERE ON A MISSION!
DOESN'T IT SEEM A LITTLE ODD TO YOU?
ワワ
HOW OBSERVANT, HARUKA. SHARP AS EVER.
SE-SETA?!
HEY THERE, GIRLS. BEEN A WHILE.
わー♡

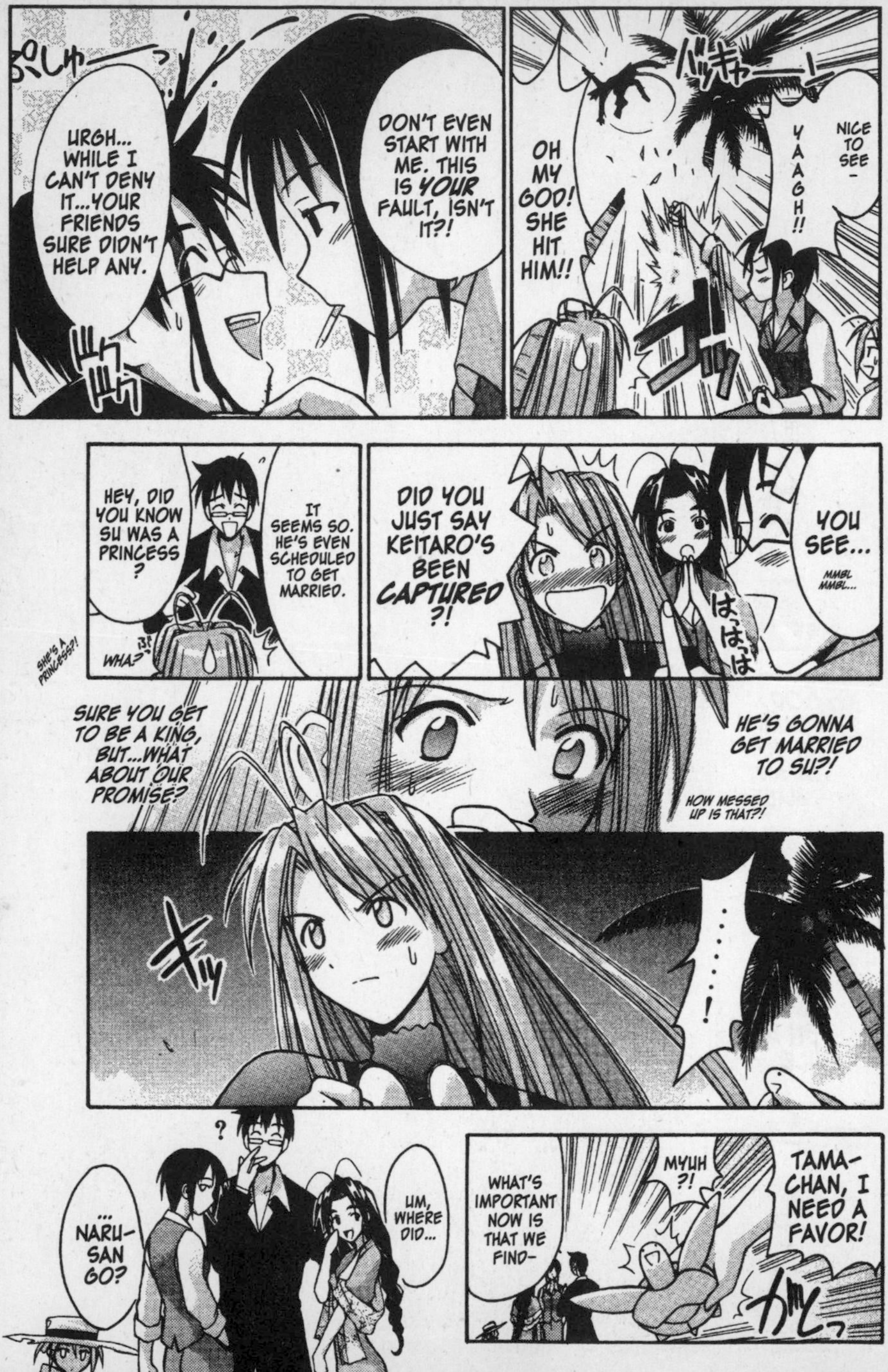
NICE TO SEE –
YAAGH!!
OH MY GOD! SHE HIT HIM!!
DON'T EVEN START WITH ME. THIS IS YOUR FAULT, ISN'T IT?!
URGH... WHILE I CAN'T DENY IT...YOUR FRIENDS SURE DIDN'T HELP ANY.
YOU SEE...
MMBL MMBL...
DID YOU JUST SAY KEITARO'S BEEN CAPTURED?!
IT SEEMS SO. HE'S EVEN SCHEDULED TO GET MARRIED.
HEY, DID YOU KNOW SU WAS A PRINCESS?
WHA?
SHE'S A PRINCESS?!
HE'S GONNA GET MARRIED TO SU?!
HOW MESSED UP IS THAT?!
SURE YOU GET TO BE A KING, BUT...WHAT ABOUT OUR PROMISE?
...!
TAMA-CHAN, I NEED A FAVOR!
MYUH ?!
WHAT'S IMPORTANT NOW IS THAT WE FIND–
UM, WHERE DID...
... NARU-SAN GO?
?

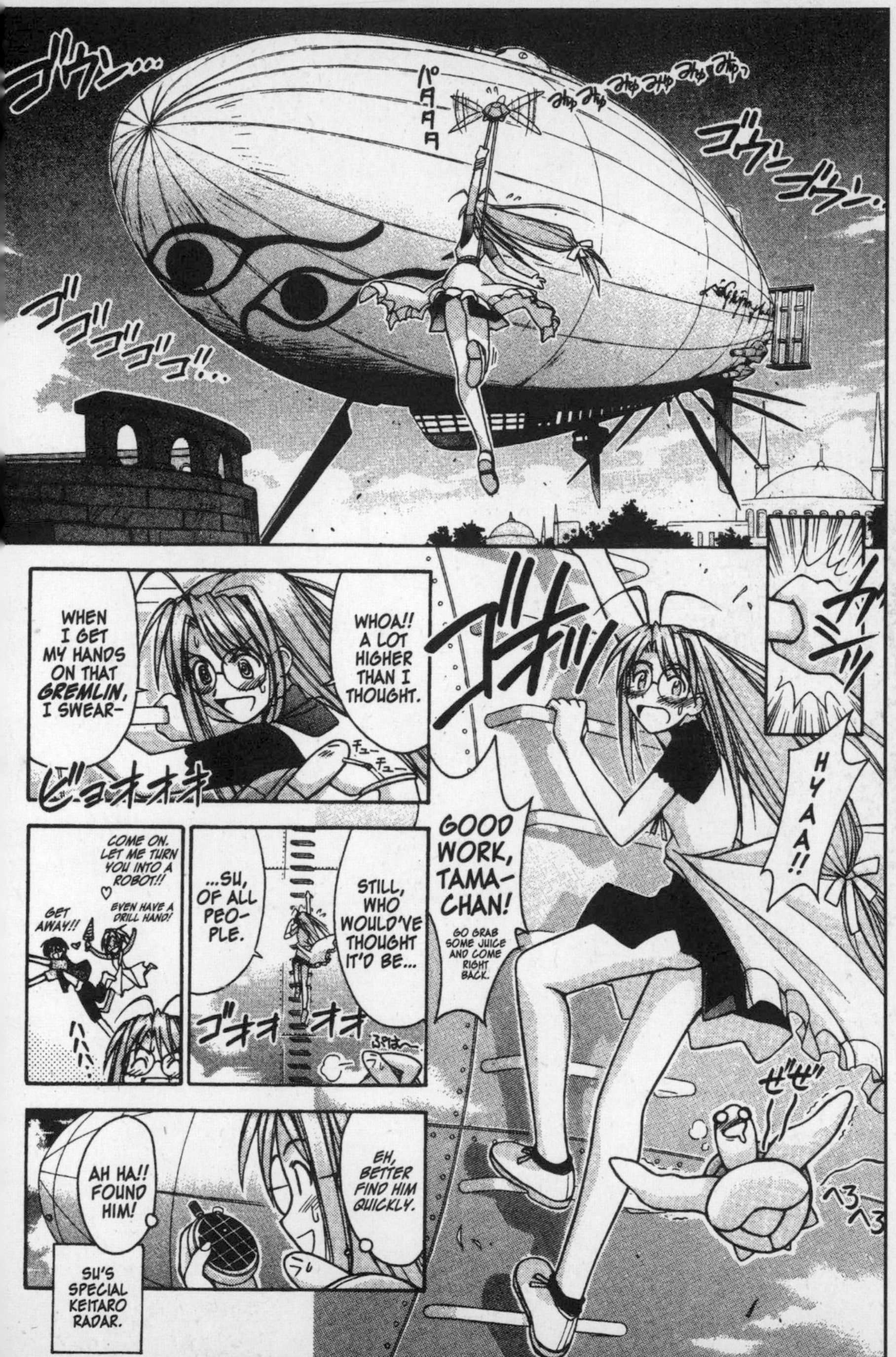
ゴウン…
パタタタ
ゴウンゴウン…
ゴゴゴゴゴ!!…
HYAA!!
GOOD WORK, TAMA-CHAN!
GO GRAB SOME JUICE AND COME RIGHT BACK.
WHOA!! A LOT HIGHER THAN I THOUGHT.
WHEN I GET MY HANDS ON THAT GREMLIN, I SWEAR-
STILL, WHO WOULD'VE THOUGHT IT'D BE...
...SU, OF ALL PEOPLE.
COME ON. LET ME TURN YOU INTO A ROBOT!! ♥
EVEN HAVE A DRILL HAND!
GET AWAY!!
EH, BETTER FIND HIM QUICKLY.
AH HA!! FOUND HIM!
SU'S SPECIAL KEITARO RADAR.

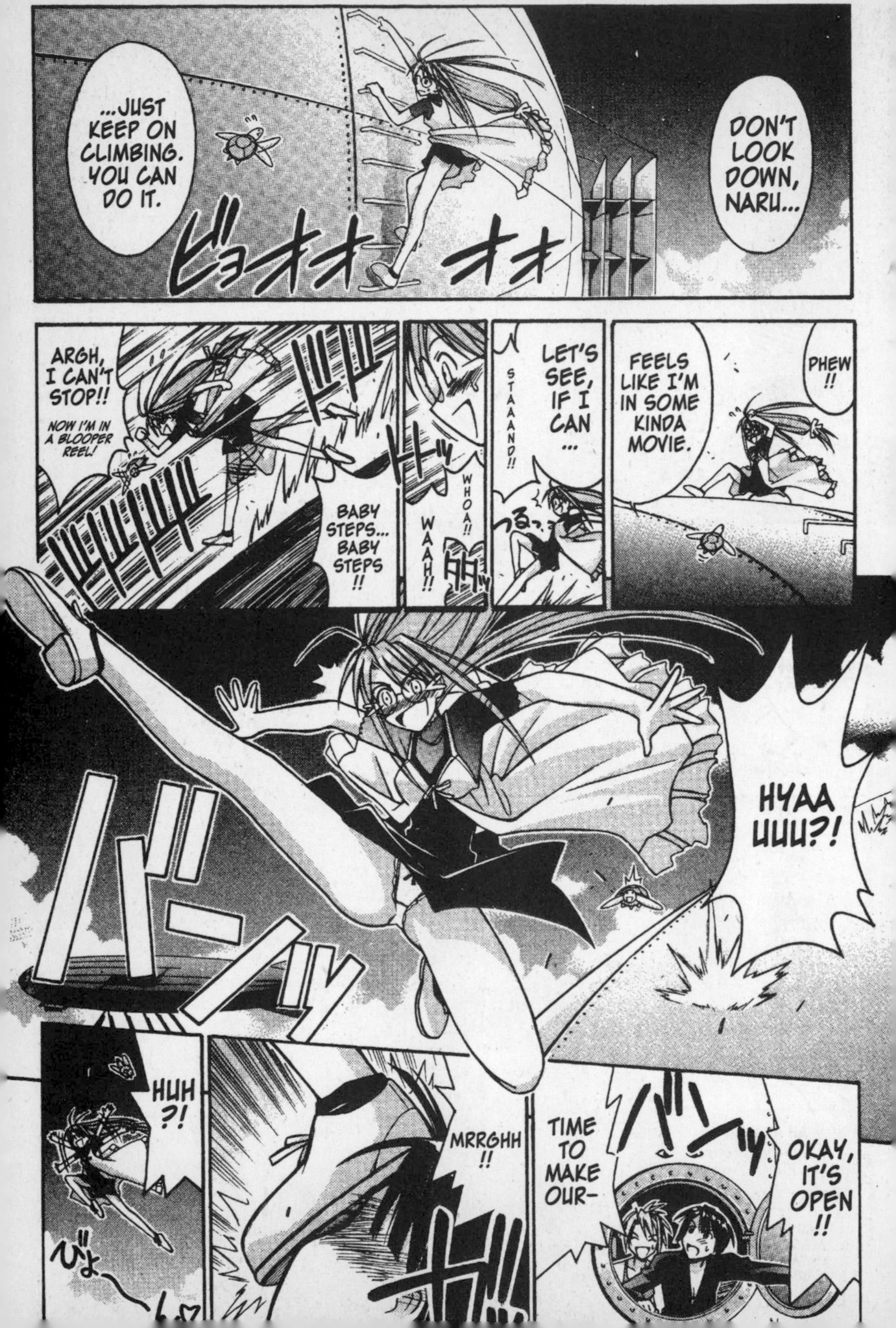
DON'T LOOK DOWN, NARU...
...JUST KEEP ON CLIMBING. YOU CAN DO IT.
ビョオオ オオ
PHEW!!
FEELS LIKE I'M IN SOME KINDA MOVIE.
LET'S SEE, IF I CAN ...
STAAAAND!!
つるっ
WHOA!!
WAAAH!!
BABY STEPS... BABY STEPS!!
ARGH, I CAN'T STOP!!
NOW I'M IN A BLOOPER REEL!
HYAA UUU?!
OKAY, IT'S OPEN!!
TIME TO MAKE OUR-
MRRGHH!!
HUH?!
ぴょ〜ん

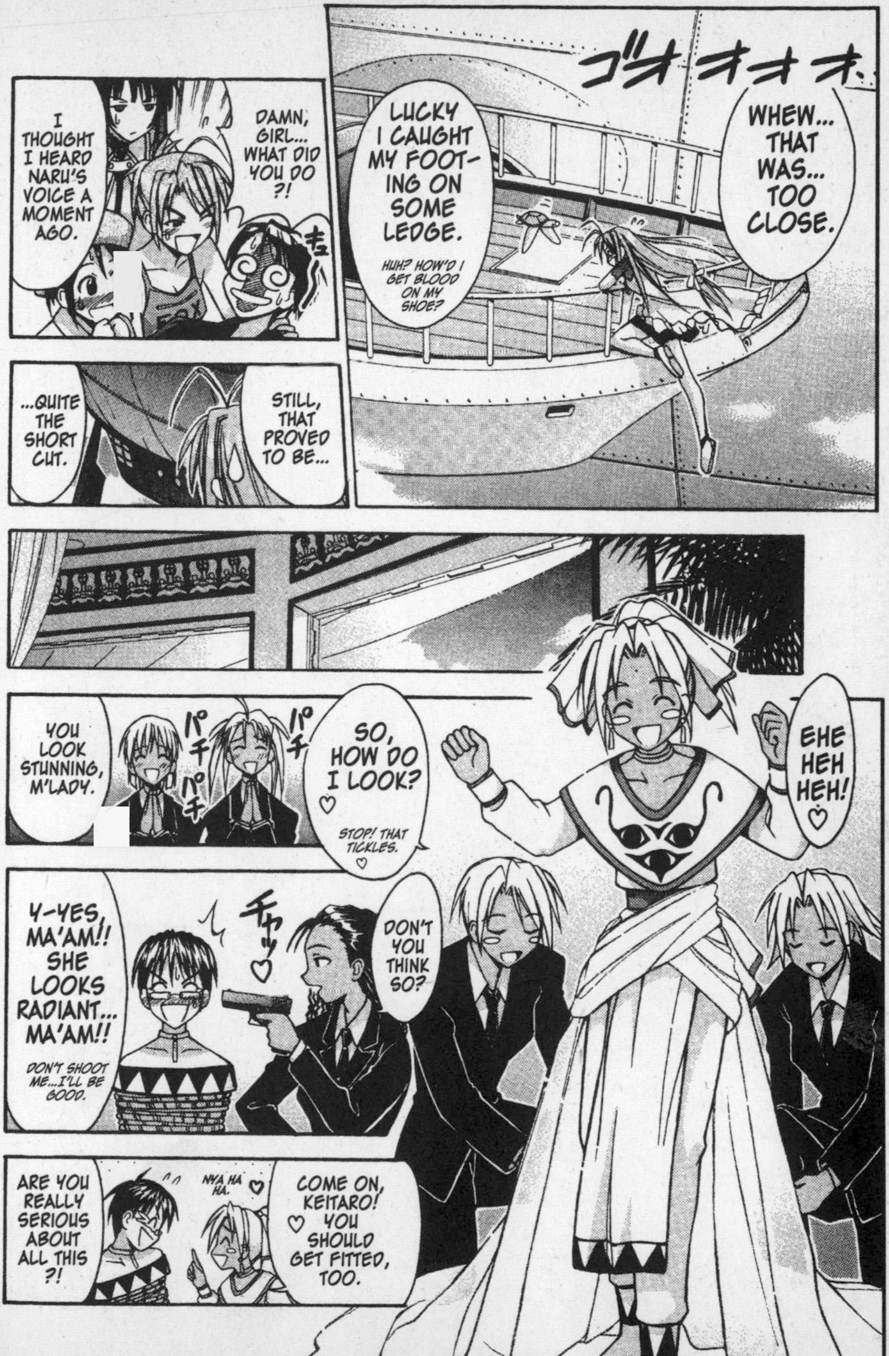
ゴオオオオ
WHEW... THAT WAS... TOO CLOSE.
LUCKY I CAUGHT MY FOOTING ON SOME LEDGE.
HUH? HOW'D I GET BLOOD ON MY SHOE?
DAMN, GIRL... WHAT DID YOU DO ?!
キュ
I THOUGHT I HEARD NARU'S VOICE A MOMENT AGO.
STILL, THAT PROVED TO BE...
...QUITE THE SHORT CUT.
EHE HEH HEH! ♡
SO, HOW DO I LOOK? ♡
STOP! THAT TICKLES. ♡
パチ
パチパチ
YOU LOOK STUNNING, M'LADY.
DON'T YOU THINK SO?
チャッ ♡
Y-YES, MA'AM!! SHE LOOKS RADIANT... MA'AM!!
DON'T SHOOT ME...I'LL BE GOOD.
COME ON, KEITARO! ♡ YOU SHOULD GET FITTED, TOO.
NYA HA HA. ♡
ARE YOU REALLY SERIOUS ABOUT ALL THIS ?!

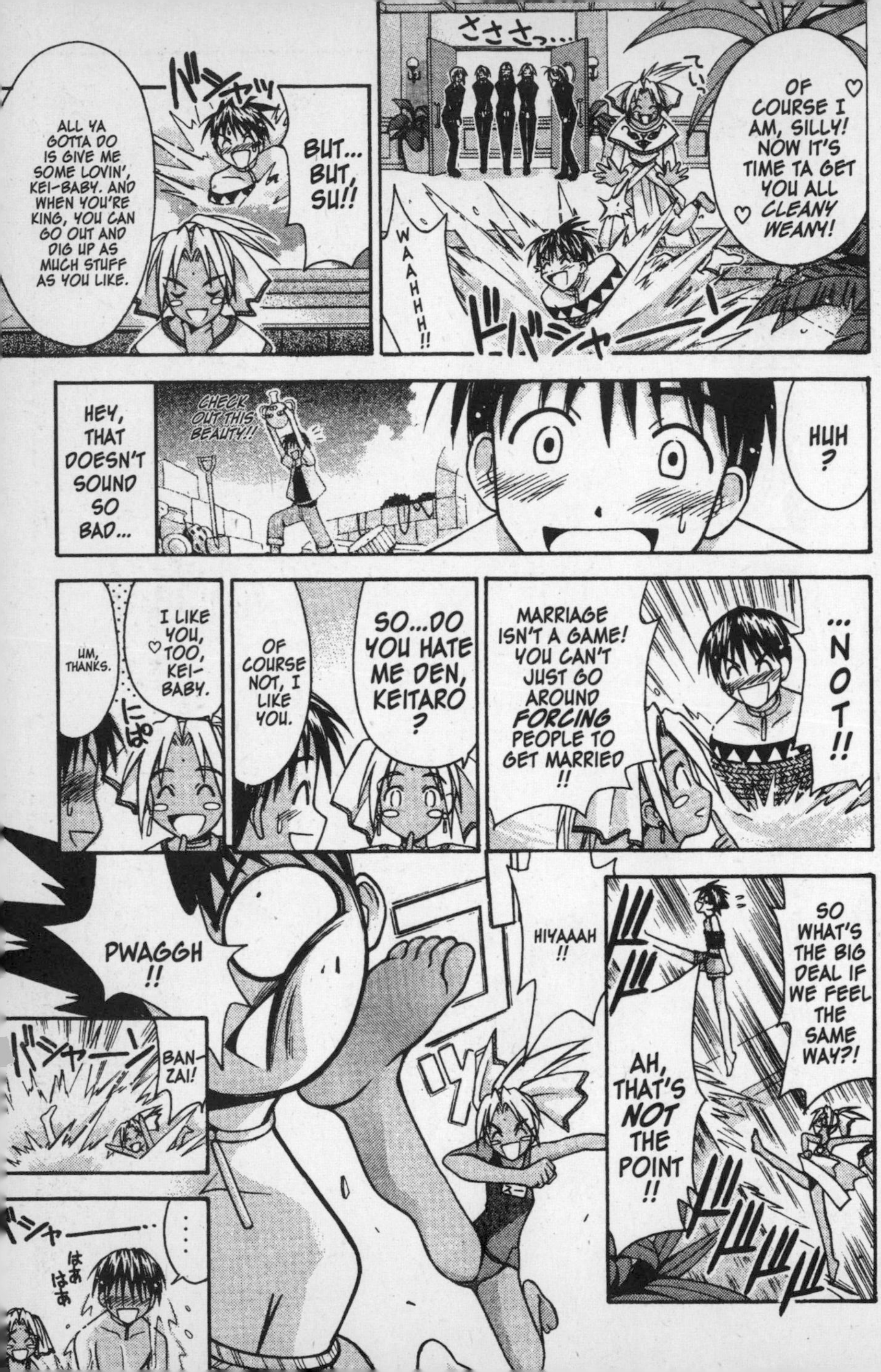
ささささっ…
てぃっ
OF COURSE I AM, SILLY! NOW IT'S TIME TA GET YOU ALL *CLEANY WEANY!*
WAAHHH!!
ドバシャ
バシャッ
BUT... BUT, SU!!
ALL YA GOTTA DO IS GIVE ME SOME LOVIN', KEI-BABY. AND WHEN YOU'RE KING, YOU CAN GO OUT AND DIG UP AS MUCH STUFF AS YOU LIKE.
HUH?
CHECK OUT THIS BEAUTY!!
HEY, THAT DOESN'T SOUND SO BAD...
...NOT!!
MARRIAGE ISN'T A GAME! YOU CAN'T JUST GO AROUND *FORCING* PEOPLE TO GET MARRIED!!
SO...DO YOU HATE ME DEN, KEITARO?
OF COURSE NOT, I LIKE YOU.
I LIKE YOU, TOO, KEI-BABY.
にぱ
UM, THANKS.
SO WHAT'S THE BIG DEAL IF WE FEEL THE SAME WAY?!
AH, THAT'S *NOT* THE POINT!!
HIYAAAH!!
PWAGGH!!
バシャーン
BAN-ZAI!
バシャー…
……
はあ はあ

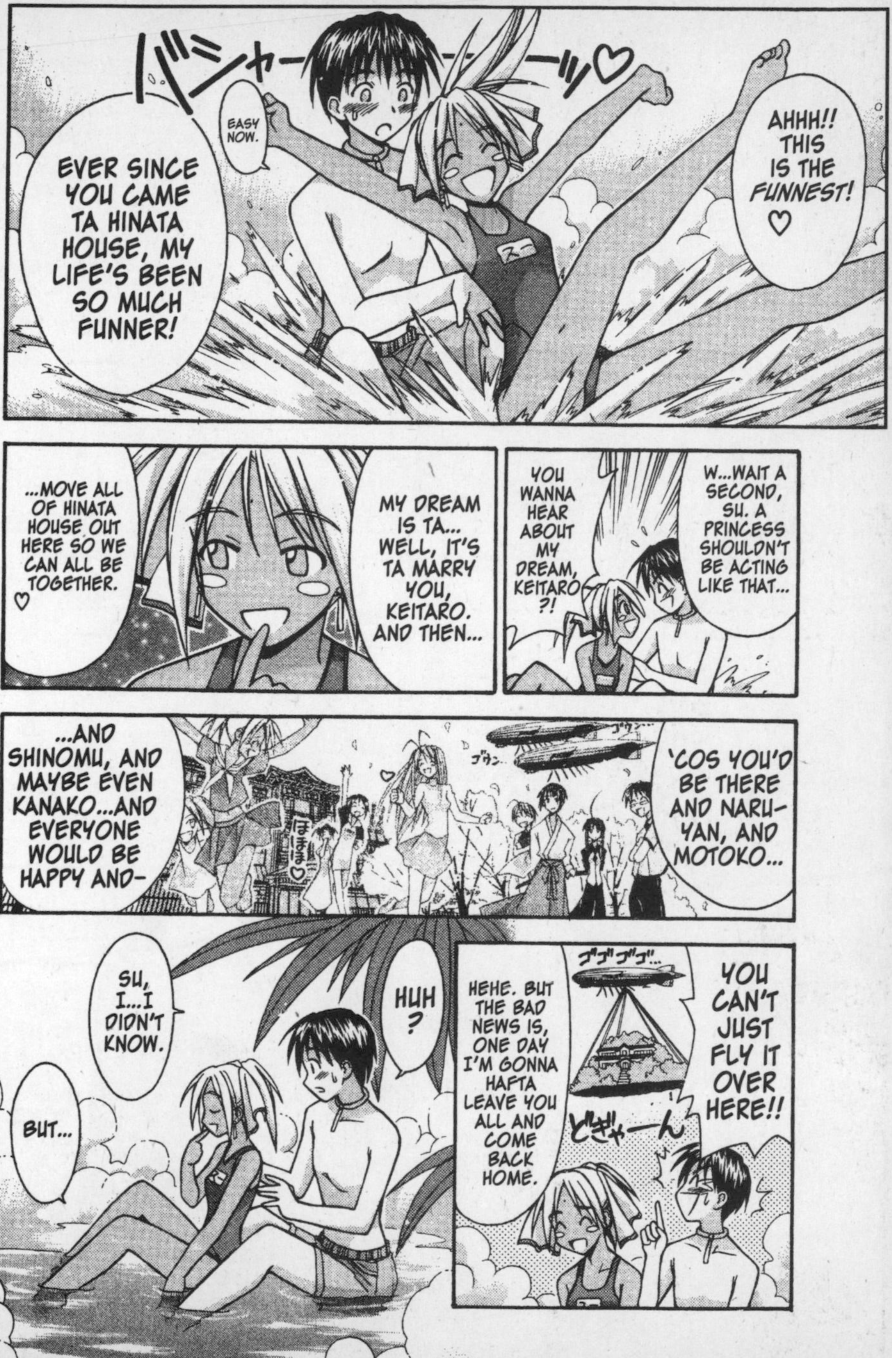
AHHH!! THIS IS THE FUNNEST! ♡
バシャーーーッ♡
EASY NOW.
EVER SINCE YOU CAME TA HINATA HOUSE, MY LIFE'S BEEN SO MUCH FUNNER!
W...WAIT A SECOND, SU. A PRINCESS SHOULDN'T BE ACTING LIKE THAT...
YOU WANNA HEAR ABOUT MY DREAM, KEITARO?!
MY DREAM IS TA... WELL, IT'S TA MARRY YOU, KEITARO. AND THEN...
...MOVE ALL OF HINATA HOUSE OUT HERE SO WE CAN ALL BE TOGETHER. ♡
'COS YOU'D BE THERE AND NARU-YAN, AND MOTOKO...
ゴウン…
ゴウン…
ほわほわ♡
...AND SHINOMU, AND MAYBE EVEN KANAKO...AND EVERYONE WOULD BE HAPPY AND-
YOU CAN'T JUST FLY IT OVER HERE!!
ゴゴゴゴ…
HEHE. BUT THE BAD NEWS IS, ONE DAY I'M GONNA HAFTA LEAVE YOU ALL AND COME BACK HOME.
どぎゃーん
HUH?
SU, I...I DIDN'T KNOW.
BUT...

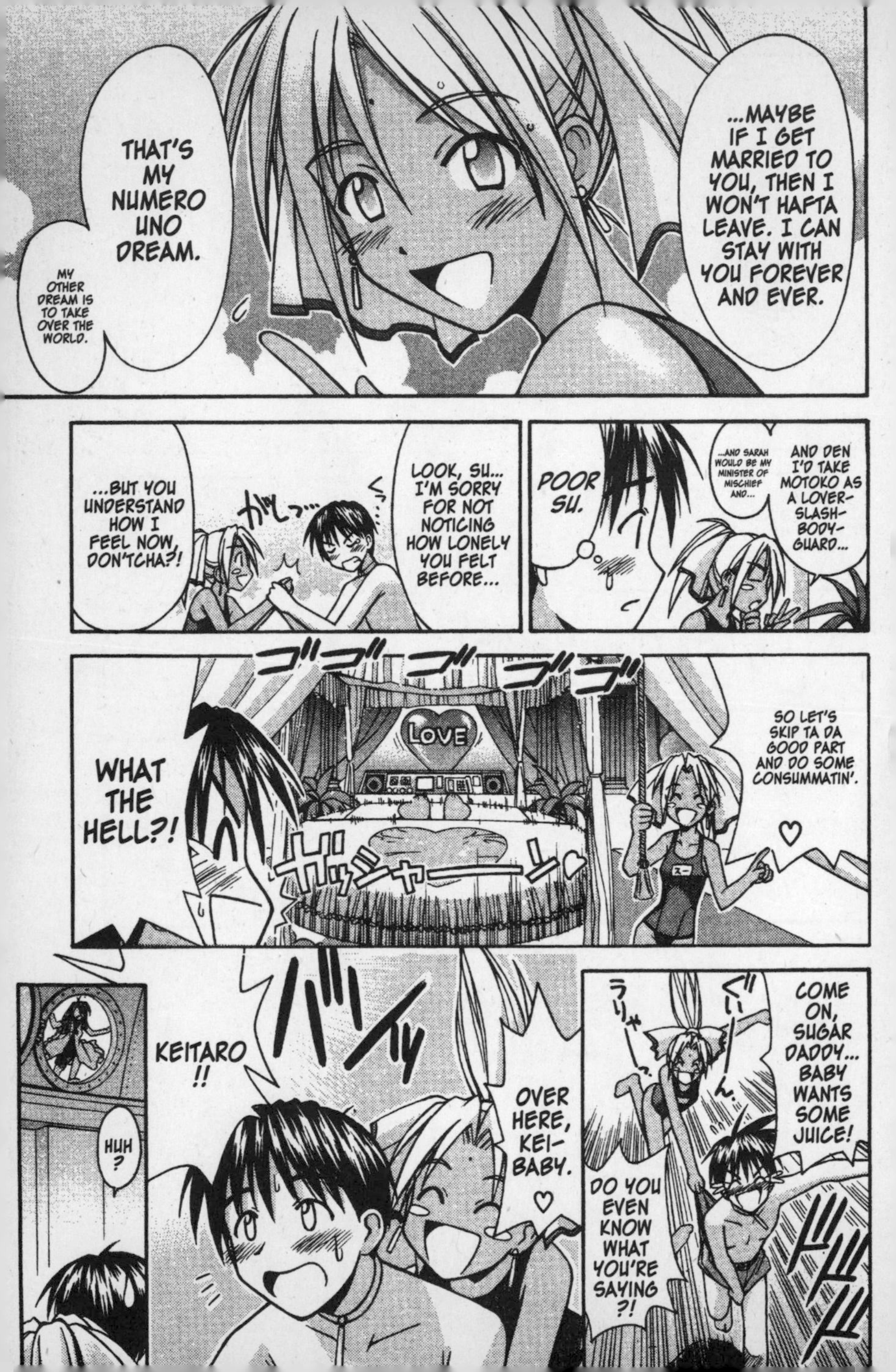
...MAYBE IF I GET MARRIED TO YOU, THEN I WON'T HAFTA LEAVE. I CAN STAY WITH YOU FOREVER AND EVER.
THAT'S MY NUMERO UNO DREAM.
MY OTHER DREAM IS TO TAKE OVER THE WORLD.
AND DEN I'D TAKE MOTOKO AS A LOVER-SLASH-BODY-GUARD...
...AND SARAH WOULD BE MY MINISTER OF MISCHIEF AND...
POOR SU.
LOOK, SU... I'M SORRY FOR NOT NOTICING HOW LONELY YOU FELT BEFORE...
...BUT YOU UNDERSTAND HOW I FEEL NOW, DON'TCHA?!
LOVE
SO LET'S SKIP TA DA GOOD PART AND DO SOME CONSUMMATIN'.
WHAT THE HELL?!
COME ON, SUGAR DADDY... BABY WANTS SOME JUICE!
DO YOU EVEN KNOW WHAT YOU'RE SAYING?!
OVER HERE, KEI-BABY.
KEITARO!!
HUH?

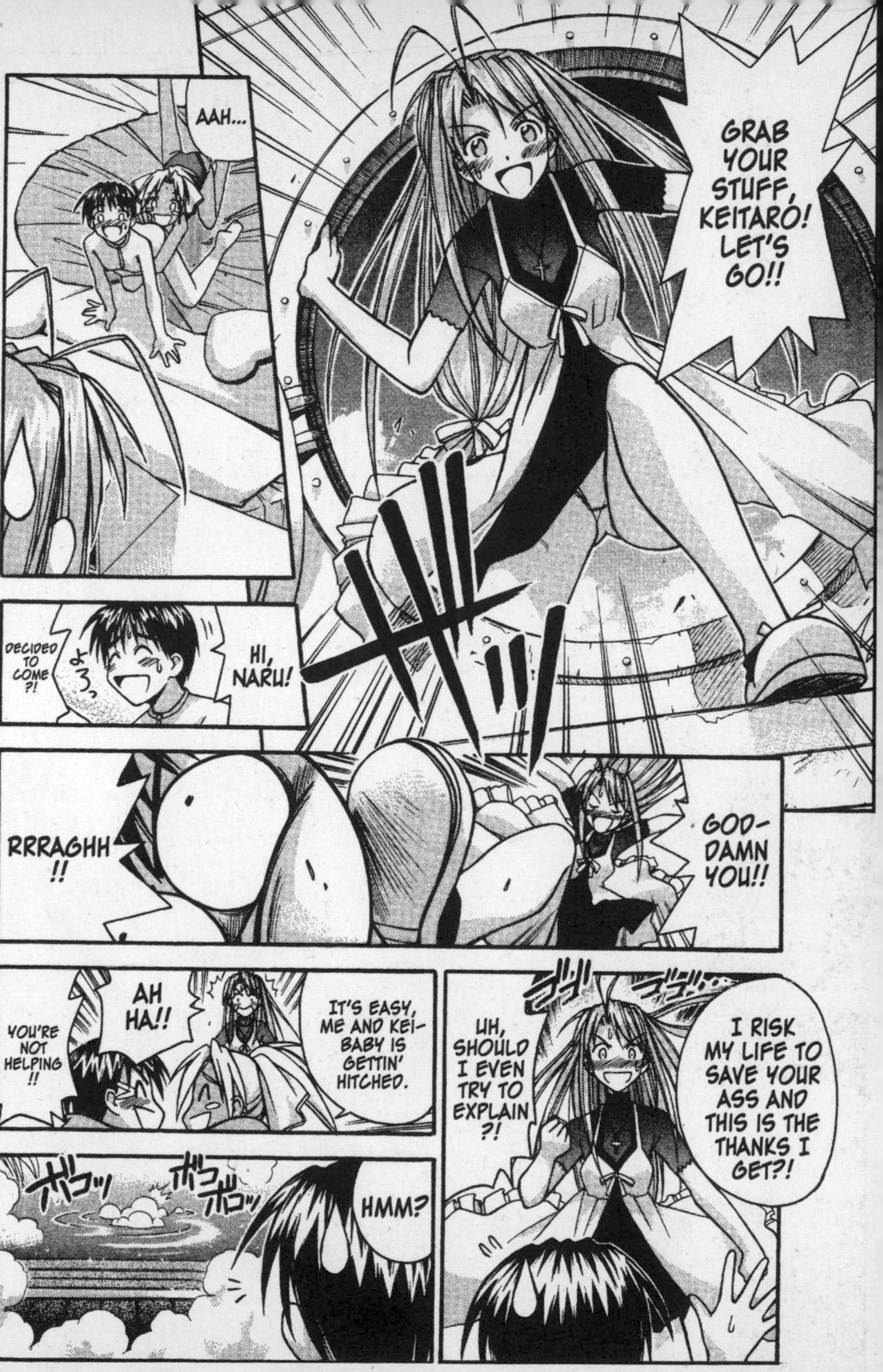
GRAB YOUR STUFF, KEITARO! LET'S GO!!
AAH...
HI, NARU!
よろっ
DECIDED TO COME ?!
GOD-DAMN YOU!!
RRRAGHH !!
I RISK MY LIFE TO SAVE YOUR ASS AND THIS IS THE THANKS I GET?!
UH, SHOULD I EVEN TRY TO EXPLAIN ?!
IT'S EASY, ME AND KEI-BABY IS GETTIN' HITCHED.
AH HA!!
YOU'RE NOT HELPING !!
HMM?

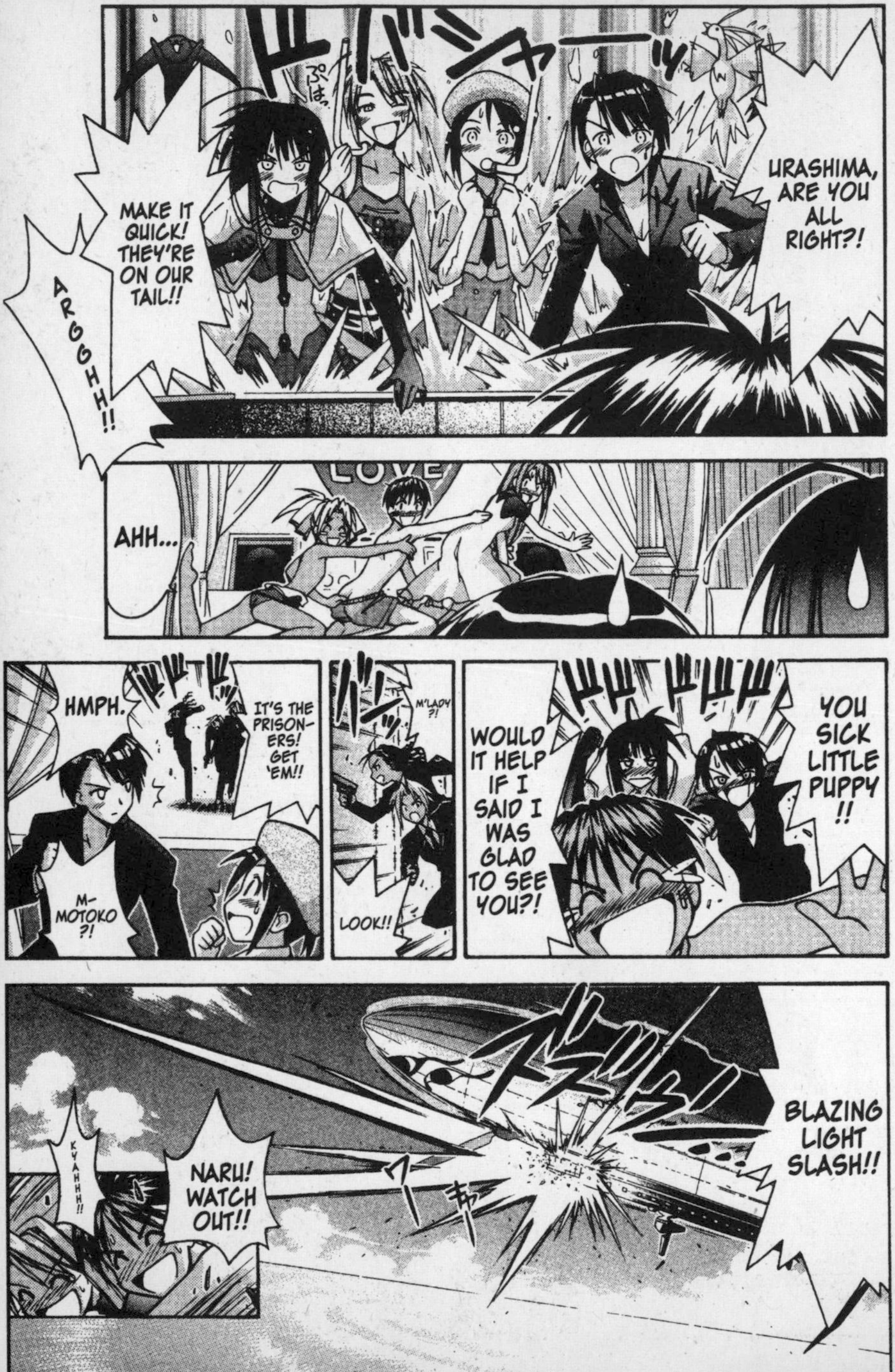

ぷはっ
URASHIMA, ARE YOU ALL RIGHT?!
MAKE IT QUICK! THEY'RE ON OUR TAIL!!
ARGGHH!!
AHH...
YOU SICK LITTLE PUPPY!!
WOULD IT HELP IF I SAID I WAS GLAD TO SEE YOU?!
M'LADY?!
LOOK!!
IT'S THE PRISONERS! GET 'EM!!
HMPH.
M-MOTOKO?!
BLAZING LIGHT SLASH!!
NARU! WATCH OUT!!
KYAHHH!!

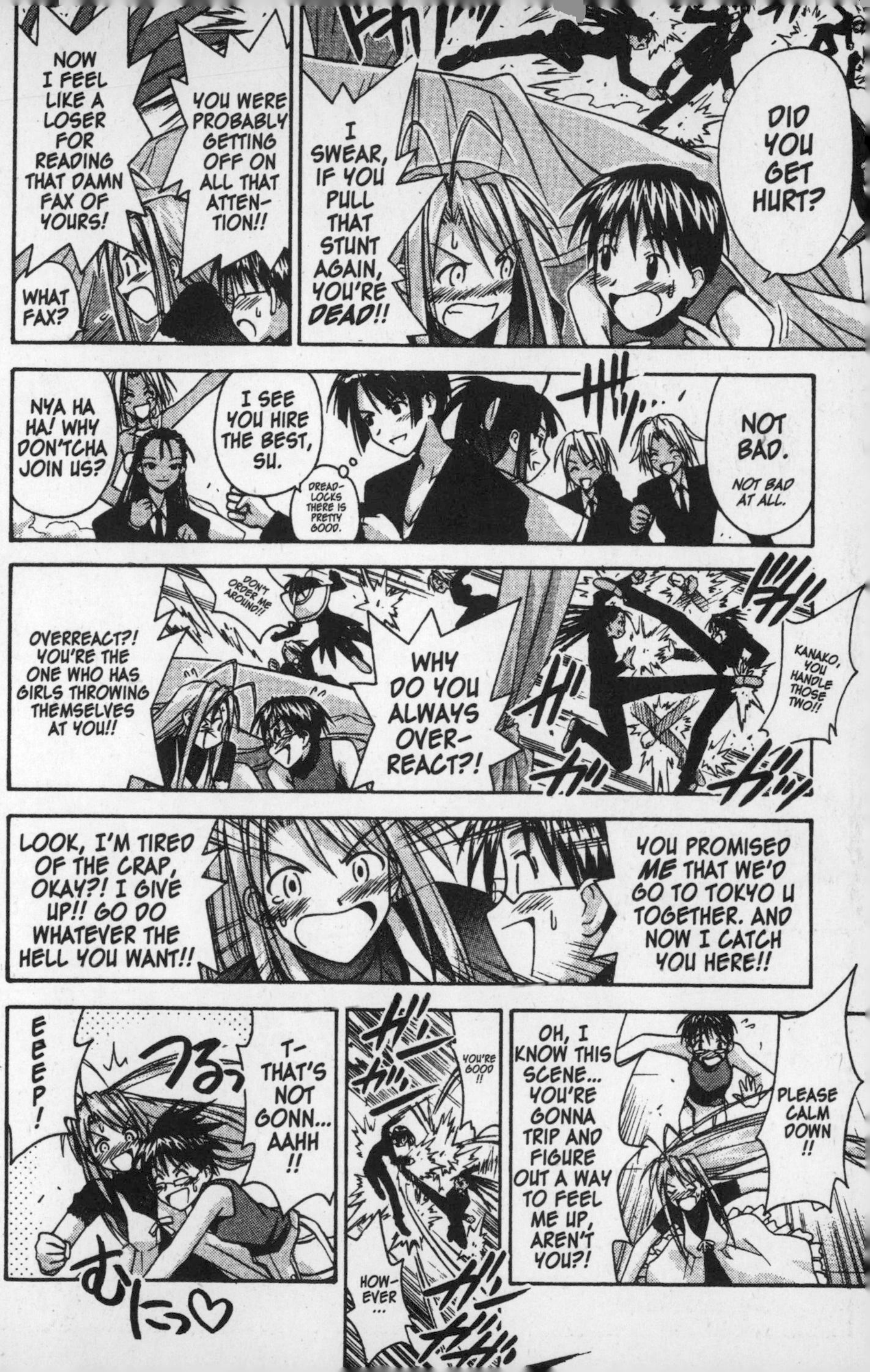
DID YOU GET HURT?
I SWEAR, IF YOU PULL THAT STUNT AGAIN, YOU'RE DEAD!!
YOU WERE PROBABLY GETTING OFF ON ALL THAT ATTENTION!!
NOW I FEEL LIKE A LOSER FOR READING THAT DAMN FAX OF YOURS!
WHAT FAX?
NOT BAD.
NOT BAD AT ALL.
I SEE YOU HIRE THE BEST, SU.
DREAD-LOCKS THERE IS PRETTY GOOD.
NYA HA HA! WHY DON'TCHA JOIN US?
KANAKO, YOU HANDLE THOSE TWO!!
WHY DO YOU ALWAYS OVER-REACT?!
DON'T ORDER ME AROUND!!
OVERREACT?! YOU'RE THE ONE WHO HAS GIRLS THROWING THEMSELVES AT YOU!!
YOU PROMISED ME THAT WE'D GO TO TOKYO U TOGETHER. AND NOW I CATCH YOU HERE!!
LOOK, I'M TIRED OF THE CRAP, OKAY?! I GIVE UP!! GO DO WHATEVER THE HELL YOU WANT!!
PLEASE CALM DOWN!!
OH, I KNOW THIS SCENE... YOU'RE GONNA TRIP AND FIGURE OUT A WAY TO FEEL ME UP, AREN'T YOU?!
YOU'RE GOOD!!
HOW-EVER...
T-THAT'S NOT GONN... AAHH!!
EEEP!
つるっ
むにっ♡

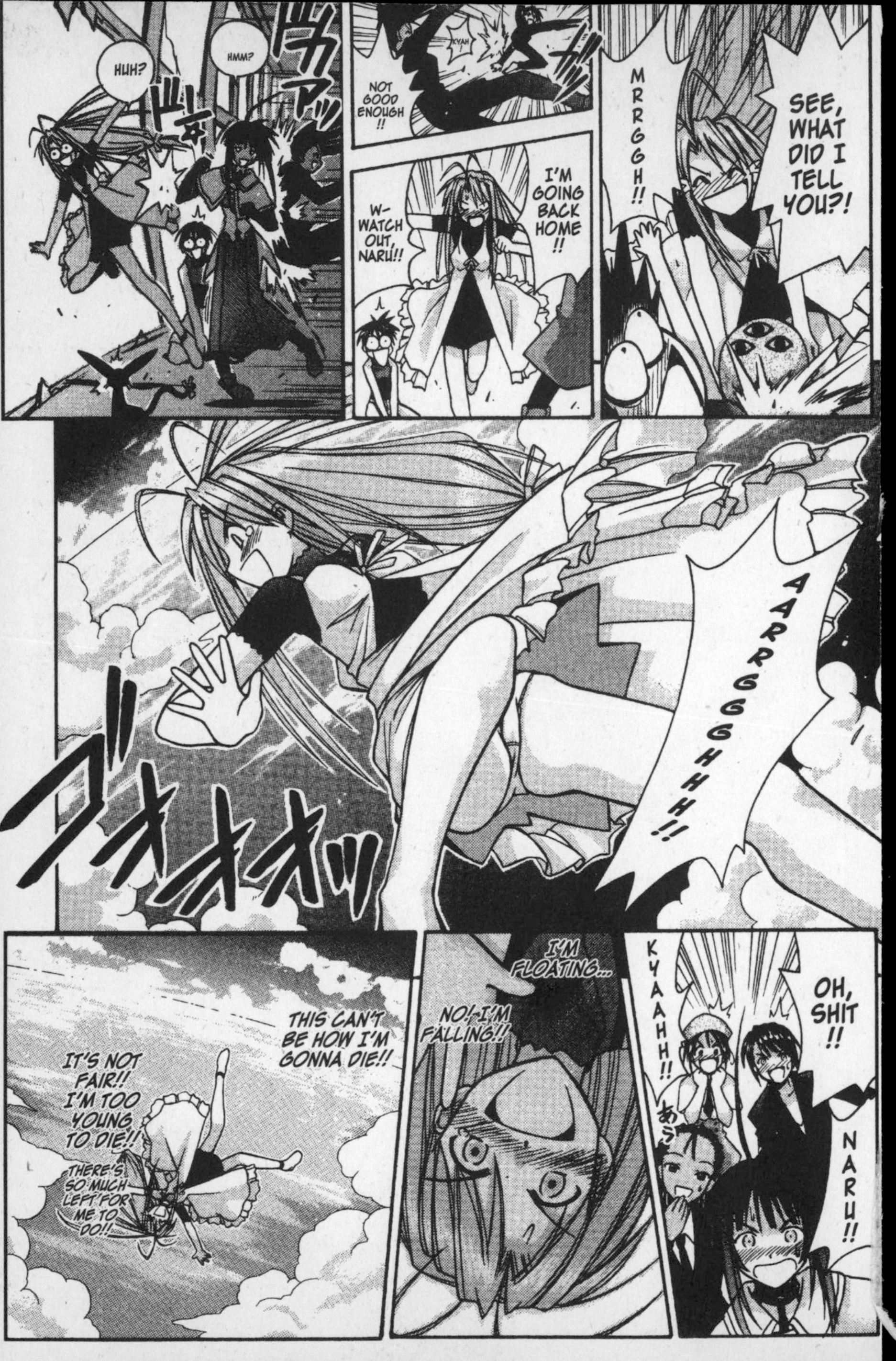
SEE, WHAT DID I TELL YOU?!
MRRGGH!!
KYAH!
NOT GOOD ENOUGH!!
I'M GOING BACK HOME!!
W-WATCH OUT, NARU!!
HMM?
HUH?
AARRGGGHHH!!
OH, SHIT!!
KYAAHH!!
NARU!!
I'M FLOATING...
NO! I'M FALLING!!
THIS CAN'T BE HOW I'M GONNA DIE!!
IT'S NOT FAIR!! I'M TOO YOUNG TO DIE!!
THERE'S SO MUCH LEFT FOR ME TO DO!!

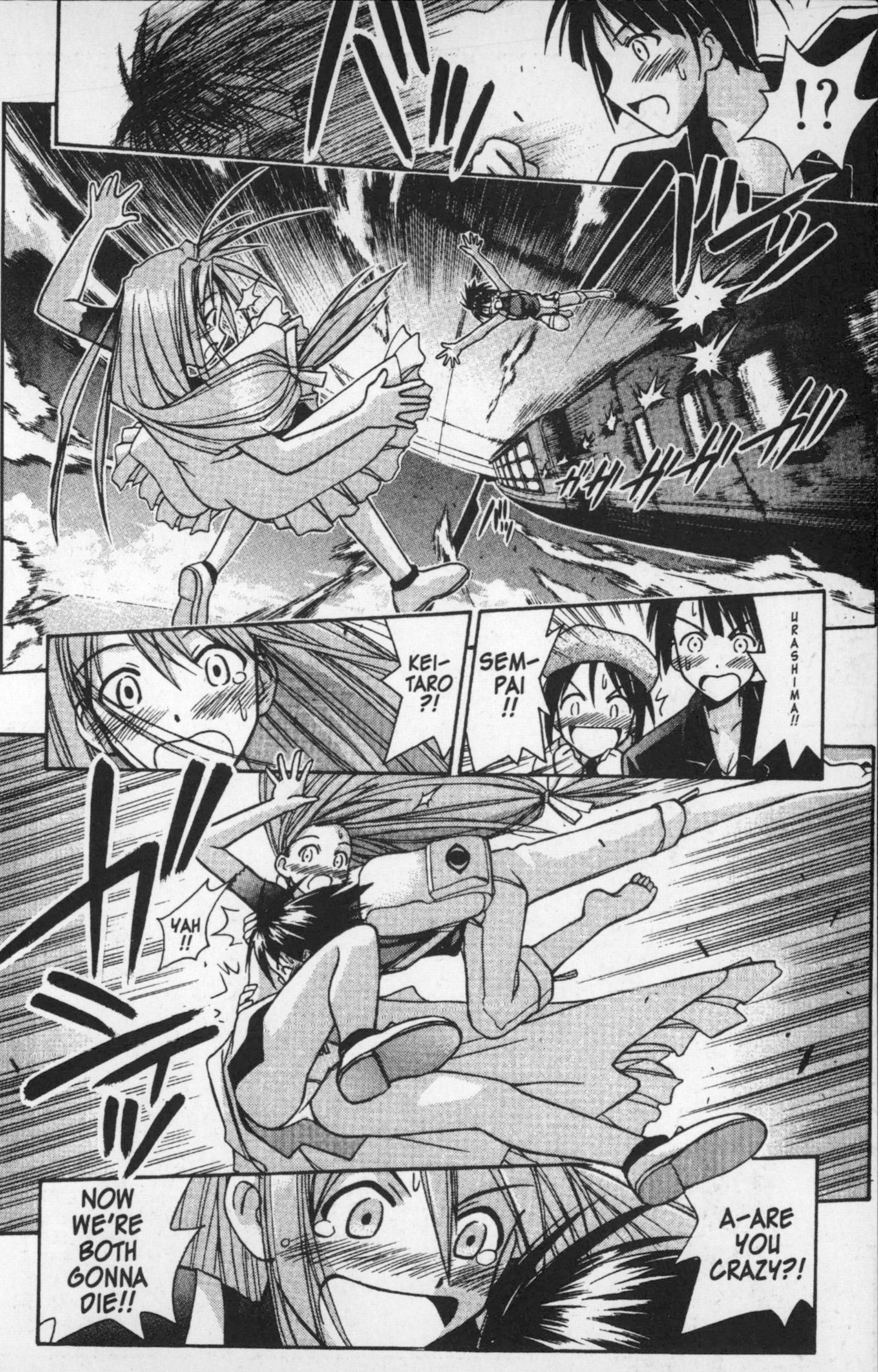
!?
URASHIMA!!
SEMPAI!!
KEI-TARO?!
YAH!!
A-ARE YOU CRAZY?!
NOW WE'RE BOTH GONNA DIE!!

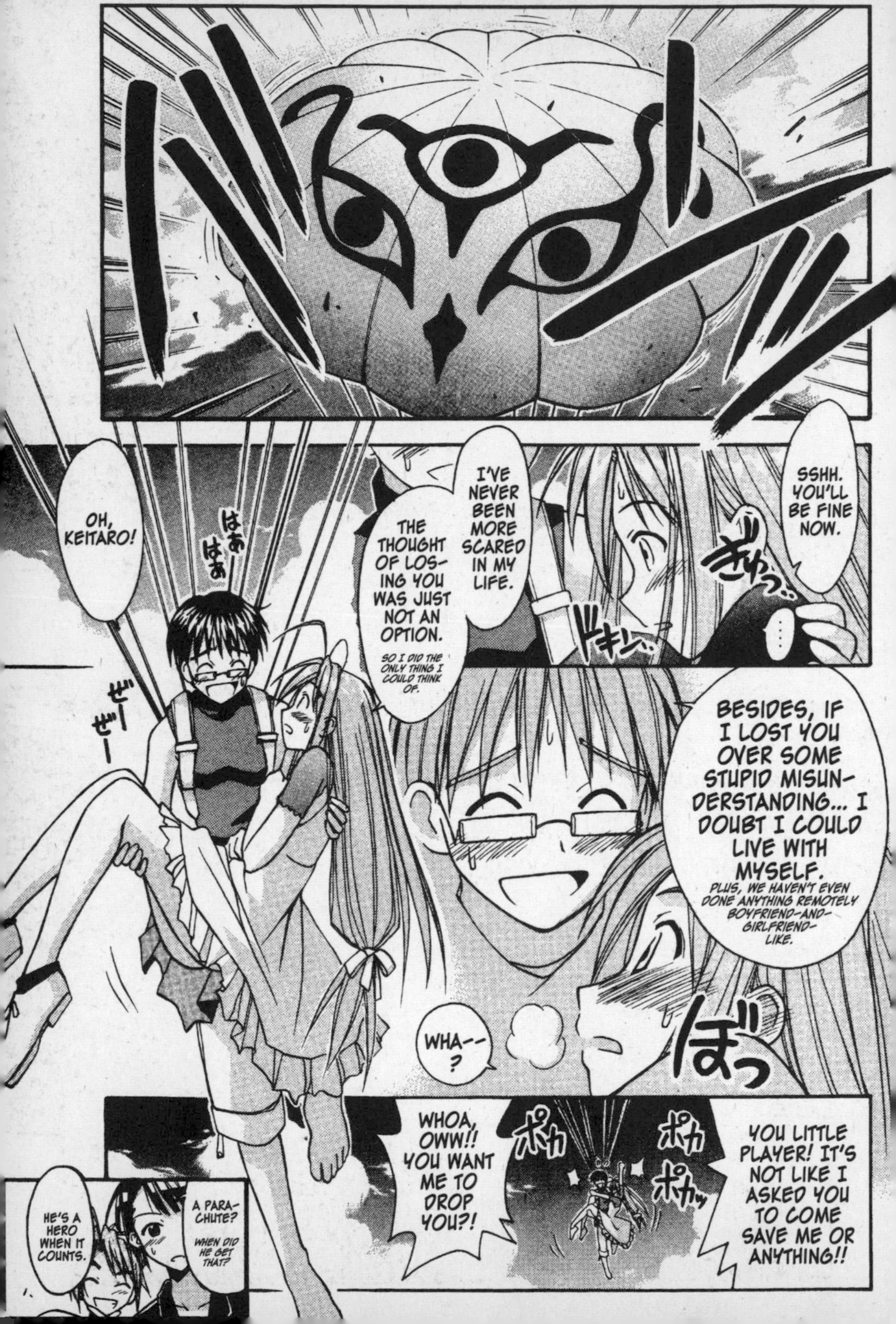
SSHH. YOU'LL BE FINE NOW.
ぎゅっ
ドキン
....
BESIDES, IF I LOST YOU OVER SOME STUPID MISUNDERSTANDING... I DOUBT I COULD LIVE WITH MYSELF.
PLUS, WE HAVEN'T EVEN DONE ANYTHING REMOTELY BOYFRIEND-AND-GIRLFRIEND-LIKE.
WHA--?
ぼっ
I'VE NEVER BEEN MORE SCARED IN MY LIFE.
THE THOUGHT OF LOSING YOU WAS JUST NOT AN OPTION.
SO I DID THE ONLY THING I COULD THINK OF.
OH, KEITARO!
はぁ はぁ
ぜー ぜー
YOU LITTLE PLAYER! IT'S NOT LIKE I ASKED YOU TO COME SAVE ME OR ANYTHING!!
ポカ
ポカッ
ポカ
WHOA, OWW!! YOU WANT ME TO DROP YOU?!
A PARA-CHUTE?
WHEN DID HE GET THAT?
HE'S A HERO WHEN IT COUNTS.

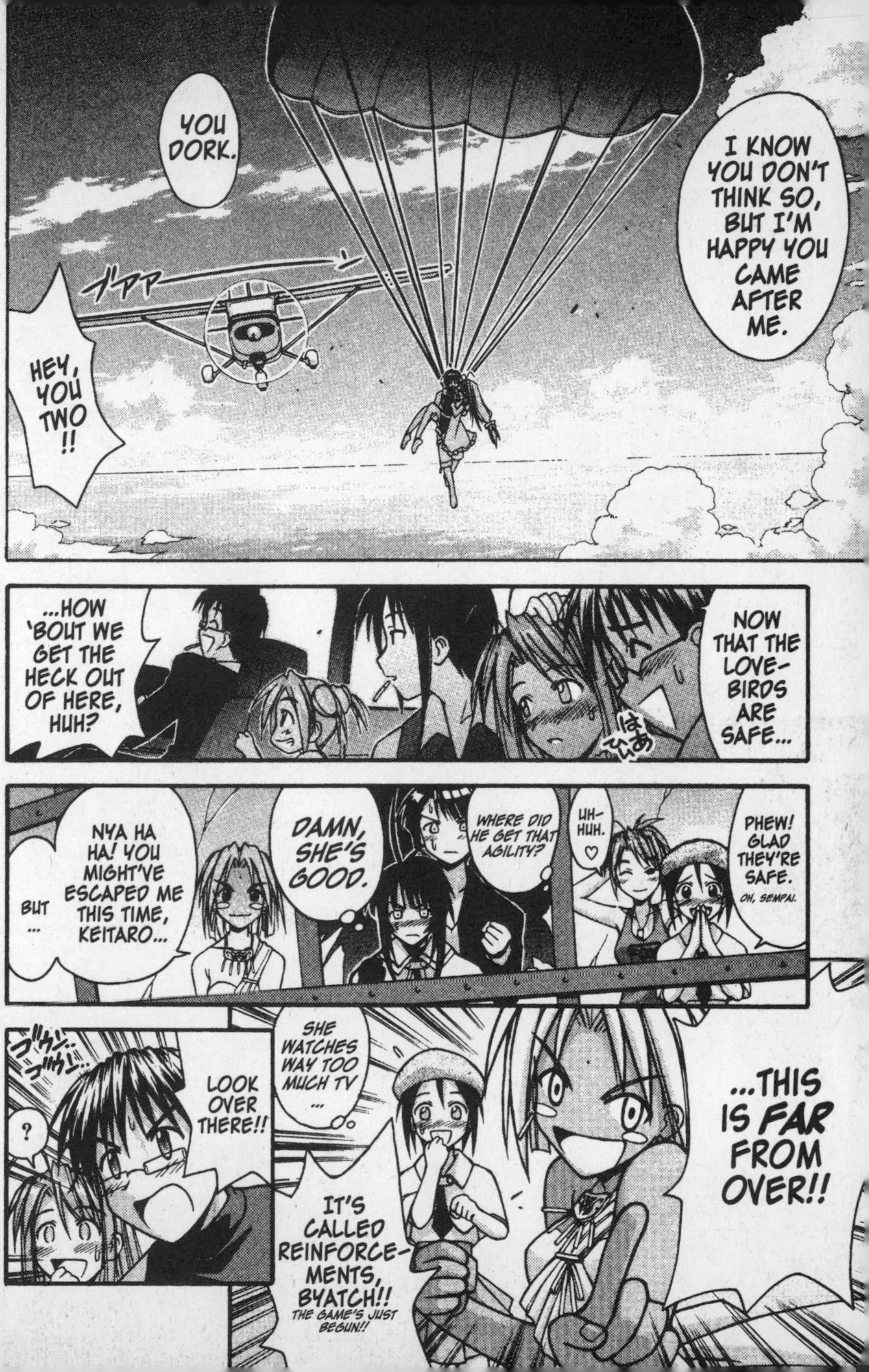
I KNOW YOU DON'T THINK SO, BUT I'M HAPPY YOU CAME AFTER ME.
YOU DORK.
HEY, YOU TWO!!
NOW THAT THE LOVE-BIRDS ARE SAFE...
はあ ひい
...HOW 'BOUT WE GET THE HECK OUT OF HERE, HUH?
PHEW! GLAD THEY'RE SAFE.
OH, SEMPAI.
UH-HUH. ♡
WHERE DID HE GET THAT AGILITY?
DAMN, SHE'S GOOD.
NYA HA HA! YOU MIGHT'VE ESCAPED ME THIS TIME, KEITARO...
BUT ...
...THIS IS *FAR* FROM OVER!!
SHE WATCHES WAY TOO MUCH TV ...
IT'S CALLED REINFORCEMENTS, BYATCH!!
THE GAME'S JUST BEGUN!!
LOOK OVER THERE!!
?

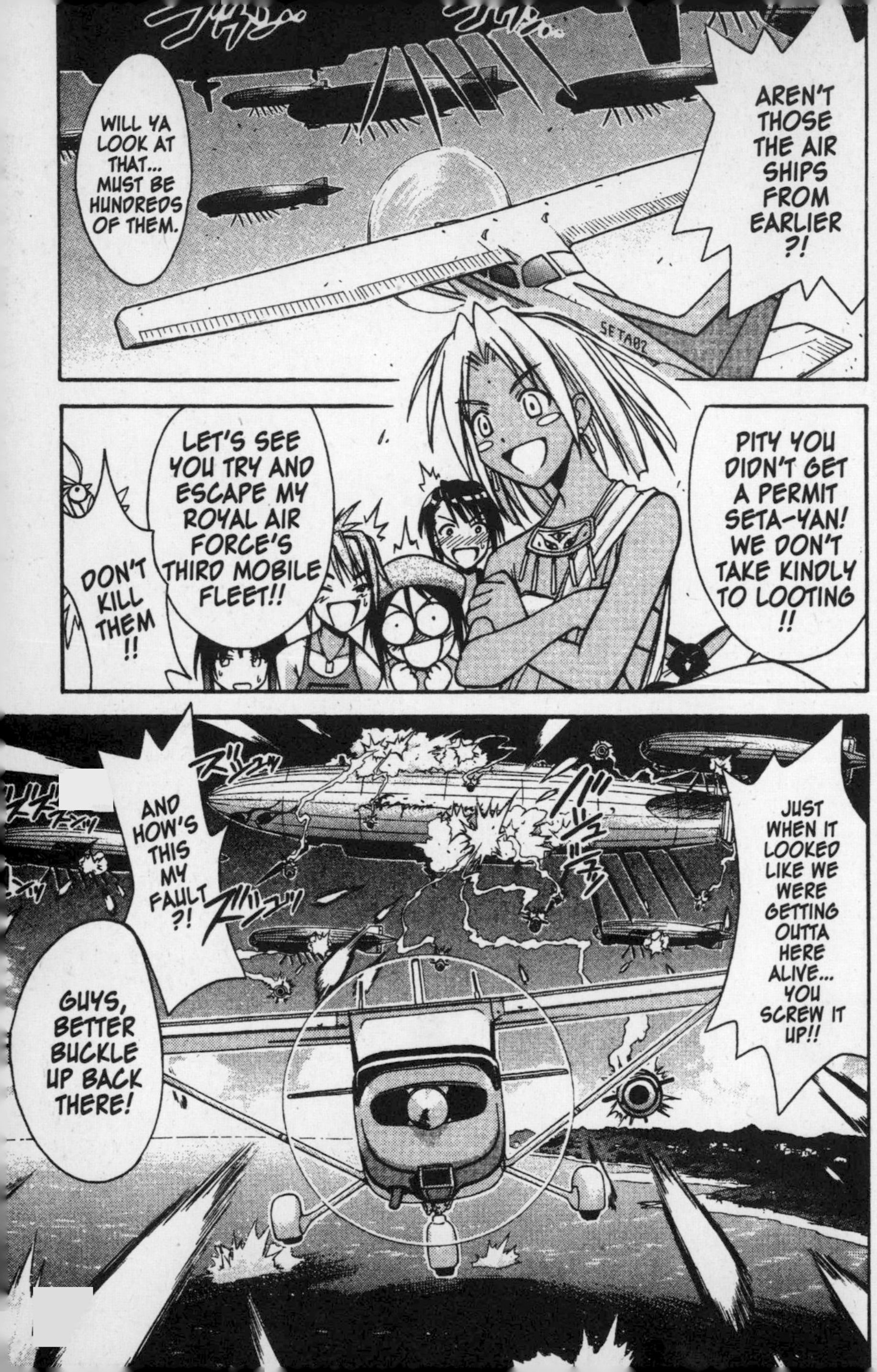

AREN'T THOSE THE AIR SHIPS FROM EARLIER ?!
WILL YA LOOK AT THAT... MUST BE HUNDREDS OF THEM.
PITY YOU DIDN'T GET A PERMIT SETA-YAN! WE DON'T TAKE KINDLY TO LOOTING !!
LET'S SEE YOU TRY AND ESCAPE MY ROYAL AIR FORCE'S THIRD MOBILE FLEET!!
DON'T KILL THEM !!
JUST WHEN IT LOOKED LIKE WE WERE GETTING OUTTA HERE ALIVE... YOU SCREW IT UP!!
AND HOW'S THIS MY FAULT ?!
GUYS, BETTER BUCKLE UP BACK THERE!

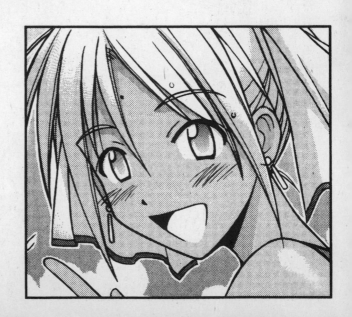

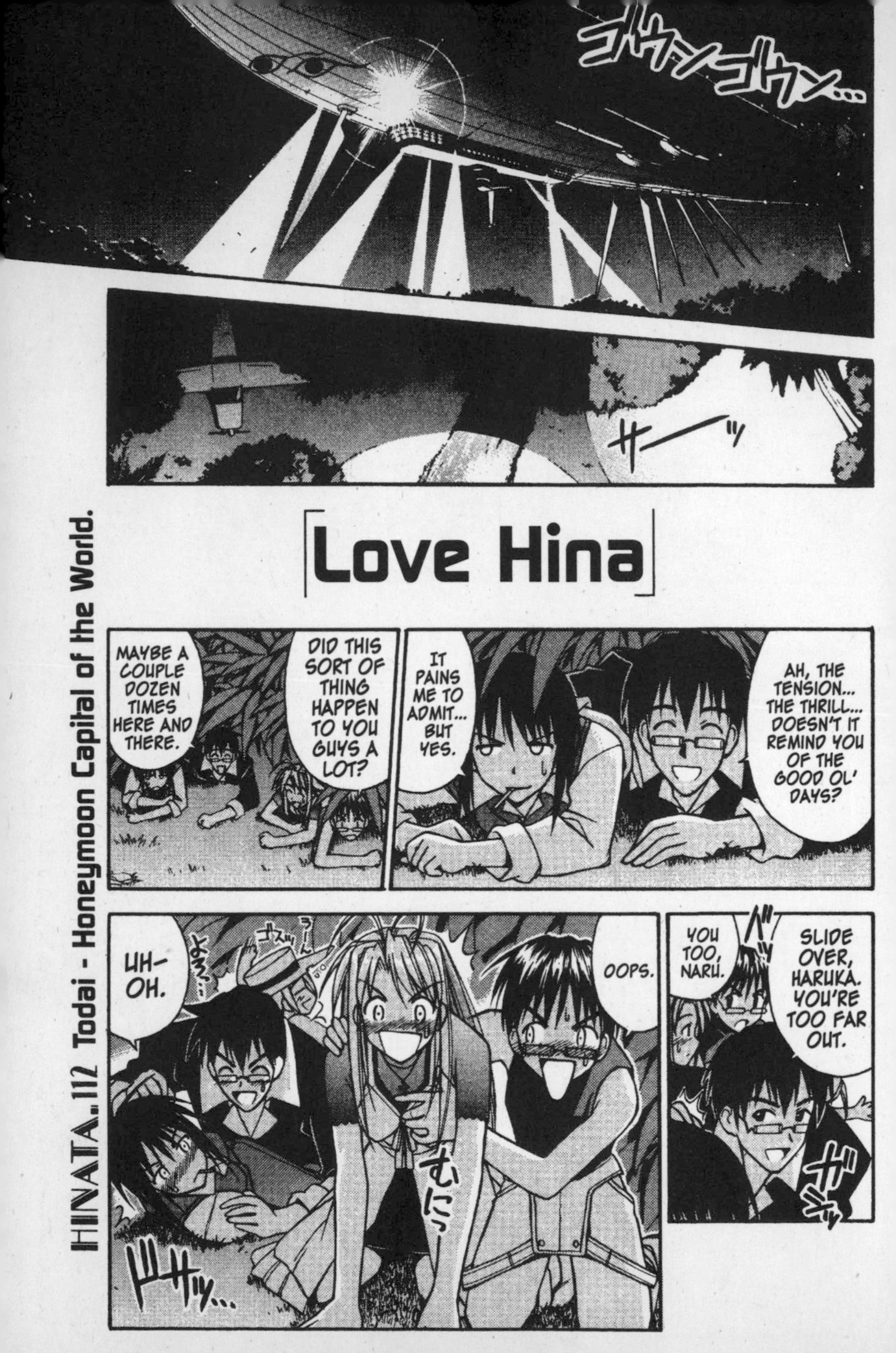
ゴウンゴウン…
サーッ
Love Hina
HINATA..112 Todai - Honeymoon Capital of the World.
AH, THE TENSION... THE THRILL... DOESN'T IT REMIND YOU OF THE GOOD OL' DAYS?
IT PAINS ME TO ADMIT... BUT YES.
DID THIS SORT OF THING HAPPEN TO YOU GUYS A LOT?
MAYBE A COUPLE DOZEN TIMES HERE AND THERE.
SLIDE OVER, HARUKA. YOU'RE TOO FAR OUT.
ベッ
YOU TOO, NARU.
ザッ
OOPS.
うーん
ゴスッ
UH-OH.
むにっ
ドサッ…

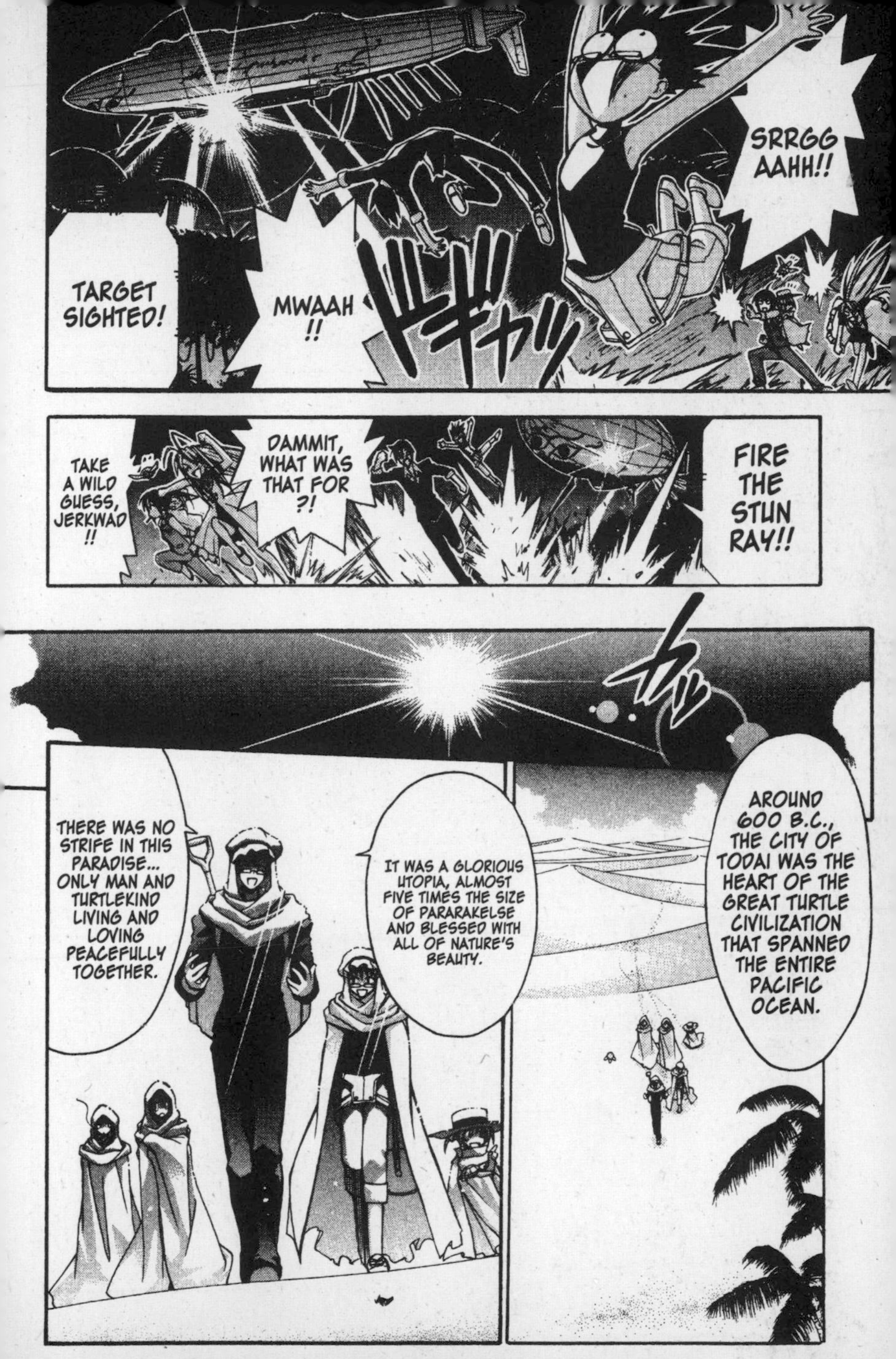
SRRGG AAHH!!
ドギャッ
MWAAH !!
TARGET SIGHTED!
FIRE THE STUN RAY!!
DAMMIT, WHAT WAS THAT FOR ?!
TAKE A WILD GUESS, JERKWAD !!
カッ
AROUND 600 B.C., THE CITY OF TODAI WAS THE HEART OF THE GREAT TURTLE CIVILIZATION THAT SPANNED THE ENTIRE PACIFIC OCEAN.
IT WAS A GLORIOUS UTOPIA, ALMOST FIVE TIMES THE SIZE OF PARARAKELSE AND BLESSED WITH ALL OF NATURE'S BEAUTY.
THERE WAS NO STRIFE IN THIS PARADISE... ONLY MAN AND TURTLEKIND LIVING AND LOVING PEACEFULLY TOGETHER.

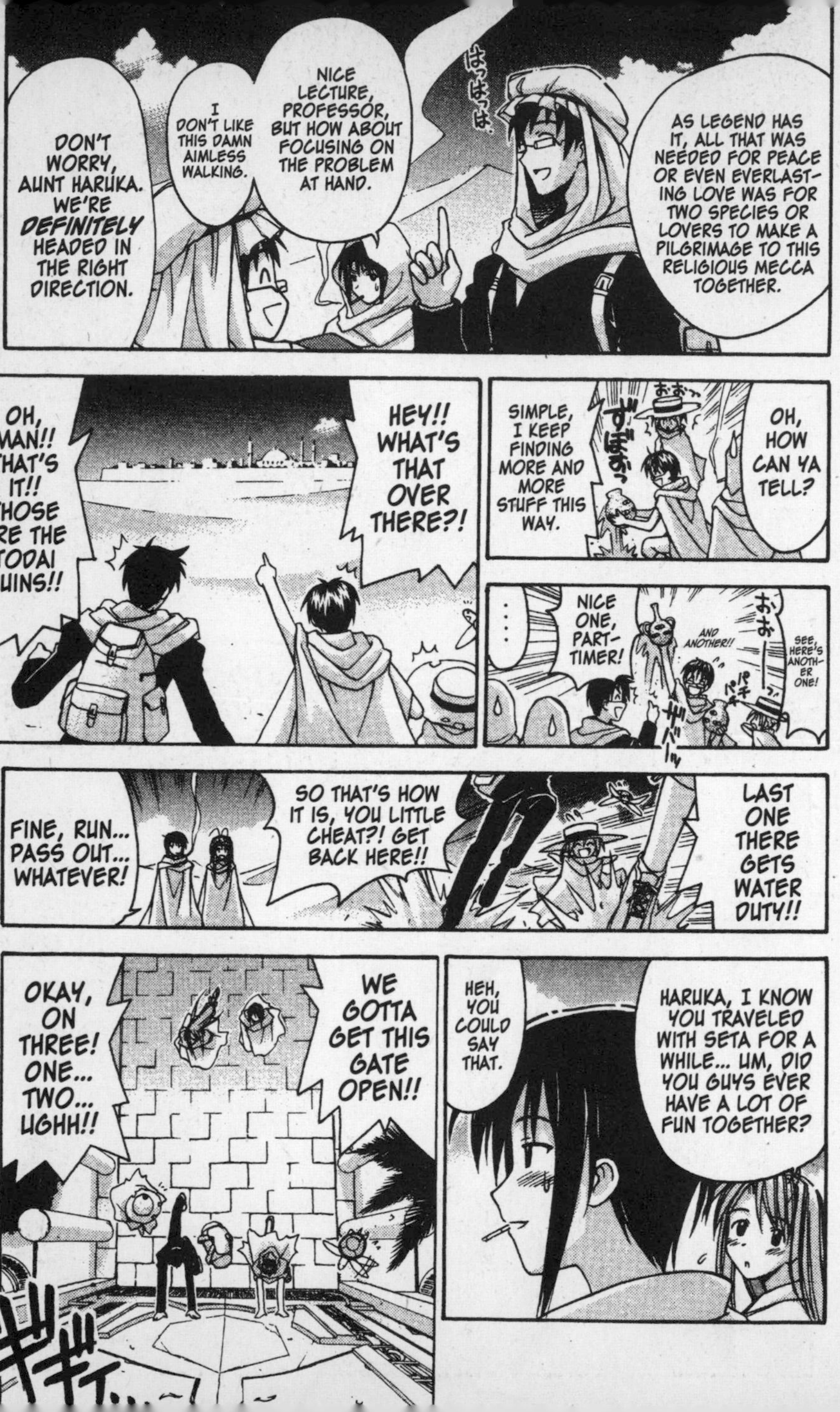

AS LEGEND HAS IT, ALL THAT WAS NEEDED FOR PEACE OR EVEN EVERLASTING LOVE WAS FOR TWO SPECIES OR LOVERS TO MAKE A PILGRIMAGE TO THIS RELIGIOUS MECCA TOGETHER.
はっはっは
NICE LECTURE, PROFESSOR, BUT HOW ABOUT FOCUSING ON THE PROBLEM AT HAND.
I DON'T LIKE THIS DAMN AIMLESS WALKING.
DON'T WORRY, AUNT HARUKA. WE'RE *DEFINITELY* HEADED IN THE RIGHT DIRECTION.
OH, HOW CAN YA TELL?
SIMPLE, I KEEP FINDING MORE AND MORE STUFF THIS WAY.
SEE, HERE'S ANOTHER ONE!
AND ANOTHER!!
NICE ONE, PART-TIMER!
....
HEY!! WHAT'S THAT OVER THERE?!
OH, MAN!! THAT'S IT!! THOSE ARE THE TODAI RUINS!!
LAST ONE THERE GETS WATER DUTY!!
SO THAT'S HOW IT IS, YOU LITTLE CHEAT?! GET BACK HERE!!
FINE, RUN... PASS OUT... WHATEVER!
HARUKA, I KNOW YOU TRAVELED WITH SETA FOR A WHILE... UM, DID YOU GUYS EVER HAVE A LOT OF FUN TOGETHER?
HEH, YOU COULD SAY THAT.
WE GOTTA GET THIS GATE OPEN!!
OKAY, ON THREE! ONE... TWO... UGHH!!

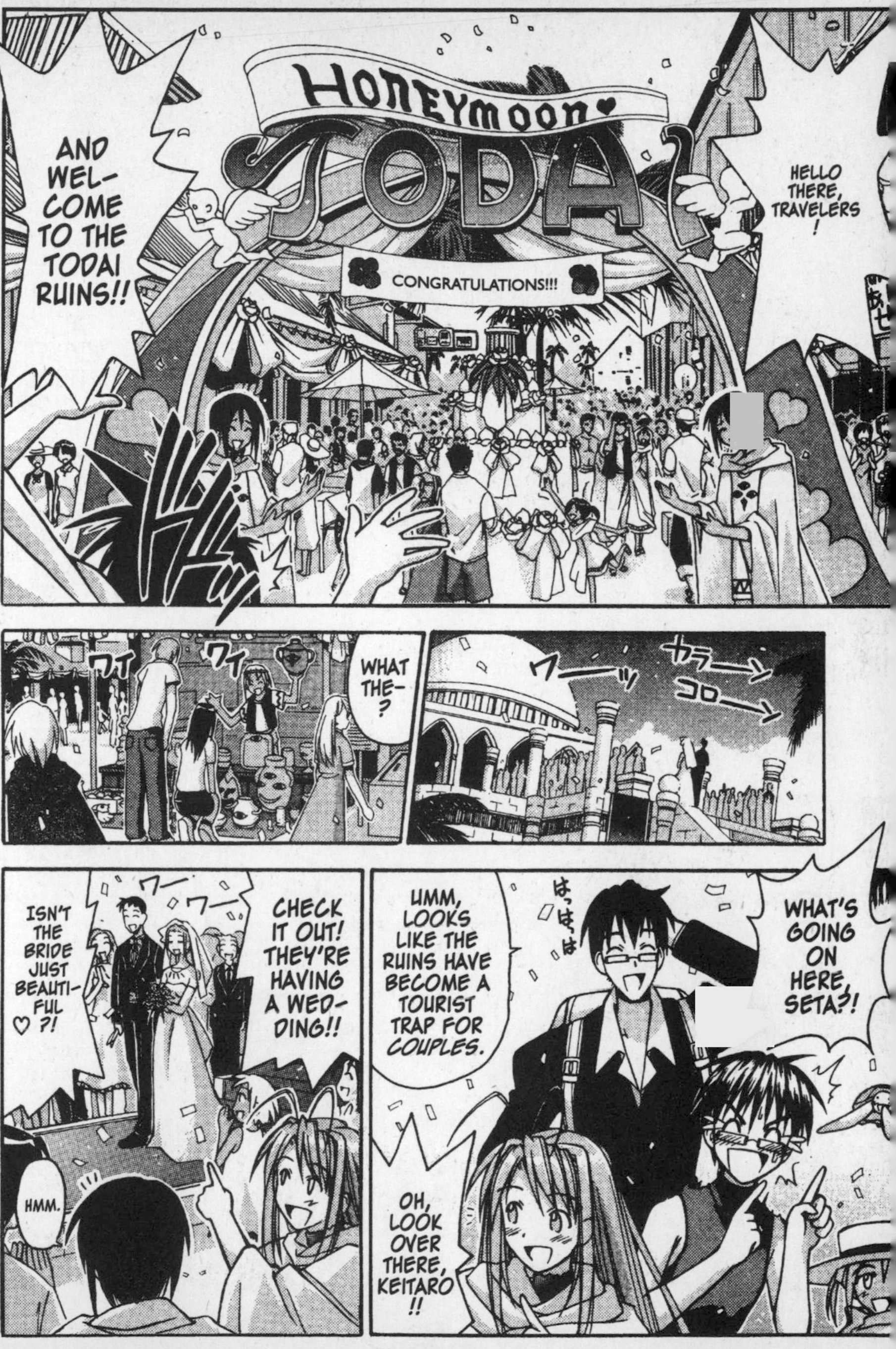
HONEYMOON ♥
TODAI
CONGRATULATIONS!!!
HELLO THERE, TRAVELERS!
AND WELCOME TO THE TODAI RUINS!!
ワーッ
カラーン
コローン
ワイ
ワイ
WHAT THE-?
WHAT'S GOING ON HERE, SETA?!
はっはっは
UMM, LOOKS LIKE THE RUINS HAVE BECOME A TOURIST TRAP FOR COUPLES.
OH, LOOK OVER THERE, KEITARO!!
CHECK IT OUT! THEY'RE HAVING A WEDDING!!
ワー
ワー
ISN'T THE BRIDE JUST BEAUTIFUL ♡?!
HMM.

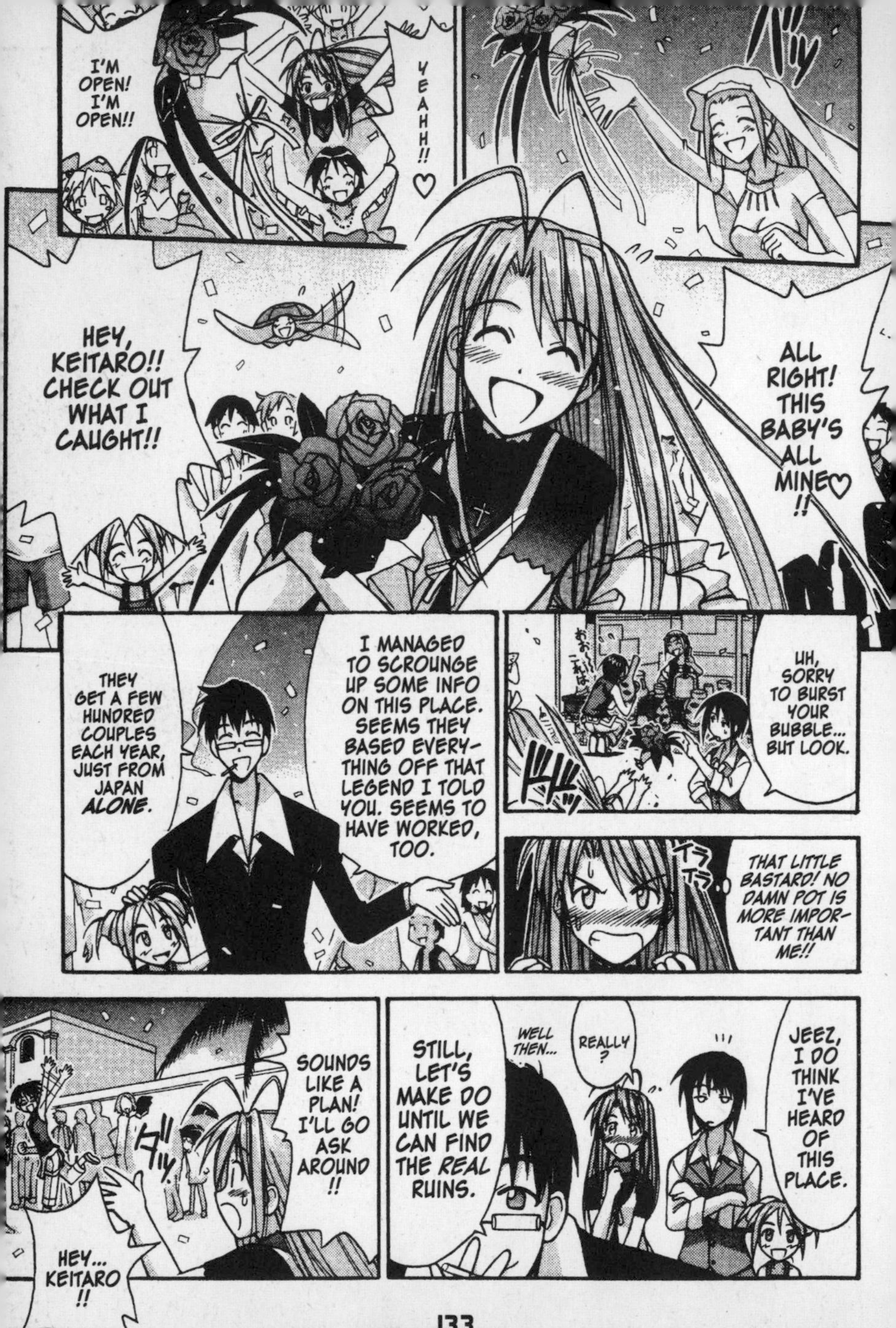
YEAHH!! ♥
I'M OPEN! I'M OPEN!!
ALL RIGHT! THIS BABY'S ALL MINE♥ !!
HEY, KEITARO!! CHECK OUT WHAT I CAUGHT!!
UH, SORRY TO BURST YOUR BUBBLE... BUT LOOK.
THAT LITTLE BASTARD! NO DAMN POT IS MORE IMPORTANT THAN ME!!
I MANAGED TO SCROUNGE UP SOME INFO ON THIS PLACE. SEEMS THEY BASED EVERYTHING OFF THAT LEGEND I TOLD YOU. SEEMS TO HAVE WORKED, TOO.
THEY GET A FEW HUNDRED COUPLES EACH YEAR, JUST FROM JAPAN *ALONE*.
JEEZ, I DO THINK I'VE HEARD OF THIS PLACE.
REALLY?
WELL THEN...
STILL, LET'S MAKE DO UNTIL WE CAN FIND THE *REAL* RUINS.
SOUNDS LIKE A PLAN! I'LL GO ASK AROUND!!
HEY... KEITARO!!

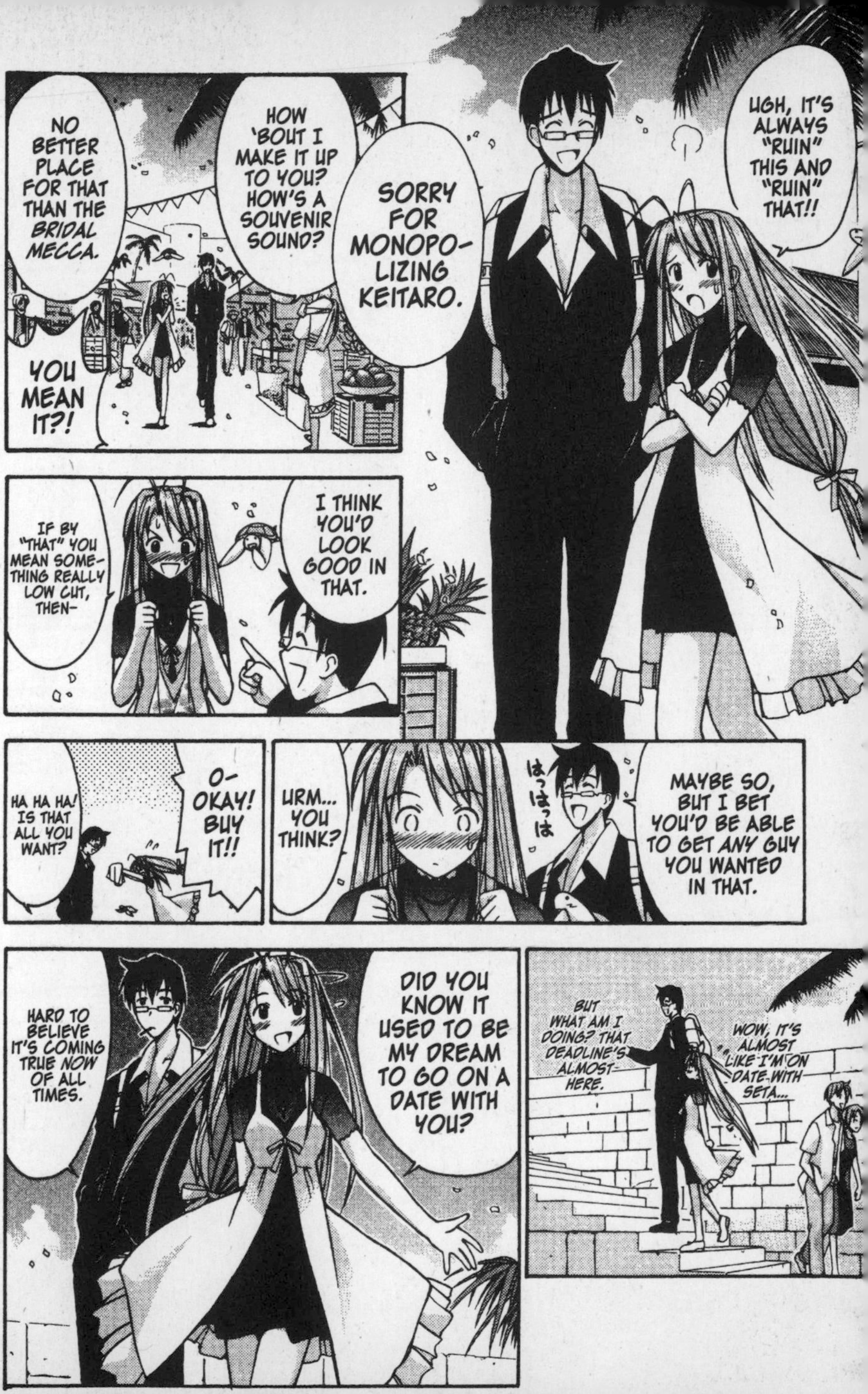
UGH, IT'S ALWAYS "RUIN" THIS AND "RUIN" THAT!!
SORRY FOR MONOPOLIZING KEITARO.
HOW 'BOUT I MAKE IT UP TO YOU? HOW'S A SOUVENIR SOUND?
NO BETTER PLACE FOR THAT THAN THE *BRIDAL MECCA.*
YOU MEAN IT?!
I THINK YOU'D LOOK GOOD IN THAT.
IF BY "THAT" YOU MEAN SOMETHING REALLY LOW CUT, THEN-
MAYBE SO, BUT I BET YOU'D BE ABLE TO GET ANY GUY YOU WANTED IN THAT.
はっはっは
URM... YOU THINK?
O-OKAY! BUY IT!!
HA HA HA! IS THAT ALL YOU WANT?
WOW, IT'S ALMOST LIKE I'M ON A DATE WITH SETA...
BUT WHAT AM I DOING? THAT DEADLINE'S ALMOST HERE.
DID YOU KNOW IT USED TO BE MY DREAM TO GO ON A DATE WITH YOU?
HARD TO BELIEVE IT'S COMING TRUE *NOW* OF ALL TIMES.

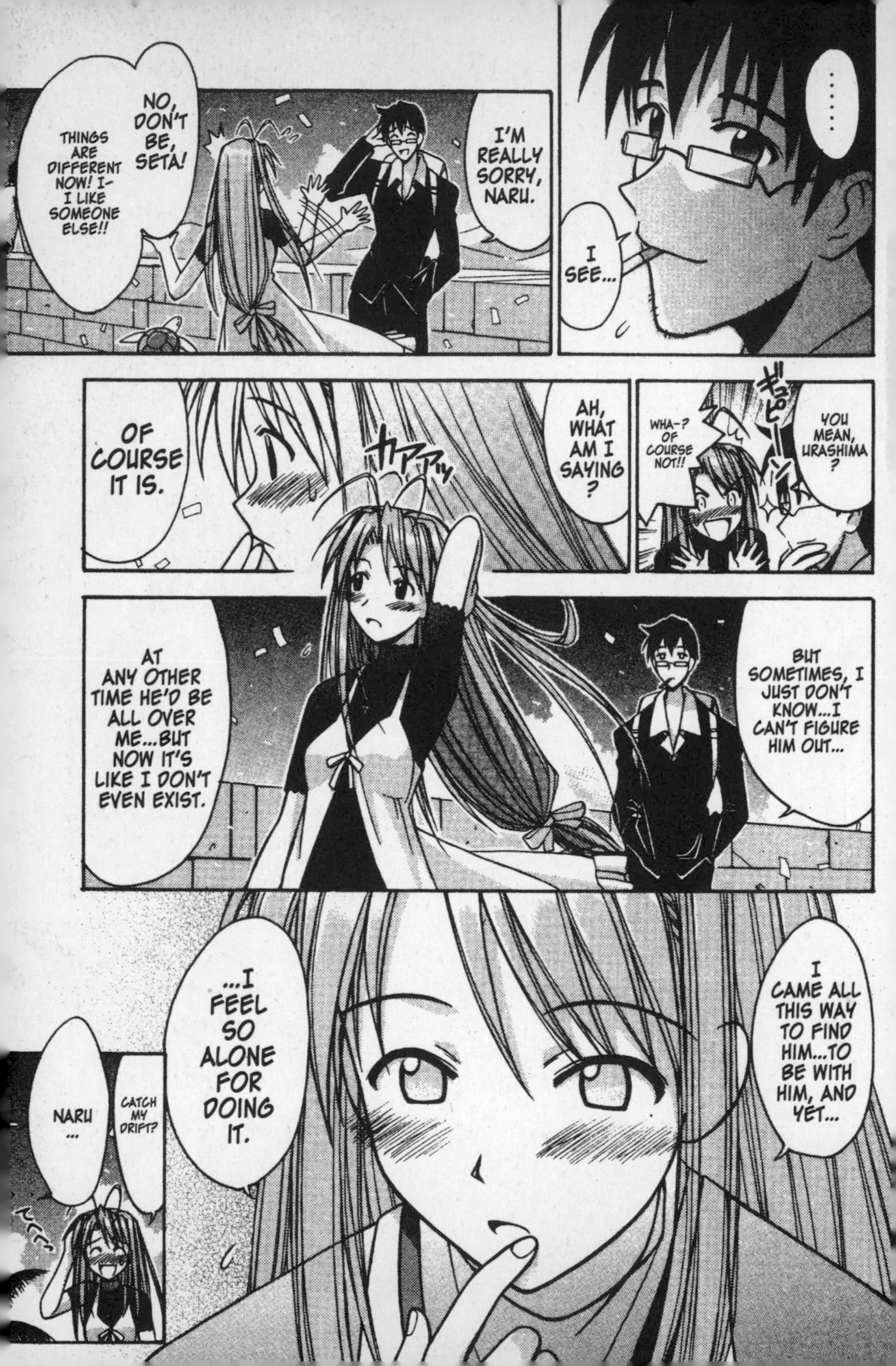
......
I SEE...
I'M REALLY SORRY, NARU.
NO, DON'T BE, SETA!
THINGS ARE DIFFERENT NOW! I-I LIKE SOMEONE ELSE!!
YOU MEAN, URASHIMA?
WHA-? OF COURSE NOT!!
AH, WHAT AM I SAYING?
OF COURSE IT IS.
BUT SOMETIMES, I JUST DON'T KNOW...I CAN'T FIGURE HIM OUT...
AT ANY OTHER TIME HE'D BE ALL OVER ME...BUT NOW IT'S LIKE I DON'T EVEN EXIST.
I CAME ALL THIS WAY TO FIND HIM...TO BE WITH HIM, AND YET...
...I FEEL SO ALONE FOR DOING IT.
CATCH MY DRIFT?
NARU ...

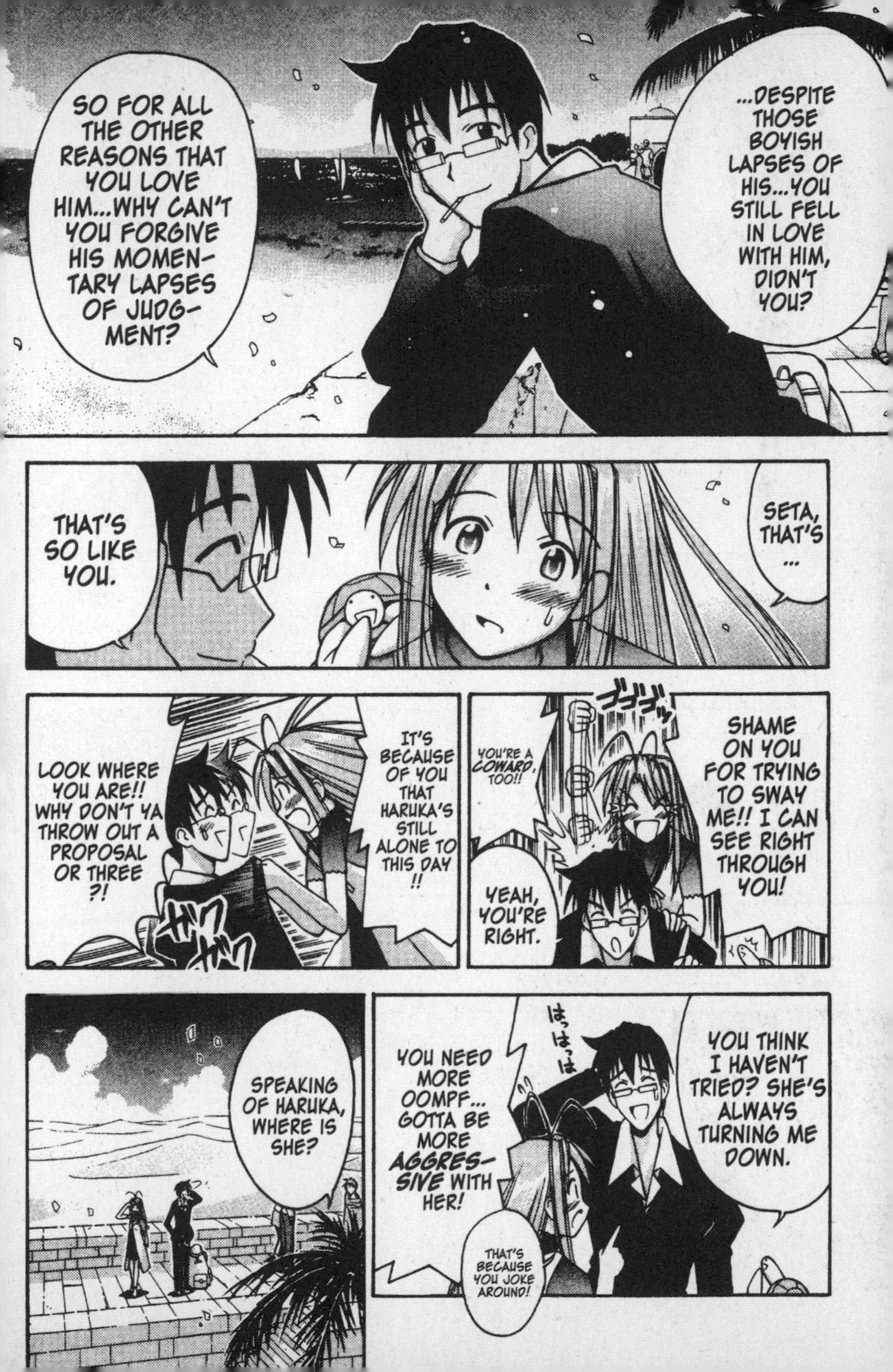
...DESPITE THOSE BOYISH LAPSES OF HIS...YOU STILL FELL IN LOVE WITH HIM, DIDN'T YOU?
SO FOR ALL THE OTHER REASONS THAT YOU LOVE HIM...WHY CAN'T YOU FORGIVE HIS MOMENTARY LAPSES OF JUDGMENT?
SETA, THAT'S ...
THAT'S SO LIKE YOU.
ゴゴゴッ
SHAME ON YOU FOR TRYING TO SWAY ME!! I CAN SEE RIGHT THROUGH YOU!
YOU'RE A COWARD, TOO!!
YEAH, YOU'RE RIGHT.
IT'S BECAUSE OF YOU THAT HARUKA'S STILL ALONE TO THIS DAY!!
LOOK WHERE YOU ARE!! WHY DON'T YA THROW OUT A PROPOSAL OR THREE?!
ガクガク
YOU THINK I HAVEN'T TRIED? SHE'S ALWAYS TURNING ME DOWN.
はっはっは
YOU NEED MORE OOMPF... GOTTA BE MORE AGGRESSIVE WITH HER!
THAT'S BECAUSE YOU JOKE AROUND!
SPEAKING OF HARUKA, WHERE IS SHE?

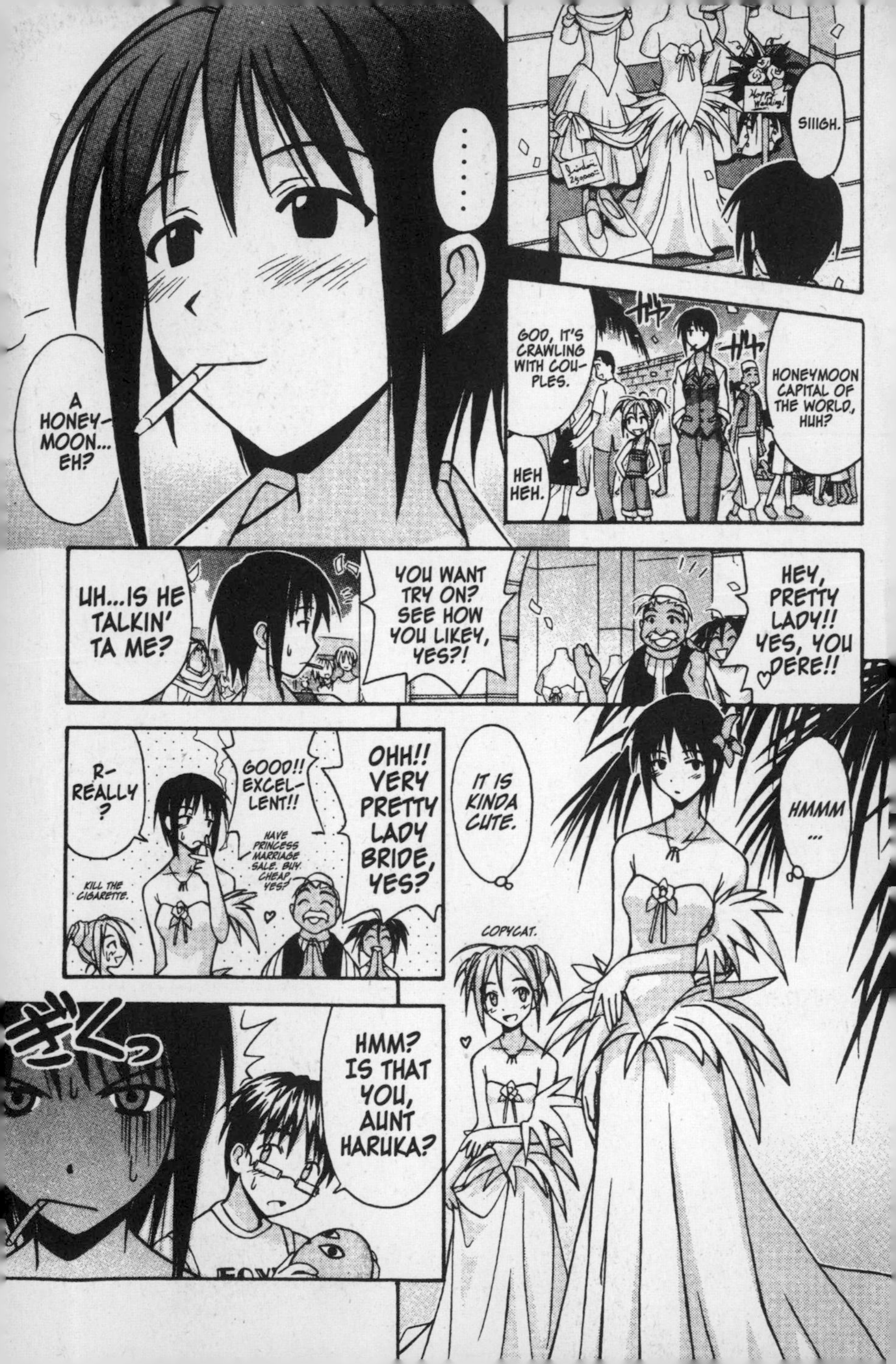

Happy Wedding!
SIIIGH.
HONEYMOON CAPITAL OF THE WORLD, HUH?
GOD, IT'S CRAWLING WITH COUPLES.
HEH HEH.
......
A HONEYMOON... EH?
HEY, PRETTY LADY!! YES, YOU DERE!!
YOU WANT TRY ON? SEE HOW YOU LIKEY, YES?!
UH...IS HE TALKIN' TA ME?
HMMM ...
IT IS KINDA CUTE.
COPYCAT.
OHH!! VERY PRETTY LADY BRIDE, YES?
GOOD!! EXCELLENT!!
HAVE PRINCESS MARRIAGE SALE. BUY CHEAP, YES?
R-REALLY?
KILL THE CIGARETTE.
HMM? IS THAT YOU, AUNT HARUKA?
ぎくっ

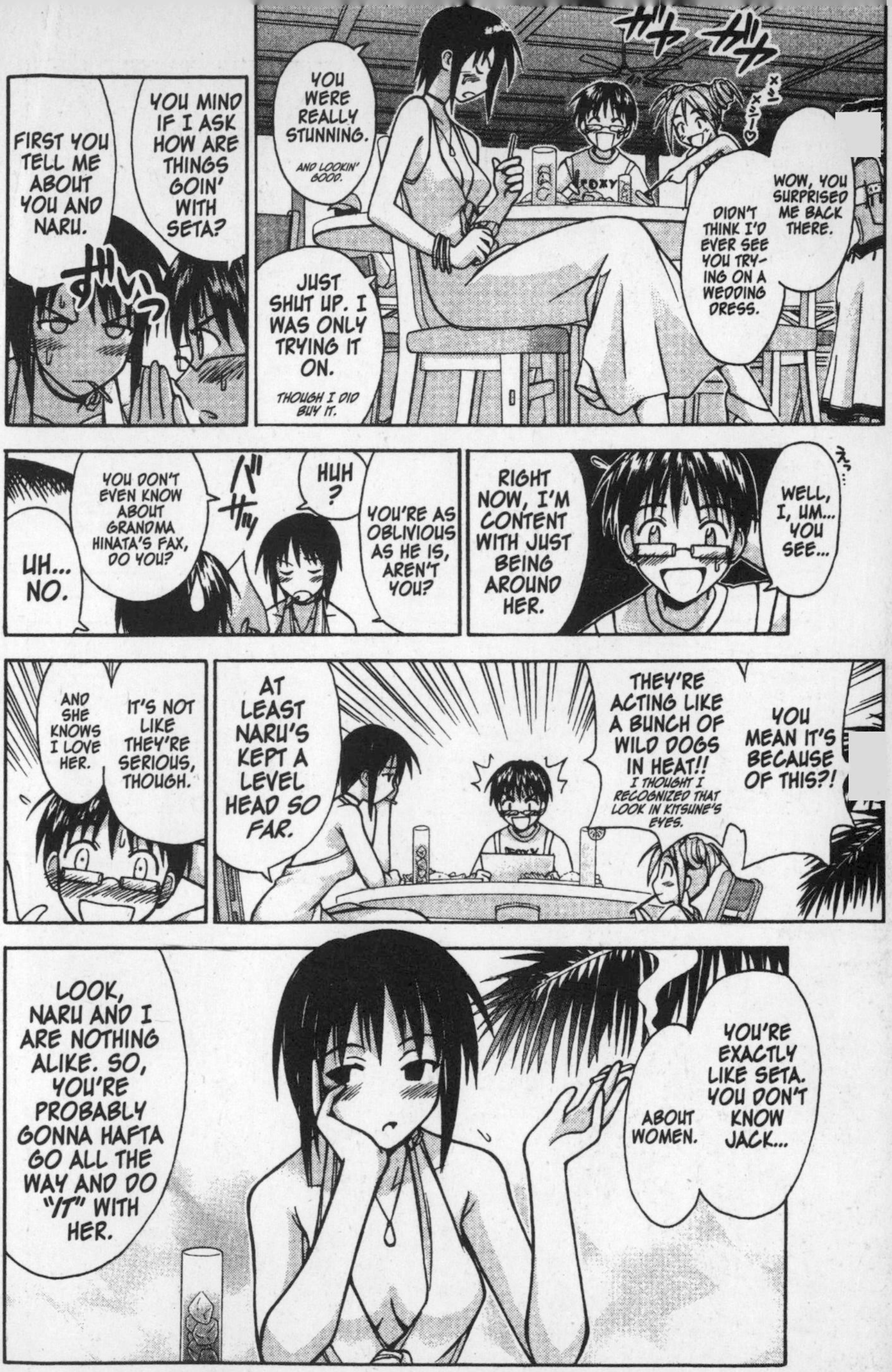
WOW, YOU SURPRISED ME BACK THERE.
DIDN'T THINK I'D EVER SEE YOU TRYING ON A WEDDING DRESS.
YOU WERE REALLY STUNNING.
AND LOOKIN' GOOD.
JUST SHUT UP. I WAS ONLY TRYING IT ON.
THOUGH I DID BUY IT.
YOU MIND IF I ASK HOW ARE THINGS GOIN' WITH SETA?
FIRST YOU TELL ME ABOUT YOU AND NARU.
WELL, I, UM... YOU SEE...
RIGHT NOW, I'M CONTENT WITH JUST BEING AROUND HER.
YOU'RE AS OBLIVIOUS AS HE IS, AREN'T YOU?
HUH?
YOU DON'T EVEN KNOW ABOUT GRANDMA HINATA'S FAX, DO YOU?
UH... NO.
YOU MEAN IT'S BECAUSE OF THIS?!
THEY'RE ACTING LIKE A BUNCH OF WILD DOGS IN HEAT!!
I THOUGHT I RECOGNIZED THAT LOOK IN KITSUNE'S EYES.
AT LEAST NARU'S KEPT A LEVEL HEAD SO FAR.
IT'S NOT LIKE THEY'RE SERIOUS, THOUGH.
AND SHE KNOWS I LOVE HER.
YOU'RE EXACTLY LIKE SETA. YOU DON'T KNOW JACK...
ABOUT WOMEN.
LOOK, NARU AND I ARE NOTHING ALIKE. SO, YOU'RE PROBABLY GONNA HAFTA GO ALL THE WAY AND DO "IT" WITH HER.

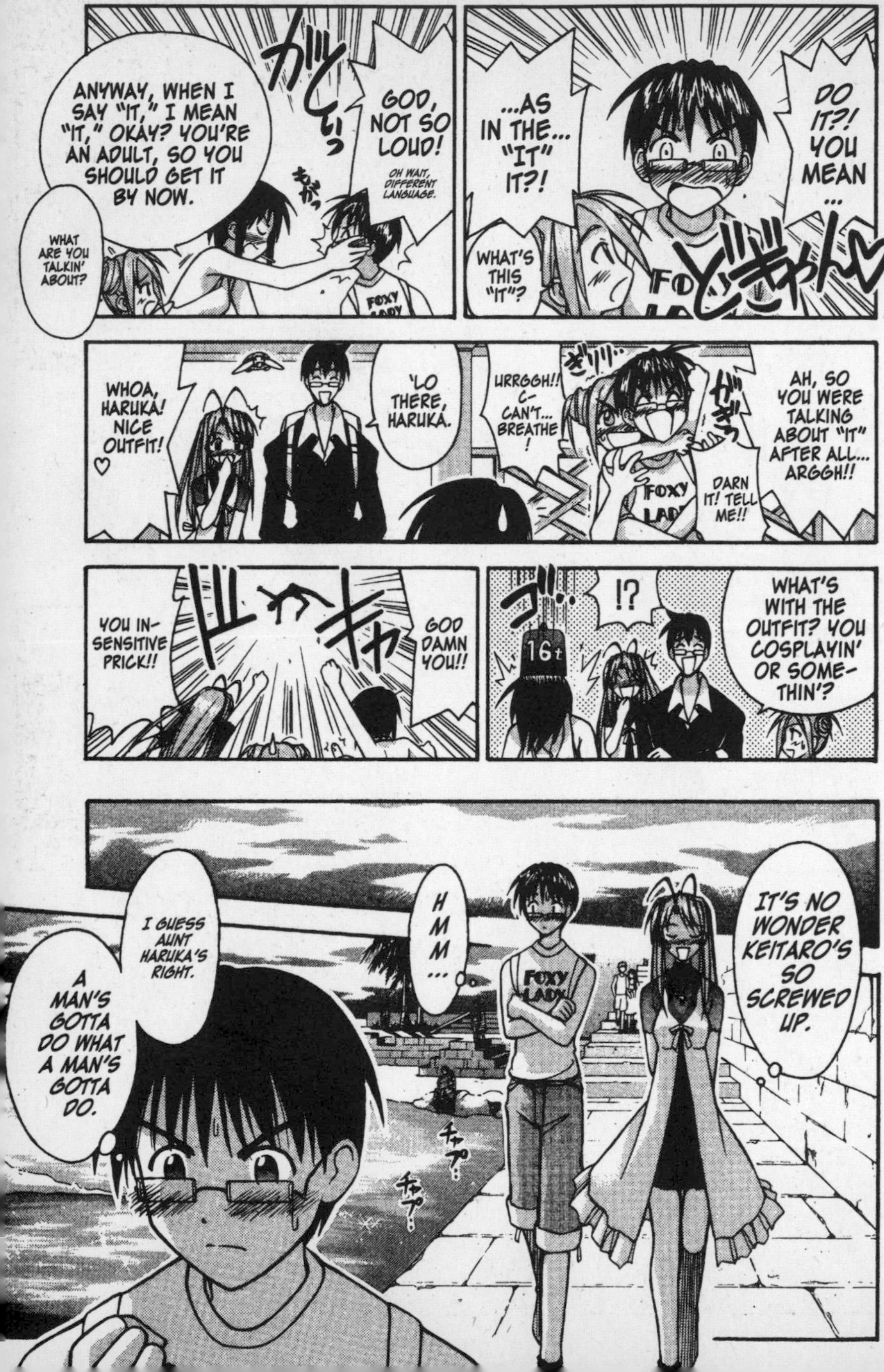
DO IT?! YOU MEAN ...
...AS IN THE... "IT" IT?!
WHAT'S THIS "IT"?
GOD, NOT SO LOUD!
OH WAIT, DIFFERENT LANGUAGE.
ANYWAY, WHEN I SAY "IT," I MEAN "IT," OKAY? YOU'RE AN ADULT, SO YOU SHOULD GET IT BY NOW.
WHAT ARE YOU TALKIN' ABOUT?
AH, SO YOU WERE TALKING ABOUT "IT" AFTER ALL... ARGGH!!
DARN IT! TELL ME!!
URRGGH!! C-CAN'T... BREATHE!
'LO THERE, HARUKA.
WHOA, HARUKA! NICE OUTFIT! ♡
WHAT'S WITH THE OUTFIT? YOU COSPLAYIN' OR SOME-THIN'?
!?
16t
GOD DAMN YOU!!
YOU IN-SENSITIVE PRICK!!
IT'S NO WONDER KEITARO'S SO SCREWED UP.
HMM...
I GUESS AUNT HARUKA'S RIGHT.
A MAN'S GOTTA DO WHAT A MAN'S GOTTA DO.

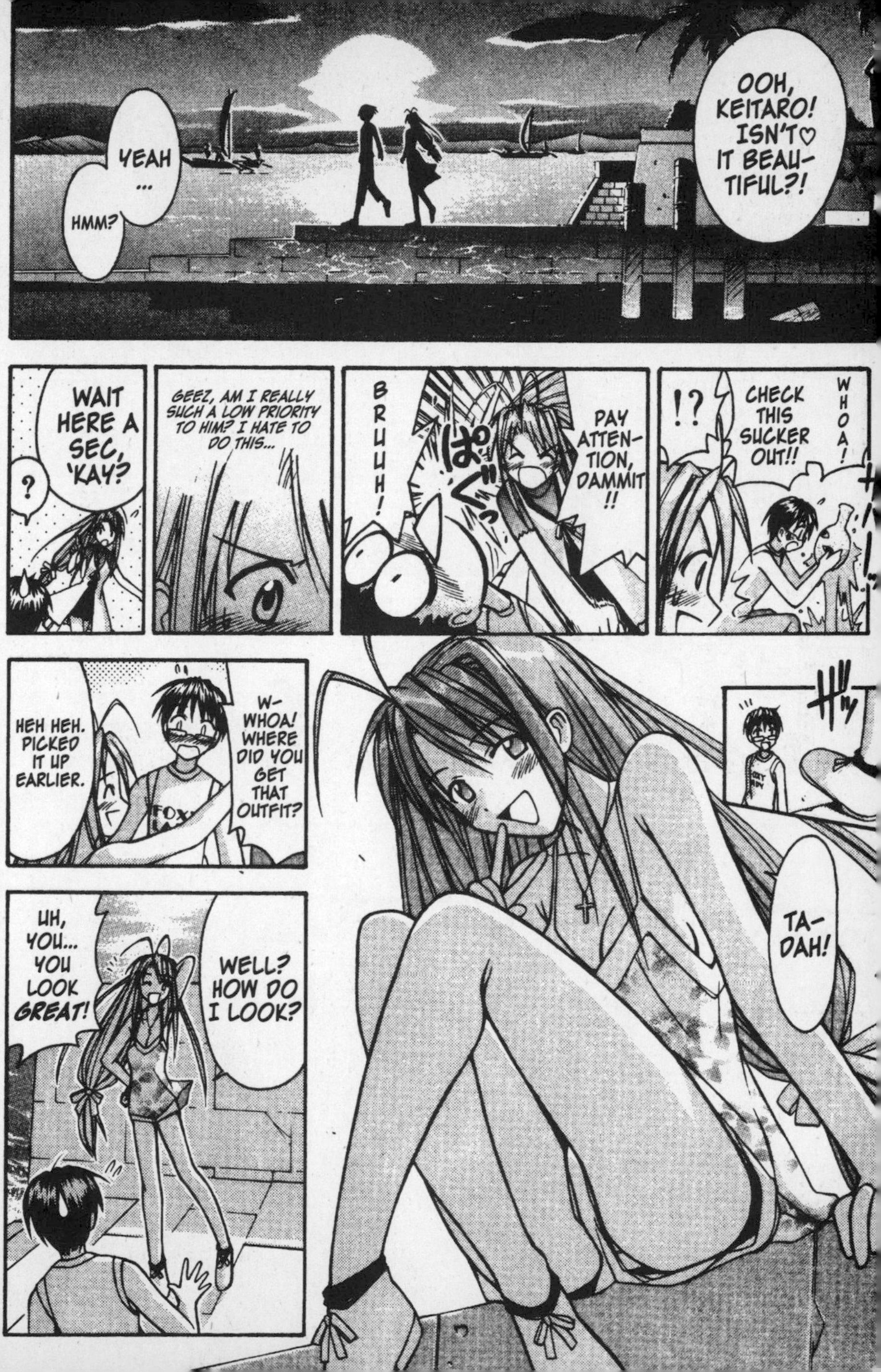
OOH, KEITARO! ISN'T♡ IT BEAUTIFUL?!
YEAH ...
HMM?
WHOA!
CHECK THIS SUCKER OUT!!
!?
PAY ATTENTION, DAMMIT!!
ぱぐっ
BRUUH!
GEEZ, AM I REALLY SUCH A LOW PRIORITY TO HIM? I HATE TO DO THIS...
WAIT HERE A SEC, 'KAY?
?
TA-DAH!
W-WHOA! WHERE DID YOU GET THAT OUTFIT?
HEH HEH. PICKED IT UP EARLIER.
WELL? HOW DO I LOOK?
UH, YOU... YOU LOOK GREAT!

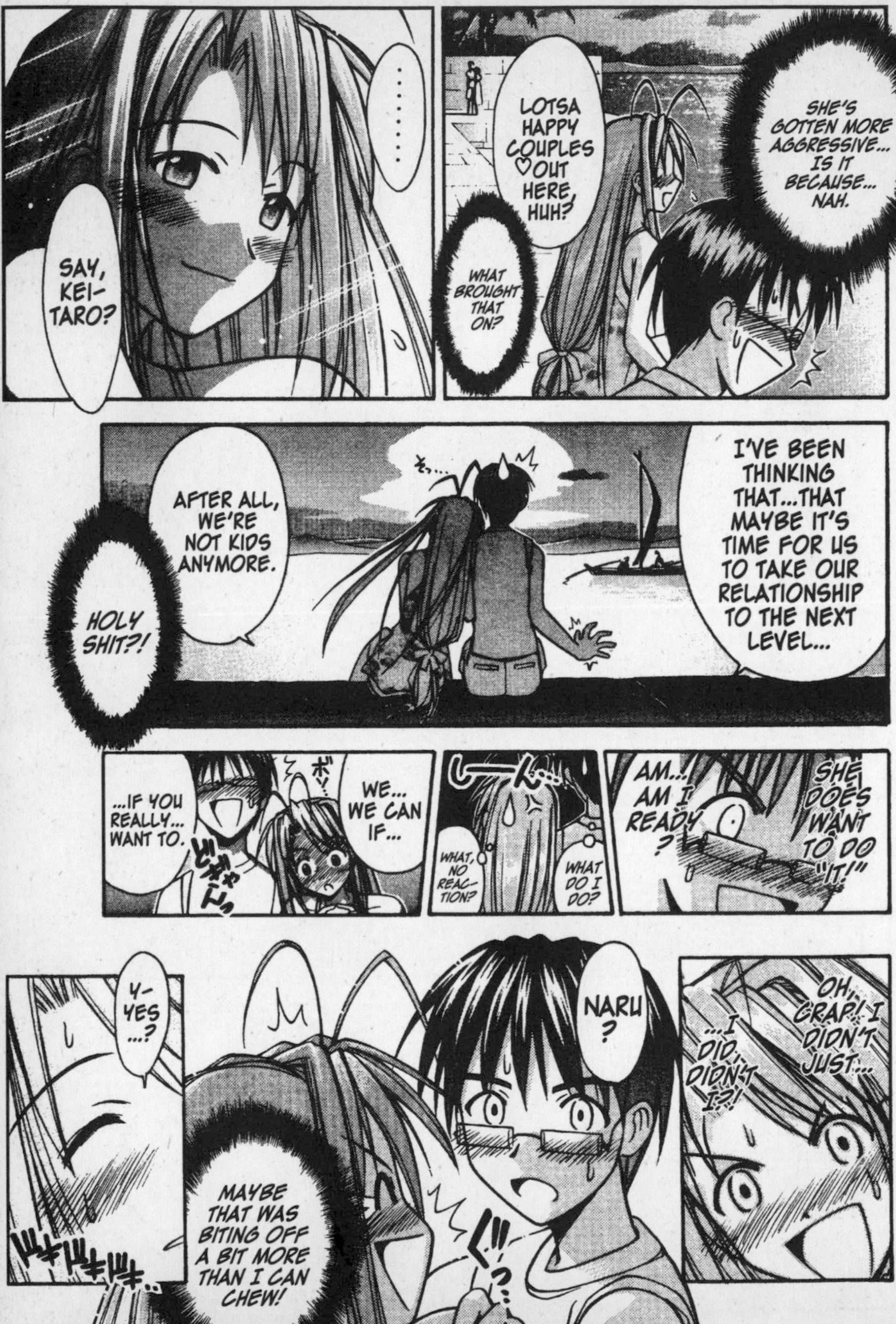
SHE'S GOTTEN MORE AGGRESSIVE... IS IT BECAUSE... NAH.
LOTSA HAPPY COUPLES ♡ OUT HERE, HUH?
WHAT BROUGHT THAT ON?
......
SAY, KEI-TARO?
I'VE BEEN THINKING THAT...THAT MAYBE IT'S TIME FOR US TO TAKE OUR RELATIONSHIP TO THE NEXT LEVEL...
AFTER ALL, WE'RE NOT KIDS ANYMORE.
HOLY SHIT?!
SHE DOES WANT TO DO "IT!"
AM... AM I READY?
WHAT DO I DO?
WHAT, NO REACTION?
WE... WE CAN IF...
...IF YOU REALLY... WANT TO.
OH, CRAP! I DIDN'T JUST...
...I DID, DIDN'T I?!
NARU?
Y-YES...?
MAYBE THAT WAS BITING OFF A BIT MORE THAN I CAN CHEW!

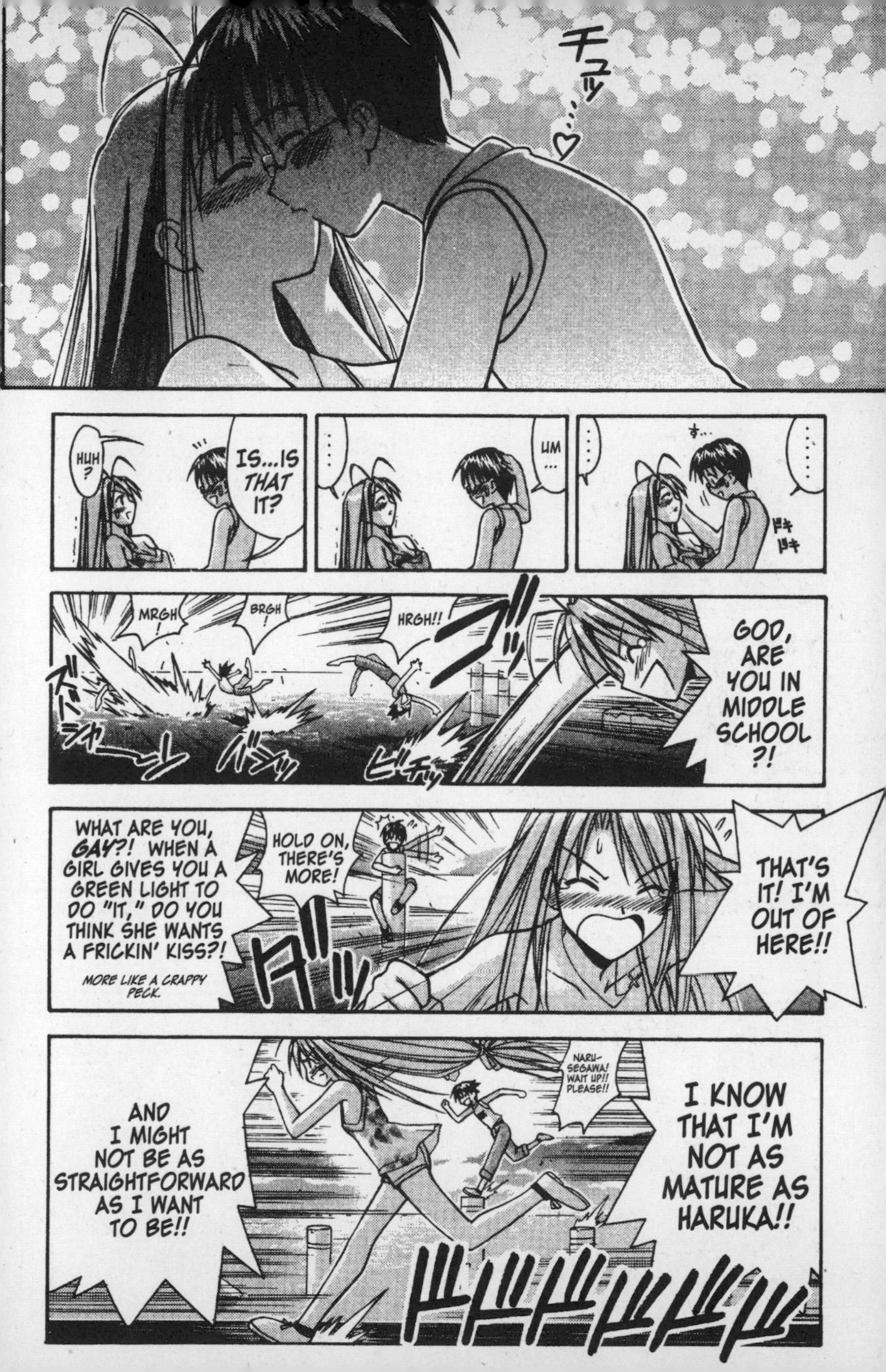
チュッ…♡
IS...IS THAT IT?
HUH ?
UM ...
....
す…
....
ドキドキ
GOD, ARE YOU IN MIDDLE SCHOOL?!
ゴッ
HRGH!!
BRGH !
MRGH !
ビチッ
バシッ
ズバシャーン
THAT'S IT! I'M OUT OF HERE!!
ダッ
HOLD ON, THERE'S MORE!
WHAT ARE YOU, GAY?! WHEN A GIRL GIVES YOU A GREEN LIGHT TO DO "IT," DO YOU THINK SHE WANTS A FRICKIN' KISS?!
MORE LIKE A CRAPPY PECK.
I KNOW THAT I'M NOT AS MATURE AS HARUKA!!
NARU-SEGAWA! WAIT UP!! PLEASE!!
AND I MIGHT NOT BE AS STRAIGHTFORWARD AS I WANT TO BE!!
ドドドドドド

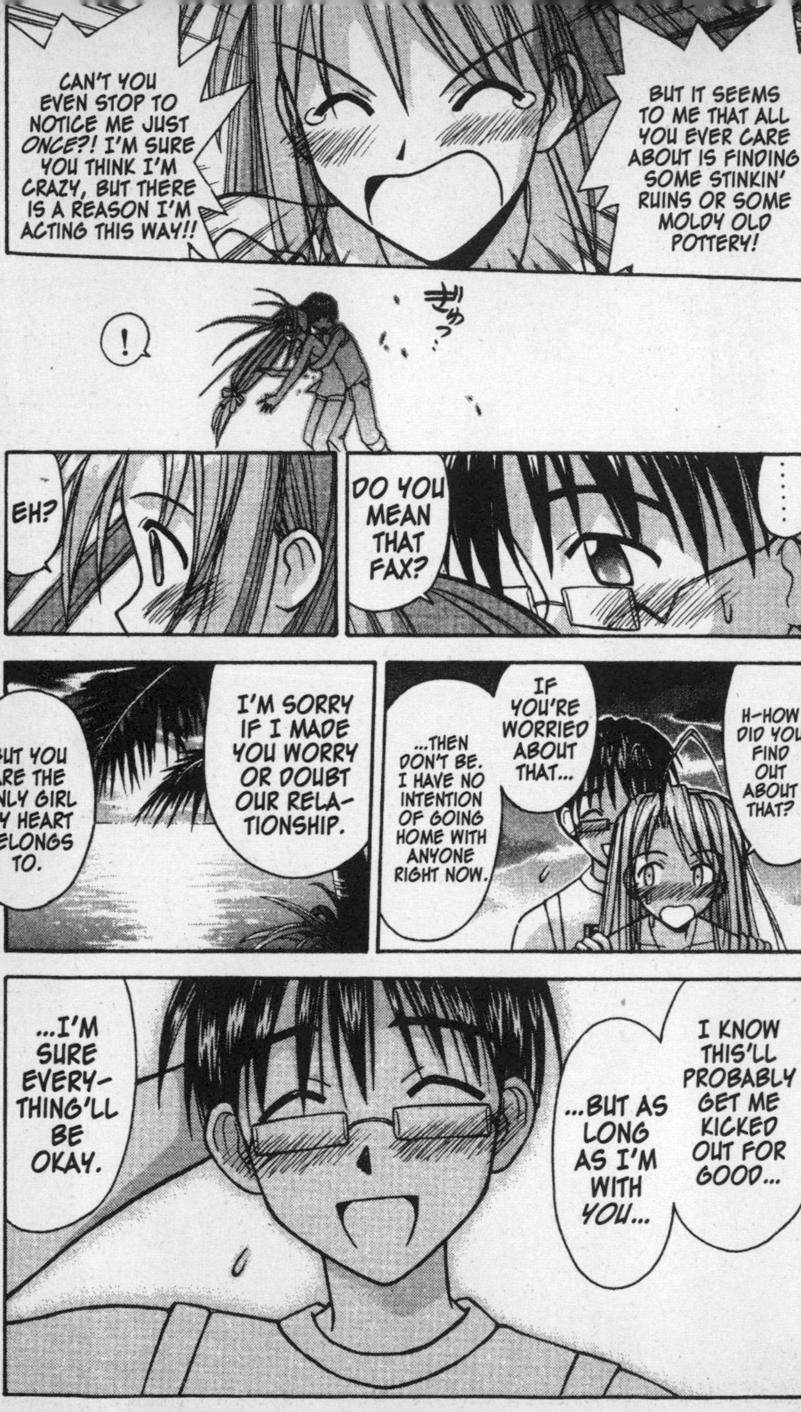
BUT IT SEEMS TO ME THAT ALL YOU EVER CARE ABOUT IS FINDING SOME STINKIN' RUINS OR SOME MOLDY OLD POTTERY!
CAN'T YOU EVEN STOP TO NOTICE ME JUST ONCE?! I'M SURE YOU THINK I'M CRAZY, BUT THERE IS A REASON I'M ACTING THIS WAY!!
ぎゅっ
!
......
DO YOU MEAN THAT FAX?
EH?
H-HOW DID YOU FIND OUT ABOUT THAT?
IF YOU'RE WORRIED ABOUT THAT...
...THEN DON'T BE. I HAVE NO INTENTION OF GOING HOME WITH ANYONE RIGHT NOW.
I'M SORRY IF I MADE YOU WORRY OR DOUBT OUR RELA-TIONSHIP.
BUT YOU ARE THE ONLY GIRL MY HEART BELONGS TO.
I KNOW THIS'LL PROBABLY GET ME KICKED OUT FOR GOOD...
...BUT AS LONG AS I'M WITH YOU...
...I'M SURE EVERY-THING'LL BE OKAY.

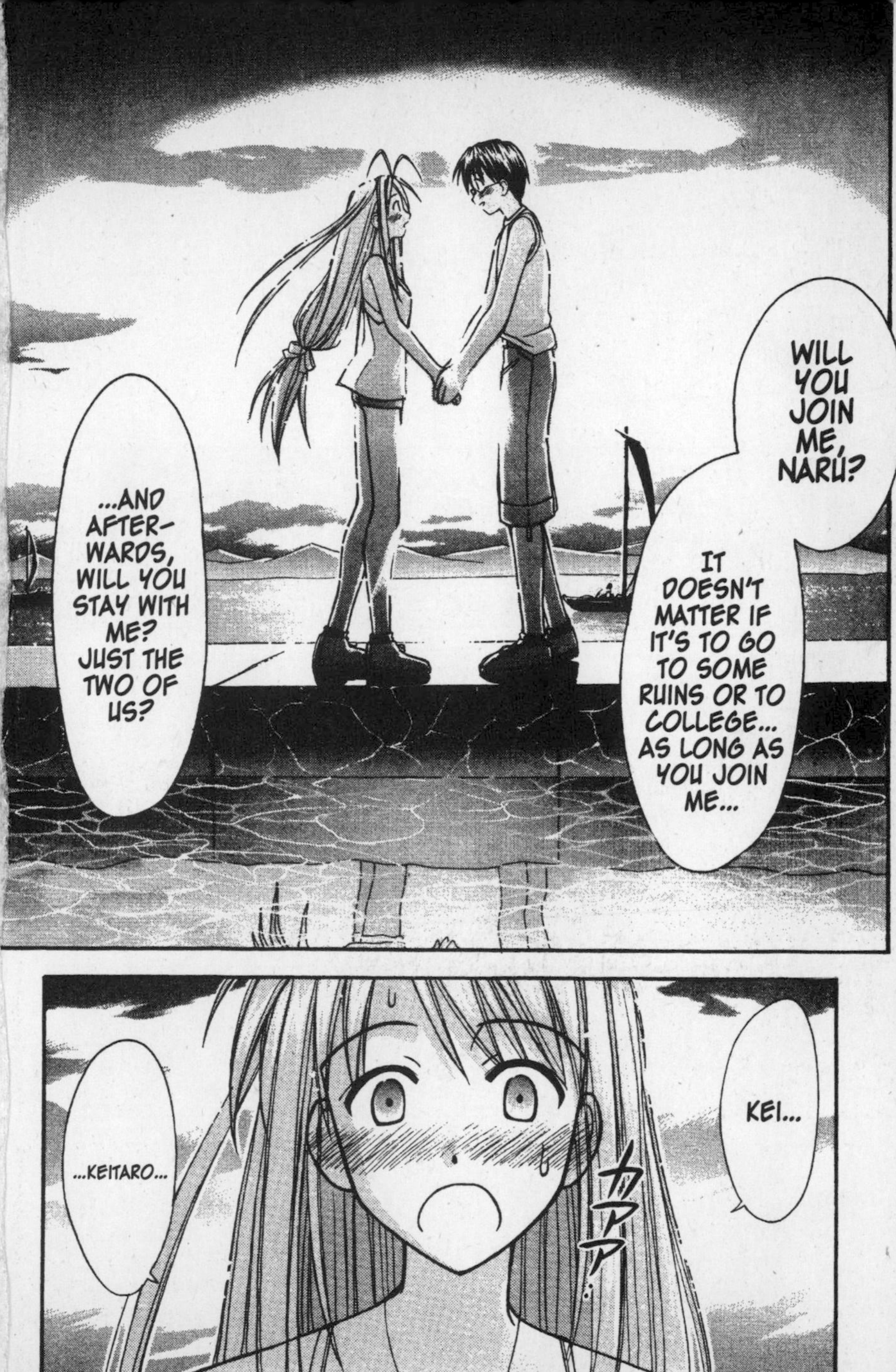
WILL YOU JOIN ME, NARÚ?
IT DOESN'T MATTER IF IT'S TO GO TO SOME RUINS OR TO COLLEGE... AS LONG AS YOU JOIN ME...
...AND AFTER-WARDS, WILL YOU STAY WITH ME? JUST THE TWO OF US?
KEI...
...KEITARO...

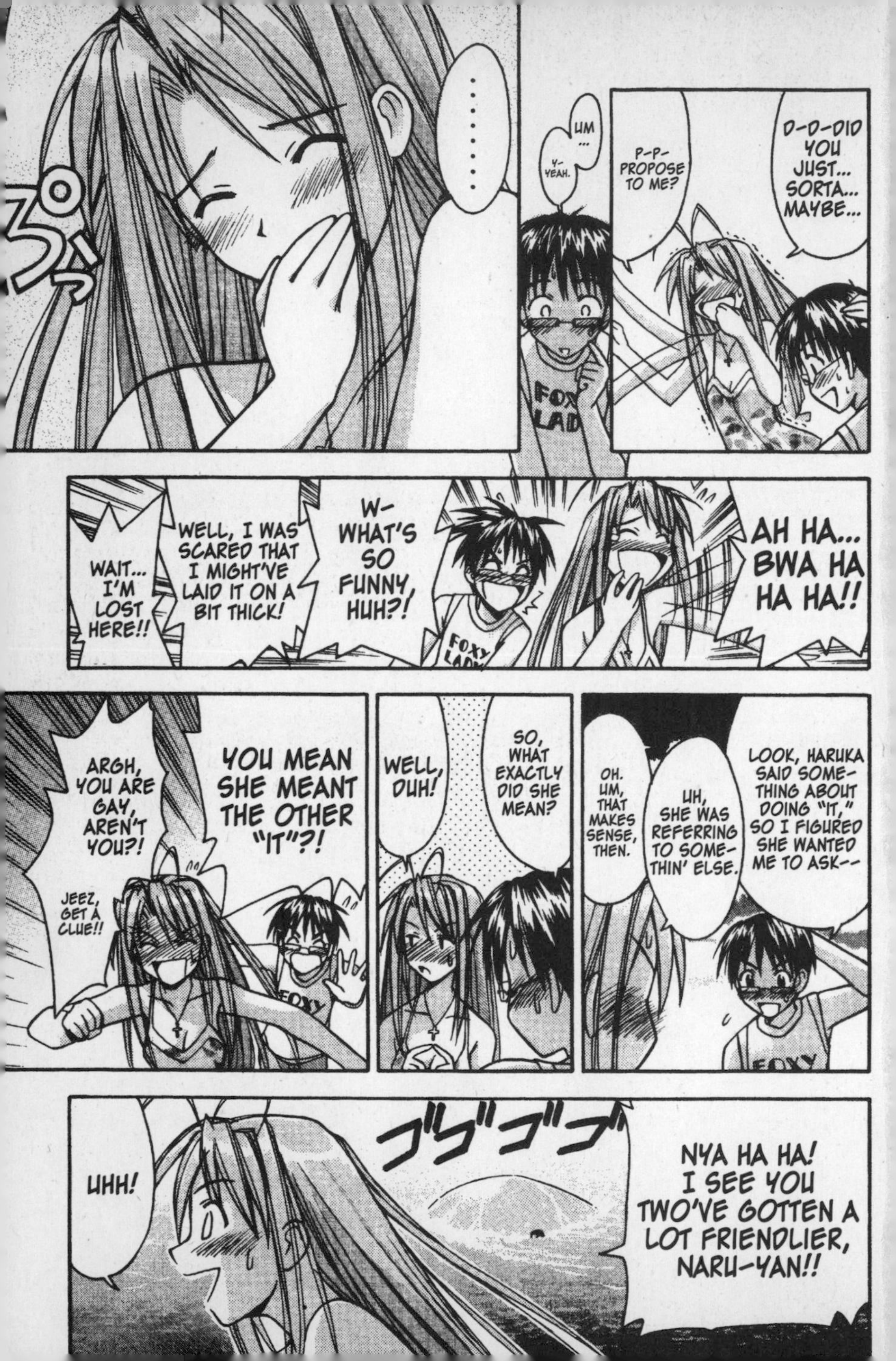
D-D-DID YOU JUST... SORTA... MAYBE...
P-P-PROPOSE TO ME?
UM ...
Y-YEAH.
......
ぷっ
AH HA... BWA HA HA HA!!
W- WHAT'S SO FUNNY, HUH?!
WELL, I WAS SCARED THAT I MIGHT'VE LAID IT ON A BIT THICK!
WAIT... I'M LOST HERE!!
LOOK, HARUKA SAID SOME-THING ABOUT DOING "IT," SO I FIGURED SHE WANTED ME TO ASK--
UH, SHE WAS REFERRING TO SOME-THIN' ELSE.
OH. UM, THAT MAKES SENSE, THEN.
SO, WHAT EXACTLY DID SHE MEAN?
WELL, DUH!
YOU MEAN SHE MEANT THE OTHER "IT"?!
ARGH, YOU ARE GAY, AREN'T YOU?!
JEEZ, GET A CLUE!!
NYA HA HA! I SEE YOU TWO'VE GOTTEN A LOT FRIENDLIER, NARU-YAN!!
ゴゴゴゴ
UHH!

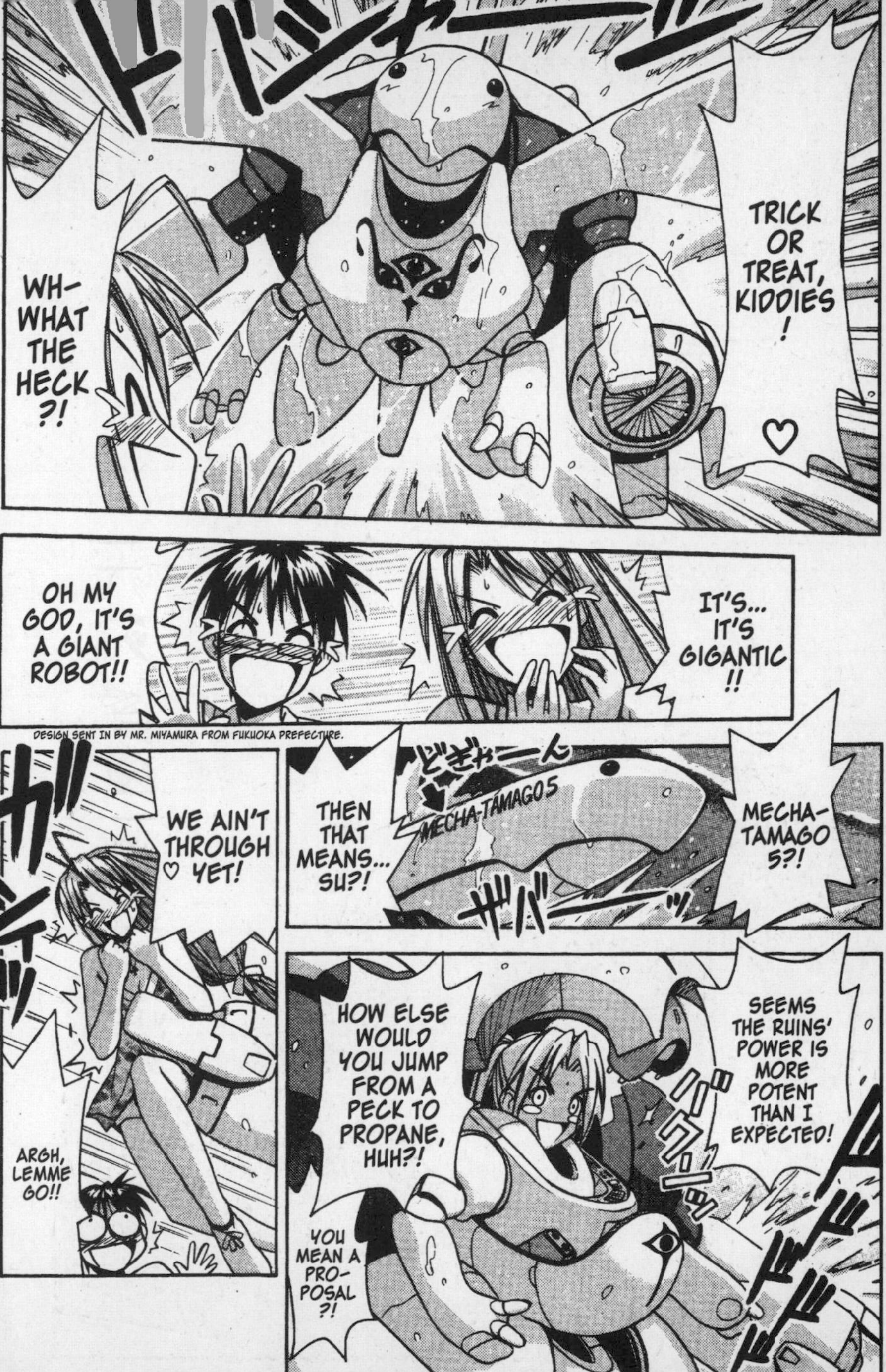
TRICK OR TREAT, KIDDIES! ♡
WH-WHAT THE HECK?!
IT'S... IT'S GIGANTIC!!
OH MY GOD, IT'S A GIANT ROBOT!!
DESIGN SENT IN BY MR. MIYAMURA FROM FUKUOKA PREFECTURE.
MECHA-TAMAGO 5?!
どぎゃーん
MECHA-TAMAGO5
THEN THAT MEANS... SU?!
SEEMS THE RUINS' POWER IS MORE POTENT THAN I EXPECTED!
HOW ELSE WOULD YOU JUMP FROM A PECK TO PROPANE, HUH?!
YOU MEAN A PRO-POSAL?!
WE AIN'T THROUGH ♡ YET!
ARGH, LEMME GO!!

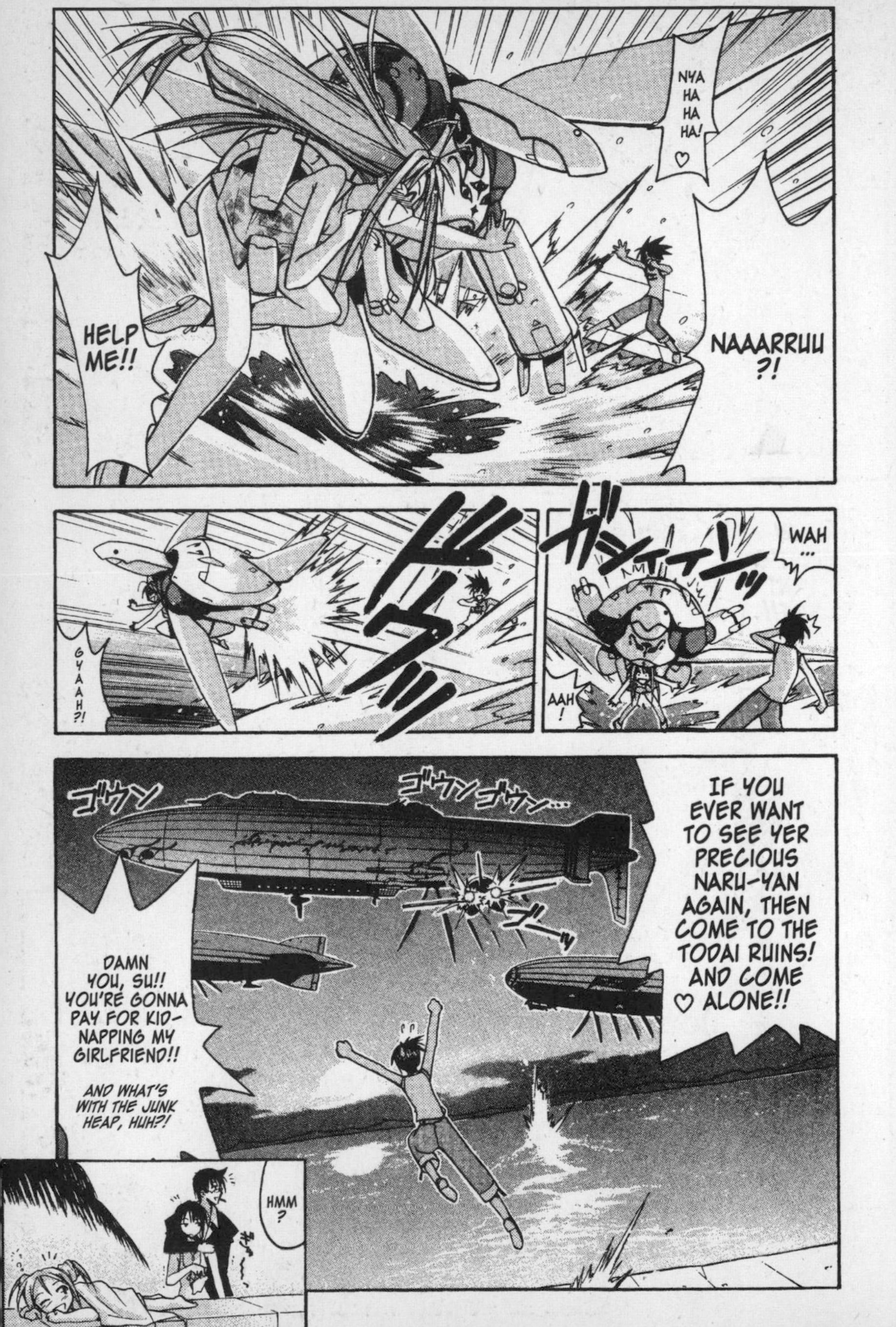
NYA HA HA HA! ♡
NAAARRUU?!
HELP ME!!
WAH ...
AAH!
ドウッ
GYAAAH?!
IF YOU EVER WANT TO SEE YER PRECIOUS NARU-YAN AGAIN, THEN COME TO THE TODAI RUINS! AND COME ♡ ALONE!!
ゴウン ゴウン…
ゴウン
ブーッ
DAMN YOU, SU!! YOU'RE GONNA PAY FOR KID-NAPPING MY GIRLFRIEND!!
AND WHAT'S WITH THE JUNK HEAP, HUH?!
HMM?

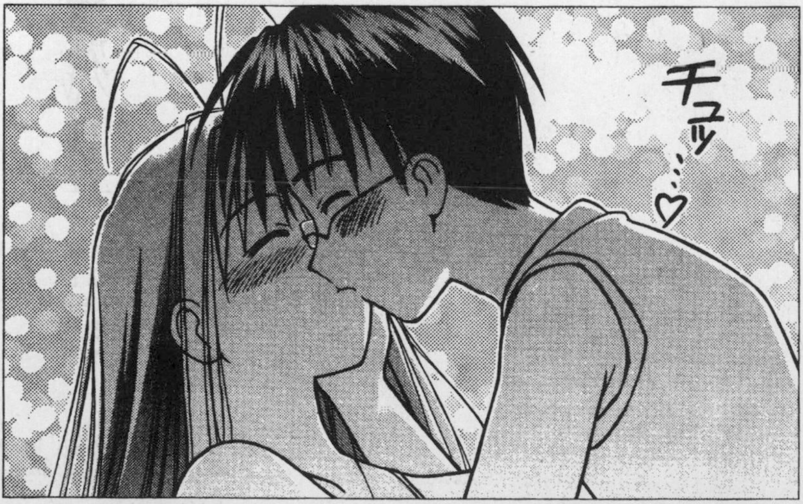
チュッ…♡

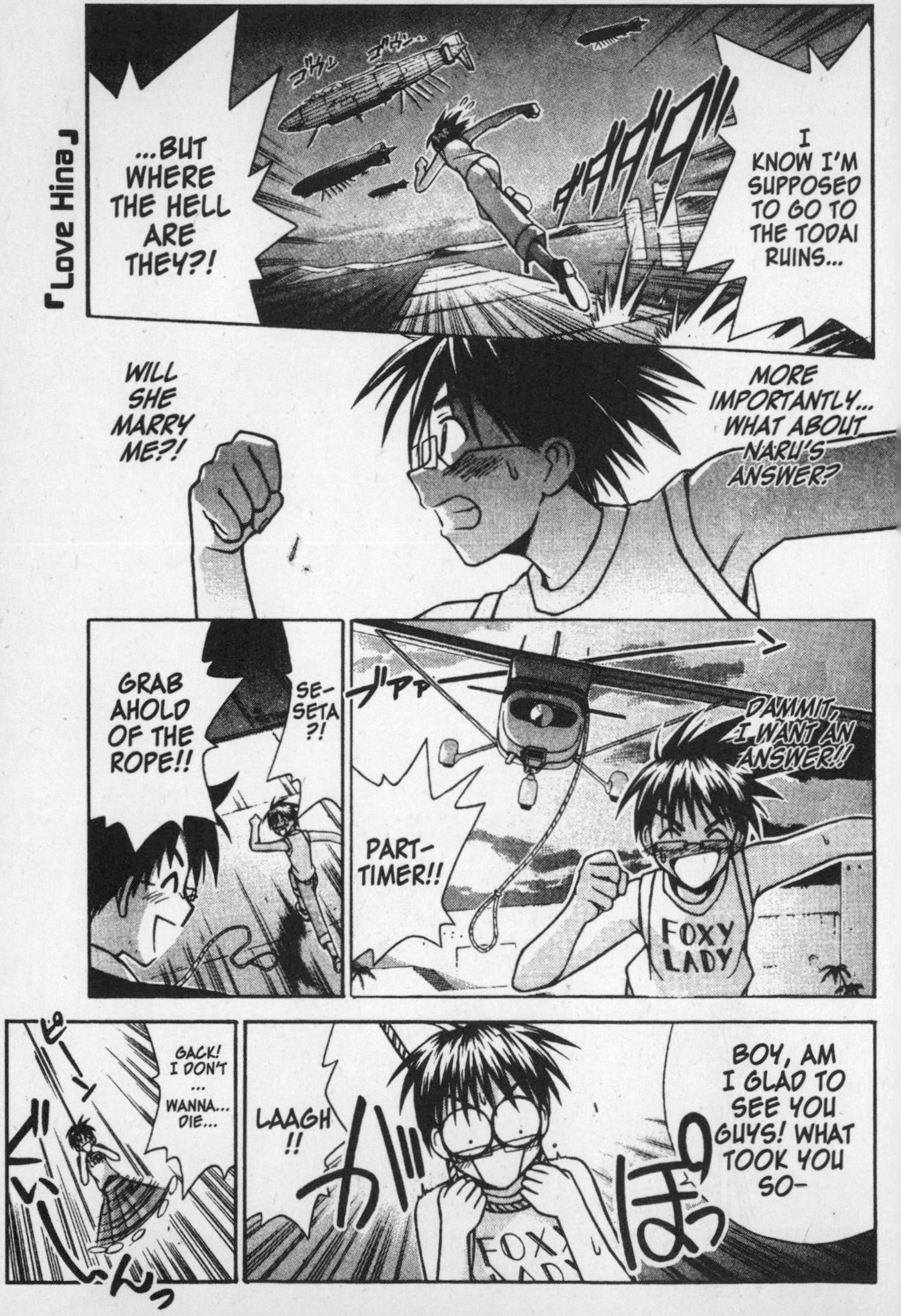
I KNOW I'M SUPPOSED TO GO TO THE TODAI RUINS...
...BUT WHERE THE HELL ARE THEY?!
MORE IMPORTANTLY... WHAT ABOUT NARU'S ANSWER?
WILL SHE MARRY ME?!
DAMMIT, I WANT AN ANSWER!!
PART-TIMER!!
SE-SETA?!
GRAB AHOLD OF THE ROPE!!
BOY, AM I GLAD TO SEE YOU GUYS! WHAT TOOK YOU SO-
LAAGH!!
FOXY LADY
GACK! I DON'T ... WANNA... DIE...

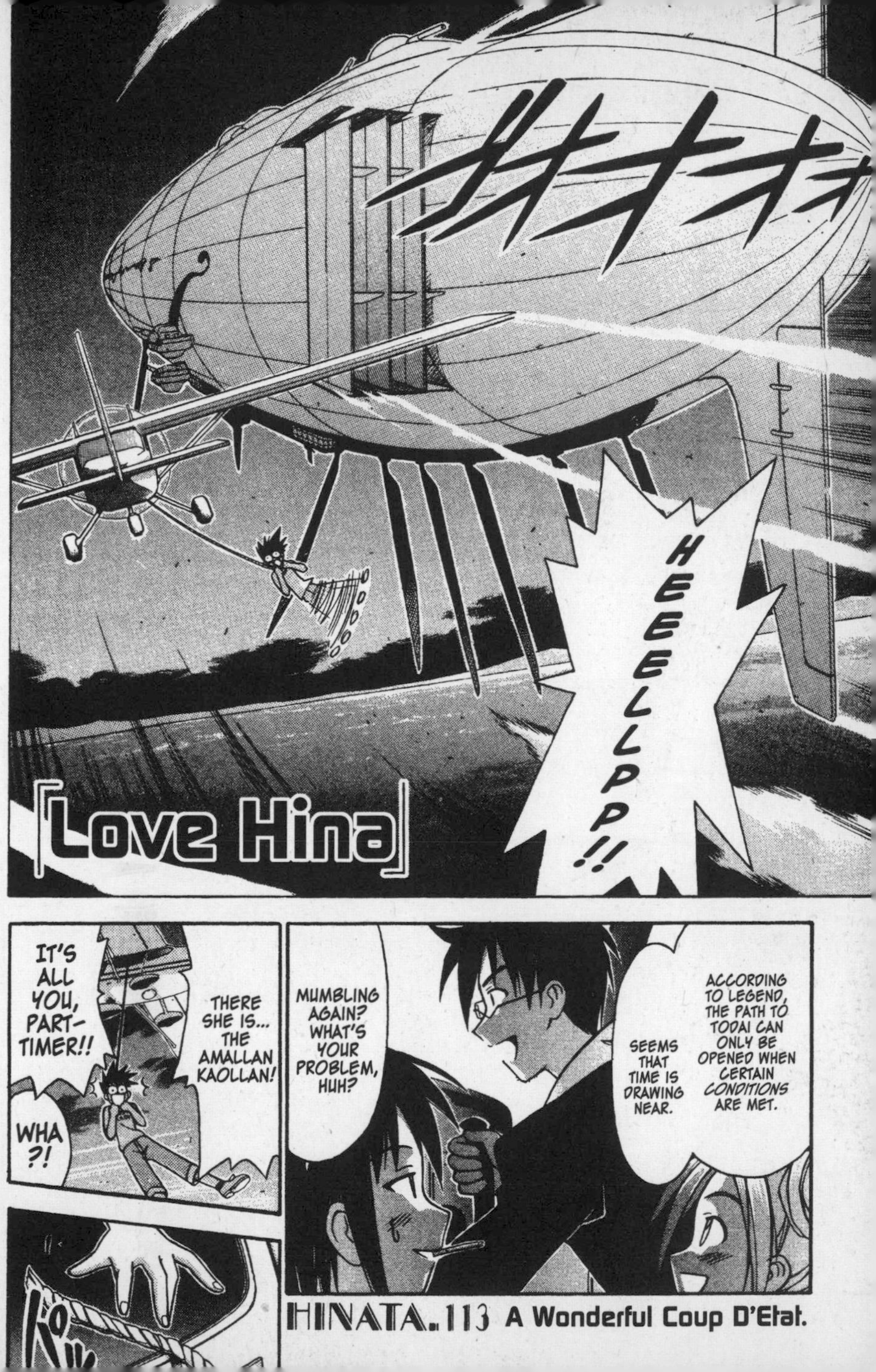
「Love Hina」
HEEELLPP!!
ACCORDING TO LEGEND, THE PATH TO TODAI CAN ONLY BE OPENED WHEN CERTAIN *CONDITIONS* ARE MET.
SEEMS THAT TIME IS DRAWING NEAR.
MUMBLING AGAIN? WHAT'S YOUR PROBLEM, HUH?
THERE SHE IS... THE AMALLAN KAOLLAN!
IT'S ALL YOU, PART-TIMER!!
WHA ?!
HINATA..113 A Wonderful Coup D'Etat.

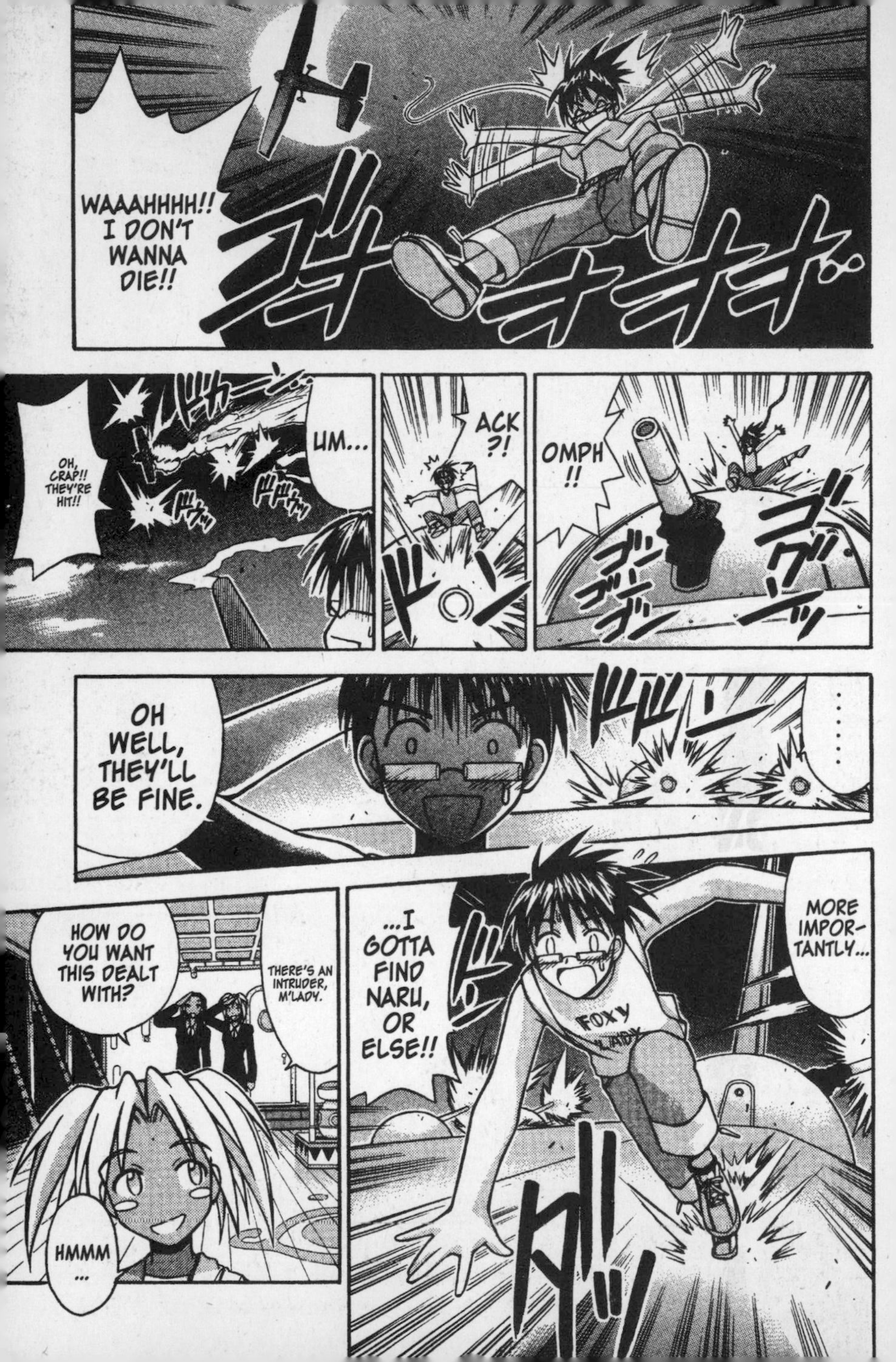
WAAAHHHH!! I DON'T WANNA DIE!!
OMPH !!
ACK ?!
UM...
OH, CRAP!! THEY'RE HIT!!
......
OH WELL, THEY'LL BE FINE.
MORE IMPOR-TANTLY...
...I GOTTA FIND NARU, OR ELSE!!
FOXY LADY
THERE'S AN INTRUDER, M'LADY.
HOW DO YOU WANT THIS DEALT WITH?
HMMM ...

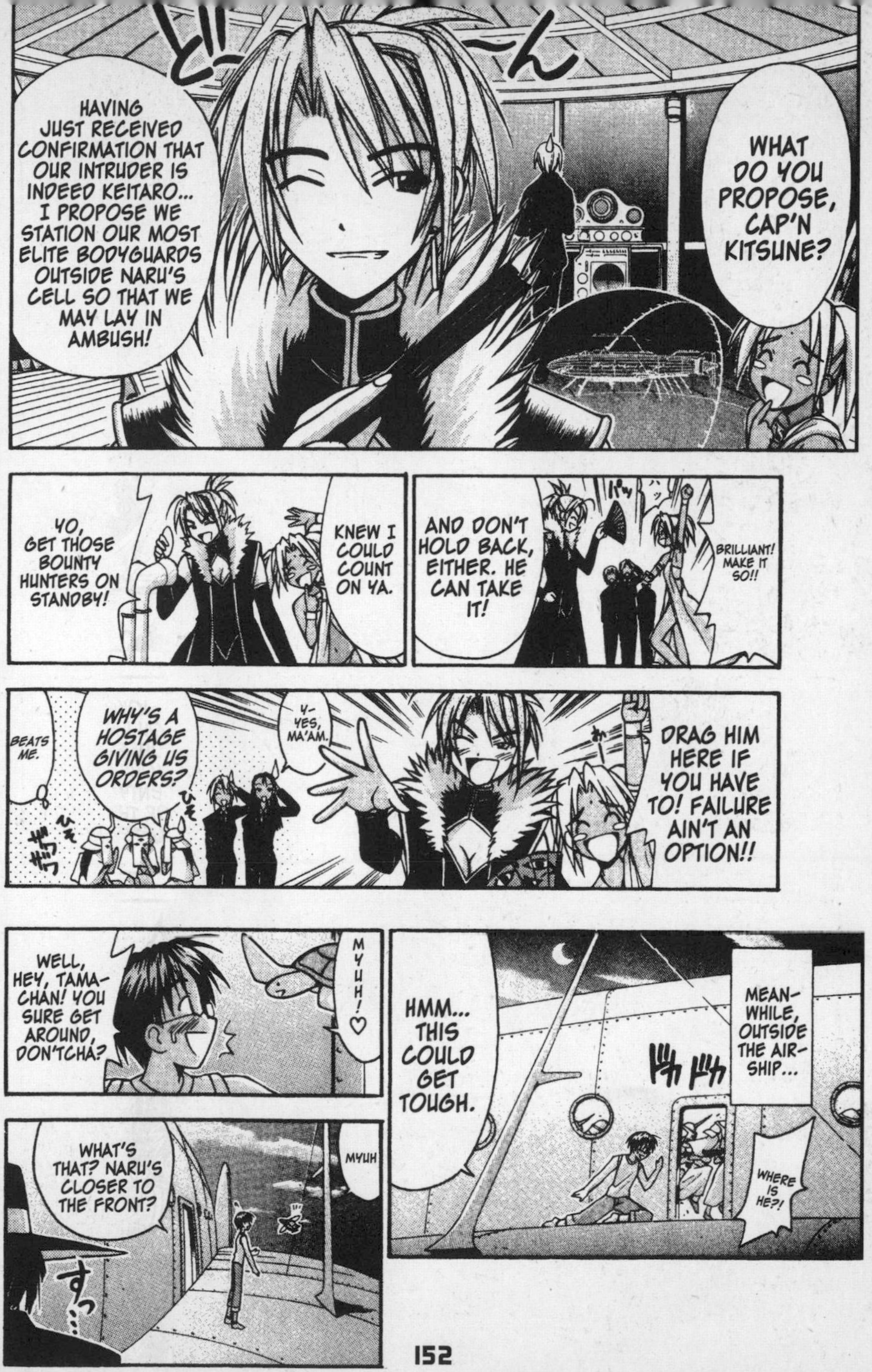
WHAT DO YOU PROPOSE, CAP'N KITSUNE?
HAVING JUST RECEIVED CONFIRMATION THAT OUR INTRUDER IS INDEED KEITARO... I PROPOSE WE STATION OUR MOST ELITE BODYGUARDS OUTSIDE NARU'S CELL SO THAT WE MAY LAY IN AMBUSH!
BRILLIANT! MAKE IT SO!!
AND DON'T HOLD BACK, EITHER. HE CAN TAKE IT!
KNEW I COULD COUNT ON YA.
YO, GET THOSE BOUNTY HUNTERS ON STANDBY!
DRAG HIM HERE IF YOU HAVE TO! FAILURE AIN'T AN OPTION!!
Y-YES, MA'AM.
WHY'S A HOSTAGE GIVING US ORDERS?
BEATS ME.
MEAN-WHILE, OUTSIDE THE AIR-SHIP...
HMM... THIS COULD GET TOUGH.
WHERE IS HE?!
MYUH! ♡
WELL, HEY, TAMA-CHAN! YOU SURE GET AROUND, DON'TCHA?
MYUH
WHAT'S THAT? NARU'S CLOSER TO THE FRONT?

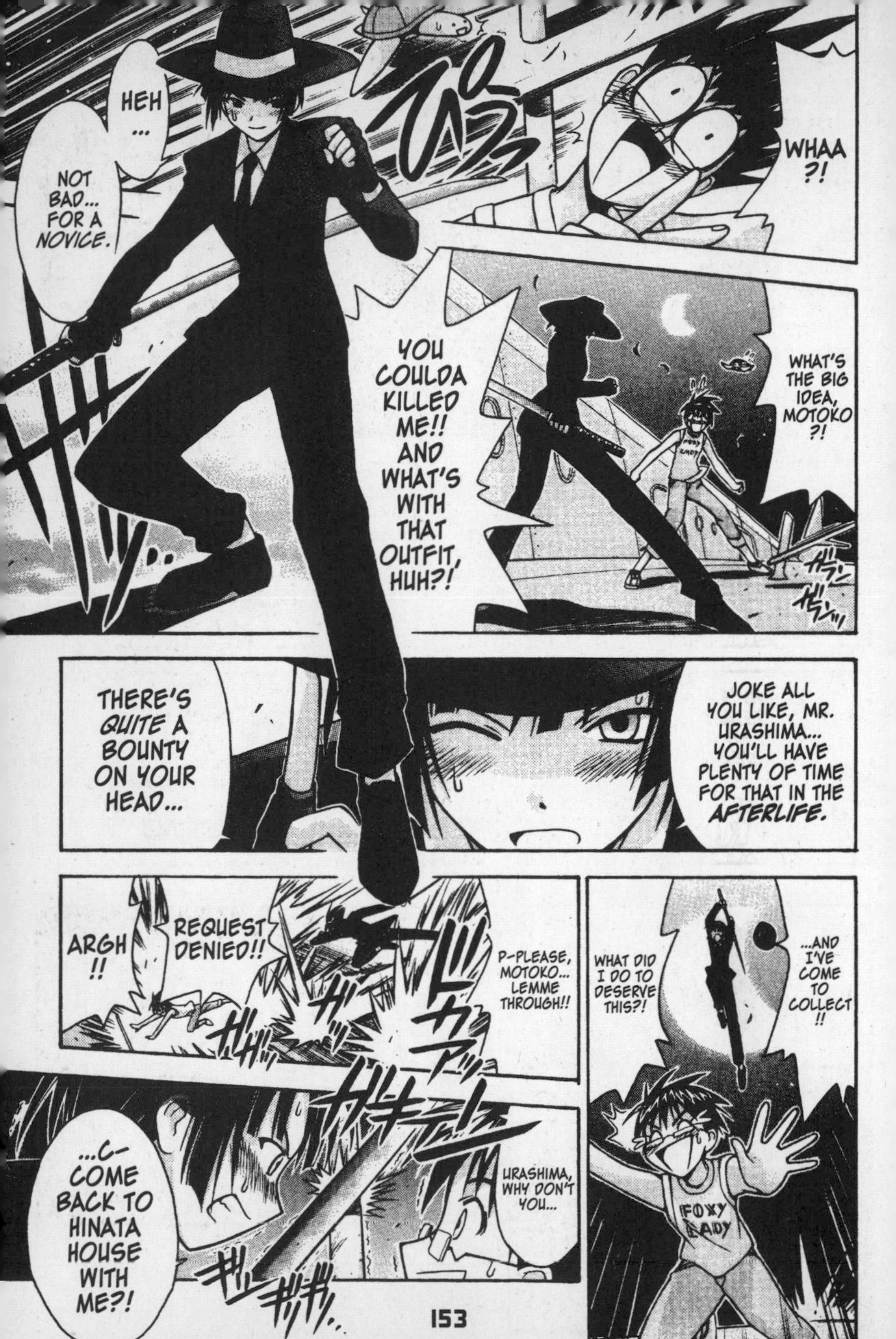
WHAA ?!
WHAT'S THE BIG IDEA, MOTOKO ?!
YOU COULDA KILLED ME!! AND WHAT'S WITH THAT OUTFIT, HUH?!
HEH ...
NOT BAD... FOR A NOVICE.
JOKE ALL YOU LIKE, MR. URASHIMA... YOU'LL HAVE PLENTY OF TIME FOR THAT IN THE AFTERLIFE.
THERE'S QUITE A BOUNTY ON YOUR HEAD...
...AND I'VE COME TO COLLECT !!
WHAT DID I DO TO DESERVE THIS?!
P-PLEASE, MOTOKO... LEMME THROUGH!!
REQUEST DENIED!!
ARGH !!
URASHIMA, WHY DON'T YOU...
...C-COME BACK TO HINATA HOUSE WITH ME?!

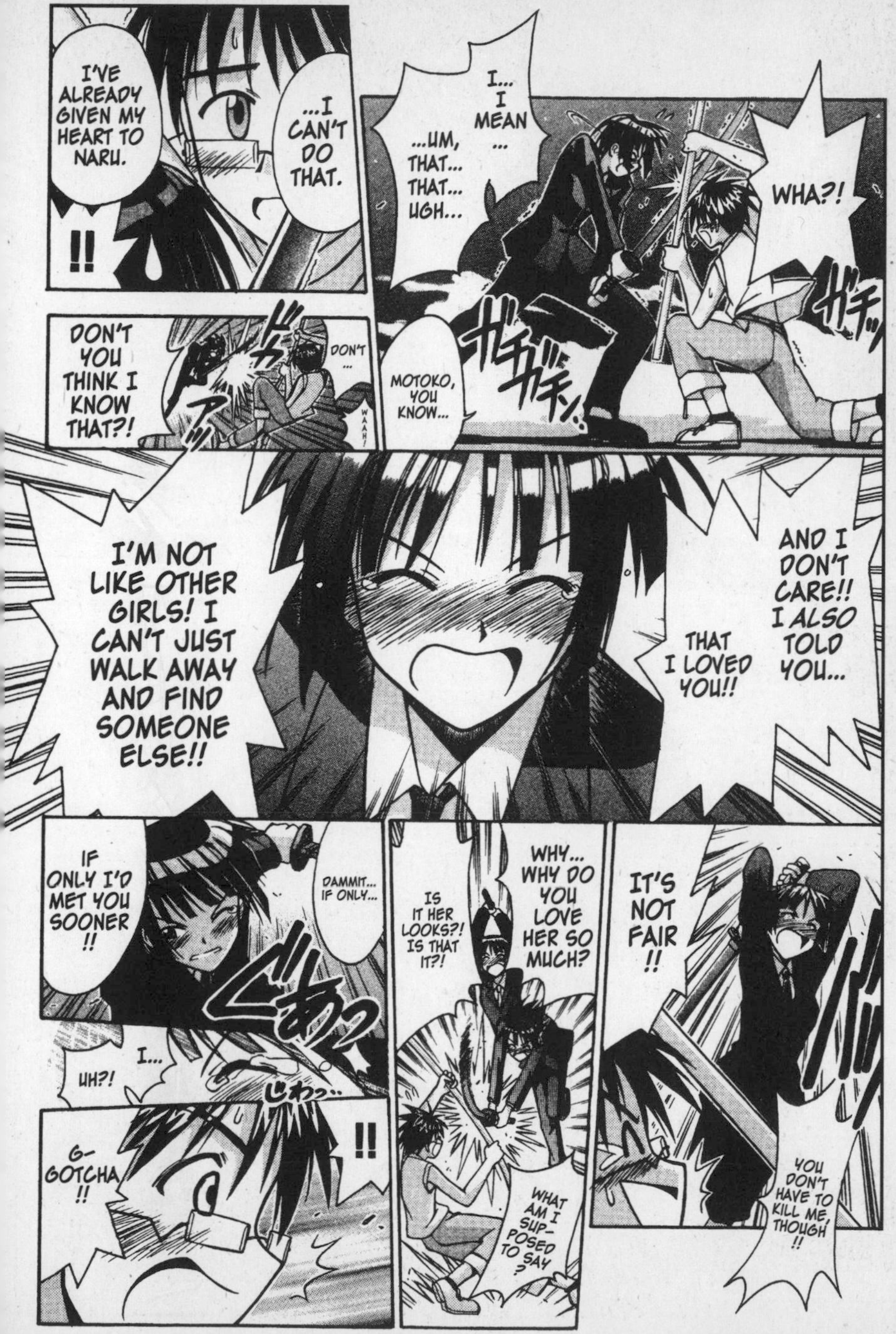
WHA?!
I... I MEAN ...
...UM, THAT... THAT... UGH...
MOTOKO, YOU KNOW...
...I CAN'T DO THAT.
I'VE ALREADY GIVEN MY HEART TO NARU.
!!
DON'T ...
WAAH!
DON'T YOU THINK I KNOW THAT?!
AND I DON'T CARE!! I ALSO TOLD YOU...
THAT I LOVED YOU!!
I'M NOT LIKE OTHER GIRLS! I CAN'T JUST WALK AWAY AND FIND SOMEONE ELSE!!
IT'S NOT FAIR !!
YOU DON'T HAVE TO KILL ME, THOUGH !!
WHY... WHY DO YOU LOVE HER SO MUCH?
IS IT HER LOOKS?! IS THAT IT?!
WHAT AM I SUP-POSED TO SAY ?
DAMMIT... IF ONLY...
IF ONLY I'D MET YOU SOONER !!
I...
UH?!
!!
G-GOTCHA !!

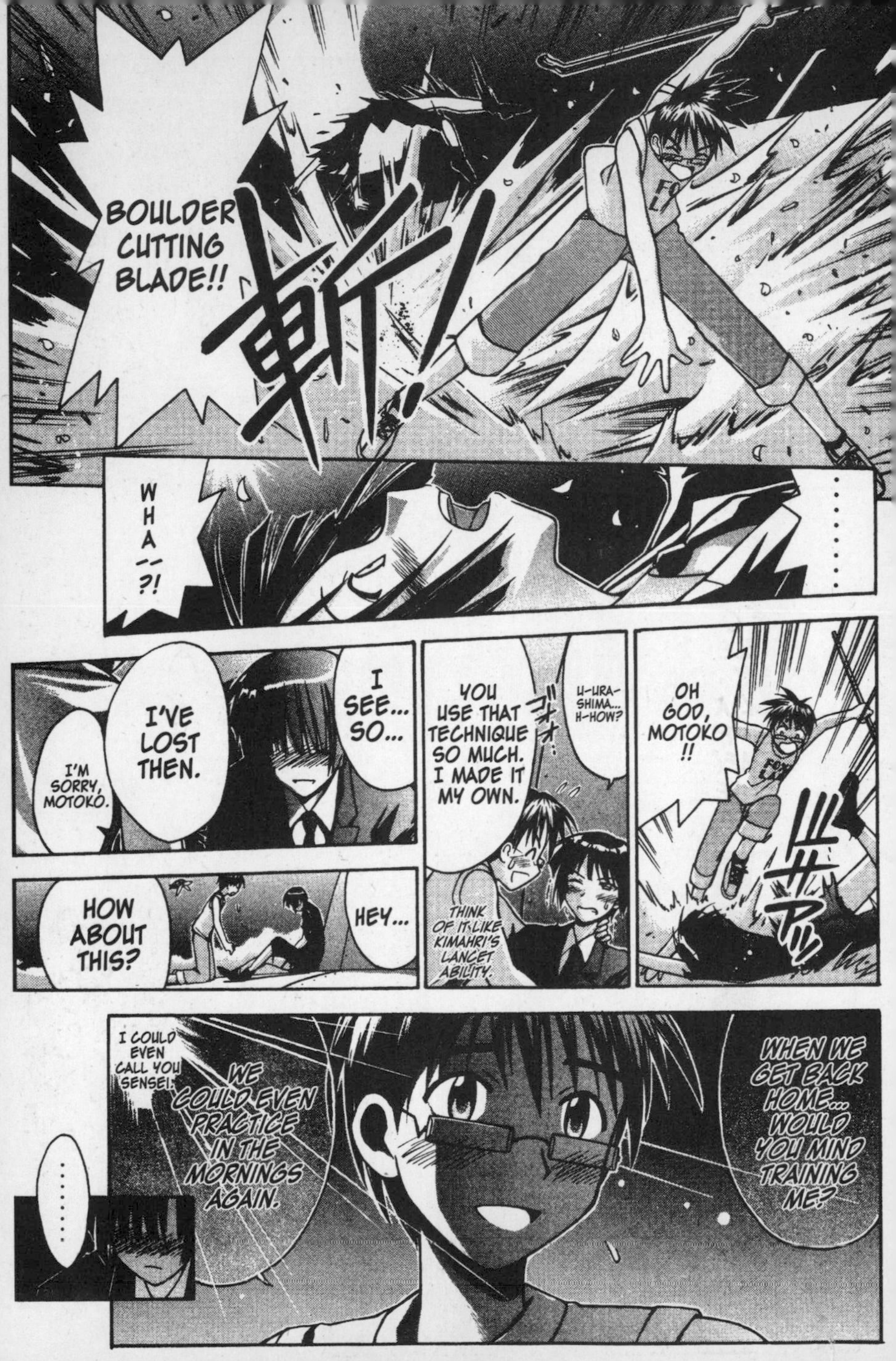
BOULDER CUTTING BLADE!!
斬
......
WHA--?!
OH GOD, MOTOKO!!
U-URASHIMA... H-HOW?
YOU USE THAT TECHNIQUE SO MUCH. I MADE IT MY OWN.
THINK OF IT LIKE KIMAHRI'S LANCET ABILITY.
I SEE... SO...
I'VE LOST THEN.
I'M SORRY, MOTOKO.
HEY...
HOW ABOUT THIS?
WHEN WE GET BACK HOME... WOULD YOU MIND TRAINING ME?
WE COULD EVEN PRACTICE IN THE MORNINGS AGAIN.
I COULD EVEN CALL YOU SENSEI.
......

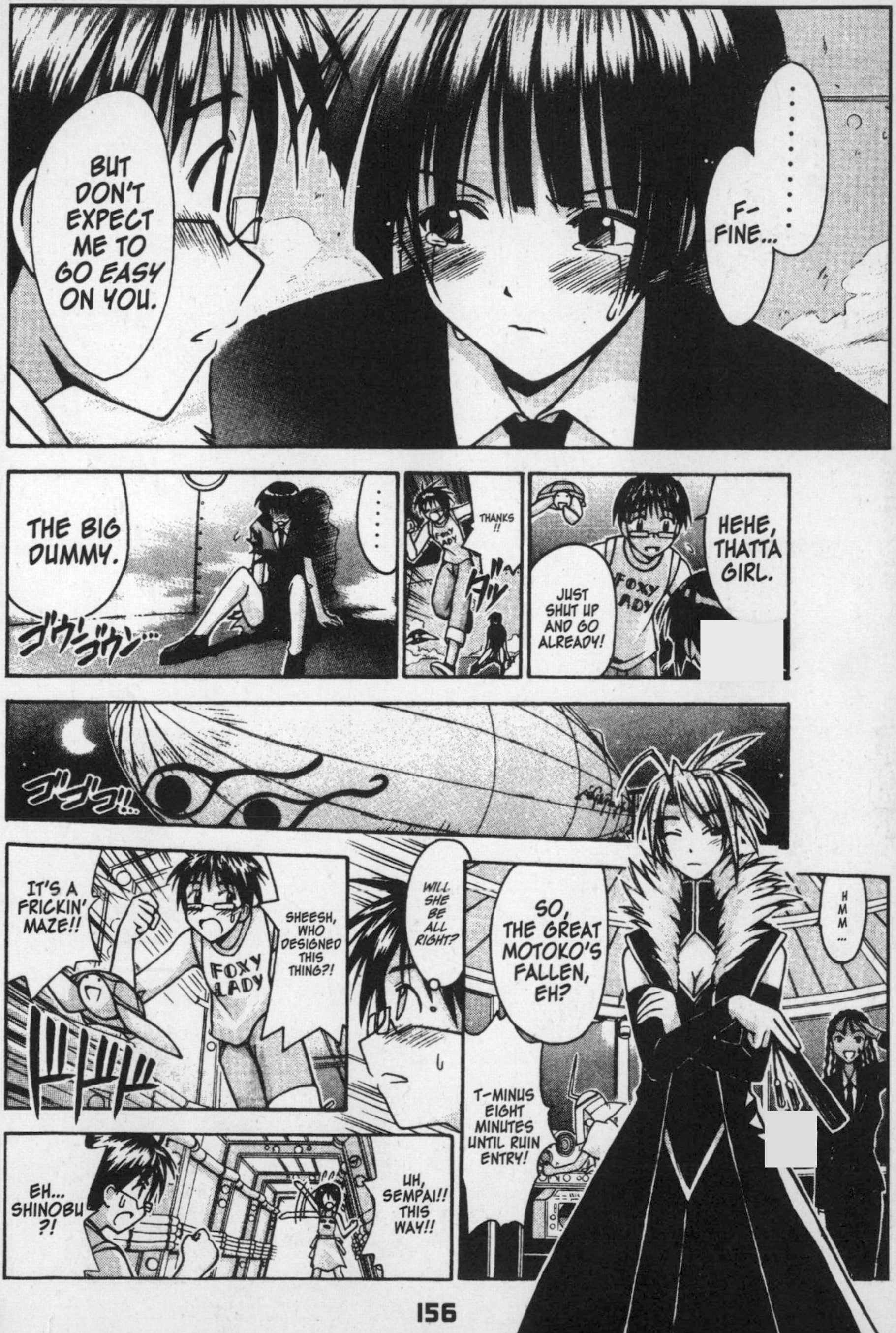
......
F-FINE...
BUT DON'T EXPECT ME TO GO EASY ON YOU.
HEHE, THATTA GIRL.
JUST SHUT UP AND GO ALREADY!
THANKS!!
......
THE BIG DUMMY.
ゴウンゴウン…
ゴゴゴ!!…
HMM...
SO, THE GREAT MOTOKO'S FALLEN, EH?
T-MINUS EIGHT MINUTES UNTIL RUIN ENTRY!
WILL SHE BE ALL RIGHT?
SHEESH, WHO DESIGNED THIS THING?!
IT'S A FRICKIN' MAZE!!
UH, SEMPAI!! THIS WAY!!
EH... SHINOBU?!

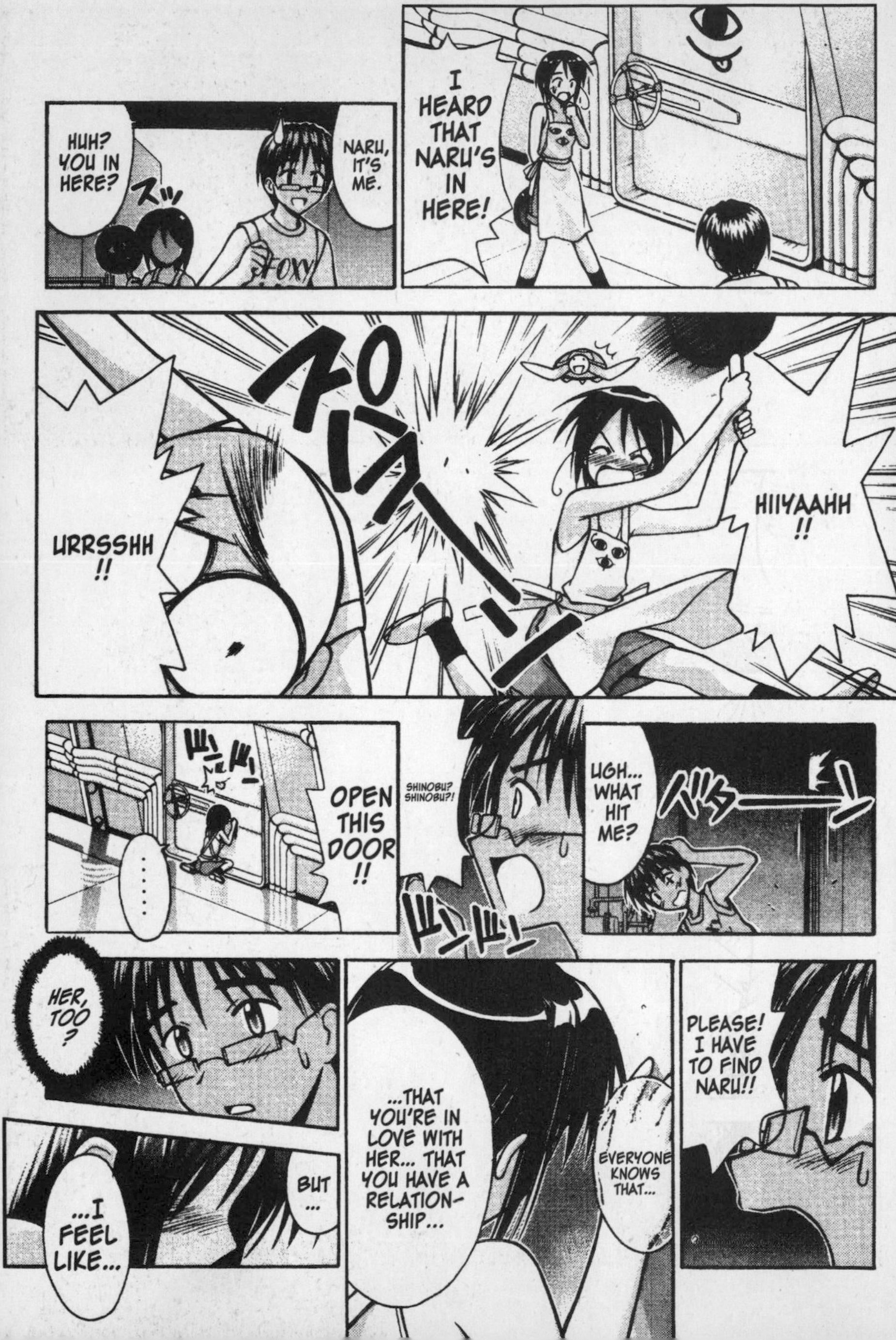
I HEARD THAT NARU'S IN HERE!
NARU, IT'S ME.
HUH? YOU IN HERE?
HIIYAAHH!!
URRSSHH!!
UGH... WHAT HIT ME?
SHINOBU? SHINOBU?!
OPEN THIS DOOR!!
......
PLEASE! I HAVE TO FIND NARU!!
EVERYONE KNOWS THAT...
...THAT YOU'RE IN LOVE WITH HER... THAT YOU HAVE A RELATION-SHIP...
HER, TOO?
BUT ...
...I FEEL LIKE...

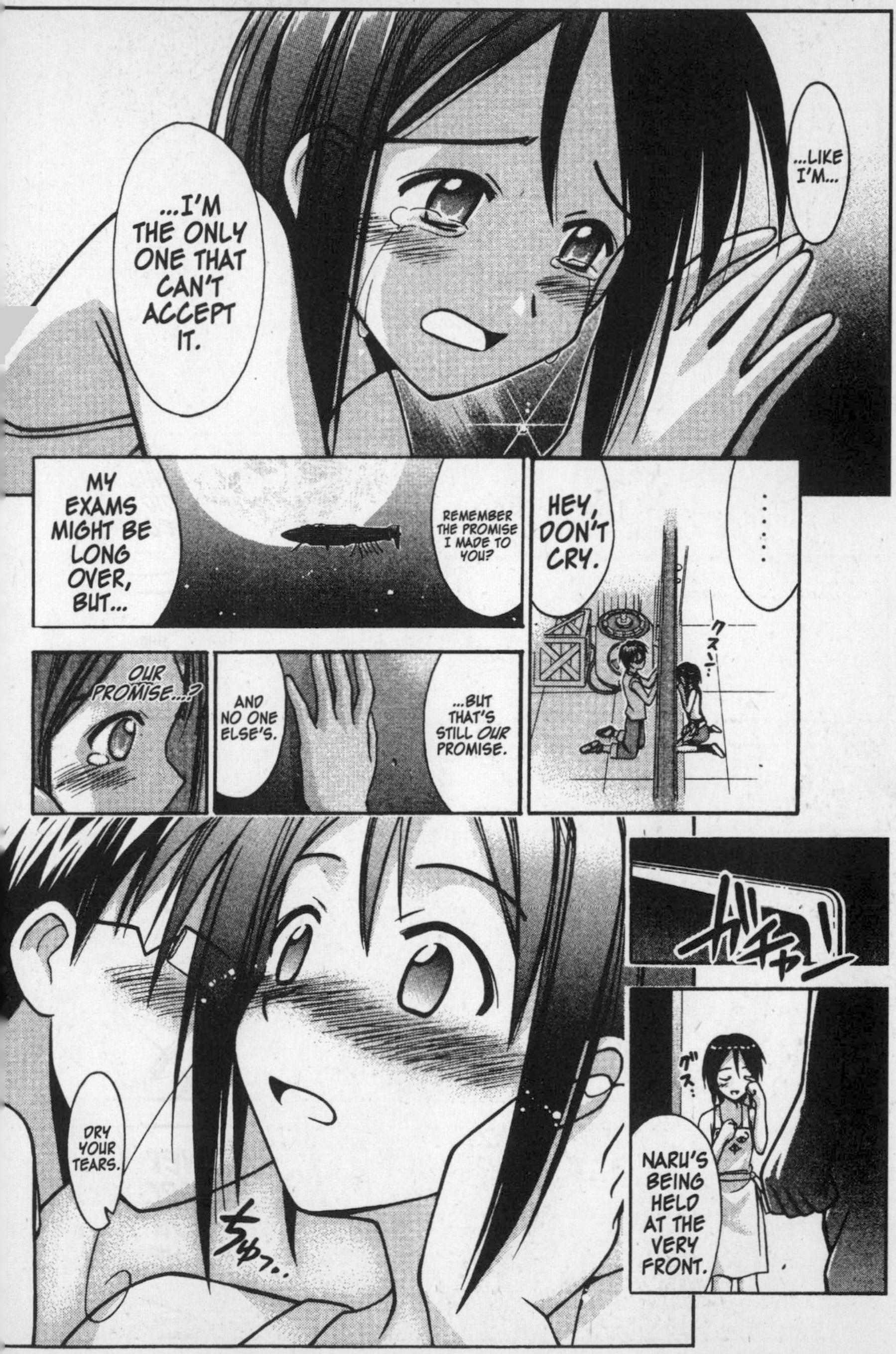

...LIKE I'M...
...I'M THE ONLY ONE THAT CAN'T ACCEPT IT.
......
クスン
HEY, DON'T CRY.
REMEMBER THE PROMISE I MADE TO YOU?
MY EXAMS MIGHT BE LONG OVER, BUT...
...BUT THAT'S STILL *OUR* PROMISE.
AND NO ONE ELSE'S.
OUR PROMISE...?
ガチャ
グス…
NARU'S BEING HELD AT THE VERY FRONT.
DRY YOUR TEARS.
ちゅっ..

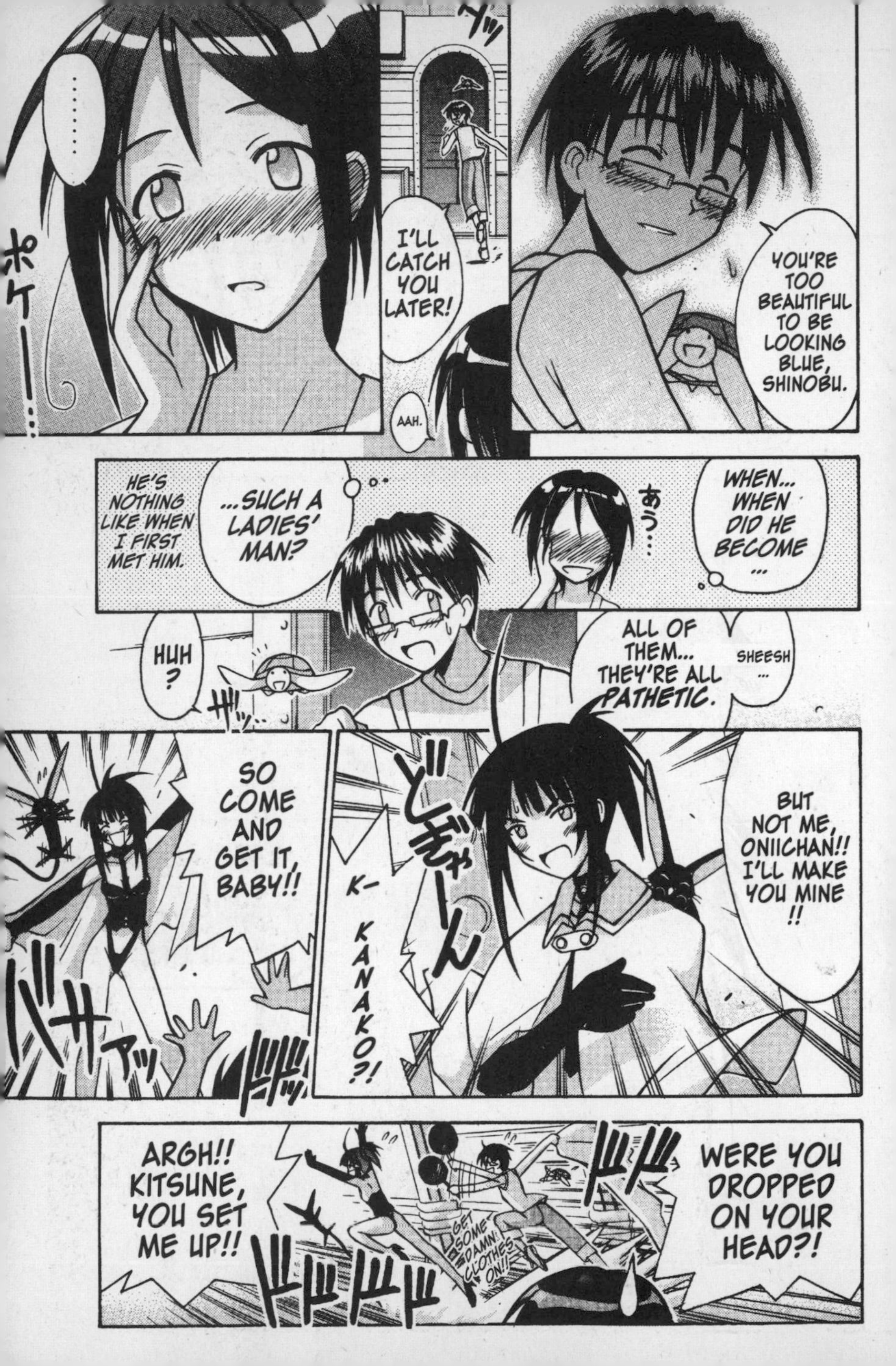
YOU'RE TOO BEAUTIFUL TO BE LOOKING BLUE, SHINOBU.
ダッ
I'LL CATCH YOU LATER!
AAH.
……
ポケー…
WHEN... WHEN DID HE BECOME ...
あう…
...SUCH A LADIES' MAN?
HE'S NOTHING LIKE WHEN I FIRST MET HIM.
SHEESH ...
ALL OF THEM... THEY'RE ALL PATHETIC.
HUH ?
ザッ…
BUT NOT ME, ONIICHAN!! I'LL MAKE YOU MINE !!
どぎゃーん
K-KANAKO?!
SO COME AND GET IT, BABY!!
バサァッ
WERE YOU DROPPED ON YOUR HEAD?!
GET SOME DAMN CLOTHES ON!!
ARGH!! KITSUNE, YOU SET ME UP!!

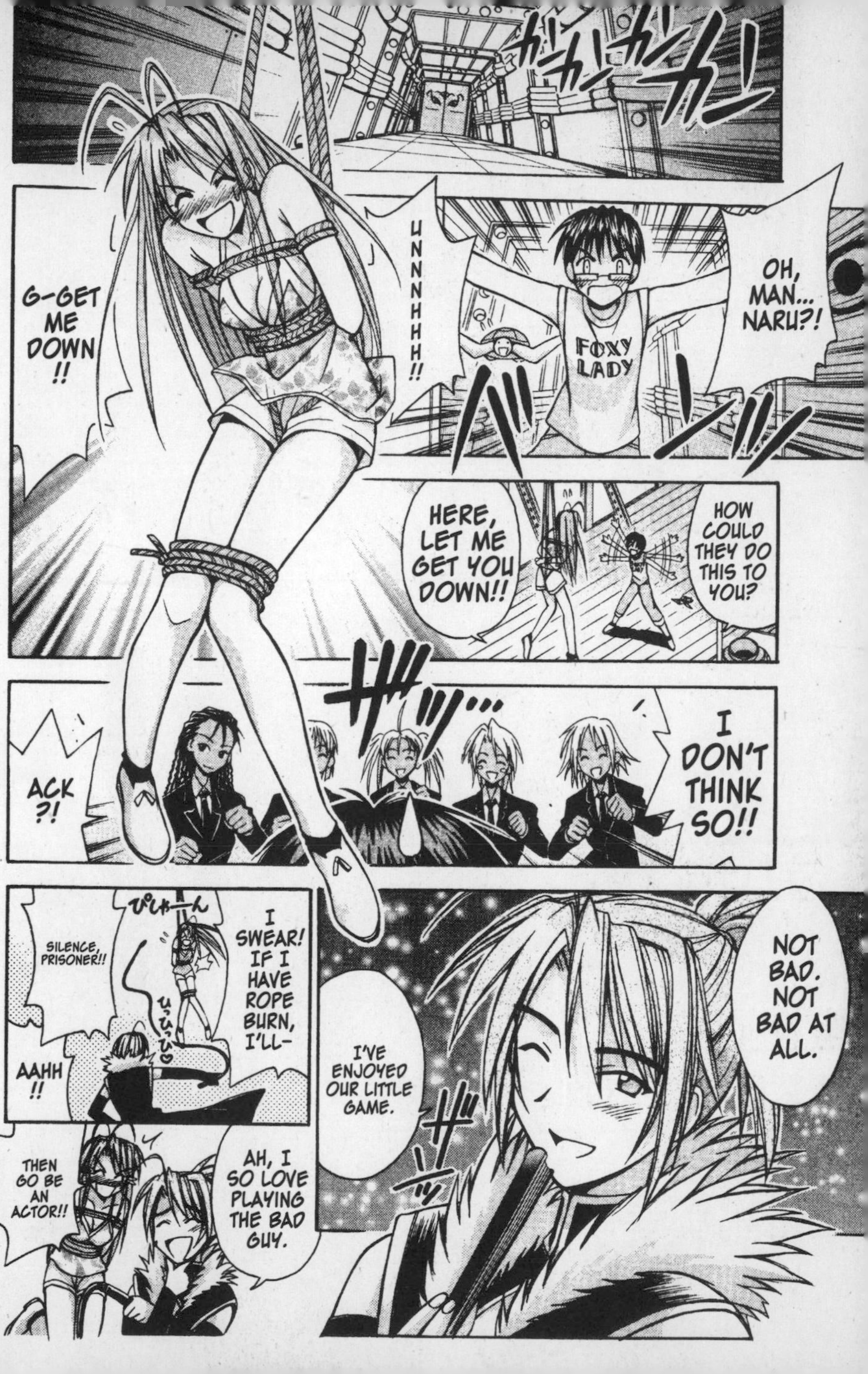
OH, MAN... NARU?!
HOW COULD THEY DO THIS TO YOU?
HERE, LET ME GET YOU DOWN!!
I DON'T THINK SO!!
ACK?!
UNNNNHHHH!!
G-GET ME DOWN!!
NOT BAD. NOT BAD AT ALL.
I'VE ENJOYED OUR LITTLE GAME.
I SWEAR! IF I HAVE ROPE BURN, I'LL-
SILENCE, PRISONER!!
AAHH!!
AH, I SO LOVE PLAYING THE BAD GUY.
THEN GO BE AN ACTOR!!

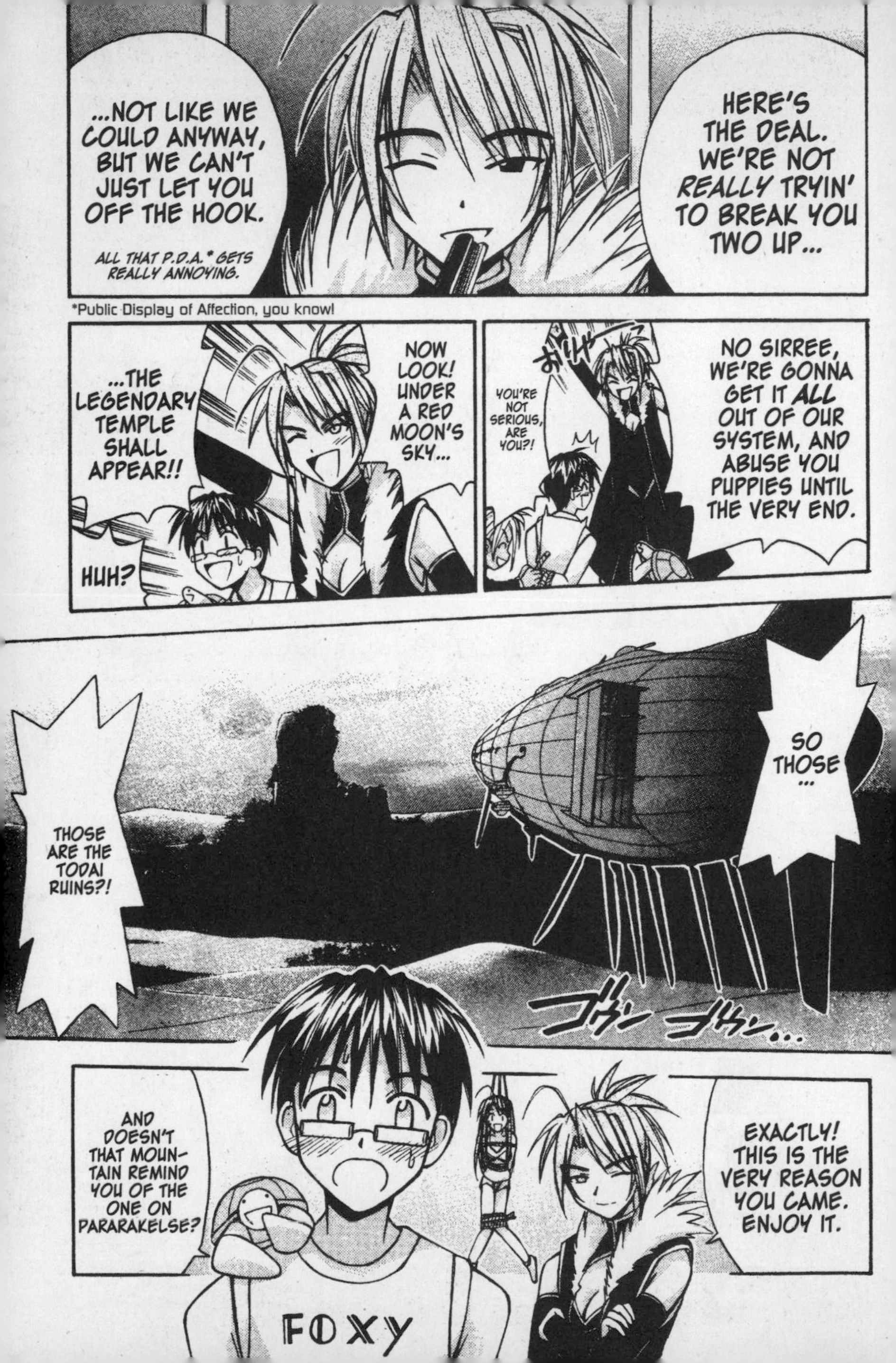
HERE'S THE DEAL. WE'RE NOT *REALLY* TRYIN' TO BREAK YOU TWO UP...
...NOT LIKE WE COULD ANYWAY, BUT WE CAN'T JUST LET YOU OFF THE HOOK.
ALL THAT P.D.A.* GETS REALLY ANNOYING.
*Public Display of Affection, you know!
NO SIRREE, WE'RE GONNA GET IT **ALL** OUT OF OUR SYSTEM, AND ABUSE YOU PUPPIES UNTIL THE VERY END.
YOU'RE NOT SERIOUS, ARE YOU?!
NOW LOOK! UNDER A RED MOON'S SKY...
...THE LEGENDARY TEMPLE SHALL APPEAR!!
HUH?
SO THOSE ...
THOSE ARE THE TODAI RUINS?!
EXACTLY! THIS IS THE VERY REASON YOU CAME. ENJOY IT.
AND DOESN'T THAT MOUNTAIN REMIND YOU OF THE ONE ON PARARAKELSE?
FOXY

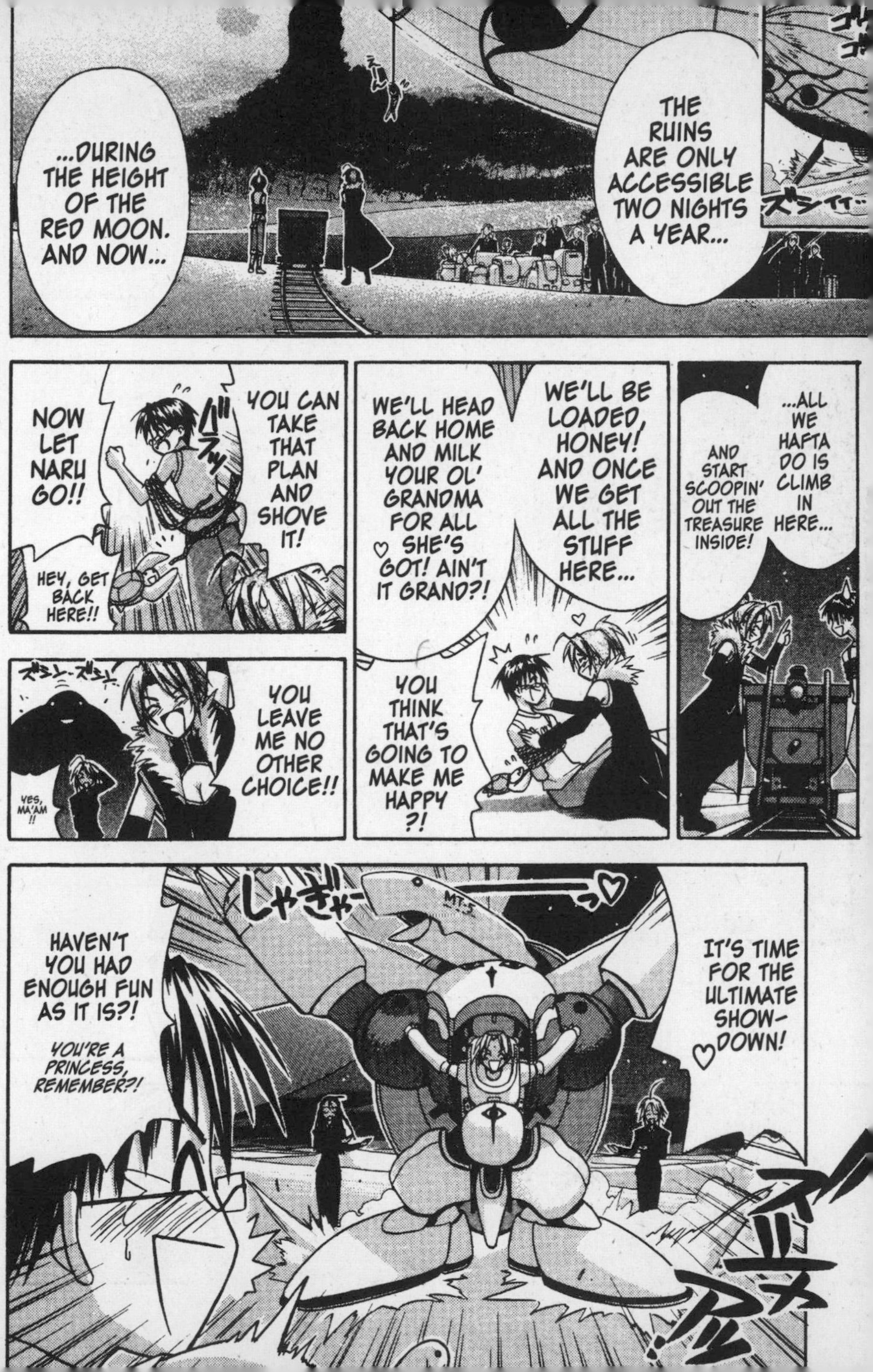
THE RUINS ARE ONLY ACCESSIBLE TWO NIGHTS A YEAR...
...DURING THE HEIGHT OF THE RED MOON. AND NOW...
...ALL WE HAFTA DO IS CLIMB IN HERE...
AND START SCOOPIN' OUT THE TREASURE INSIDE!
WE'LL BE LOADED, HONEY! AND ONCE WE GET ALL THE STUFF HERE...
WE'LL HEAD BACK HOME AND MILK YOUR OL' GRANDMA FOR ALL SHE'S GOT! AIN'T IT GRAND?!
YOU THINK THAT'S GOING TO MAKE ME HAPPY?!
YOU CAN TAKE THAT PLAN AND SHOVE IT!
NOW LET NARU GO!!
HEY, GET BACK HERE!!
YOU LEAVE ME NO OTHER CHOICE!!
YES, MA'AM!!
IT'S TIME FOR THE ULTIMATE SHOW-DOWN!
HAVEN'T YOU HAD ENOUGH FUN AS IT IS?!
YOU'RE A PRINCESS, REMEMBER?!

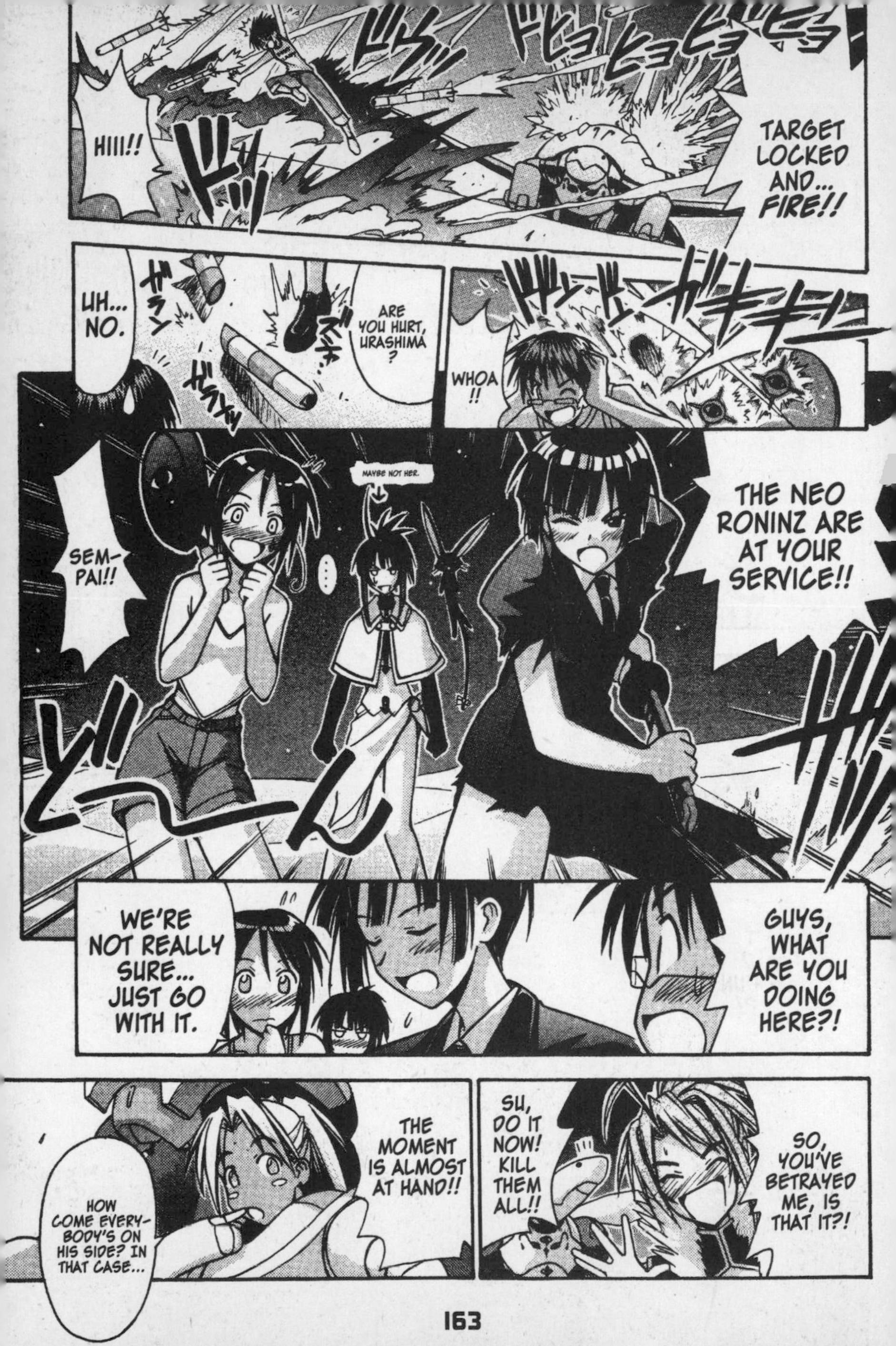
TARGET LOCKED AND... FIRE!!
HIIII!!
WHOA !!
ARE YOU HURT, URASHIMA?
UH... NO.
THE NEO RONINZ ARE AT YOUR SERVICE!!
MAYBE NOT HER.
...
SEM-PAI!!
GUYS, WHAT ARE YOU DOING HERE?!
WE'RE NOT REALLY SURE... JUST GO WITH IT.
SO, YOU'VE BETRAYED ME, IS THAT IT?!
SU, DO IT NOW! KILL THEM ALL!!
THE MOMENT IS ALMOST AT HAND!!
HOW COME EVERY-BODY'S ON HIS SIDE? IN THAT CASE...

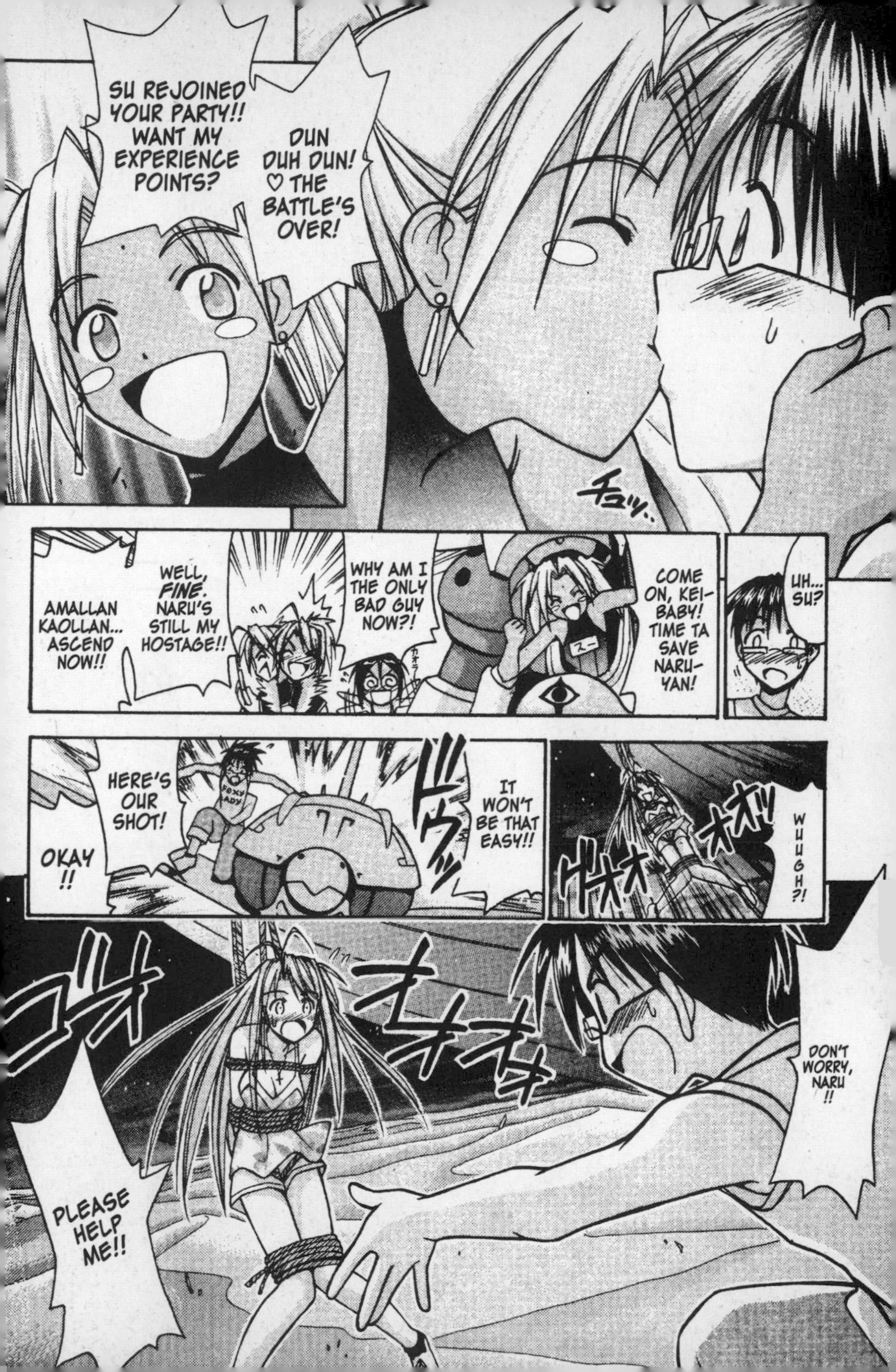

DUN DUH DUN! ♡ THE BATTLE'S OVER!
SU REJOINED YOUR PARTY!! WANT MY EXPERIENCE POINTS?
UH... SU?
COME ON, KEI-BABY! TIME TA SAVE NARU-YAN!
WHY AM I THE ONLY BAD GUY NOW?!
WELL, FINE. NARU'S STILL MY HOSTAGE!!
AMALLAN KAOLLAN... ASCEND NOW!!
WUUGH?!
IT WON'T BE THAT EASY!!
HERE'S OUR SHOT!
OKAY!!
DON'T WORRY, NARU!!
PLEASE HELP ME!!

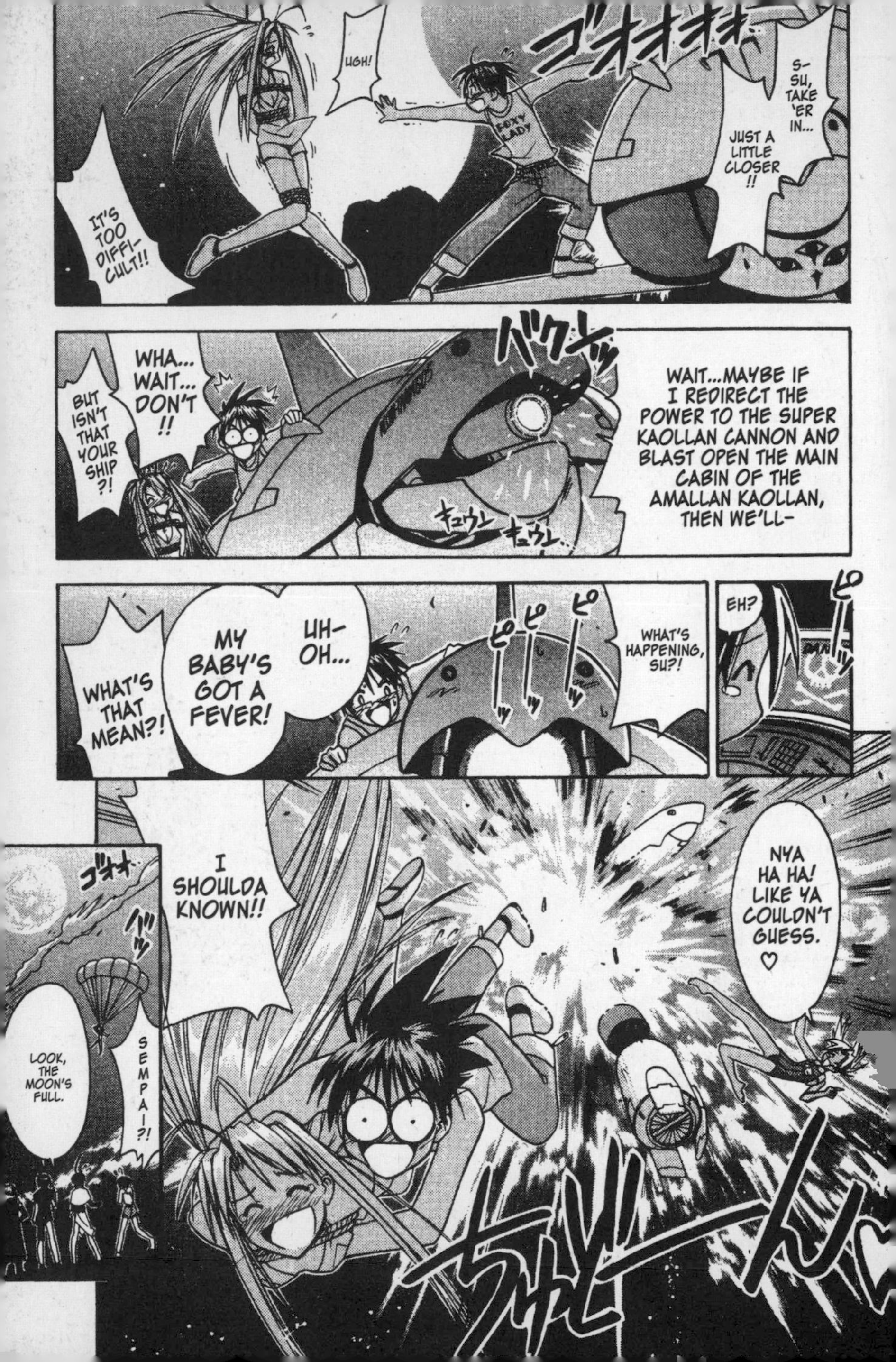
S-SU, TAKE 'ER IN...
JUST A LITTLE CLOSER!!
UGH!
IT'S TOO DIFFI-CULT!!
WAIT...MAYBE IF I REDIRECT THE POWER TO THE SUPER KAOLLAN CANNON AND BLAST OPEN THE MAIN CABIN OF THE AMALLAN KAOLLAN, THEN WE'LL-
WHA... WAIT... DON'T!!
BUT ISN'T THAT YOUR SHIP?!
EH?
WHAT'S HAPPENING, SU?!
UH-OH...
MY BABY'S GOT A FEVER!
WHAT'S THAT MEAN?!
NYA HA HA! LIKE YA COULDN'T GUESS. ♡
I SHOULDA KNOWN!!
SEMPAI?!
LOOK, THE MOON'S FULL.

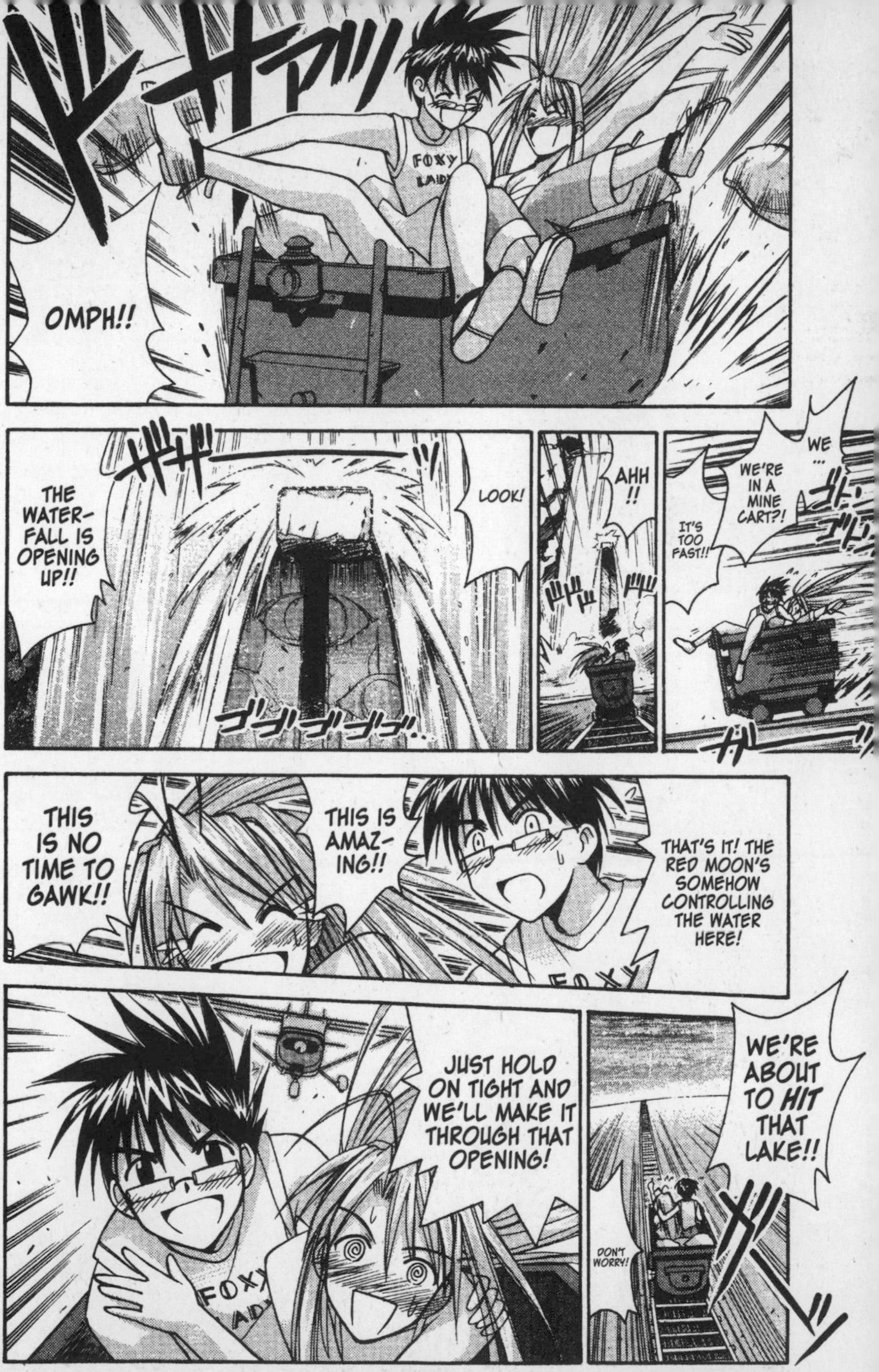

OMPH!!
WE ...
WE'RE IN A MINE CART?!
IT'S TOO FAST!!
AHH !!
LOOK!
THE WATER-FALL IS OPENING UP!!
THAT'S IT! THE RED MOON'S SOMEHOW CONTROLLING THE WATER HERE!
THIS IS AMAZING!!
THIS IS NO TIME TO GAWK!!
WE'RE ABOUT TO *HIT* THAT LAKE!!
DON'T WORRY!
JUST HOLD ON TIGHT AND WE'LL MAKE IT THROUGH THAT OPENING!

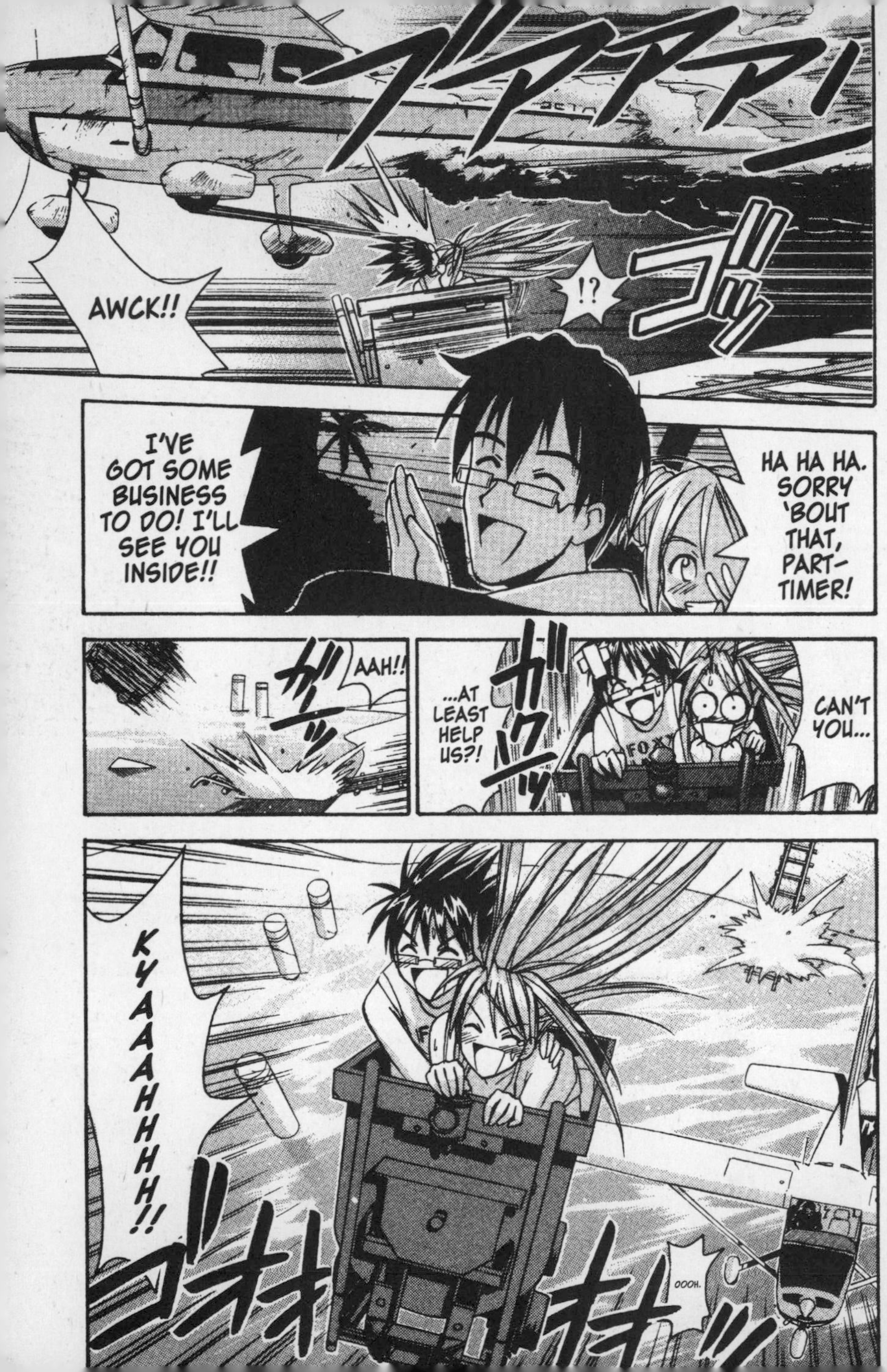
AWCK!!
!?
HA HA HA. SORRY 'BOUT THAT, PART-TIMER!
I'VE GOT SOME BUSINESS TO DO! I'LL SEE YOU INSIDE!!
CAN'T YOU...
...AT LEAST HELP US?!
AAH!!
KYAAAAHHHHH!!
OOOH.

Hinata.108. Outfit Collection.

MAGI Name Stage Version

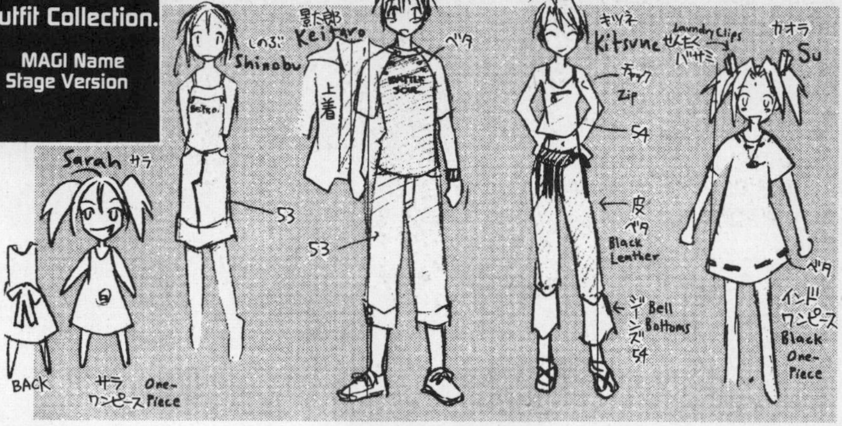

しのぶ Shinobu
53
景太郎 Keitaro
上着
ベタ
53
キツネ Kitsune
チャック Zip
54
皮 ベタ Black Leather
ジーンズ 54
Bell Bottoms
カオラ Su
Laundry Clips せんたくバサミ
ベタ
インドワンピース Black One-Piece
Sarah サラ
BACK
サラ ワンピース One-Piece

Keitaro - Final Battle Design

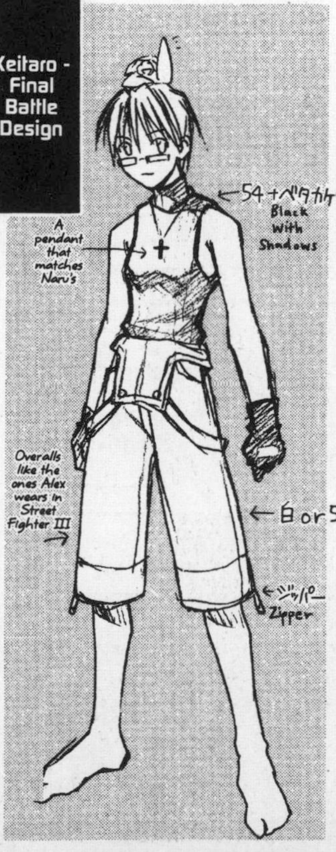

54＋ベタカゲ Black With Shadows
A pendant that matches Naru's
Overalls like the ones Alex wears in Street Fighter III
白 or 53
ジッパー Zipper

A postcard, sent to us by Takashi Miyamura from the Fukuoka Prefecture, inspired the design for the Mecha-Tamago 5. The unit traces all of Su's actions within the cockpit, and relays them into direct actions.

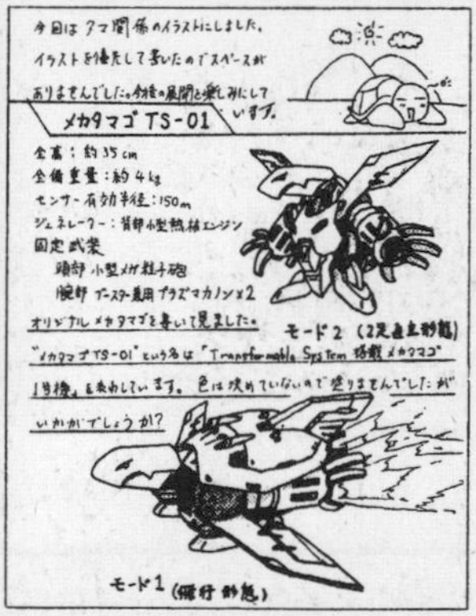

今回はタマ関係のイラストにしました。
メカタマゴ TS-01
全高：約35cm
全備重量：約4kg
センサー有効半径：150m
固定武装
オリジナルメカタマゴを書いて見ました。
モード2
いかがでしょうか?
モード1

Here is the original design for the ceremonial altar found within the Todai Ruins (Hinata.114). At first I envisioned it as a sunken pyramid with the floor and glyphs visible through the water. However, the end result turned out quite different.

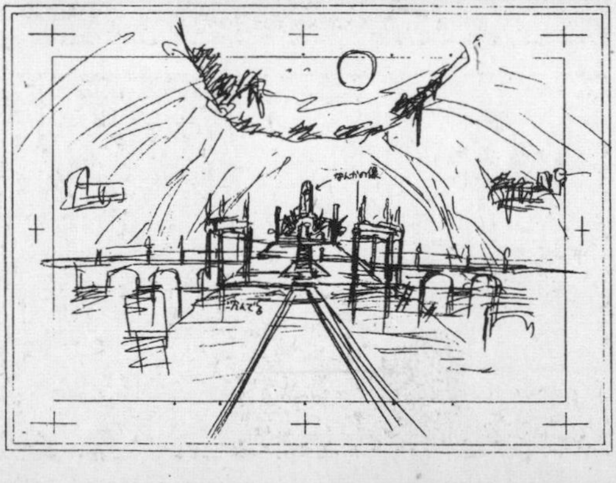

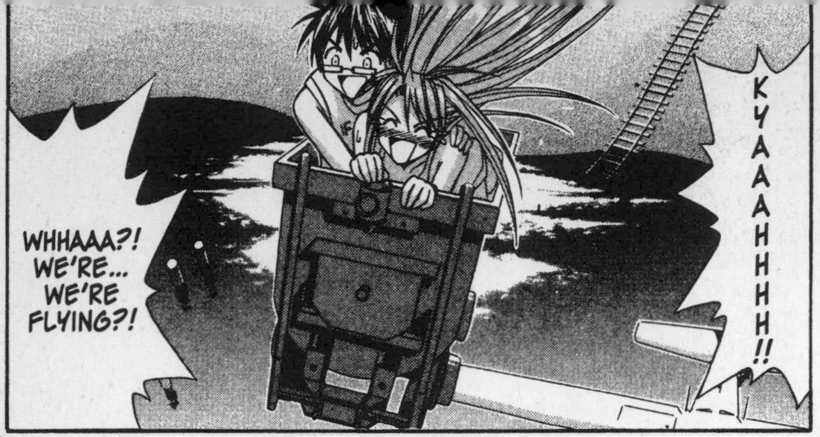
KYAAAAHHHHH!!
WHHAAA?! WE'RE... WE'RE FLYING?!

Love Hina

HINATA..114 A Happy Todai Wedding

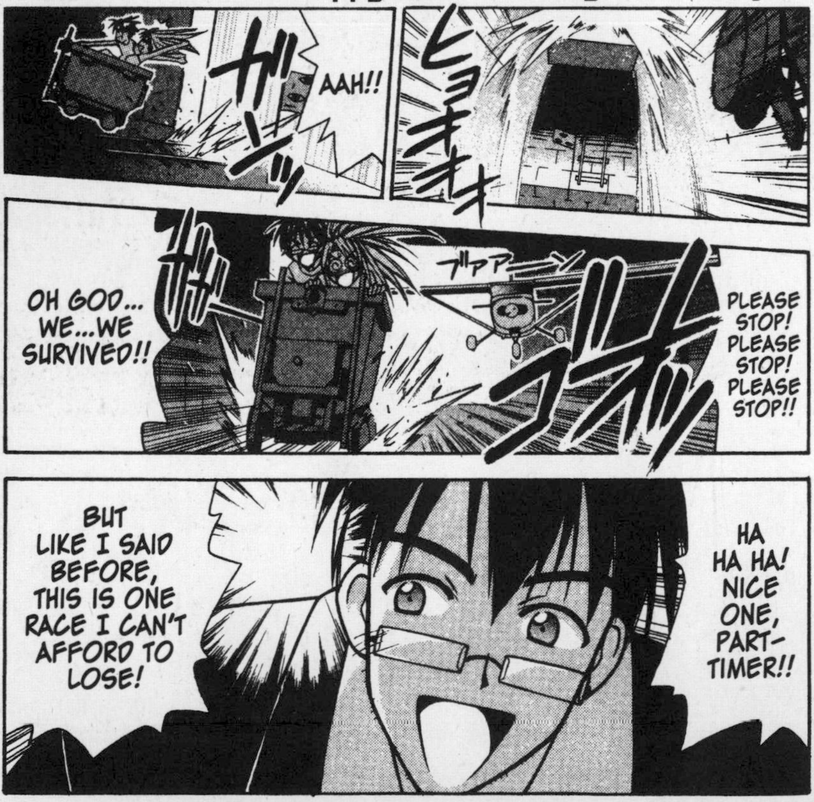
AAH!!
PLEASE STOP! PLEASE STOP! PLEASE STOP!!
OH GOD... WE...WE SURVIVED!!
HA HA HA! NICE ONE, PART-TIMER!!
BUT LIKE I SAID BEFORE, THIS IS ONE RACE I CAN'T AFFORD TO LOSE!

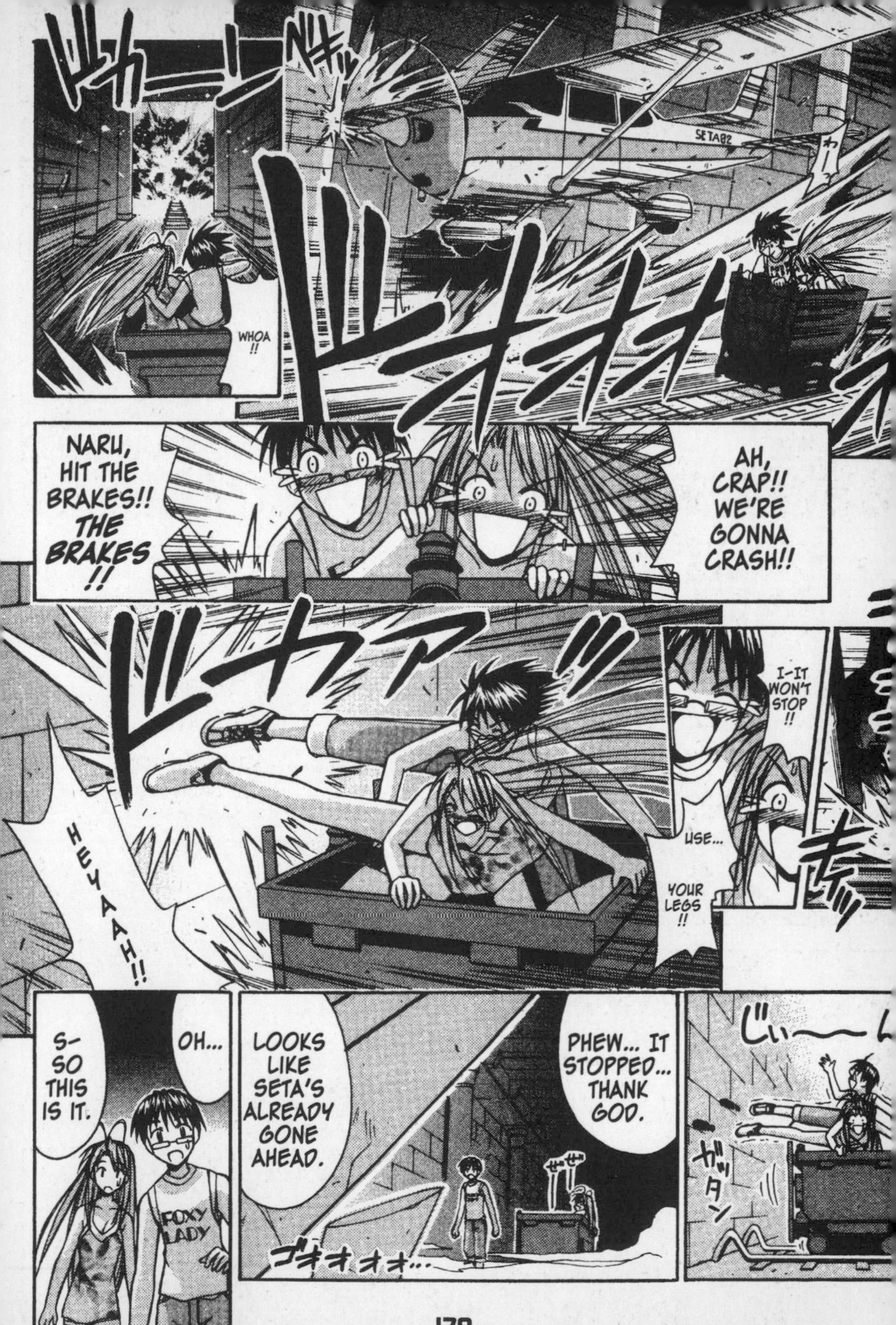
SETA82
WHOA !!
AH, CRAP!! WE'RE GONNA CRASH!!
NARU, HIT THE BRAKES!! THE BRAKES !!
I-IT WON'T STOP !!
USE...
YOUR LEGS !!
HEYAAAH!!
PHEW... IT STOPPED... THANK GOD.
LOOKS LIKE SETA'S ALREADY GONE AHEAD.
OH...
S-SO THIS IS IT.
FOXY LADY

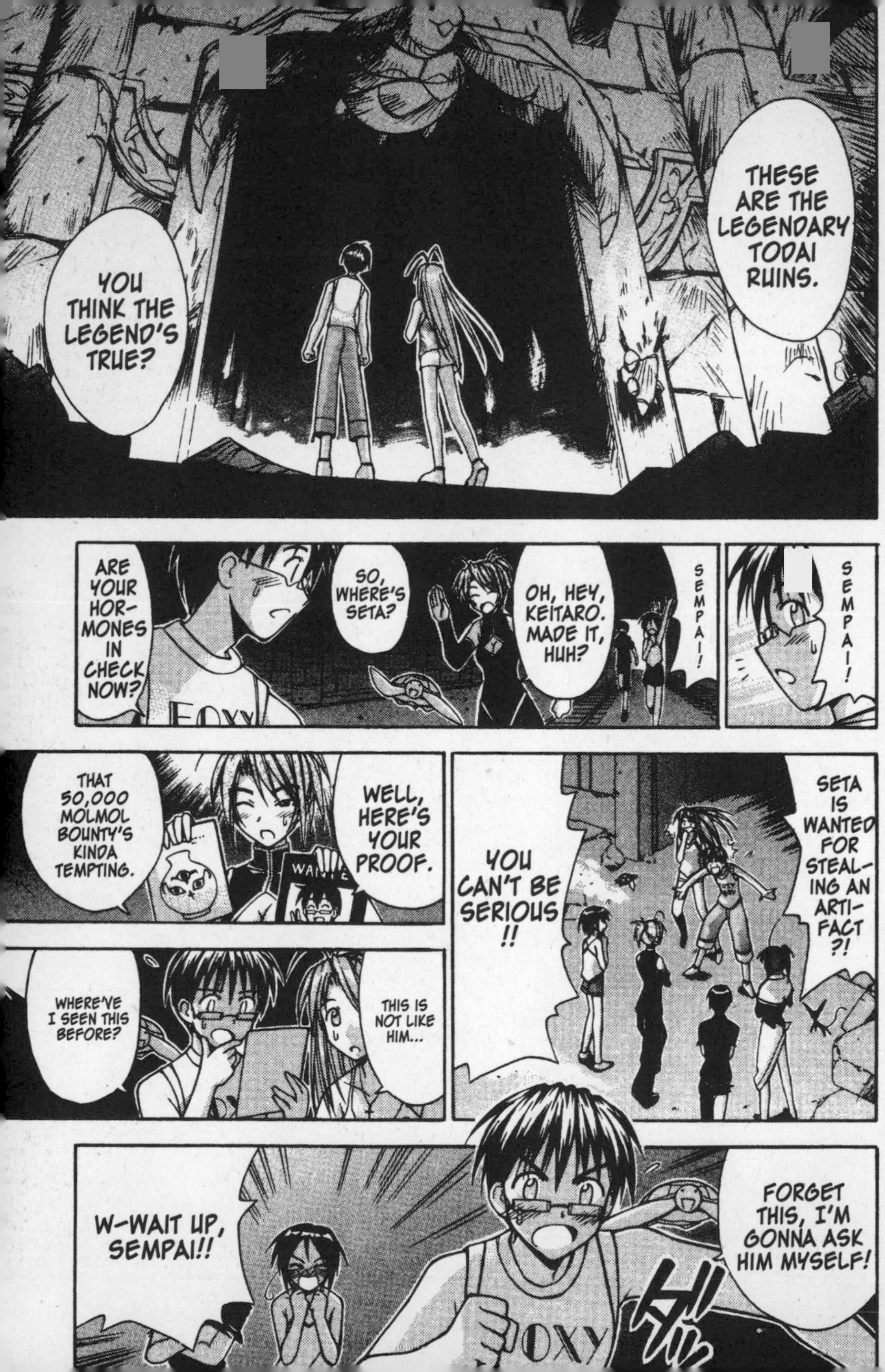
THESE ARE THE LEGENDARY TODAI RUINS.
YOU THINK THE LEGEND'S TRUE?
SEMPAI!
SEMPAI!
OH, HEY, KEITARO. MADE IT, HUH?
SO, WHERE'S SETA?
ARE YOUR HOR-MONES IN CHECK NOW?
SETA IS WANTED FOR STEAL-ING AN ARTI-FACT?!
YOU CAN'T BE SERIOUS!!
WELL, HERE'S YOUR PROOF.
THAT 50,000 MOLMOL BOUNTY'S KINDA TEMPTING.
THIS IS NOT LIKE HIM...
WHERE'VE I SEEN THIS BEFORE?
FORGET THIS, I'M GONNA ASK HIM MYSELF!
W-WAIT UP, SEMPAI!!

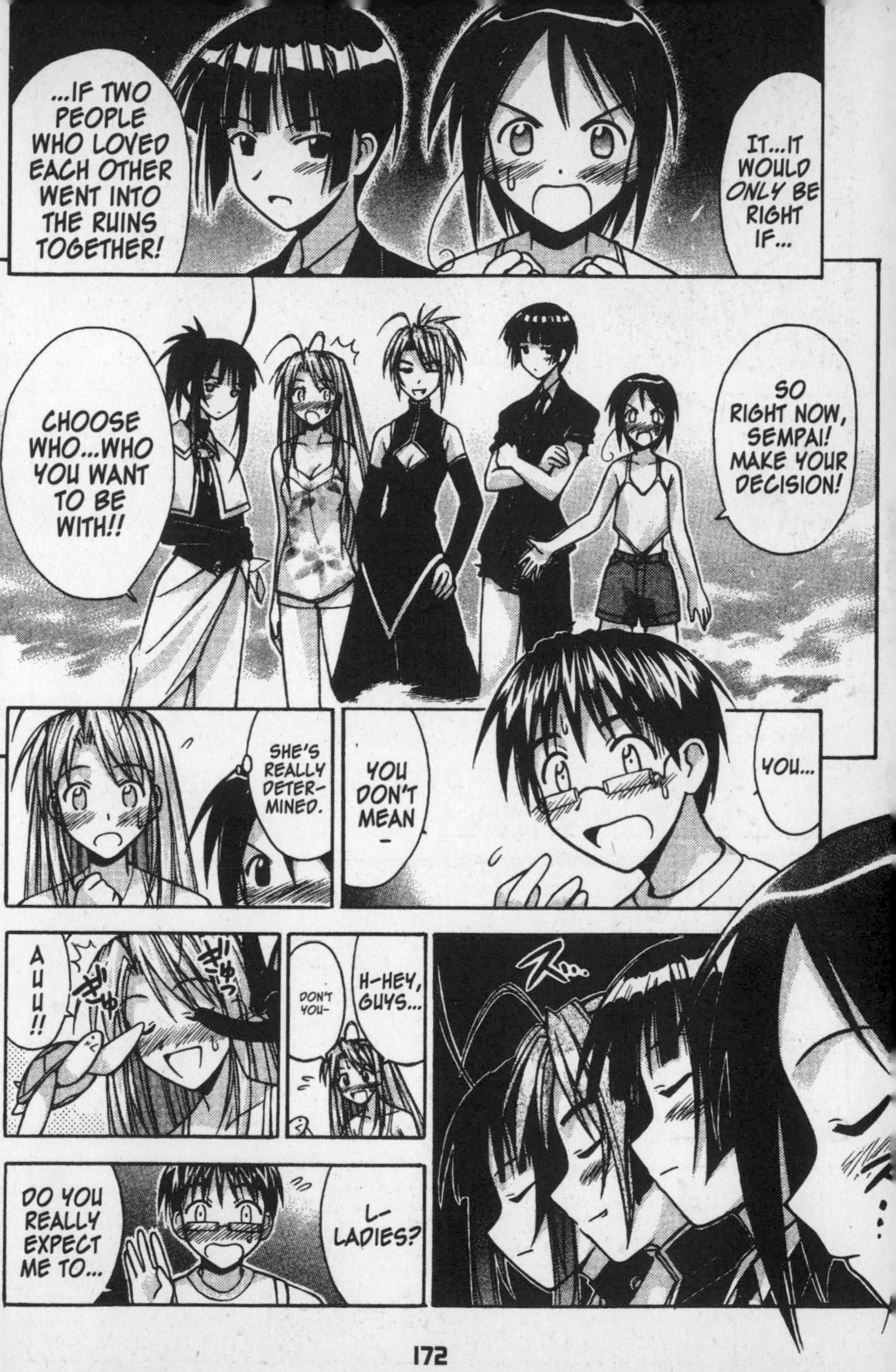
IT...IT WOULD ONLY BE RIGHT IF...
...IF TWO PEOPLE WHO LOVED EACH OTHER WENT INTO THE RUINS TOGETHER!
SO RIGHT NOW, SEMPAI! MAKE YOUR DECISION!
CHOOSE WHO...WHO YOU WANT TO BE WITH!!
YOU...
YOU DON'T MEAN –
SHE'S REALLY DETERMINED.
H-HEY, GUYS...
DON'T YOU-
AUU!!
L-LADIES?
DO YOU REALLY EXPECT ME TO...

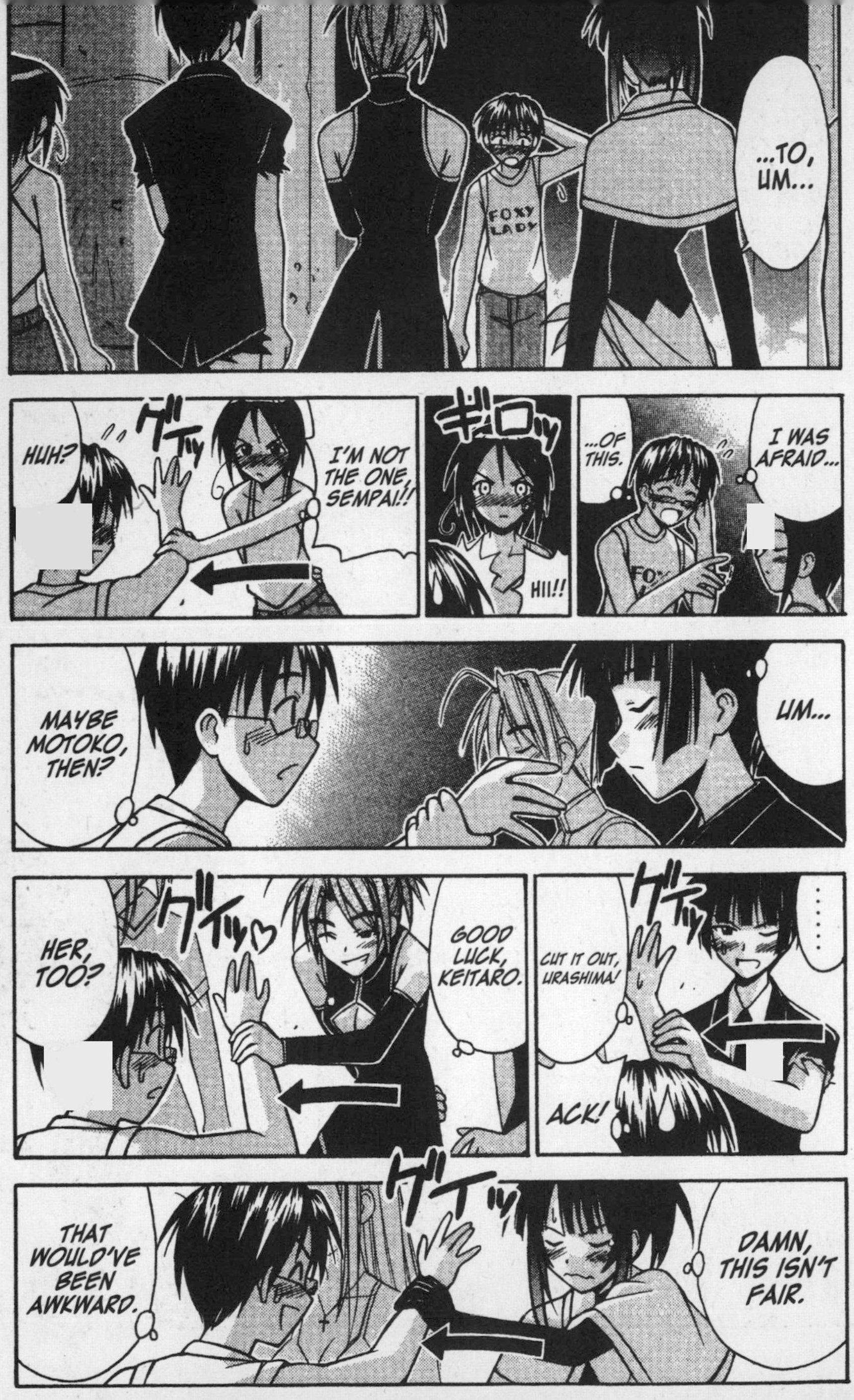
...TO, UM...
I WAS AFRAID...
...OF THIS.
ギロッ
HII!!
I'M NOT THE ONE, SEMPAI!!
グイッ
HUH?
UM...
MAYBE MOTOKO, THEN?
......
グイッ
CUT IT OUT, URASHIMA!
ACK!
GOOD LUCK, KEITARO.
グイッ♡
HER, TOO?
DAMN, THIS ISN'T FAIR.
グイッ
THAT WOULD'VE BEEN AWKWARD.

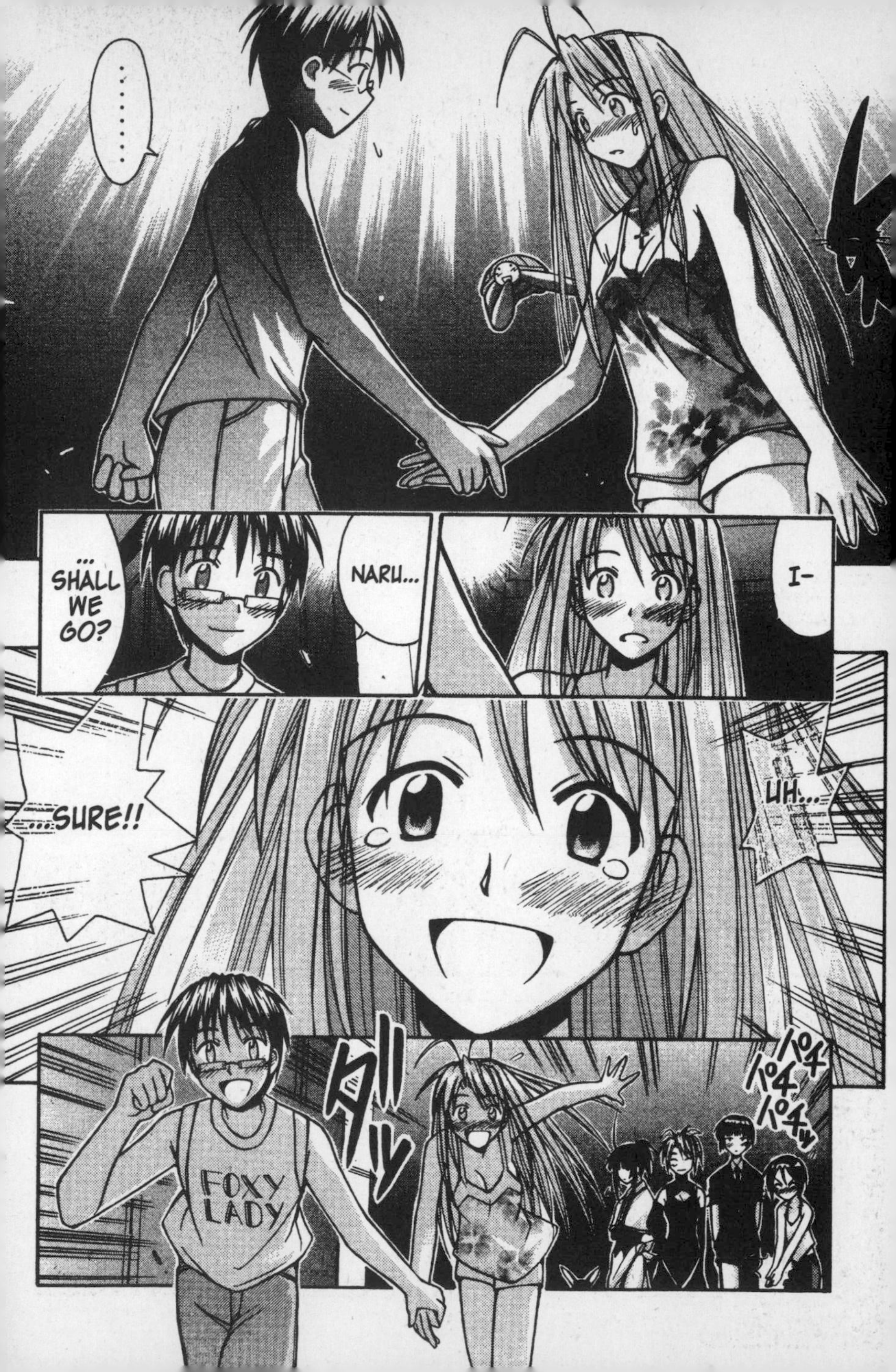
......
I-
NARU...
...SHALL WE GO?
UH...
...SURE!!
パチ
パチ
パチッ
ダッ
FOXY LADY

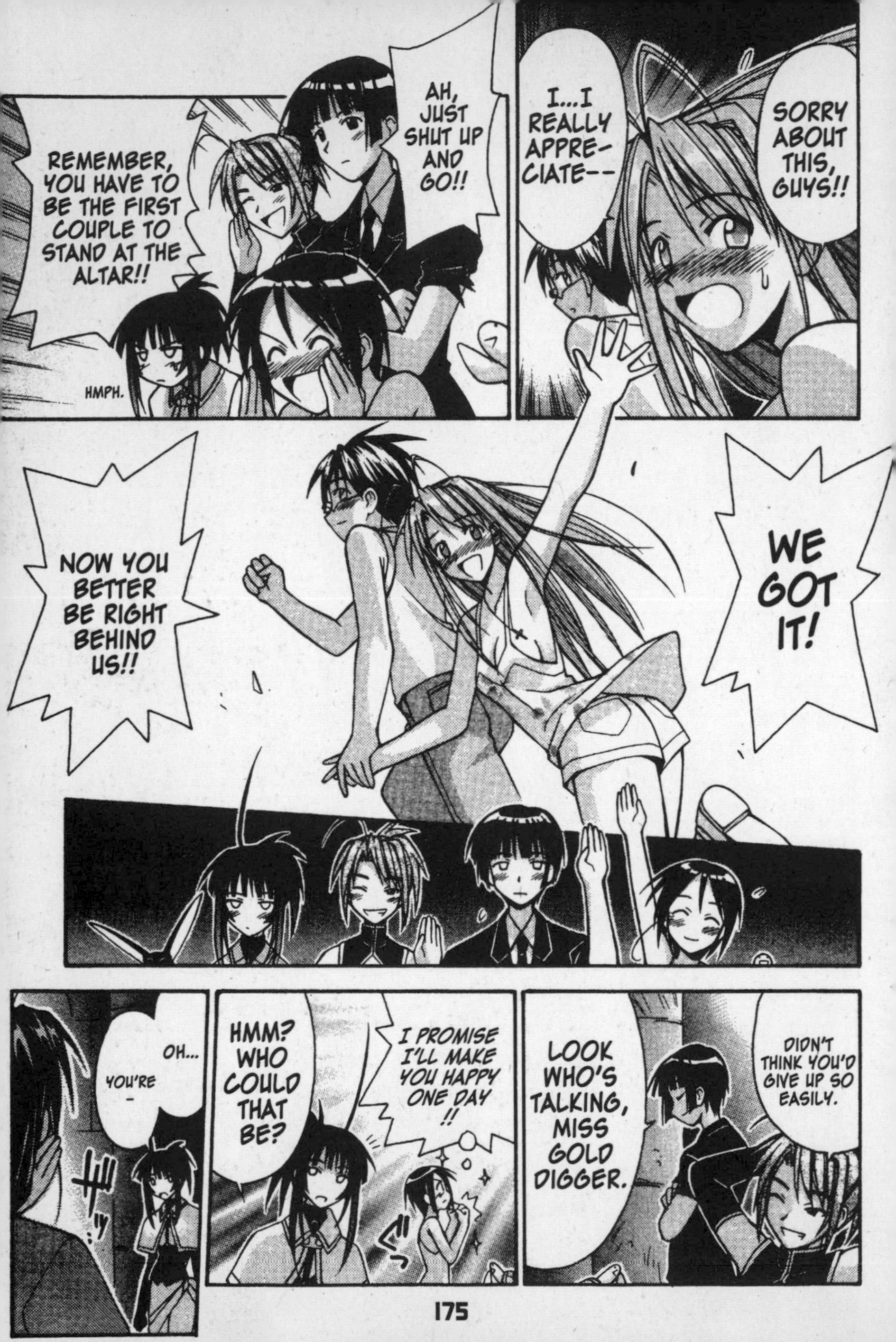
SORRY ABOUT THIS, GUYS!!
I...I REALLY APPRE-CIATE--
AH, JUST SHUT UP AND GO!!
REMEMBER, YOU HAVE TO BE THE FIRST COUPLE TO STAND AT THE ALTAR!!
HMPH.
WE GOT IT!
NOW YOU BETTER BE RIGHT BEHIND US!!
DIDN'T THINK YOU'D GIVE UP SO EASILY.
LOOK WHO'S TALKING, MISS GOLD DIGGER.
I PROMISE I'LL MAKE YOU HAPPY ONE DAY!!
HMM? WHO COULD THAT BE?
OH...
YOU'RE -

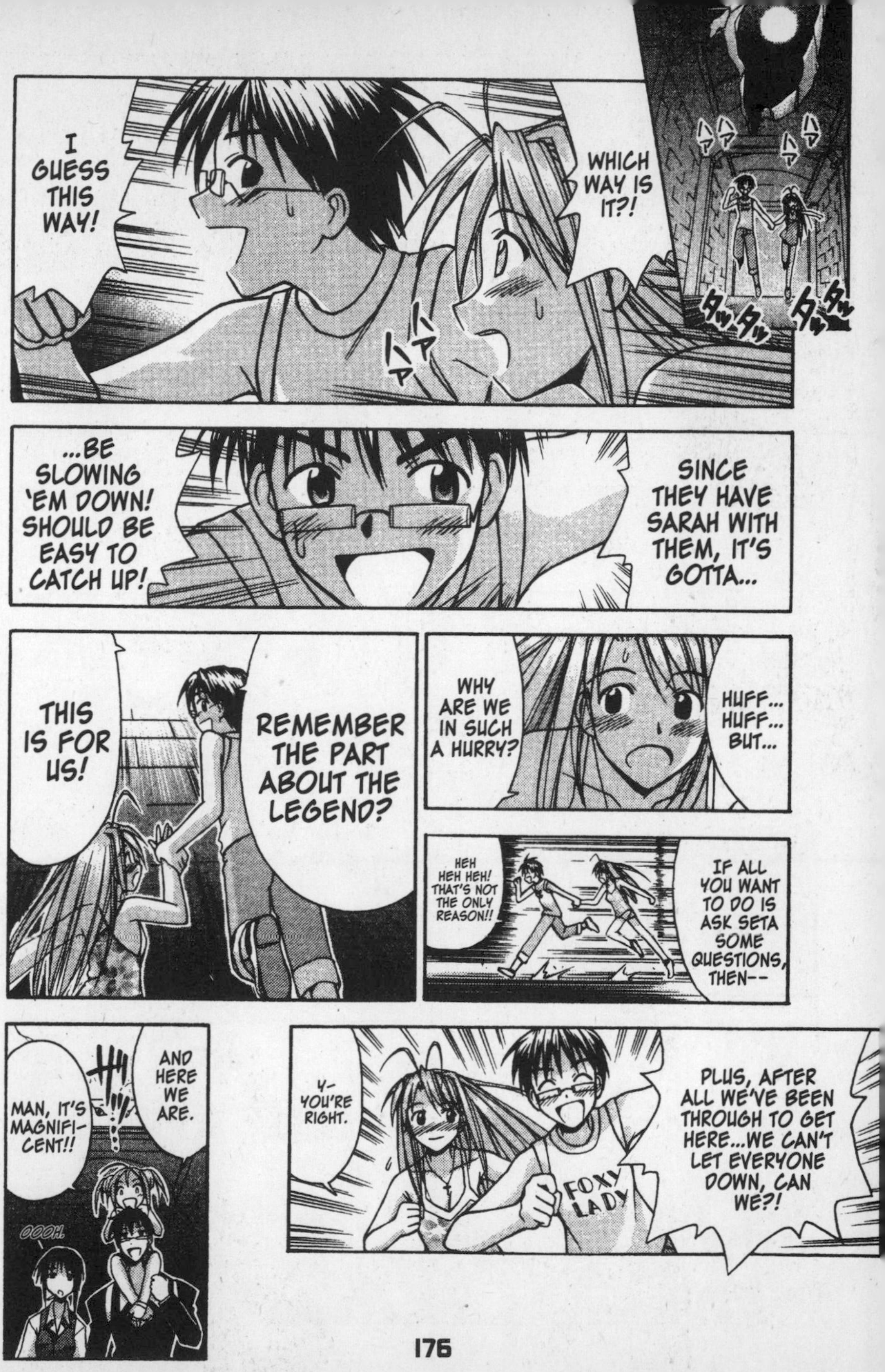
WHICH WAY IS IT?!
I GUESS THIS WAY!
SINCE THEY HAVE SARAH WITH THEM, IT'S GOTTA...
...BE SLOWING 'EM DOWN! SHOULD BE EASY TO CATCH UP!
HUFF... HUFF... BUT...
WHY ARE WE IN SUCH A HURRY?
IF ALL YOU WANT TO DO IS ASK SETA SOME QUESTIONS, THEN--
HEH HEH HEH! THAT'S NOT THE ONLY REASON!!
REMEMBER THE PART ABOUT THE LEGEND?
THIS IS FOR US!
PLUS, AFTER ALL WE'VE BEEN THROUGH TO GET HERE...WE CAN'T LET EVERYONE DOWN, CAN WE?!
FOXY LADY
Y-YOU'RE RIGHT.
AND HERE WE ARE.
MAN, IT'S MAGNIFI-CENT!!
OOOH.

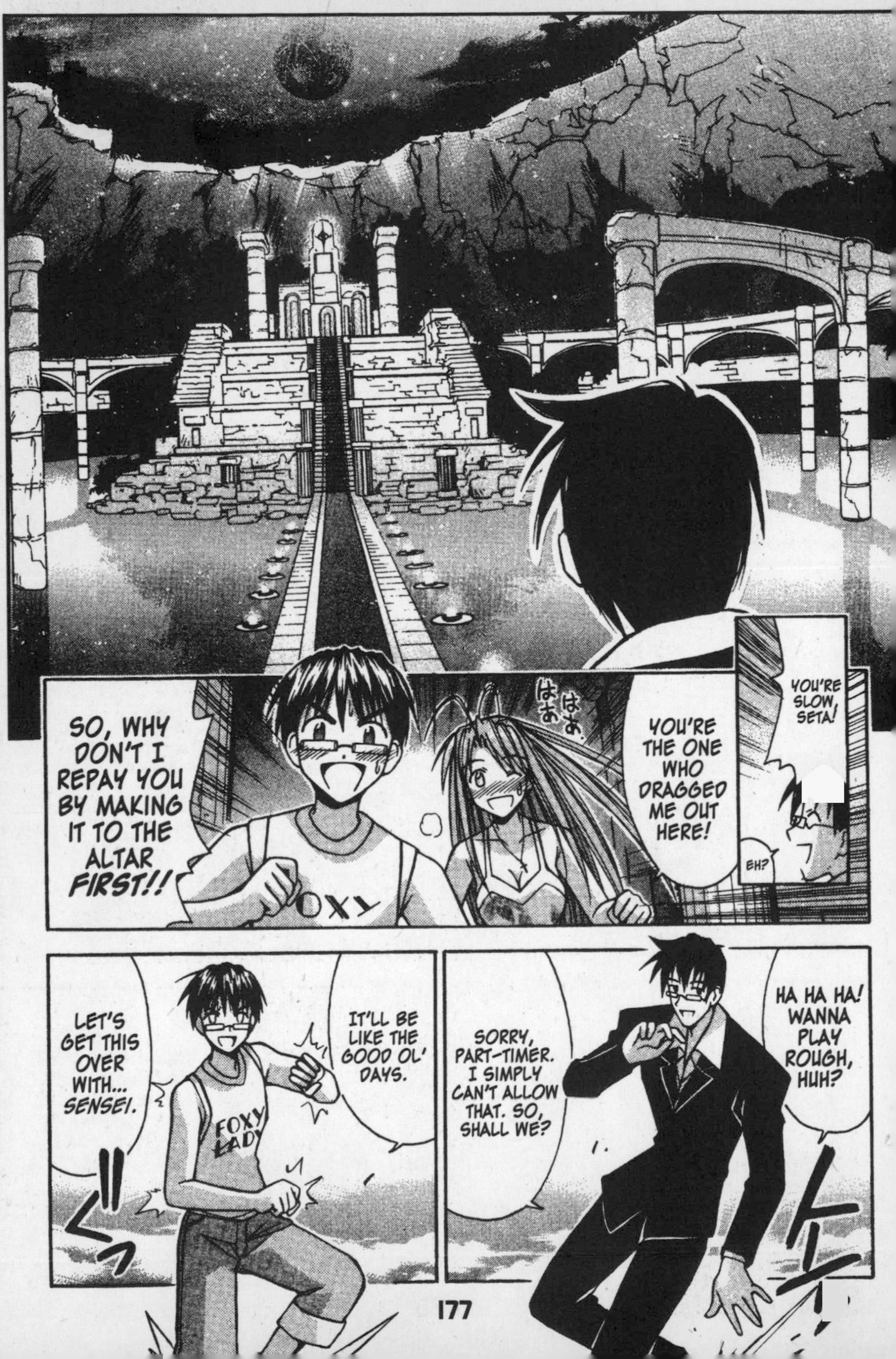
YOU'RE SLOW, SETA!
EH?
YOU'RE THE ONE WHO DRAGGED ME OUT HERE!
はあ はあ
SO, WHY DON'T I REPAY YOU BY MAKING IT TO THE ALTAR FIRST!!
HA HA HA! WANNA PLAY ROUGH, HUH?
SORRY, PART-TIMER. I SIMPLY CAN'T ALLOW THAT. SO, SHALL WE?
IT'LL BE LIKE THE GOOD OL' DAYS.
LET'S GET THIS OVER WITH... SENSEI.

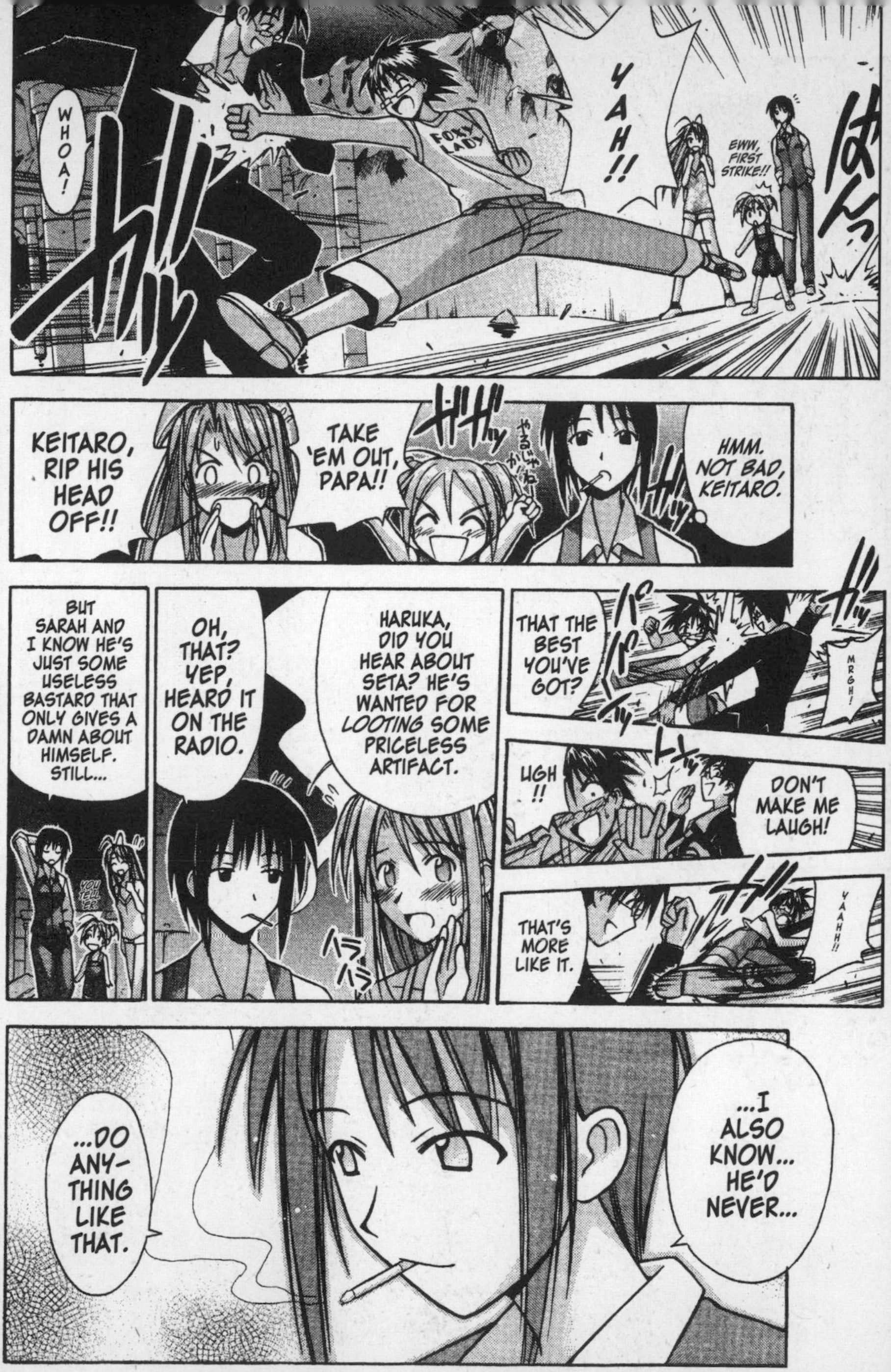
EWW, FIRST STRIKE!!
YAH!!
WHOA!
HMM. NOT BAD, KEITARO.
TAKE 'EM OUT, PAPA!!
KEITARO, RIP HIS HEAD OFF!!
THAT THE BEST YOU'VE GOT?
MRGH!
DON'T MAKE ME LAUGH!
UGH!!
YAAHH!!
THAT'S MORE LIKE IT.
HARUKA, DID YOU HEAR ABOUT SETA? HE'S WANTED FOR *LOOTING* SOME PRICELESS ARTIFACT.
OH, THAT? YEP, HEARD IT ON THE RADIO.
BUT SARAH AND I KNOW HE'S JUST SOME USELESS BASTARD THAT ONLY GIVES A DAMN ABOUT HIMSELF. STILL...
...I ALSO KNOW... HE'D NEVER...
...DO ANY-THING LIKE THAT.

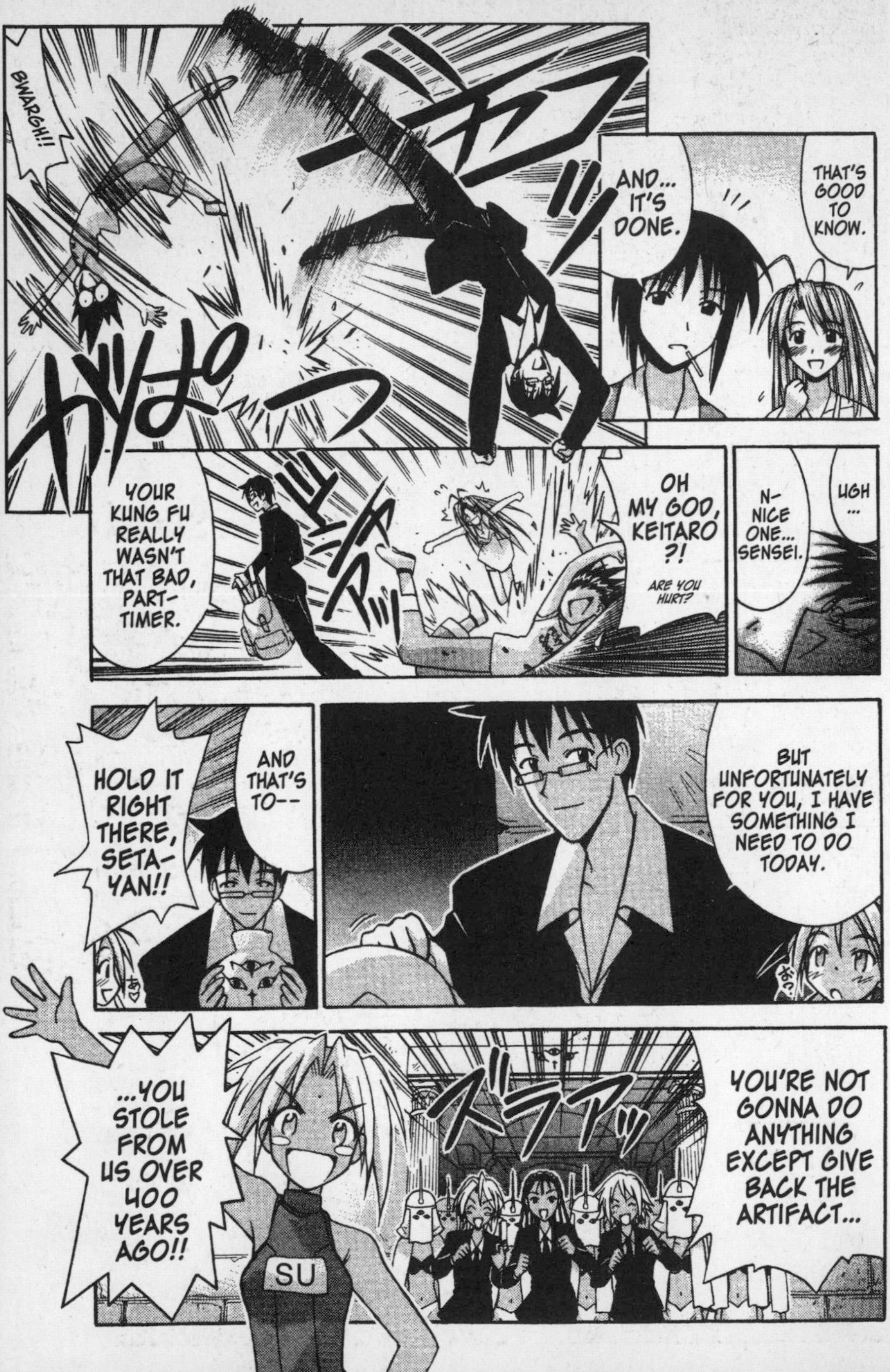
THAT'S GOOD TO KNOW.
AND... IT'S DONE.
BWARGH!!
UGH ...
N-NICE ONE... SENSEI.
OH MY GOD, KEITARO?!
ARE YOU HURT?
YOUR KUNG FU REALLY WASN'T THAT BAD, PART-TIMER.
BUT UNFORTUNATELY FOR YOU, I HAVE SOMETHING I NEED TO DO TODAY.
AND THAT'S TO--
HOLD IT RIGHT THERE, SETA-YAN!!
YOU'RE NOT GONNA DO ANYTHING EXCEPT GIVE BACK THE ARTIFACT...
...YOU STOLE FROM US OVER 400 YEARS AGO!!
SU

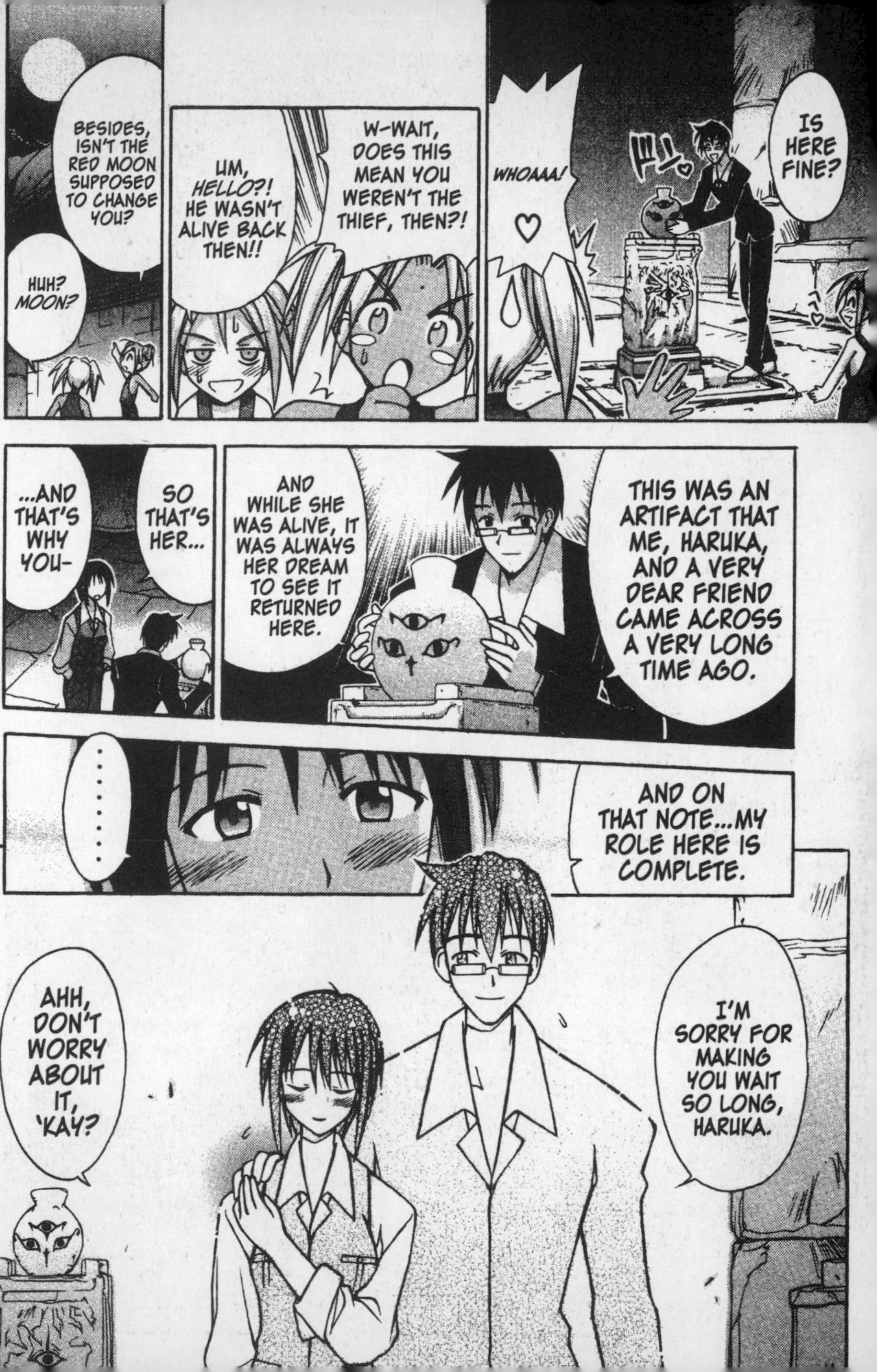
IS HERE FINE?
WHOAAA!
W-WAIT, DOES THIS MEAN YOU WEREN'T THE THIEF, THEN?!
UM, HELLO?! HE WASN'T ALIVE BACK THEN!!
BESIDES, ISN'T THE RED MOON SUPPOSED TO CHANGE YOU?
HUH? MOON?
THIS WAS AN ARTIFACT THAT ME, HARUKA, AND A VERY DEAR FRIEND CAME ACROSS A VERY LONG TIME AGO.
AND WHILE SHE WAS ALIVE, IT WAS ALWAYS HER DREAM TO SEE IT RETURNED HERE.
SO THAT'S HER...
...AND THAT'S WHY YOU-
AND ON THAT NOTE...MY ROLE HERE IS COMPLETE.
......
I'M SORRY FOR MAKING YOU WAIT SO LONG, HARUKA.
AHH, DON'T WORRY ABOUT IT, 'KAY?

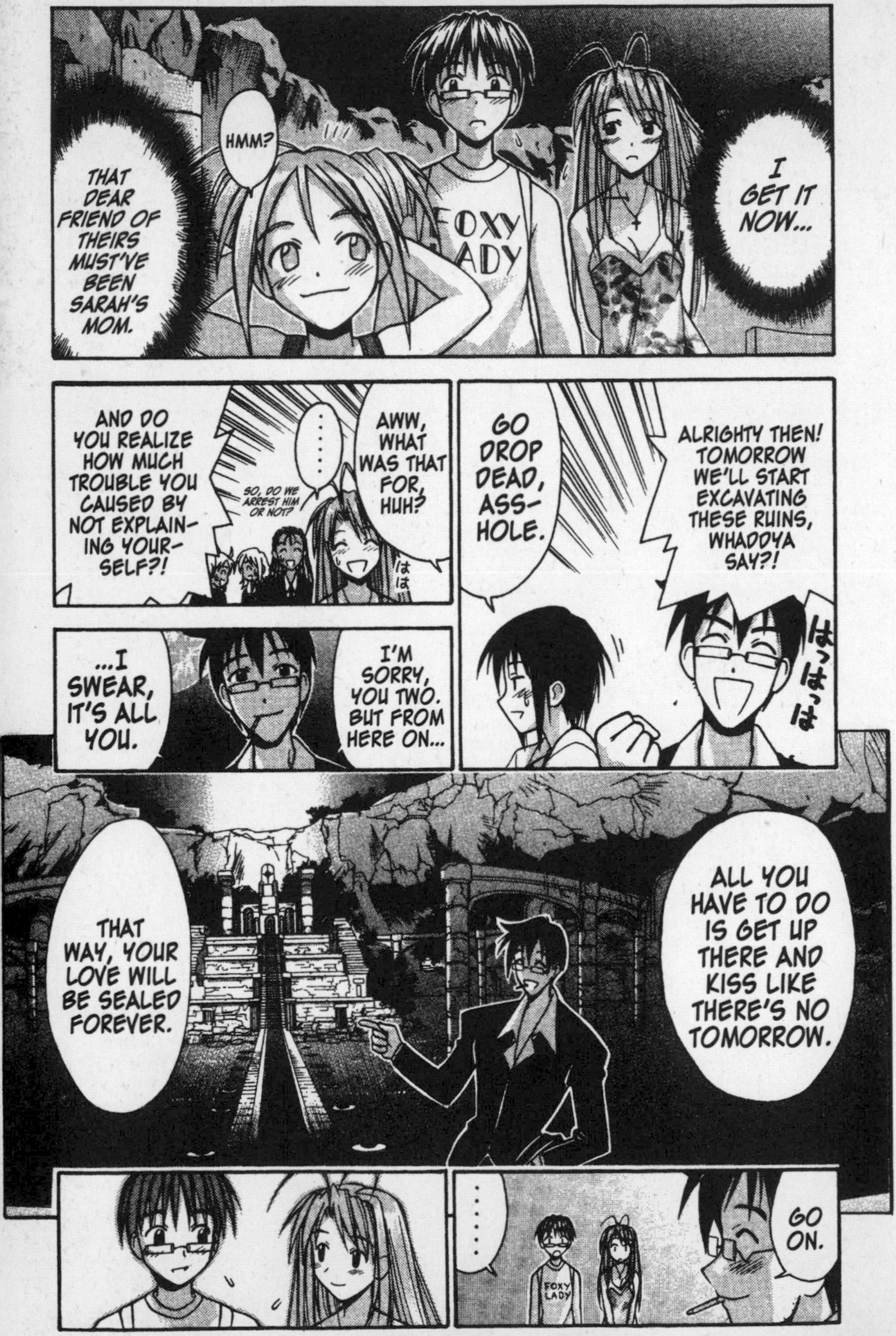
I GET IT NOW...
THAT DEAR FRIEND OF THEIRS MUST'VE BEEN SARAH'S MOM.
HMM?
ALRIGHTY THEN! TOMORROW WE'LL START EXCAVATING THESE RUINS, WHADDOYA SAY?!
GO DROP DEAD, ASS-HOLE.
はっはっは
AWW, WHAT WAS THAT FOR, HUH?
はは
......
SO, DO WE ARREST HIM OR NOT?
AND DO YOU REALIZE HOW MUCH TROUBLE YOU CAUSED BY NOT EXPLAIN-ING YOUR-SELF?!
I'M SORRY, YOU TWO. BUT FROM HERE ON...
...I SWEAR, IT'S ALL YOU.
ALL YOU HAVE TO DO IS GET UP THERE AND KISS LIKE THERE'S NO TOMORROW.
THAT WAY, YOUR LOVE WILL BE SEALED FOREVER.
GO ON.
......

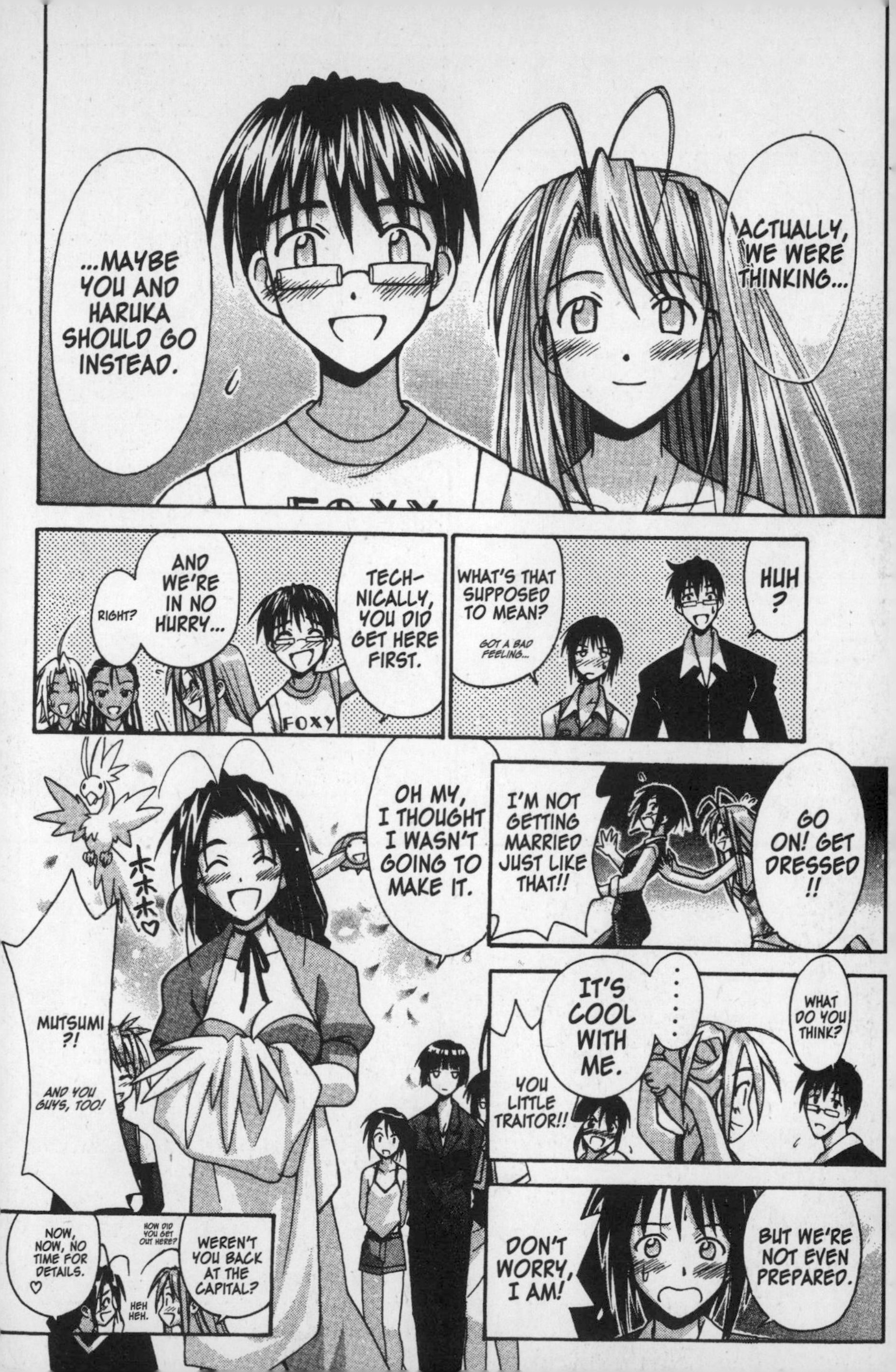

ACTUALLY, WE WERE THINKING...
...MAYBE YOU AND HARUKA SHOULD GO INSTEAD.
HUH?
WHAT'S THAT SUPPOSED TO MEAN?
GOT A BAD FEELING...
TECH-NICALLY, YOU DID GET HERE FIRST.
AND WE'RE IN NO HURRY...
RIGHT?
GO ON! GET DRESSED!!
I'M NOT GETTING MARRIED JUST LIKE THAT!!
WHAT DO YOU THINK?
......
IT'S COOL WITH ME.
YOU LITTLE TRAITOR!!
BUT WE'RE NOT EVEN PREPARED.
DON'T WORRY, I AM!
OH MY, I THOUGHT I WASN'T GOING TO MAKE IT.
ホホホ♡
MUTSUMI?!
AND YOU GUYS, TOO!
WEREN'T YOU BACK AT THE CAPITAL?
HOW DID YOU GET OUT HERE?
NOW, NOW, NO TIME FOR DETAILS. ♡
HEH HEH.

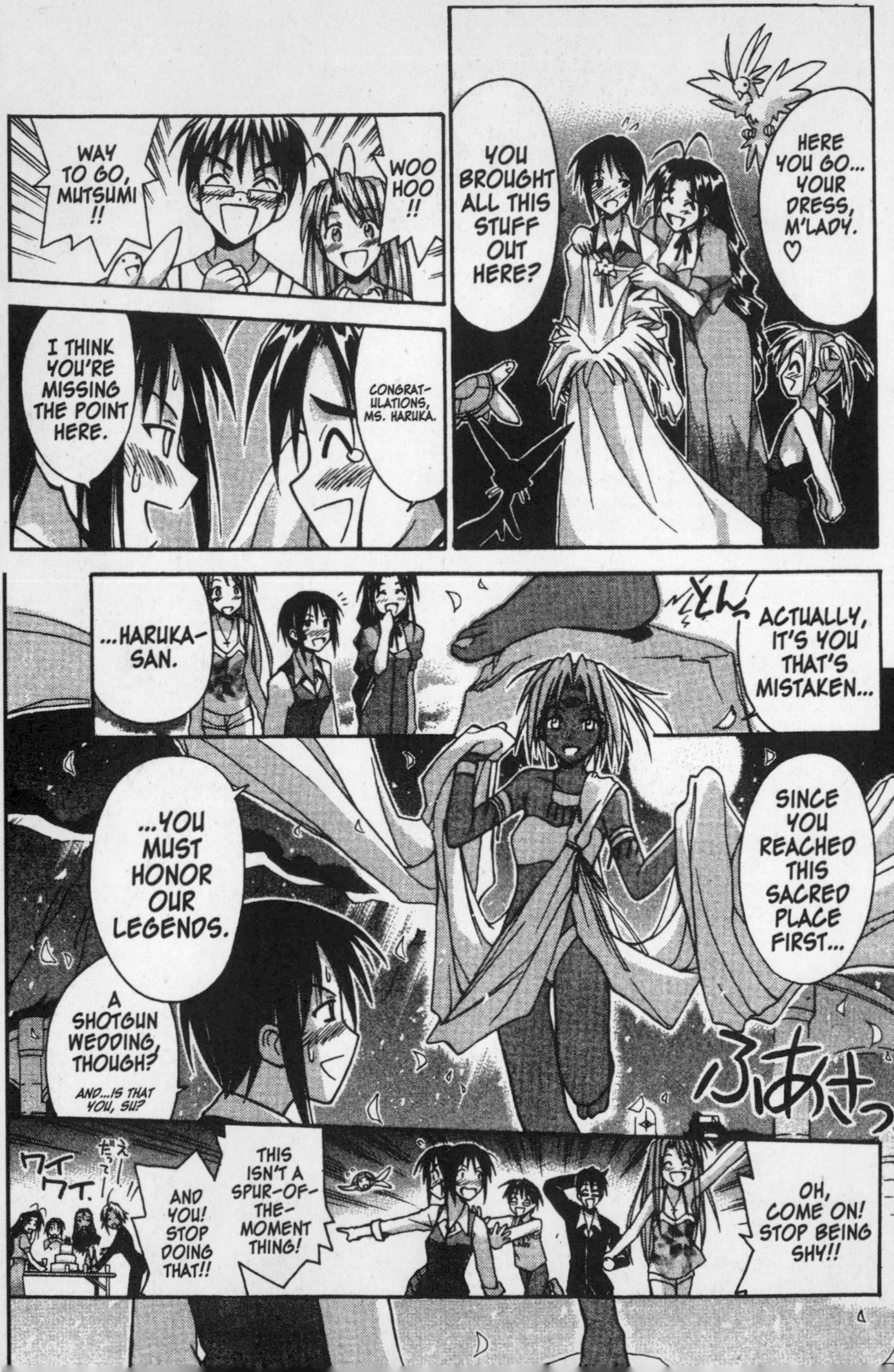
HERE YOU GO... YOUR DRESS, M'LADY. ♡
YOU BROUGHT ALL THIS STUFF OUT HERE?
WOO HOO !!
WAY TO GO, MUTSUMI !!
CONGRAT- ULATIONS, MS. HARUKA.
I THINK YOU'RE MISSING THE POINT HERE.
とん
ACTUALLY, IT'S YOU THAT'S MISTAKEN...
...HARUKA-SAN.
SINCE YOU REACHED THIS SACRED PLACE FIRST...
...YOU MUST HONOR OUR LEGENDS.
ふぁさっ
A SHOTGUN WEDDING, THOUGH?
AND...IS THAT YOU, SU?
OH, COME ON! STOP BEING SHY!!
THIS ISN'T A SPUR-OF-THE-MOMENT THING!
AND YOU! STOP DOING THAT!!
だって～！
ワイワイ.

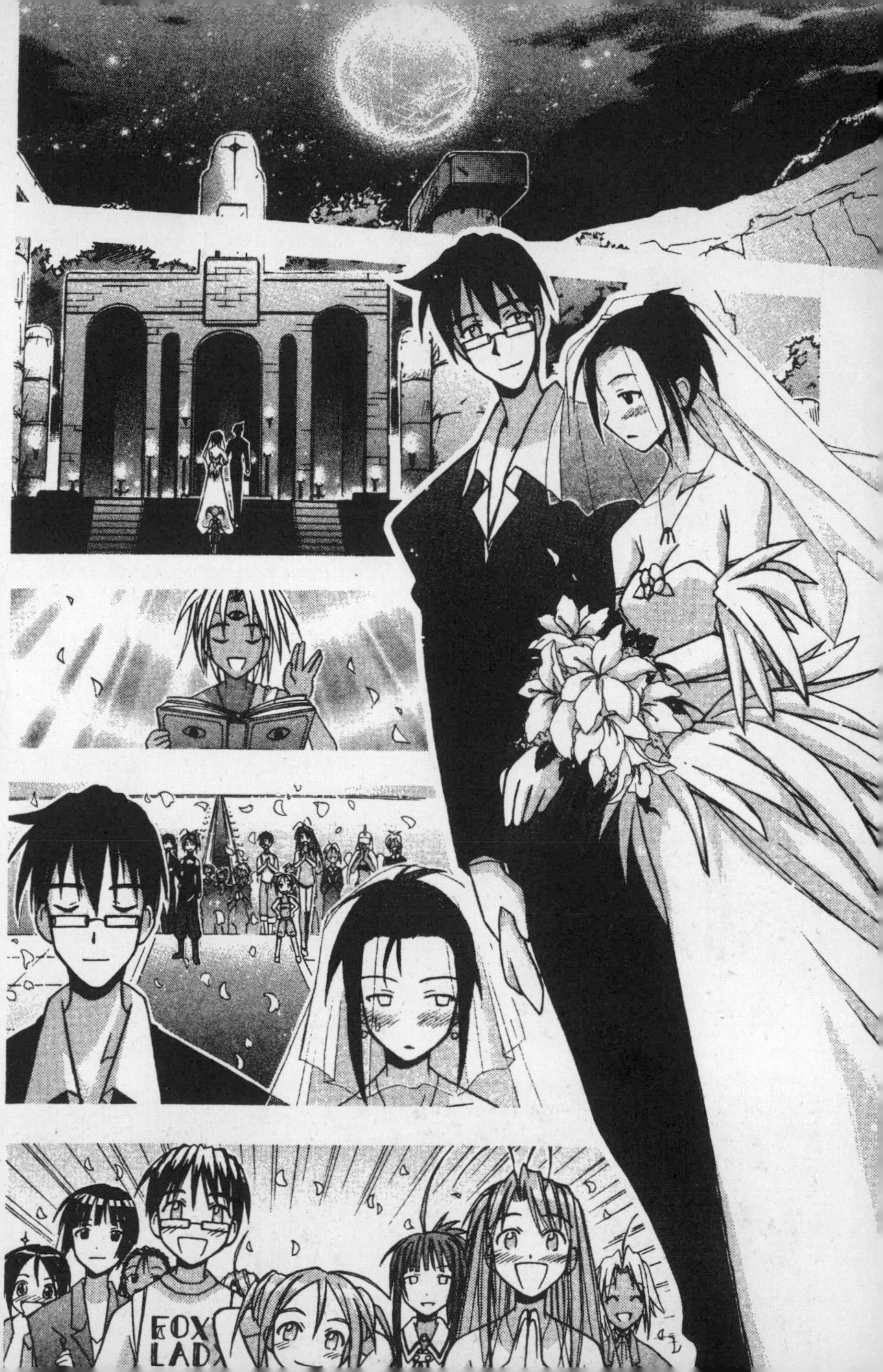

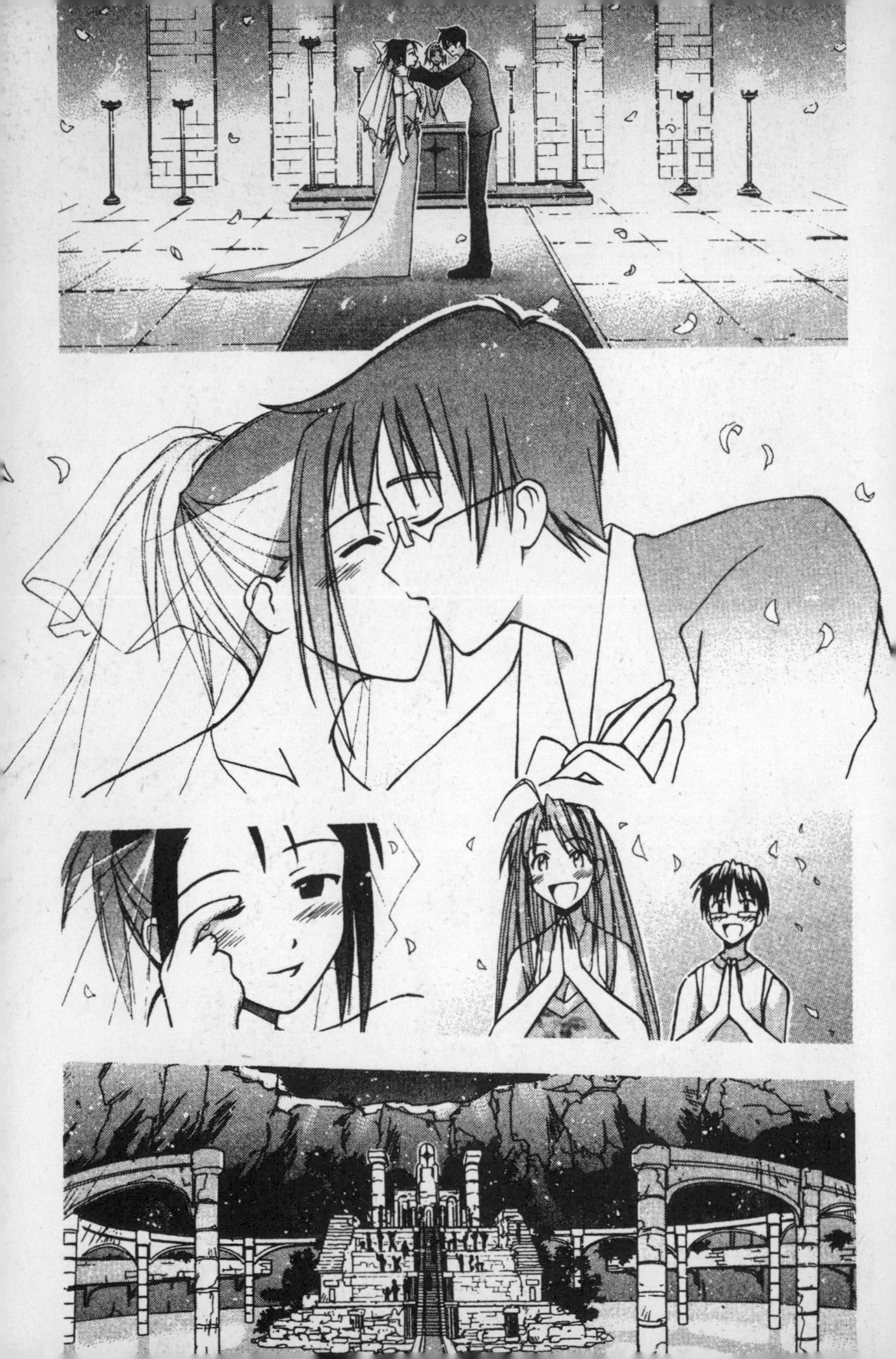

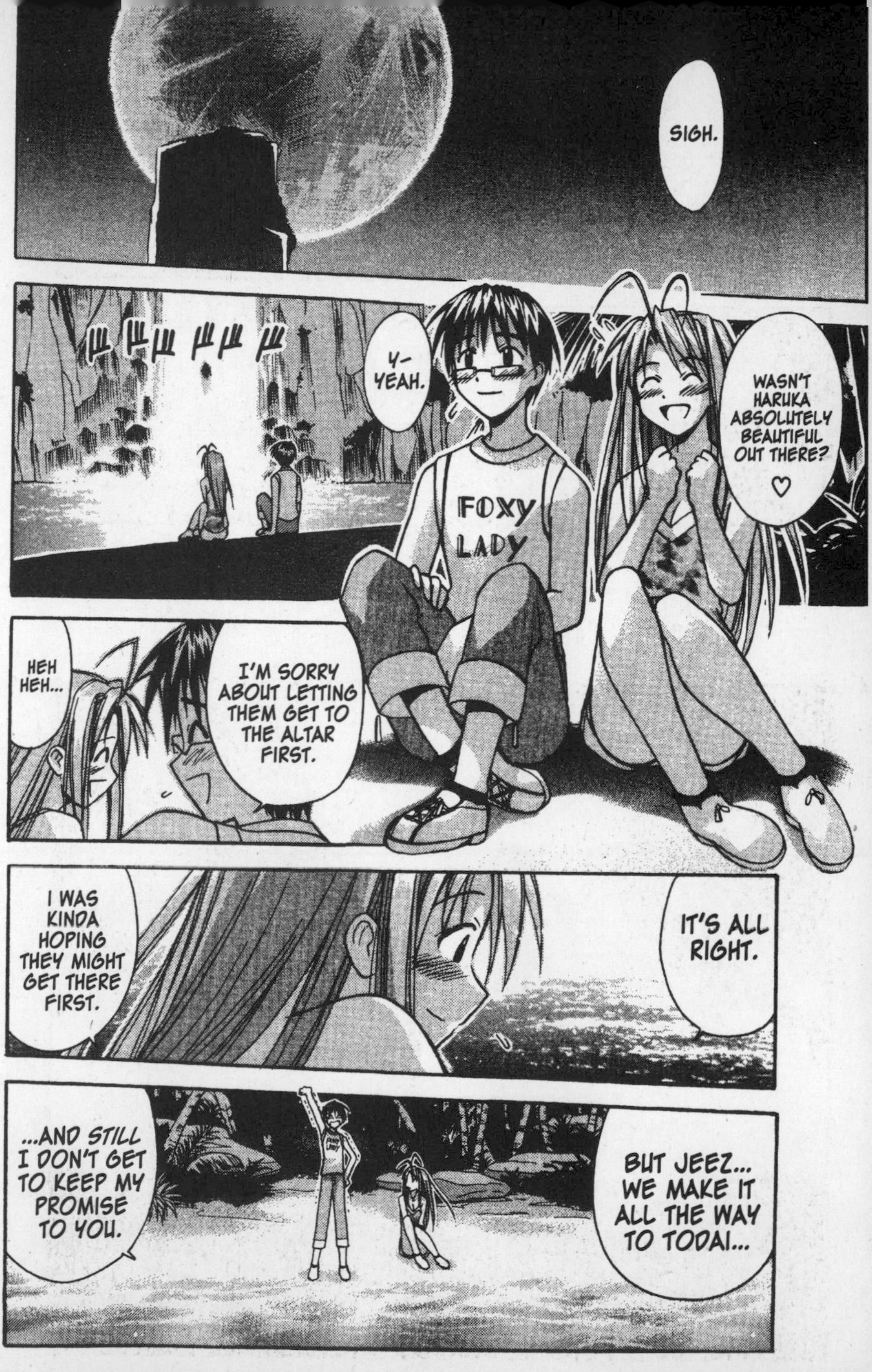
SIGH.
WASN'T HARUKA ABSOLUTELY BEAUTIFUL OUT THERE? ♡
Y-YEAH.
I'M SORRY ABOUT LETTING THEM GET TO THE ALTAR FIRST.
HEH HEH...
IT'S ALL RIGHT.
I WAS KINDA HOPING THEY MIGHT GET THERE FIRST.
BUT JEEZ... WE MAKE IT ALL THE WAY TO TODAI...
...AND STILL I DON'T GET TO KEEP MY PROMISE TO YOU.

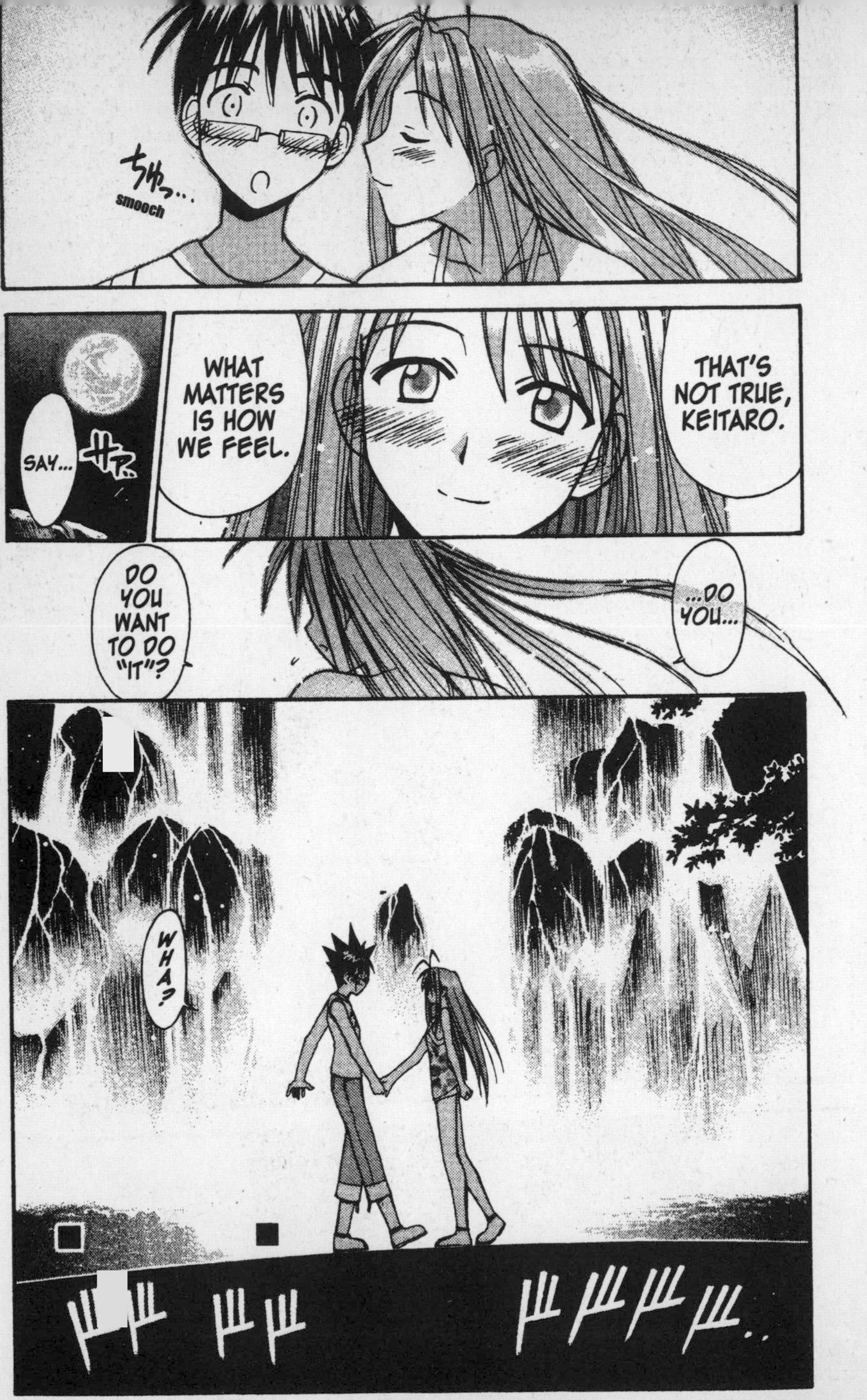

ちゅっ...
smooch
THAT'S NOT TRUE, KEITARO.
WHAT MATTERS IS HOW WE FEEL.
SAY...
...DO YOU...
DO YOU WANT TO DO "IT"?
WHA?

STAFF

Ken Akamatsu
Takashi Takemoto
Kenichi Nakamura
Takaaki Miyahara
Tomohiko Saito
Masaki Ohyama
Ran Ayanaga

EDITOR

Noboru Ohno
Masakazu Yoshimoto
Yasushi Yamanaka

KC Editor

Mitsuei Ishii

In the next volume of

Love Hina

The Promise Girl

Every relationship has its ups and downs, but for Keitaro and Naru, their roller coaster romance could shatter a long-standing friendship. Having just seen their mentors, Haruka and Seta, get married, the aspiring young couple is on a mad dash to make it back to Hinata House before Grandma Hinata arrives. But when Keitaro gets his days mixed up, he ends up missing her visit completely!

Royally screwed, Naru and Keitaro head to Tokyo University and finally seal their promise once and for all...or do they? A surprise phone call brings Keitaro in contact with his grandmother for the first time in years. And when Grandma Hinata lets on that she knows about Keitaro's childhood promise, Naru cuts the phone call short.

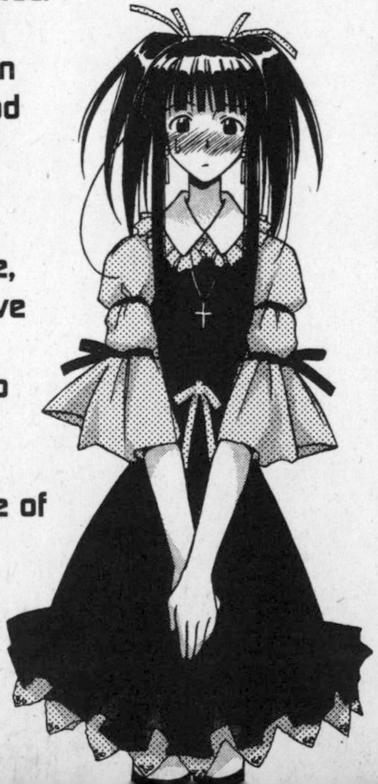

As Naru and Keitaro's seemingly star-crossed romance begins to slowly erode, the other residents of Hinata House leave in a mass exodus. Will Hinata House ever be the same? Will Naru and Keitaro ever find happiness? And who is the promise girl? The answers are finally revealed in this last sidesplitting volume of Love Hina!

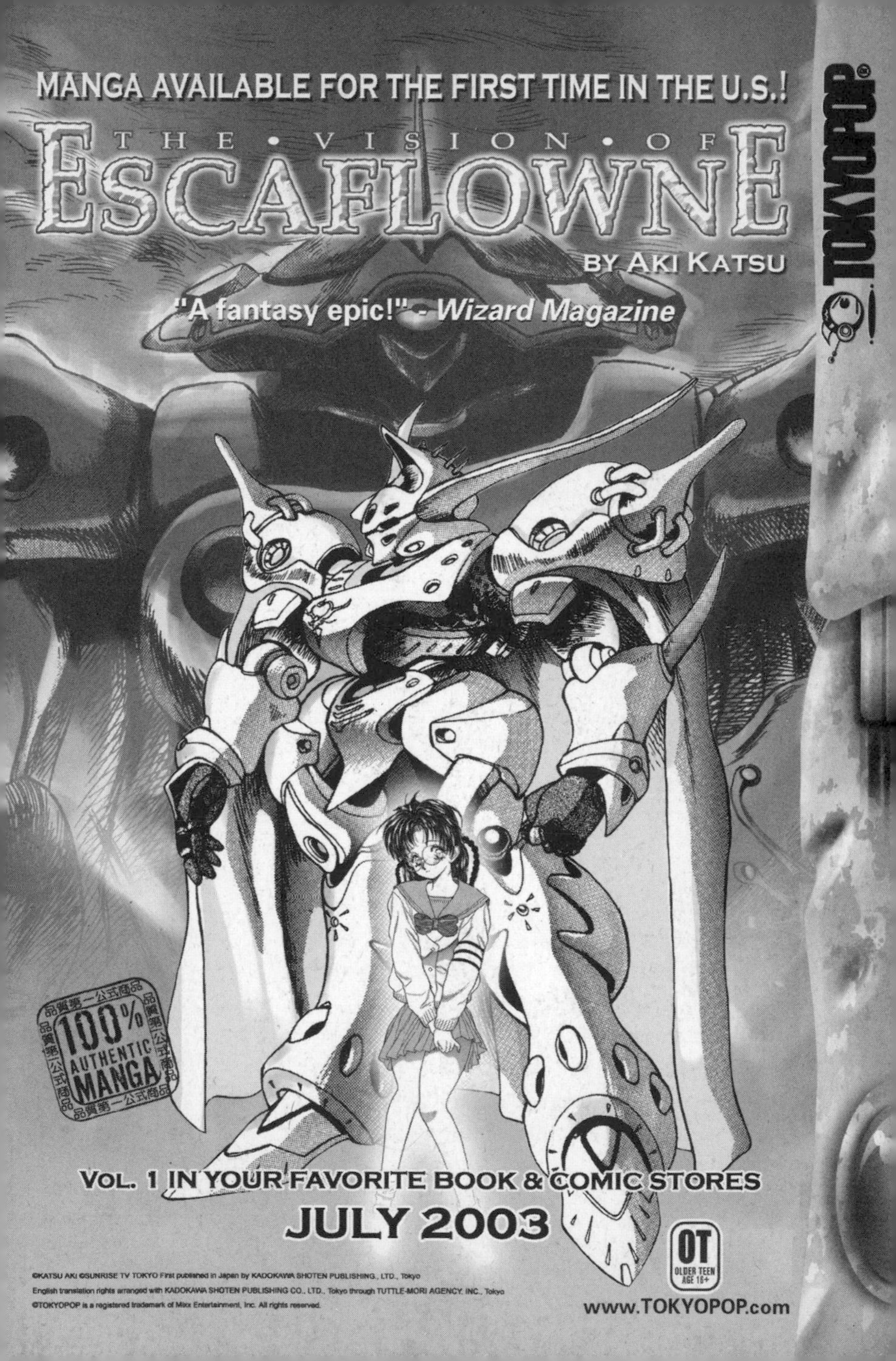

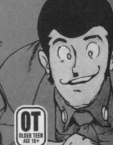

STOP!

This is the back of the book.
You wouldn't want to spoil a great ending!

This book is printed "manga-style," in the authentic Japanese right-to-left format. Since none of the artwork has been flipped or altered, readers get to experience the story just as the creator intended. You've been asking for it, so TOKYOPOP® delivered: authentic, hot-off-the-press, and far more fun!

DIRECTIONS

If this is your first time reading manga-style, here's a quick guide to help you understand how it works.

It's easy... just start in the top right panel and follow the numbers. Have fun, and look for more 100% authentic manga from TOKYOPOP®!

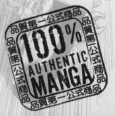

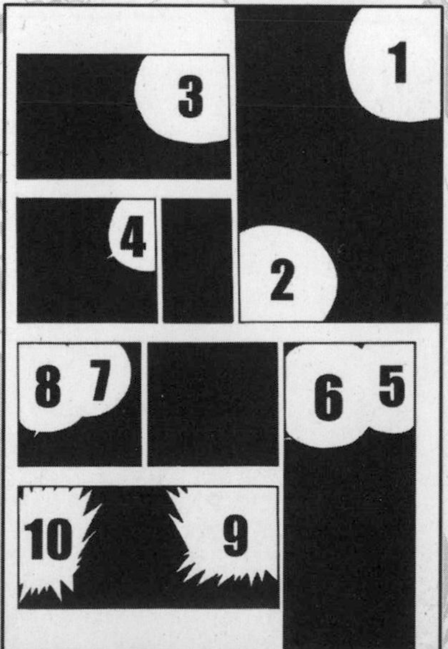